Sex

ROUGH GUIDES

www.roughguides.com

Credits

Rough Guides Reference

Reference Director: Andrew Lockett
Editors: Kate Berens, Peter Buckley, Tracy Hopkins,
Matthew Milton, Joe Staines and Ruth Tidball

The Rough Guide to Sex

Editing: Joe Staines, Peter Buckley
Design and layout: Peter Buckley, Diana Jarvis, Dan May
Picture research: Joe Staines
Diagrams: Katie Lloyd-Jones
Cover design: Tom Cabot
Proofreading: Susanne Hillen
Production: Rebecca Short

Cover Credits

Front cover: Fitzwilliam Museum, Cambridge (Indian couple);
Brand X Pictures (kiss); PhotoAlto (lingerie)
Back cover: Frédéric Cirou/PhotoAlto/Corbis
Inside front cover: BreBa/beyond/Corbis

Publishing Information

This first edition published January 2010 by
Rough Guides Ltd, 80 Strand, London WC2R 0RL
375 Hudson St, 4th Floor, New York 10014, USA
Email: mail@roughguides.com

Distributed by the Penguin Group:
Penguin Books Ltd, 80 Strand, London WC2R 0RL
Penguin Putnam, Inc., 375 Hudson Street, NY 10014, USA
Penguin Group (Australia), 250 Camberwell Road, Camberwell,
Victoria 3124, Australia
Penguin Books Canada Ltd, 90 Eglinton Avenue East, Toronto,
Ontario, Canada M4P 2YE
Penguin Group (New Zealand), Cnr Rosedale and Airborne
Roads, Albany, Auckland, New Zealand

Printed in Singapore by Toppan Security Printing Pte. Ltd.

Typeset in Berthold Akzidenz Grotesk, Kabel and Minion

408 pages; includes index

A catalogue record for this book is available from the British
Library

ISBN: 978-1-84836-564-3

1 3 5 7 9 8 6 4 2

Sex

by

James McConnachie

Contents

Introduction

While researching *The Book of Love*, my history of the *Kamasutra*, I was struck by a complaint in the opening pages. Its author, Vatsyayana, bemoaned the fact that, on the one hand, moralizers thought books about sex shouldn't be written at all. On the other hand, the books about sex which did exist all divided the subject up into little specialist areas of interest, thus separating it from everything else that was important or interesting about the world. So Vatsyayana decided to write a book which would encompass everything that was known about the subject, which would also place sex in the context of life in general: the *Kamasutra*.

Sex guides, today, still exhibit the same tendencies which bothered Vatsyayana, in the third century AD. The more popular kind will happily list the Hundred Hottest Tips for a Great Blow Job or sensationally sell you their Sauciest Sex Secrets. But few have any sense of history, or culture, or ethics, or politics – any sense of how all this fits in with the rest of our lives. The more serious books, by contrast, might discuss the masturbation hysterias of the nineteenth century, or sex science in the twentieth. But they would never extrapolate their findings into practical, hands-on advice.

SEX is my attempt to do it all, to bring everything together. It offers history, culture, relationship counselling, sex advice, religion, discussion of ethical and religious issues, psychology, neuroscience, health information and some personal experiences. It tries to be relevant for the twelve-year old with questions, the young gay man with questions, the middle-aged couple with questions, the post-pregnancy or post-menopausal woman with questions… You get the picture. If you haven't got questions, this book probably isn't for you.

This doesn't mean that a reader of this book is expected to be at the threshold of some great phase in sex exploration. Most sex guides you'll find in the shops are written by sex professionals: people, by and large, who have made sex the centre of their careers or their lives. Some are radicals, campaigners, ultra-liberals. Others produce their own pornography, sell sex toys on their websites or organize sex parties. So you'll hardly get started on finding out how to kiss someone nicely before you're being encouraged to slip in a butt plug. According to one prolific author, "every bedroom should contain a treasure chest" containing bondage gear, a blindfold, erotica and a dental dam – which, if you're not already aware, is a kind of condom for oral sex.

This book will tell you about such things. But it will put these kinds of add-ons and extras in context – as add-ons and extras. *SEX* is mainly addressed to the people you might call the silent sexual majority, to those who are open to learning more and who may like to experiment from time to time – but for whom trying out new sex toys and new contortions aren't priorities. That's not to say that the book is morally conservative. It stands for the notion that what people do in bed (or out of it) is entirely up to them as long as it doesn't hurt anyone else. It believes sex for pleasure and sex for love are both valid pursuits, offering different kinds of rewards. It believes that people should be free to have sex with men, women or both, and to define their sexuality as they choose – or not to define it at all. It believes in freedom of expression, including sexual expression. It also believes that we should teach children about sex just as we teach them about everything else that's important and wonderful about life.

We should probably teach ourselves, too. My hope is that a little sex education – by which I mean real knowledge and understanding, not the health advice and anatomy lessons dished out in schools, nor the "naughty" sex tips purveyed by the sexperts – will eventually be seen as a crucial part of every well-rounded individual's life. In my book on the *Kamasutra*, I concluded that this most venerable of

sex manuals was really unique because it saw sex as an integral part of civilization. You weren't a truly civilized person unless you were skilled at sex, it said, and unless you understood it's purpose, and its place in the greater scheme of things. I think that message is still good today. If we set sex apart from the rest of civilization, I believe, we can't hope to be truly civilized about sex.

Inevitably there will be omissions or mistakes in the first edition of a book. So tell me where I've got it wrong. Tell me what I haven't told you. Tell me what you wish your partner knew. Email me at sex@roughguides.com.

James McConnachie

Acknowledgements

I would like to thank all the many people who so generously offered their expertise, discussed issues with me, or read and commented on my text: Nick Brook of Southampton University Hospital Trust, Charlie Comins, Imogen Cooper, Sofia Dyson, Melissa Edwards, Michael Edwards of The London Lighthouse, James Hall, Lucy Handford of the Terence Higgins Trust, Ford Hickson of Sigma Research, Sally Jones, Jane Knight of Fertility UK, Jim MacSweeney of Gay's the Word, Charlie Marshall, Julie Penman, Richard Scholar, David Smith of Norm UK, Nikki Sutcliffe and Anna Whitelock. All eccentricities of viewpoint, glaring gaps in knowledge and errors of fact or judgment are, of course, entirely my own.

I'd also like to thank all the many people – friends, friends of friends, friends of contacts, contacts of friends, contacts of contacts – who talked me through their personal experiences over a coffee or a glass of wine, or who allowed me to interview about their sexual history more formally; their honesty and insight hasn't been credited by name, but the book undoubtedly couldn't have been written without them.

I want to say a particularly heartfelt thank you to an exceptional group of editors at Rough Guides: Andrew Lockett, who commissioned this book and so completely shared and supported my vision of it from beginning to end; Ruth Tidball, who provided valuable feedback on initial drafts; Peter Buckley, who edited a crucial section and did some fine design work; Kate Berens, who provided some excellent editorial comments and drew up the index; and Joe Staines, who not only took on the final master edit with such wisdom and good humour, but found exactly the images I'd hoped for and generally helped me across the finishing line. Thanks also to Susanne Hillen, who is far more than a proof reader, and Kel Dyson, who did such painstaking work on the illustrations.

Above all, I'd like to thank my family, who have unflinchingly supported my decision to embark on this sometimes difficult topic: my generous, clear-sighted and ever-encouraging parents; my parents-in-law, who never raised an eyebrow; my inspiring wife, and my dear daughter, whose arrival in the world during the course of writing this book threw my schedule into such joyous disarray.

1

Laws of

attraction

Laws of attraction

If a gap exists between the mind and the body it is nowhere narrower than in the realm of sex. Love and desire are felt, powerfully, in the body – and may even be created there. Scientists can now see exactly where a brain "lights up" when its owner sees or thinks about a lover, and they can measure the flows of the hormones which regulate not only our primal urges, but also the complex emotions of love itself. Biologists are tracing how we use scent and smell to sniff out a partner. Psychologists are using computer-generated images to work out exactly what "gorgeous" really looks like. And evolutionary theorists are starting to come up with plausible answers as to why people might fancy the people they do.

Yet who actually gets it on with who is still highly unpredictable. Sexual desire and attraction is fascinating because it is so incredibly varied. Why some men prefer men – and why some women prefer men, and vice versa – is one of the most hotly debated questions of the age. Sexuality in its broader sense is an equally alluring subject. It covers some of the biggest and most puzzling questions people ever ask themselves. Are men and women different in bed? Do they think about sex differently? Do they want more or less of it? And, ultimately, does sexuality define us – is it about who we are or what we do? Or is sexuality a question of what it is that we really desire?

Hearts and minds: love and desire

Most societies seem to distinguish between a "pure" love of the heart and mind, and an "animal" desire of the body. Love is supposed to be selfless and altruistic while lust is all about satisfying the hunger of the beast within. But scientists are now confirming what poets and philosophers have known for centuries: love and desire go hand in hand. "Falling" in love is less a matter of a plummeting, downward trajectory and more like being propelled skywards by the rocket fuel of desire. It's often said that the best sex happens when you're in love. It's less often pointed out that the reverse is also true: the best kind of love is the one that's both crowned and underpinned by sex.

Sexual desire

Sexual desire has had a bad rap down the centuries. It has been called a "passion", a word which covers any kind of intense, elevated emotion but usually means a recklessly uncontrolled one. The Roman philosopher Cicero reckoned that passions were "agitations of the soul", and "contrary to nature". Similarly, the word "lust" is tainted by how violently Christianity loathed it (see p.321), yet in origin it just means "longing".

The word "desire" encompasses similar qualities of yearning. People tend to conceive of their own sexual desire as a kind of mysterious force or energy, a libidinous, primeval, evolutionary "drive" which pushes them towards reproduction. But desire may be more of a push than a pull. The seventeenth-century philosopher Thomas Hobbes argued that it was not so much an inner motor as an instinctive reaction to a person's essentially attractive qualities. It was the anticipation of the pleasure which another person might produce.

Searching for "The One"

Ancient myths around the world have imagined that humanity began as one perfect, androgynous being and only later split – or was divided – into male and female. The Bible carries an echo of this myth. In Genesis, before God creates Eve as an afterthought using Adam's spare rib, it describes how God made man – that is, humanity – "in his own image", as both male and female. By eating the forbidden apple of the tree of knowledge, Adam and Eve effectively become conscious of their separation from each other. At the same moment, sex (or sin) enters the world, because they start to desire each other in a forlorn attempt to recreate their lost unity.

In his *Timaeus*, the Greek philosopher Plato speculated that sexual desire was all about the urge of a split species to combine once again in the original wholeness. Modern psychoanalysis has sometimes taken a similar line, though here it's not divinity that humans seek through sex, but a reuniting with or recreation of a kind of wholeness-of-self that was lost in infancy. Most blame the infantile development of consciousness and language for this modern-day "fall" from innocence.

The French philosopher-psychoanalyst Jacques Lacan developed the idea into his theory of

jouissance, meaning a kind of delirious or blissful merging. It is characterized by painful pleasure or pleasurable suffering, and goes beyond the usual, socially delimited kinds of enjoyment towards a more mystical and transgressive state. Through *jouissance*, we taste the almost-possibility – and, simultaneously the tragic impossibility – of the recovery of our lost, inner absence.

It is no accident that Lacan concocted his term from the French word *jouir*, which means not only to "enjoy" or "delight in" but also, in slang, to orgasm. The Buddha took a not dissimilar line. He called desire *tanha* or "thirst" and felt that *kama-tanha* or sexual thirsting was its key constituent. He pointed out that in an impermanent world, desire could never be wholly realized. His Second Noble Truth, in fact, maintained that desire was the ultimate origin of all suffering.

Craving pleasure: ancestral brains and libidinous ids

The American neuroscientist Paul D. Maclean argued that sexual desire, for the beast within, is all about the seeking of pleasure. He proposed that the human brain had evolved in three stages, and retained a triune structure. The ancient, "reptilian" brain stem controls the instinctive, in-the-moment necessities of sheer existence. The topmost neocortex, part of the cerebral cortex, is the seat of reason, speech and all the other higher, human faculties. In the middle lies the "limbic" system, the original core of the mammalian brain. It drives and controls behavioural essentials like seeking prey or sexual reproduction, and does this by perceiving the world as either good or bad, as pleasurable or painful: as something to be avoided or sought.

It's true that if someone has the anterior temporal lobe of their cerebral cortex removed, they often start behaving in relatively untrammelled, exaggeratedly sexual ways. The surgery seems to act like the release of a safety valve or inhibitor, letting the mammalian brain seek its pleasures free of social or rational concerns.

Around the beginning of the twentieth century, Sigmund Freud turned a similar conception of desire into a key principle of his psychoanalytic theories. For Freud, too, the human psyche was divided into three parts: the moral superego, the rational ego, and the boiling, churning, lawless id, the unconscious seat of the libido. By means of what Freud called the "pleasure principle", the libido continually drives the body to seek sexual gratification. And dreams, of course, can allow the interpreter a window into the desires of the id.

What's the point?

As far as evolution is concerned, sex exists because it increases the chance that the genes in the care of any two individuals will survive to breed again another day. Sexual, as opposed to asexual, reproduction muddles up the genes every generation. This helps smooth out random genetic mutations – a process known as Muller's ratchet – and allows a population to keep one step ahead of the parasites co-evolving to take advantage of it. Genetic variation may also allow a group of genetically non-identical organisms – a family or village, say – to find and exploit slightly different evolutionary niches. Some think this grand genetic shuffle also speeds up the process of adaptation itself. Attraction has evolved to make us attempt our curious genetic swaps with the best DNA we can get hold of, after all.

The seat of desire

René Descartes, the seventeenth-century "Father of Modern Philosophy", might have agreed. For him, six "primitive passions" ruled the mind, prompting the body to seek out things which gave it pleasure (or which were useful) and avoid those which caused pain (or were harmful). They did this by means of "animal spirits" which, in cooperation with the nervous system, talked to the "primary seat" of the brain, lodged in the pineal gland. Among Descartes' six passions was desire.

Recent neuroscientific studies have tended to confirm the notion that the desire for pleasure is located in a specific place in the brain. Not in Descartes' pineal gland, however, but in the hypothalamus. A less-than-entirely-unkind animal experiment made rats ejaculate by merely stimulating the hypothalamus. Other rats with an electrode implanted in the same area would self-stimulate it, and themselves, by switching it on again and again. One rat "pleasured" itself in this way more than 2000 times an hour for 24 hours.

When it comes to humans, there are intriguing cases of medical patients with similar electrodes implanted in the brain experiencing unmediated sexual pleasure and arousal. One male psychiatric patient turned himself on, quite literally, over a thousand times an hour, apparently "begging for a few more jolts" as the machine was taken away. It's not quite up there with the heroic rat, but definitely beats the average masturbatory capacity.

Which came first: desire or arousal?

The 1960s sex researchers William Masters and Virginia Johnson were the first to put humans in a laboratory and observe them having sex. They hooked them up to heart monitors and cameras and even devised an artificial coital machine with a see-through plastic penis and a "photoplethysmograph" – not a dinosaur, but an instrument for measuring vaginal blood flow. What they came up with was a model for how sexual response develops, beginning with desire and moving to arousal before entering a four-stage "sexual response cycle": excitement, plateau, orgasm, resolution.

Later critics felt that this linear development was a very male approach, arguing that women have a rather more complex pattern of arousal which might better be described as circular. Desire might come before arousal, but it might equally well come after it. As for the idea that sex progressed inevitably from excitement to orgasm, this was nonsense. For women, it was said, satisfaction could be found at any stage, and orgasm wasn't inevitable.

Some, in turn, felt that this analysis was wrongheaded. Younger women, who'd grown up in a more liberated sexual culture and felt comfortable and confident about their sexuality, certainly didn't need to be "turned on" by their partner before they felt desire. And they weren't going to be "satisfied" with yet more orgasm-free sex.

Sexual love

For an activity that's central to most people's lives, not to mention the life and survival of the human species, most languages have a shockingly inadequate vocabulary for discussing what is sometimes called "romantic" or "passionate" love, or being "in love" – the kind of love, in other words, that's distinguished from all others by taking place within a sexual relationship. You might call it sexual love.

Some loves are noble and uplifting: the comforting and comradely love for a pet cat; the tender and pitiful love for a vulnerable child; the generalized, humanitarian love that makes you put your hand in your pocket for flood victims. This is what the Bible means by love as "charity" (the old translation of the Latin *caritas*), the love which "suffereth long, and is kind", which "envieth not, vaunteth not itself, is not puffed up". But the word love also covers more tangled bonds: the parent's possessive love for a child; the lover's jealous love for someone whose desires they can't imagine wholly fulfilling; the desperate addiction of unrequited love; the complex love for a sibling you can't quite get along with, or the ex-partner you can't quite leave behind.

The sexual kind of love is supposed to encompass all these feelings. It is the über-love. The American psychologist Robert Sternberg, an arch-categorizer of human behaviour, proposed the term "consummate love" to mean the love which combines all three of what he thought were love's major constituents: intimacy, passion and commitment. On its own, passion (or sexual desire) produces Infatuation; commitment alone creates Empty Love; and intimacy alone gets you mere Liking. The combinations produced by the

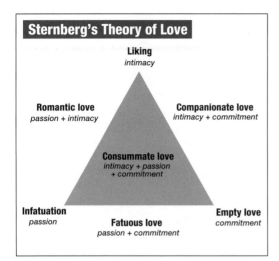

Sternberg's Theory of Love

Liking
intimacy

Romantic love
passion + intimacy

Companionate love
intimacy + commitment

Consummate love
intimacy + passion + commitment

Infatuation
passion

Fatuous love
passion + commitment

Empty love
commitment

Love, madness and biology

Sexual love is perhaps less the blending of sexual desire with different kinds of love, and more a phenomenon in its own right. It has often been compared to a disease, an infection, a madness or a form of possession. That's certainly how the ancients conceived of it, with their notions of Cupid (or, in India, the god Kama) shooting off his darts and poisoning or inciting mortals to love. Plato quoted Sophocles as saying how glad he was that age had rid him of love, as if he had "escaped from a mad and savage master".

This kind of intense, romantic, sexual love is sometimes accused of being a Western cultural concoction. The philosopher Michel Foucault, for instance, thought sexual love was a kind of tool through which Western bourgeois values could be asserted. He clearly hadn't read much Sanskrit or Chinese poetry. The anthropologists Jankowiak and Fischer, frustrated by colleagues who made references to love-free, non-Western cultures, analysed studies of more than 160 societies and found evidence of sexual love in almost 90 percent of them.

Such universality strongly suggests that sexual love is biological. Brain scans conducted in recent years by the biologist and love-researcher, Helen Fisher, have shown how early-stage love ramps up hormones in the brain to extraordinary levels. This charged-up, effervescent state usually either blows its lid, and dissipates, or settles into a calmer state of "attachment" – but it can also persist, a nugget of slow-release intensity which can potentially help fuel partner bonding over a lifetime.

Fisher believes that falling in love has three stages, beginning with the trigger, "lust", and

triangle can be rather revealing about the need for balance in love: passion and intimacy without commitment form Romantic Love, it appears, while the admittedly unlikely combination of commitment and passion without liking results in what is dubbed Fatuous Love.

The triangle also underlines the curious fact that sexual desire is an integral part of what most people imagine as complete or full (or indeed consummate) love. But it doesn't take much account of love's dynamics. It doesn't show how infatuation can turn into intimacy – out of which commitment may develop. It also separates sex, or "passion", from intimacy and commitment, whereas it's arguable that the intimacy found within a sexual relationship is of a different kind from the one found within a friendship. Sex itself, arguably, is a kind of intimacy, and commitment without an element of passion, equally, may not be the same as commitment with it.

Falling into limerence

Fisher admits that love can begin with attachment or attraction just as much as it can with lust. But the classic symptoms of "falling in love" are marked by a particular kind of craving. In the 1970s, the American psychologist Dorothy Tennov interviewed hundreds of people about their experience of love. She concluded that a particular psychological state existed which was more extreme than a mere "infatuation" yet wasn't characterized by the bonding and altruism of full romantic/sexual love. She coined the term "limerence" to describe it – but given that many of its features are disturbingly familiar to anyone who has fallen in love, "falling in love" might be just as good a term.

The limerent, or falling lover, experiences aching in the chest, churning in the stomach, obsessive thoughts, hyper sensitivity to looks and comments, and fear of rejection. Positive qualities in the beloved are dwelled on and imaginatively intensified; negative ones are ignored or justified. Panting desire gives way to trembling anxiety about performance. Paralysing shyness in the presence of the beloved veers towards wild risk taking. Pounding despair suddenly soars to an elation so extreme as to feel as if the limerent is actually walking on air.

This appalling state lasts about eighteen months to three years, on average, intensifying from a first, surprising wave to a state of virtual addiction some months later. Some get accustomed to their addiction after a couple of years, and find they can move on – which, for some, explains the phenomenon of the four-year peak in Western divorces. Some manage to transform limerence to committed, intimate love.

Tennov pointed to two ways in which to escape limerence. One is to take a decision never to even

Cupid tried to make the mortal Psyche fall in love with a monster but accidentally fell for her himself. Canova's delicate marble (1796) shows Cupid waking his lover.

moving through romantic "attraction" as bonded "attachment" develops. Each state, she says, gradually flows into the next. Her explanation is straight out of evolutionary psychology: lust puts you out there, in other words, attraction persuades you to find a mate, and attachment keeps you together long enough for the children to survive.

The poetry of love denied

Far and away the greatest outpourings of poetic love in western literature are by poets courting mistresses who frankly did not want to know. The origins of this curious culture of despair and hankering reach back to the medieval ideal of "courtly love", which basically meant desiring another man's wife – or indeed his queen, in the case of Lancelot and Guinevere.

What mattered about courtly love was that it was both illicit and, if not unrequited, at least unconsummated. The courtly lover would worship his lady from a safe distance, vowing his constancy to her even while she, very properly, rejected him. After coming close to death – through both or either despair and deeds of reckless heroism – she might deign to respond to his advances. But the affair should not proceed beyond kisses and stolen embraces. That said, some of those kisses were described in powerfully erotic ways – as in all that business about the lady and her girdle, in the fourteenth-century English classic, *Sir Gawain and the Green Knight*.

The basic message of courtly love was that the erotic urge was dangerous but not a bad thing in essence. If allied to other virtues, it could be transfigured into something far loftier. But the erotic instinct was necessary if the noble, upward journey was to begin at all. It was just as Plato had said: the instinct for the appreciation of actual, real, physical beauty, or eros, is the same instinct which inspires the love of a higher, moral, ineffable Beauty.

Loving despair in poetry reached its peak with the sonnet craze. The fad began in thirteenth- and

Courtly love? The kneeling Lancelot (Franco Nero) clasps the hands of King Arthur (Richard Harris) and his wife Guinevere (Vanessa Redgrave), a scene from the 1967 film musical *Camelot*.

fourteenth-century Italy, chiefly thanks to Dante (who loved Beatrice from afar) and Petrarch (whom Laura rejected), but swept across Europe, finally reaching England in the sixteenth century. It provoked an outpouring of poems of frustrated love from the greatest writers and courtiers of the Elizabethan age – Shakespeare chief among them. Only the lid of denial, it seems, could bring love to the hottest of rolling boils. Either that or successful lovers were too busy doing it to write about it.

go there. The firmly married and comfortably single are relatively safe. The last-ditch chance is to cut off all contact as soon as the limerent feelings start rising. Controlled, limited contact just isn't possible; cold turkey is the only way. Once hooked, you're in for the full ride, and a few limerents stay on the track for many painful years. Some would even say that, just like alcoholism, once you're in love you're in love for ever.

Sex and drugs and hormones

At its most brutish, desire is pretty short-lived. One quick, self-administered orgasm can quickly level out any major spikes. Plenty of animals live and breed in just this way, giving themselves up to furious bouts of copulation which they're no more able to control than a starving man confronted with a plate of food. Human desire is different: slower-acting, longer-lasting and less insistent.

This slowness is partly the result of hormones. These chemical signallers work on a longish timescale, allowing human sexual feelings to be absorbed into the mind and considered by the will. Hormones motivate human behaviour but they don't cause it. Take women's hormonal cycle, which has a rather confusing and loose relationship with actual sexual behaviour. The biggest statistical peak in lovemaking, for instance, does not occur around ovulation but at the weekend.

Far more urgent is the role of faster-acting neurotransmitters, the signal chemicals of the brain. When humans fall in passionate love, especially, levels of the neurotransmitters

dopamine, norepinephrine and oxytocin soar, causing, arguably, the extraordinary behaviour of new lovers.

Sex hormones: testosterone and oestrogen

In 1848, the German scientist A.A. Berthold castrated some cockerels to see what would happen. Not only did their distinctively male crests and wattles disappear, so did their sex drives. Something in the testes was clearly driving both "maleness" and sexuality – unless both were the same thing. That something turned out to be testosterone, which in men is largely cooked up in the testicles. It works on boys as well as roosters, turning them into men at puberty. It fuels a certain kind of activeness in behaviour (stereotypically manifested as aggression), builds muscle and makes men's voices lower.

Testosterone levels ramp up in the morning (fuelling waking erections), before sleep (encouraging bedtime wanking) and during adolescence (when it can fuel frequent if not obsessive sexual thoughts). The hormone feeds sexuality right through a man's life, fading only in extreme old age. Falling in love, getting overstressed and taking certain drugs can interfere with production, however. Some countries use testosterone blockers to treat socially unacceptable behaviour – paedophile activity, for instance.

It would seem natural, therefore, if oestrogen, produced by a woman's ovaries, lay at the root of female sexuality. To some extent, it does. Relatively high levels of oestrogen enable women to be more responsive to oxytocin than men – a fact which may help explain the reported tendency for women to feel more "cuddly" after sex than men. Removing the ovaries may dampen some women's libido, while hormone replacement therapy can help restore it.

To boost sexual desire in women, however, giving testosterone is far more effective than giving oestrogen. This has nothing to do with turning women into men. The gendering of hormones as "male" or "female" is a handy way to differentiate them, but it's misleading. Men use oestrogen for maintaining bone health as well as fertility, for instance, while women secrete testosterone naturally, in their ovaries and adrenal glands.

Although it's something of a grey area, women's sex drives seem to be fuelled by oestrogen and testosterone working in combination. Both peak at around ovulation, when many women say they feel at their horniest – and studies show their behaviour to be sexier, too. Whether or not oestrogen plays a role in male sexuality is even less clear.

Love drugs: norepinephrine, PEA, oxytocin, dopamine, serotonin

The closest humans get to being out of control, or rather in the grip of their sexuality, is when they're in the early throes of passionate love. In this intense period, lovers' brains are awash with some of the most exciting chemicals going: norepinephrine, dopamine and oxytocin.

Under its popular name, adrenaline, the fast-acting hormone norepinephrine is well known as a kind of nerve tonic. It winds up all the senses and encourages risk taking and decisive action.

It's also responsible for the classic thumping heart, stomach "butterflies", wakefulness and lack

Wanna buy some O?

Oxytocin's powers of encouraging trust, attraction and arousal have led, inevitably, to it being sold online as a kind of recreational love drug or "pulling pill" (in much the same way as it's sold, legitimately, to promote breastfeeding) in the form of a nasal spray. The idea of the scam is that if you spray oxytocin on your clothes or somehow get it into your victim's bloodstream, you'll create – and be able to enjoy – instant intimacy. Of course, delivering oxytocin to the brain isn't as simple as dabbing it on a handkerchief like eau de cologne. One reason may be that natural release of oxytocin in the brain follows a rhythmic pulse. Drugs which raise the brain's own production of oxytocin, like MDMA, however, do seem to cause users to enjoy its effects. Hence MDMA's street name, ecstasy. Unfortunately for people taking ecstasy, it seems to dampen desire even as it stokes up feelings of empathy and elation.

of appetite of the brand-new lover – not to mention the single-mindedness, the exhilaration and the compulsive behaviour. Norepinephrine also peaks at orgasm. And it's actually addictive.

People thrilling to the rush of norepinephrine seem to be more sexually suggestible, too. In a famous psychology experiment of 1974, an attractive female researcher approached young men standing on one of two bridges: the terrifying Capilano Canyon Suspension Bridge, and an ordinary, lower bridge. They were asked to describe a picture and told they could call her afterwards if they had any questions. The men on the suspension bridge gave

Telling it to Mr Coolidge

The story goes that US president Calvin Coolidge and his wife were being given a farm tour some time in the late 1920s. Grace Coolidge saw a cockerel servicing a hen with considerable vigour. She asked, astonished, if he did that often, and upon being told that indeed he did, dozens of times a day, she quipped: "Tell that to Mr Coolidge". On being shown the same cockerel, her husband was similarly impressed. His wife's message was passed on. Coolidge asked, innocently, whether it was with the same hen every time. It wasn't. "Tell that", he murmured, "to Mrs Coolidge".

The story became the "Coolidge Effect", whereby lovers supposedly lose interest in their partners over time. It probably says more about the Coolidges' relationship than sexual desire, however. "Silent Cal" was famously cold and reserved – as if he'd been "weaned on a pickle", Roosevelt's daughter said. Grace was sociable and fashionable, fond of bright red dresses and interested in women's issues. When a journalist requested stories of their romantic courtship, she asked him, "Have you ever met my husband?"

President Coolidge and his feisty wife Grace on their way to his inauguration.

much more erotic interpretations of the picture – and four times as many rang back later.

The role of the hormone PEA, or beta-phenylethylamine, is related. It revs up the system by increasing levels of norepinephrine and dopamine. There's some evidence that people whose PEA systems are faulty may be "love blind". Unfortunately, people get used to PEA's effects in two to three years – just long enough, curiously, to conceive and raise a child beyond infancy.

The neurotransmitter dopamine – the "happy hormone", as it's sometimes called – is part of the brain's self-administered reward system. It's linked to steadier – if no less pushy – desires and motivations than adrenaline. Waiting for a big win at the races, surfing a cocaine rush or, indeed, getting it on with a partner, all boost levels of dopamine. In sex, it seems to fuel not just initial lust but attachment, as it increases motivation alongside pleasure.

The drawback of dopamine is that the brain gets used to it. Just as heroin addicts need higher and higher doses, eventually the dopamine threshold is above anything that the presence of the lover can actually stimulate. Passionate love, in short, wears off. If attachment hasn't occurred in the meantime, the "love junkie" will seek a new partner so as to experience that initial high. Some relate this to promiscuity and the so-called Coolidge Effect (see box, opposite).

The famous "cuddle hormone", oxytocin, surges when holding hands, cuddling, breast feeding, holding a child and watching a romantic film. It promotes feelings of warmth and intimacy, and its bonding powers are so strong that people given oxytocin can even find complete strangers trustworthy, attractive and likeable. It also surges when you come, which is one of the reasons why sleeping around can be risky: you honestly don't know who you might end up falling in love with. As sex researcher Jim Pfaus puts it: "you think someone made you feel good, but really it's your brain that made you feel good."

Psychiatrist Donatella Marazziti of the University of Pisa found that new lovers had unusually low levels of serotonin – levels that pretty well matched those of obsessive compulsives. (She also discovered that, in terms of testerone levels, men in love become slightly more like women, and women in love like men.) Marazziti's serotonin findings explain an unfortunate side effect of serotonin-boosting antidepressants like some SSRIs: it seems they can actually block passionate love. Given that SSRIs may also interfere with desire and orgasm, some sufferers from depression are being given an unenviable choice between a life and a sex life.

Attraction

What attracts or fails to attract one person to another would seem to be too complex a phenomenon to describe, still less explain. Yet the mechanisms of attraction are increasingly well understood. Genetic science has restored that often ignored sense, smell, to its proper prominence in the field of sexuality. And the social sciences are increasingly able to explain patterns of visual attraction – not to mention attraction to wealth, status and intelligence, which are perhaps the strongest pulls of all. The pseudoscience of body language is lagging somewhat behind, but have just about managed to sketch out the art of reading the unconscious sexual minds of others.

I put a smell on you

Smell is famously the most evocative of all the senses, and the most emotional. It may be the most sexual as well, certainly if other mammals are anything to go by. The noses of many monkeys swell and redden alongside their genitals, and many use their vomeronasal organ to smell out whether a potential partner is on heat, curling back their lips in a curious grimace known as flehming.

Normal people don't flehm, but they may sniff out potential partners unconsciously, either sensing the (much disputed) presence of "pheromones" or simply picking up on other, less mysterious olfactory cues without quite realizing it. Sigmund Freud, for one, was convinced the nose was intimately linked with the sexual subconscious – he even thought a stuffy nose was one sign of a compulsive masturbator. Neurological science agrees that smell is well connected to the primitive "limbic" parts of the brain. It's as if the nose offers an ancient pathway towards desire, one that persists despite the more heavily trafficked and evolutionarily improved highway offered by the eyes.

Sniffing out partners

When people greet each other with a kiss, you could argue that they were subconsciously sniffing each other out, almost like dogs. Kissing not only allows nose and breath to meet, intimately, but brings the nose close to the aprocine-type, or scent-producing, glands, which are found on the eyelids,

Scent is an essential ingredient of attraction.

nose and upper lip. Even an airy, apparently more formal cheek kiss wafts the nostrils around the nook of the ear and neck – exactly where perfume is usually dabbed. But the musky smell of fresh sweat in the armpit, the "axillary odour", is usually considered the sexiest perfume of all. Traditional partner dancing not only allows bodies to be held close, it puts the man's nose roughly on top of the woman's hair (or beside her ears and neck), and it brings her nose within sniffing distance of the man's chest and armpits.

Freud protested that modern fastidiousness blocked the natural conduits of scent attraction, and thus contributed to neurosis. Soaps and deodorants today are widely accused of blocking the body's "signature odour", while perfumes supposedly create a deceptively artificial mask. Yet this is nothing new. Many ancient civilizations went to great lengths to replace natural odours with artificial ones. Depilation, being a form of odour control, has long been practiced across the Middle East and Asia, while the lace cap and hair veil, as used across medieval Europe and the Islamic world, are, arguably, devices to trap the rich scent of a woman's hair.

Many cultures fetishized particular perfumes. Sandalwood paste was de rigueur in ancient India, while pharaonic Egypt employed a range of essential oils and rich waxes, from jasmine, rose and lily to myrrh, incense, storax and galbanum. The ancient Egyptians even employed perfumed waxy cones, which could be placed on the head and allowed to melt over the course of a long soirée, slowly releasing their seductive odours.

Reproductive roses and beavers' balls

Since 2006, when L'Oreal persuaded a French court that its scents could be protected by copyright, perfumes have officially been works of art. But perfumes are also expressions of sexuality: not just in being used to attract and seduce, but in their very essence.

Traditionally, the essential oils that underpin perfumes are made of bits of sexual anatomy. From flowers, the seductive petals and the inner, reproductive parts are taken and distilled into essences of jasmine, rose, iris, lily, orange and the rest of the floral family of scents. Secretions of the sexual parts of animals are also used: musk from the abdominal/genital sacs of the musk deer; civet from the perineal glands of the mongoose-like African civet; castoreum from the anal gland of the beaver. All three animals use these secretions to attract partners. Humans merely borrow.

Animal welfare aside, most natural essences are too expensive to be sold in millions of litres, so synthetic alternatives are now used instead. Possibly the two most influential and best-loved perfumes ever made, François Coty's Chypre and Ernest Beaux' Chanel No. 5 were both made with distinctive-smelling, synthesized aldehydes. It wasn't just a cost-saving exercise. Coco Chanel, who commissioned No. 5, famously declared that "women do not want to smell of a bed of roses". Neither do they want to smell of a deer's bottom, it seems. The keynote aldehyde in No.5, 2-methylundecanal, smells famously "clean" – like "lemon juice on strawberries", Beaux reckoned. Chanel No. 5 has a musky note, but it is artificial, a "nitro musk" known as Musk Ketone.

The best perfume is said to be the one that complements your own natural body odour, but perfumes are also supposed to express personality and style. Perfumiers also like to link perfumes with skin tone and hair colour. Dark and red-haired women are supposed to suit more earthy, musky "erogenic" perfumes; blondes are encouraged towards floral or citrus scents. Whether or not these divisions have any basis in fact is unclear, although it's certain that people have long connected colouring and odour. The pioneer sexologist Iwan Bloch thought blondes smelled naturally of amber and brunettes of violets or musk. His British counterpart, Havelock Ellis, considered brunettes to smell audacious and fatiguing, redheads sharp and fierce, and blondes "heady as some sugared wines".

Pheromones

A spray that magically makes people fancy you sounds like something from an X-rated fairy tale, but this product is actively marketed by a number of companies of varying degrees of reputability. They sell perfumes impregnated with "pheromones", hormone-type extracts that supposedly turn people on without them even realizing why. Unfortunately for the perfume people, most scientists think pheromones don't exist, or not in humans. The pheromones used in these perfumes come largely from other sources: pig urine, for instance. In fact, the whole pheromone concept comes from insects, which excrete chemicals to make other insects have sex with them.

Some mammals can sense pheromones, however, using the vomeronasal organ, or VNO, which is a kind of extra set of mini-nostrils located inside the nose. If you take the VNO out of a hamster it's as effective as castration. Humans, however, don't have a working VNO – at least, they have the slits, but seem to lose the necessary connections to the brain while still in the womb (much as they lose the spinal parts that might become a tail).

And yet there is all sorts of circumstantial evidence that people do respond to some kind of smell trigger while being quite unaware of it. In one classic study, "exotic dancers" who were ovulating made more in tips than those who were not: $70 per hour as against $50, or a paltry $35 for women who had their period. Did the dancers in the study give off some kind of secret olfactory signal? Or did they, as the sceptics think, simply behave more sexily?

BoarMate and sweaty T-shirts

Many of the most famous human pheromone experiments have been criticized for their lack of rigour – but they're intriguing anyway. In one early experiment, a chair in a dentist's waiting room was sprayed with the synthetic steroid androstenone (as found in human sweat and, in much more massive quantities, in boar's saliva – it's the killer ingredient in BoarMate, which pig farmers use on sows they're trying to have impregnated.) Those humans who can smell androstenone at all think it smells rank. Yet more women than men sat on the impregnated chair. Were they "attracted" to it?

Another experiment asked women to rate men's attractiveness. Some, unbeknown to them, were doing so with a cloth soaked in male sweat close at hand, and they rated men consistently and considerably higher than the control group. Another study smeared swabs taken from male armpits on the upper lips of female volunteers. Surprisingly, they reported improved mood, and their levels of luteinizing hormone – which normally surges naturally at ovulation – were shown to have risen.

Whether it's just ordinary smell doing the work or "pheromones", ovulation is clearly an important factor in the sexuality of smell. It affects how as well as what women smell. At ovulation, levels of "copulins" or fatty acids in vaginal secretions, rise, and it's possible that men can sense this. Men who were given T-shirts to sniff that had been worn by women found the ones from ovulating women smelled more pleasant or sexy. Ovulation also sharpens women's own sense of smell. One study found that ovulating women rated the smell of a pad impregnated with androstenone as less unappealing than did women who weren't ovulating. Another group of women, in Prague, were given pads worn in sweaty male armpits. There were no strong patterns of who liked what – except that women who were ovulating during the test thought that pads worn by men classed as "dominant" were sexiest.

Perhaps the best evidence that humans use some kind of secret sexual signalling comes from gene research. A region on the genome called the Major Histocompatability Complex works as a kind of signal of the immune system, influencing a person's "signature perfume". The more different two people's MHC is, the more appealing they seem to find each other's smell. Intriguingly, a rival study found that women preferred the smell of men with somewhat, but not very, similar genes.

Beer goggles and pecking orders

"Beer goggles" are a kind of legendary spectacles which have the power to turn even unattractive people into beauties. Or, to put it another way, they lower the "beauty standard" which people are prepared to accept before they'll engage in a sexual encounter. The effect was long thought to be a pretty simple result of drinking alcohol, which reduces inhibition, increases excitement and, according to a mould-breaking Yale study, "encourages riskier sexual behaviour".

A Manchester University study – commissioned, suspiciously, by an eyewear manufacturer – found that visual deterioration also plays a part. Drunk people, it seems, actually can't see so well. And they're often drinking in low-lit or smoky environments too. Another study suggested the beer-goggle effect wasn't just about sex: people who have been drinking find people of their own sex more attractive as well. They're happy, in other words. And yet another study worked out that the "standards" of people drinking in a bar were dropping not simply because they were getting more drunk, but because it was getting later. Effectively, the further down the beauty pecking order someone appeared to be rated (given that they were still alone as the evening wore on), the less attractiveness they'd demand from a potential partner.

Looking good

Visual attractiveness isn't quite the same thing as beauty. Beauty is both hugely subjective and culturally determined. Attractiveness is more about assessing someone as a potential sexual partner – and people around the world seem to agree much more about who "looks good" in this way than on who looks "beautiful". The Gandan men of Uganda may admire pendulous breasts and the Victorians may have fetishized freakishly small waists, but cross-cultural surveys have found other, universally approved signs of attractiveness. Symmetry in the face is a constant, so too is youthfulness and the body types that signal it.

When attractiveness translates into actual partner-matching and bonding, there's a wild card.

For longer-term relationships people don't seek the jaw-droppingly gorgeous, on the whole. They seek a partner who stands on roughly the same rung of the attractiveness ladder as themselves. The risk of losing a relatively more attractive partner to a higher-status rival is surely a factor. But evolutionary pressures may also be at work. Everyone may be trying to get it together with the highest-status partner possible. But no one is likely to score with someone much more attractive than themselves (as that person will themselves be seeking someone more attractive) and neither is anyone much inclined to dip down. So in the great shuffle, everyone usually ends up with someone at roughly the same level.

Facial symmetry

If you take a group of passport photos of a random collection of men, some good-looking, others less so, and then, using a bit of imaging wizardry, blend their faces together to form an average or composite, a strange thing happens. A fantasy face emerges, and it's almost always rated as attractive (if not necessarily "beautiful"), no matter who's looking, or what their sex or ethnicity – even babies stare for that little bit longer. The same effect applies to a collection of women's faces.

The reason for this odd effect, say the evolutionary psychologists, is that a composite face is relatively symmetrical. And symmetry is an excellent indicator of genetic health because it proves that relatively little has gone awry in the lifelong process of cell replication and division; it proves the strength of the immune system. A symmetrical face, it appears, flags up a good person to breed with. The effect may be boosted by another indicator of good health that the program creates: clear, even-toned skin.

The sexual advantage of high bilateral symmetry is very marked in the animal kingdom, but even a small degree in humans is apparently effective. Men with relatively symmetrical faces have, according to one study, a marginally higher number of sexual partners. And they tend to lose their virginity three or four years earlier than men with asymmetrical faces. Women with asymmetrical partners were found to fantasize about other men (symmetrical men, presumably) around the time of their ovulation, while the smug women with relatively symmetrical partners did not.

Masculine mugs and feminine faces

If faces of *both* sexes are merged using image manipulation software, the result is typically pleasant but rarely sexually compelling. The imaginary faces are just too sexually ambiguous – and masculine-looking men are generally thought to be sexually attractive, as are feminine-looking women.

Curiously, people at the masculine and feminine extremes of looks are often read as being more up for casual sex as well – and, according to psychologist Lynda Boothroyd of Durham University, may actually be so. Her 2008 study found that men with relatively promiscuous attitudes had squarer jaws, larger noses and smaller eyes; women who were open to casual sex, meanwhile, tended to be those whose photographs were judged "attractive". Sceptics wondered if these men and women were less restricted sexually simply because they enjoyed more chances.

Thanks to pubertal testosterone, adult men tend to have more marked bone structure: a larger jaw, more pronounced cheekbones and a more jutting brow. Female faces are softened (and, incidentally, made more symmetrical) by a padding of soft tissue, and by the effect of oestrogen, which limits bone growth in the upper and lower face. On average, women have bigger eyes, fuller lips, a smaller gap between nose and mouth and mouth and chin, and smaller noses. Make-up for women mimics these classic feminine traits, and cosmetic surgery attempts to enhance it by reversing the ageing process. Essentially, in seeking to "look attractive" women are making themselves look more feminine.

Hyper-masculinity isn't always valued in a man's face, however. Assessment of male

Like seeks like

It's said that opposites attract but "like seeks like" would be a truer adage. People are not only attracted to those with similar attitudes and values, they're also likely to have a longer-lasting relationship if they get together with them. There are only two major exceptions. People with low self-esteem sometimes appear to seek partners whose qualities "fill in" for the ones they feel are lacking in themselves. And dominant types tend to do better with submissives, and vice versa. The reason is pretty obvious: two people with dominant personalities are likely to fight all the time, while two submissives will never get anything done.

Psychoanalysts take a slightly different view. They believe that people don't seek partners who are like themselves so much as people like their parents – or, specifically, like their opposite-sex parent. The mother supposedly provides a "romantic template" or "love map" for her son, and the father for his daughter, and these "working models" guide adult sexual preferences. Actual research only suggests a weak correlation, however. One study found that teenage girls in love did tend to love boys with the same eye colour as their dad. Another found that mixed-race men and women were more likely to marry into the ethnic group of their opposite-sex parent. But other evidence suggests that if romantic templates exist at all, the mother is providing them for boy and girl alike – unless a woman had a particularly strong relationship with her father.

Even more telling than similarity or difference, however, is sheer presence. Psychologists have long demonstrated the exposure or propinquity effect, in which people are more likely to get together with somebody the longer they spend with them. To paraphrase the sitcom *Seinfeld*, people are like product jingles: it doesn't even matter if you're pretty irritating in yourself, if you stick around long enough someone will eventually be humming you in the shower. The drawback is longer-term over-exposure. Noone likes to have a bad tune stuck in their head for a lifetime.

attractiveness seems to depend more on who's looking, what qualities they're seeking in a potential partner – and what time of the month it is. Very masculine-looking men may be seen as sexy; men with more feminine faces may be perceived as better parenting material.

Young blondes

Men, on the whole, strongly equate youthfulness with sexiness. Youth correlates, of course, with high fertility but it may produce a different kind of attractiveness from oestrogen-rich womanliness. Blonde hair is often said to be sexy, and some think this is because hair, in general, darkens and coarsens with age. Blonde says young which says fertile ... Sceptics of this kind of evolutionary guesswork point out that blonde hair also signals "Scandinavia", which is one of the world's wealthiest and most sexually liberal regions – not to mention being a major producer of porn.

Clear, unlined skin also signals youth and attractiveness – leaving aside teenage acne. So too does pale skin, which many cultures rate very highly. Skin-lightening creams are found all over Africa, Asia and the Caribbean. In the West, too, a porcelain complexion was until recently seen as the height of feminine beauty (the recent cult of the tan is largely about signalling ownership of the resources necessary to go on frequent beach holidays). It might have been because young skin tends to be paler. It might have been because it indicated the kind of wealth that allowed you to lounge about indoors while other people worked your fields.

Headless copulating turkeys

The old, misogynist aphorism has it that "you don't look at the mantelpiece while you're stoking the fire". If humans are anything like turkeys, however, that's exactly where you look. Faces are crucial to arousal. Such, at any rate, was the finding of a bizarre 1960s experiment, which persuaded male turkeys to mate with an increasingly abstracted series of model females. Researchers discovered that you could take away the tail, the feet, the wings and even the body – as long as the turkey cock had a turkey hen's head to focus his arousal on, he'd be up for it. It didn't even have to be much of a head. The scientists, po-faced, reported that a real head, freshly severed, worked best. A dried-out male head was slightly less attractive, but better at least than a "discoloured, withered and hard" female head. Least arousing of all was a plain old head knocked up in balsa wood – but even that would get the gallant turkey going.

Waists and hips

Despite plentiful evidence from art that people have admired different body shapes at different eras and in different places, some evolutionary psychologists are fixated on the notion of a universal ideal of female beauty. Once you strip away cultural obsessions with particular features, they say – American frat-boy culture is obsessed with large, round breasts, for instance, while many African societies have long venerated a generous female bottom – one core beauty standard remains: the waist–hip ratio. As long as women's waists are significantly smaller than their hips, it's thought, men will find them basically attractive.

One survey of cultures around the world agreed: a broad pelvis on a woman was thought to be a good thing by six times as many societies as thought it was unattractive. An American survey found that between the 1960s and 1980s, Playboy models and Miss America contestants have almost always had waists that were roughly 70 percent the size of their hips, even though overall size had gone up or down in line with fashions. The argument runs that this golden ratio reflects healthy levels of oestrogen (which helps determine where fat is deposited on the body). And good oestrogen equates with fertility – and thus with male attraction, as triggered by preferences shaped by evolution

Fat or thin?

Waist fat is closely associated with susceptibility to diseases like diabetes, with hormone levels and, indeed, with fertility. It's also true that waist-reducing corsetry was hugely popular in the nineteenth-century. But assessments of attractiveness are more complex than evolutionary psychology tends to grant. Narrow waists are also associated with young women who haven't given birth and perhaps haven't had sex – long a cultural fixation for the male of the species.

As for overall size, men aren't necessarily attracted to models, or not in the flesh. One survey found that men prefer a woman who wears a dress size roughly two up from the size women think they like. They prefer an average woman, in short,

Different cultures, different standards of female beauty: Rubens' *The Three Graces* (c.1639).

to a slim one. And fatness preference is certainly shaped by culture more than biology. In calorie-rich societies, thinness is usually idealized. In societies where food is scarce (or has been in living memory), fatness equates with wealth, and is usually thought to look attractive. The Indian sari, tellingly, is deliberately cut to reveal the rounded attractions of the female belly, while a recent Jamaican scandal involved the discovery that young women were taking "fowl pills", or chicken-fattening hormone supplements, to enhance their sexual appeal.

Ideals of male bodily beauty tend to be a version of classic masculinity: narrow hips, muscularity and broad shoulders figure highly in most hit lists. All these features relate to testosterone levels. But as with facial preferences, a lot may depend on what a woman is looking for. An extremely masculine figure, shaped by very high testosterone (and, perhaps, extreme narcissism in the gym), may communicate fertility – but it's not necessarily the figure of someone you'd want to live with, or who you'd trust to care about your pleasure, or, indeed, bring up your children.

Body language

The body "talks" all the time and, in courtship or flirtatious encounters, it talks loudest of all. If you can learn its language, it may speak more honestly than the mouth: a phenomenon called "non-verbal leakage". That said, mastering body language also means you can start to manipulate it.

Showing attraction is typically a deepening or extension of the way the body expresses other kinds of interest. Smiling, holding the gaze, opening the stance, moving closer, echoing the other person's posture: these moves occur in all kinds of non-sexual situations, they just get bigger or more intimate when attraction is added. Men are famously liable to misinterpret friendliness as sexual interest, partly because they're relatively bad at interpreting social situations and partly because they interpret the world more sexually in general.

To avoid misinterpretation, context is the best clue. People usually only flirt in situations where it's normal to do so. Anthropologists call this "cultural remission", meaning there's a slackening of the usual social rules in certain places and situations, such as bars or parties. A disproportionate number of couples get together in these environments because they are allowed – or allow themselves – to communicate sexual interest.

Correctly gauging attraction is also about reciprocity and escalation. If they don't do it back, or they never take it to the next level, they're probably not interested. The key to successful flirtation is a slow deepening of intimacy, matched with a sensitivity to the other person's response. You can force the pace to a certain extent, but you can't accelerate too hard. The flirtation-killer, by the same token, is any kind of backwards step.

Speaking with the face

Cultures vary hugely as to how long it's socially acceptable to hold the gaze, but holding it longer than normal is a universal signal of sexual interest. (Holding the gaze *much* longer than normal, of course, is a universal sign of the axe murderer.) Social eye contact generally escalates. People usually begin by scanning each other's faces: the eyes dart from point to point, taking it all in. In more formal encounters, the look rarely strays far beyond the eye area. But the bigger and slower the scan, the greater the sexual interest.

A lingering, triangular flick from eye to eye and down to mouth, for instance, is very friendly. If the eyes rove down as far as the body, or focus on the mouth, it's definitely flirtatious. The ultimate extension, "elevator eyes" from breasts to mouth and back up, is simply lascivious. Looking askance, obviously, signals lack of interest. (People find photos with a marginally less-than-direct gaze slightly less attractive than those looking full-on,

Pick-up artists and speed seducers

The pseudosciences of body language, gender relations and evolutionary psychology have proved a rich mine for a subculture of men who have turned meeting women into something of a competitive sport. The techniques of "pick-up artists", or PUAs, as they call themselves, mostly boil down to a hackneyed mix of flattery, directness, wit and boasting, combined with unusual attentiveness to body language and verbal signals – or "indicators of interest" as they're called in the jargon. Some techniques, such as toting around a piece of lint in order to pick it off a woman's shoulder, smack of desperation.

Great store is set by establishing the PUA as an "alpha male", and marking him out from the AFC, or "Average Frustrated Chump". The golden rule is to behave in an unusually assertive way, perhaps by asking direct or surprisingly intimate questions. Making less-than-subtle references to wealth, popularity and high-status work or hobbies is also crucial. Some techniques are borrowed from spurious sciences such as "neuro-linguistic programming" and hypnosis. One such is "negging", or making negative remarks, often combined with flattery in order to put the "target" on the back foot: "Your hair looks amazing! Is it real?" Another is to set up supposedly hypnotic associations by using "trance words" such as "allow", "think", or "feel"; simply talking about romance or sex is supposed to prime the target for sexual response. PUAs also borrow heavily from sales and marketing psychobabble, employing "patterns" designed to elicit certain responses, for instance, and staying focused on the desired outcome.

At its most innocuous, playing "the Game", as it has been called, gives men the confidence to start talking to people they're attracted to. The mantra employed by original "speed seducer", Ross Jeffries – "compliment, introduction, question" – isn't such a bad way to get started. Fears that men are somehow tricking women into bed are based on an overestimate of how effective this kind of patter could ever actually be.

Terry-Thomas (left) gives a master class in caddish charm in the British comedy classic *School for Scoundrels* (1960). Janette Scott is the delighted recipient as Ian Carmichael looks on, tight-lipped.

probably because they're interpreting the look as sexually uninterested.) If the person looks away and flicks back again, however, everything changes: alternating expressing interest and witholding it is the very stuff of flirtation.

The "eyebrow flash" is a classic sign of recognition. Used on someone unfamiliar, however, it says "I'd like to get to know you". The return look is crucial: if the other person looks puzzled, wondering where they met you perhaps, it's not looking good. A return flash, by contrast, is a come-hither, as is a prolonged flash, or a quizzically asymmetrical one. Eyelids speak volumes, too. People blink more when they're interested in or attracted to what they're looking at. Eyes also help reveal a true smile from a forced one, which doesn't crinkle the eyes in quite the same way.

Mirrors and echoes, preening and pointing

Hair-touching is one of the best-known signals of attraction, and in the world of amateur human zoology that is the study of body language, it's called preening. It may once have been linked to the release of natural scent from the hair, but it's also a form of display. People who are interested often expose their palms or wrists, for instance, which may be about showing vulnerability and encouraging intimacy.

Some movements seem uncompromisingly sexual. Women may unconsciously arch their backs or cross and uncross their legs, calling attention to their breasts and legs. Men often stand so as to emphasize their size and physical presence. And both sexes engage in the alarming-sounding genital pointing – which can mean anything from

standing face-on to shifting the hips forward. Most obviously, people relax and open their stance when they're with someone they like.

The least ambiguous signals of attraction are reciprocated ones, such as "mirroring". People have a sip of their drink in tandem, maybe, or lean on the same elbow, or unconsciously both reach up to touch their face at the same time. Psychologists call this "interactional synchrony" or the "gestural dance". If it's done deliberately, it can actually help create intimacy or attraction.

Everyone maintains a certain "personal space", a distance from their face or body within which they feel at ease with people. The "social" zone is usually comfortable talking – but not smelling – distance. Only friends or intimates are acceptable in the closer "personal zone". Touching brings people within what you might call the "zero zone". This is usually restricted to good friends or lovers – leaving aside socially codified contact like handshakes. Penetrative sex, of course, gets closest of all, which is partly why it's usually regarded as the ultimate in intimacy.

Different cultures acccept different social and personal distances, but moving across a boundary, wherever it's set, indicates a desire to increase intimacy. Flirts and seducers use transgression of these boundaries to show – and simultaneously encourage – sexual interest. This transgression could be anything from the choice of tight or revealing clothing to the touch of an arm or the asking of an unexpectedly intimate question.

However, it's usually not the person apparently driving the encounter who sets the pace. Studies show that whoever has the lower social status in an encounter is generally the first to touch. In flirtatious contexts, it's almost always the woman – however much the man may think he is doing all the work.

Sexuality

In biology, the term "sexuality" describes an evolutionary choice to follow a particular strategy of reproduction – and the physical consequences of that choice. The Welsh freshwater pearl mussel, for instance, may be "notoriously celibate" (to quote the UK environment agency) but it's not asexual. When the males get around to it, they release sperm into the water; if it happens to float by them, the female mussels will draw it up through their siphons and reproduce. Mussels, in short, have sexuality. Yeast, by contrast, which employs mere cell division to reproduce itself, is asexual.

Sexuality is not just a means of reproduction, however, it is also the instinct which drives sexual behaviour, and the expression of it. It is both something humans have and something they do. The word lies somewhere between, or curls around, the concepts of behaviour and identity. Sexuality shapes, describes and defines an individual's predilections, the quality of their fantasies and the expression of their preferences.

Nowadays, the word "sexuality" is most commonly used to define a gender preference for sexual partners. Yet this is very narrowing definition. It might be more useful to say that sexuality is like a signature perfume. It is a scent created from a unique combination of ingredients yet which strikes distinctive and recognizable notes: a musky masculinity matched with a certain floral charm, perhaps. And like a perfume, sexuality is intimately tied to branding and presentation – to the market in which it is discussed and sold. Ultimately, human sexuality is a matter of how people conceive of themselves as sexual beings, of how they present themselves to the world – and of how the world, and potential partners, especially, perceives them.

Homosexuality and identity

In most Western countries, homosexuality is generally regarded as a state of being. You "are" gay or straight. (Unless you're one of those

Asexuals and sexaholics

At the extraordinary extremes of human sexuality stand the asexual and the sexaholic. Asexuals aren't necessarily without any sexual feelings whatsoever. Some find the idea of sex repulsive, others are merely indifferent. Some sense a particular orientation – to men or women – but feel it as more emotional than sexual. Some are capable of arousal and may even masturbate for the pleasurable sensations it gives – but don't feel the classic sexual urge to do so. The point is that asexuals don't experience sexual *attraction* to the extent that they want to do anything about it.

Asexuals are often accused of being in denial, or of having a physiological or psychological problem. If their "condition" causes them distress, they may even be told they have hypoactive sexual desire disorder. Groups like AVEN, the Asexuality Visibility and Education Network exist to support those who want their sexual lifestyle to be respected. They cite studies among animals that show that lack of sexual behaviour is almost as common as homosexuality, or surveys which show that one or two percent of people have never had a sexual experience – and a healthy proportion of them are entirely happy about it.

"Sexaholics" have had just as big a battle on their hands for recognition. It hasn't helped that the idea of sexual addiction was born in conservative 1980s America, when infidelity or enthusiastic masturbation could get labelled "problem sex". Sexual expression that's getting out of control, however, or causing distress or hurt to others, is calling out for treatment. Various twelve-step programmes now exist, on the model of alcohol or narcotics anonymous, to help people who have been engaging in endless fruitless affairs, enjoying excessively risky sex, making repeated visits to sex workers or even subjecting others to frotteurism, exhibitionism or assault.

Unlike alcoholics, sexaholics are usually told to moderate their behaviour rather than abstain altogether. And sexaholics aren't hooked on taking a drug – or not an external one. In this, they may be more like problem gamblers, who start to need the adrenaline and dopamine rush provided by a punt. Sex provides a similar hormonal cocktail, with the added euphoria of orgasmic oxytocin.

Extreme behaviour can be a response to childhood sexual abuse, or it can express a psychological disorder, such as Obsessive Compulsive Disorder – a type of anxiety in which sufferers have repetitive thoughts and may feel compelled to perform personal "rituals" – which can include sexual ones. Histrionic and Narcissistic Personality Disorder are both characterized by personal grandiosity and the seeking of admiration – which can be expressed sexually.

rare bisexuals, but they're somehow counted as exceptional.) Many, many gay men and lesbian women feel this way. Their sexuality is part of them: it comes from their body and creates who they are.

It isn't really surprising that this attitude, known as essentialism, prevails in the West. If gay rights are to put down strong roots in society, they have to be planted on solid ground – and Protestant cultures especially are rarely comfortable with ambiguities of identity. Yet many other cultures, and many "men who have sex with men" (to use the jargon), take a rather different view. Some sex, they say, is just that: sex. It doesn't necessarily define who you are – and they're not just saying that because they're persecuted or in denial.

Queer theorists talk about different kinds of homosexuality. Opposing the essentialist position is behavioural theory: you are homosexual, it says, if you're a man having sex with men – regardless of what you call yourself. Others prefer to talk about sexuality in terms of orientation, locating innate sexuality in fantasies and preferences or patterns of arousal. In truth, sexuality is a mixture of all these things: to put it glibly, it is who you *are*, who you *do*, who you *say* you are and who you *want* to do.

Male homosexuality and the third gender

Homosexuality takes many forms. In Asia and the Americas, especially, men who take male lovers may dress or act as women – so-called gender-reversed homosexuality. These traditions are very ancient: the *Kamasutra* describes a "third gender" (traditionally mistranslated as "eunuchs") known for its excellence in giving men oral sex. The classical Greek playwright Aristophanes mocks "wide-arsed men", especially if they dress effeminately or wear their hair long. The Qur'an and other Islamic texts describe *mukhannathun*, feminine men who are not attracted to women (and who may or may not have sex with men).

The young, male actor-prostitutes of Edo-era Japan's *nanshoku* tea houses would often wear kimonos, blurring questions of sexuality and gender. As the great poet Basho asked, "Plum and willow, *washaku* [youth] or woman?". Today, the most famous reverse-gender groups are the *kathoeys* or "ladyboys" of Thailand, the *travestis* of Brazil and Argentina and the *hijra* of south Asia, and all of these groups encompass people born as men but who consider themselves to be a third gender – and who dress, for the most part, as women. Members of all three groups, interestingly, often work as male prostitutes, and their intermediate gender may be sustained by the fact that they tend to receive rather than penetrate. A minority have themselves castrated or seek gender reassignment surgery.

In some societies male transgender homosexuals may play a particular role in the life of a community – as shamans or priests, perhaps. India's *hijras*, for instance, traditionally perform certain religious ceremonies (as well as often engaging in male prostitution). The shamans of the Chukchi people of the Russian Arctic regions may dress and behave as women and have sexual relationships – including marriage – with men. Among the Mohave of north America, a male, homosexual shaman might be considered more powerful than a heterosexual one.

Men and boys, givers and receivers

Age-structured homosexuality, in which men or women take lovers of the same sex but of a different age, is best known from ancient Greece and Rome, and from the medieval Arab world. In Greece, the tradition was known as pederasty, meaning the sexual love of boys – though the evidence suggests

Sexuality: who you are, who you do, who you say you are or who you want to do?

that it was actually "striplings" in their late teens rather than young boys who were admired most. In classical Athens, eighteen-year-olds would run naked from the altar of love in the gymnasium to the city walls, while the city's seniors watched – and the scene probably encapsulates the one-way direction which is believed to have characterized Greek homosexual eroticism.

In fact, criticism of young men who responded in kind to the seductive advances of their older admirers – not to mention the plentiful erect penises seen on painted pots – is strong evidence that full sexual relationships were fairly common. Troth-plighting or ritual marriage took place between men, and older, more experienced soldiers often had younger lovers. The Roman emperor Hadrian had the youthful and divine Antinous. (He was quite literally divine: Hadrian decreed him a god

after his death.) Spartan soldiers regularly took male lovers, but the custom was for non-penetrative sex and a cloak was laid between them when they slept together. So too did two of the greatest of all ancient warriors: Achilles and Alexander the Great, whose loves for Patroclus and Hephaestion, respectively, are literally legendary. As for the Greek gods, one scholar has triumphantly announced that only one god never fell in love with a young man: Ares, the god of war.

The Umayyad, Seljuk and Ottoman courts of the Golden Age weren't far behind the Greeks in their love of boys – even if the Prophet himself warned of the danger of their attractions. Poets such as Rumi, Sa'di and Hafez praised the delights of young men, while the eighth-century Persian poet Abu Nawas, "of the Dangling Locks", went so far as to lovingly describe untying the trouser-bands of beardless young men so as to reveal "each man's quivering backside oscillating supplely like a green bough". (Abu Nawas was not exclusive in his orientation, however, describing the vaginas of prostitutes with similar glee as being like split pomegranates which smelled of "crushed amber".)

Pederasty quietly died out of Arab poetry in the nineteenth century, but still exists underground (because of political and religious restrictions) among Arab men who have sex with men – few of whom would identify as "gay" in a Western sense. In many cultures – including that of ancient Rome, and some contemporary Mediterranean, Latino and Islamic societies – the receptive partner would generally be considered effeminate, or homosexual, while the man doing the penetrating would not. Julius Caesar, for instance, was derided for allegedly receiving anal sex whereas the emperor Hadrian, as the older, active partner, was scarcely criticized for his relationship with Antinous. The non-homosexual self-identification of the penetrator is often reinforced if the person being penetrated is younger, lower class (a prostitute, perhaps) or a foreigner. Abu Nawas, typically, rhapsodized about the saqi, or Christian boys, he picked up in wine taverns.

condition, or simply a minority grouping. The former view, as espoused by sexologist Havelock Ellis, won out – partly in the hope that it would protect "inverts" from being criticized or attacked.

This argument still holds sway today: if biological roots can be found for homosexuality, then no one is "to blame" and discrimination can no longer be justified. For much of the twentieth century, however, psychoanalysis monopolized the study of homosexuality, so same-sex desire was often treated as a problem to be solved by analysis. Surprisingly, perhaps, Freud himself assumed humans were basically bisexual, but that most people "sublimated" their homosexual desires, redirecting them into other areas such as sports or friendship.

Predictably, those who "failed" to do so had their childhood to blame. Either they hadn't outgrown a childish, ambivalent model of sexuality – thanks, in men, to an excessively close relationship with a domineering mother or, in women, thanks to a failure to identify with their mother. Or they had "developed" homosexuality due to certain formative sexual experiences. This latter, specious, argument would underpin irrational fears among conservatives that predatory homosexuals could "turn" children gay.

Queer science

Almost since the word was coined, science has wanted to believe that homosexuality is hard-wired – either created by the parents' genes or formed in the womb. As far back as 1897, the authors of the pioneering study, *Sexual Inversion*, argued about whether to present homosexuality as a congenital or pathological

Gay genes, gay minds

Research has found no link between the dynamics of the family and homosexuality, and precious little between sexual preference and infantile experience. Instead, it has delved into the brain and the human genome, with major "discoveries" trumpeted in the early 1990s.

The secret history of lesbianism

Queer history has done much to rescue male homosexuality from censorship or historical obscurity, but the task is that much harder when it comes to lesbianism. The old urban myth about Queen Victoria's refusal to believe that lesbians even existed really is just a myth, but a revealing one. If the lives of women are shockingly under-represented in pre-twentieth-century history, the lives of lesbian women are almost entirely absent.

The wellspring of lesbianism is the Greek poet Sappho, who wrote richly homoerotic verses. She lived on the island of Lesbos in around the seventh-century BC, surrounded by a community of admirers. A contemporary poet addressed her as "you with strands of hair in violet, O holy one, you with the honey-sweet smile" and she has been pretty much worshipped ever since – to such an extent that both her name and the island she lived on have lent themselves to female homosexuality. If "Sapphic" isn't much used today, "lesbian" is pretty much the standard term.

There are more solid descriptions of lesbianism from ancient India and China. The Indian law book, *Arthashastra*, sets a fine for women having sex with women – at half the rate of men. The *Kamasutra* admits, rather sniffily, that women in harems sometimes dress as men and use dildoes. Early Chinese sex manuals describe women having sex with each other in some detail, as when "Lady Precious Yin" and "Mistress White Jade" lie intertwined, pressing their "jade gates" together "like fishes gobbling flies or water plants from the surface". (Unfortunately, in this instance, "Great Lord Yang" soon comes thrusting between them with his jade root.)

The best early evidence from Europe, is found in early medieval penitentials, rule books establishing how sinners should seek penance for specific sins. Sex between women is not as fiercely condemned as sex between men, but the authorities were definitely more upset if dildoes were involved. Convent records and letters can be revealing in a more positive way. In the twelfth century, a Bavarian nun recalled another's kisses, and how "with tender words you caressed my little breasts". Most extraordinarily, the seventeenth century Italian abbess Benedetta Carlini adopted the persona of a beautiful male angel called Splenditello, and carried on a highly spiritualized (and equally sexual) relationship with her cell mate.

Lesbians were rarely criminalized in Europe, and even more rarely prosecuted, though women masquerading as men crop up in criminal records from time to time – such as the Irish seventeenth-century lovers and partners in piracy Anne Bonny and Mary Read. A few lesbian couples even appear in marriage registers, or linked as married couples on tombs. Westminster Abbey houses a little-known memorial to the "close union and friendship" of Mary Kendall and Lady Catherine Jones, who did not wish their ashes to be divided after death.

Lesbians have also been "outed" by men attacking or mocking them. Frances Brudenell, Duchess of Newburgh, was attacked in verse in 1736 for presiding over a cabal of Dublin "tribades" (an archaic word for lesbians, though technically it means women who rub their vulvas together). But poetry, letters and diaries provide the richest source of lesbian testimony. In her love poem "To the Fair Clorinda", the seventeenth-century writer Aphra Behn tells the androgynous young woman of the title how "In pity to our Sex sure thou wer't sent/That we might Love, and yet be innocent./ For sure no Crime with thee we can commit; / Or if we shou'd – thy Form excuses it." In the nineteenth century, American poet Emily Dickinson addressed many ardent poems and letters to the love of her life, Susan Gilbert.

Until recently, scholars tended to dismiss such expressions of love as merely "passionate friendship". Then, the diaries of Yorkshirewoman Anne Lister turned up. Among detailed descriptions of love affairs, she described in February 1821 "that soft intercourse which blends us into one", sighing that "there is no feeling like it". Only a week before, she confessed that "I love, and only love, the fairer sex and thus beloved by them in turn, my heart revolts from any other love than theirs." This kind of clarity was prophetic. Before the century was out, lesbianism would no longer be a matter of private confession only.

Sapphic love: the poet Sappho and her lover Erinna as depicted by gay pre-Raphaelite painter Simeon Solomon.

How many people are gay?

The great American sex researcher Alfred Kinsey told an astonished – and fascinated – American public that 4 percent of men were homosexual. And 37 percent of men had reached orgasm with another man. Kinsey's figures now look as if they may have been slight overestimates. Depending on the survey, between 2 and 4 percent of Western men and 1 and 2 percent of women identify as homosexual (though they may have had sex with someone of the opposite sex), while some 20 percent of men and 10 percent of women have had sex with someone of their own gender.

Biologist Dean Hamer found that gay men were twice as likely to have gay relatives on the mother's side, suggesting that any genetic material would be on the maternally inherited X-chromosome. True enough, men with gay brothers were shown to share the same DNA sequences in the "Xq28" region. It was inevitably dubbed the "gay gene". Psychologists J. Michael Bailey and Richard Pillard, meanwhile, found that half of gay identical twins had a twin who was also gay. Compared to non-identical twins (one in five) and adoptive siblings (one in ten), this suggested that genes influenced sexual orientation to a strong degree.

Both studies were later criticized. Having similar DNA in a particular region doesn't amount to a "gay gene". And other researchers failed to replicate Hamer's findings and reckoned that, in fact, only a fifth of gay identical twins had a gay twin after all. Similar criticisms met the research of neuro-anatomist Simon Le Vay, who found that an area of the brain's hypothalamus known as INAH-3 was smaller in gay men than in straight men, and more like that of a woman. Critics pointed out that he had examined just 41 brains, belonging to men who had died of AIDS and whose testosterone had been low due to treatment. Le Vay himself pointed out that brain differences could as well be a result of homosexual behaviour as the cause of homosexual orientation.

But a series of studies in the 2000s found other similarities: both between the brains of gay men and straight women, and between those of straight men and lesbian women. The corpus callosum, which connects the two halves of the brain, was one such area, as was the amygdala, which seems to process emotional memories. In various tests lesbian women were found to be like straight men and gay men like straight women.

In 2008, Stockholm neuroscientists Ivanka Savic and Per Lindström announced that gay men and straight women had symmetrical brains, while lesbian women and straight men were asymmetric. The study was hailed as significant because these structures were fixed at birth, so couldn't be shaped by life experiences or behaviour. Yet another Swedish study – which surveyed every single identical twin in the country in the same year – worked out that the genetic component of same-sex behaviour in men could amount to no more than 35 percent. The rest was made up of "other individual-specific environmental factors." It looked as if the gay gene had come to the end of the helix.

Hormosexuality?

What Savic's study still couldn't answer was the most hotly debated question: was homosexual orientation genetic (or partly so), or was it the result of exposure to hormones in the womb, as many scientists argued. Some think the "default setting" for humans is to be attracted to males, but that prenatal exposure to male hormones triggers attraction to females. If that exposure were to be altered in some way (perhaps by the hormone levels themselves, perhaps by a genetic predisposition not to react to them), then men with same-sex orientation might be the result.

This theory could explain the mysterious fraternal birth-order effect. The more elder brothers a man has, the more likely he is to be gay – and having older brothers is one of the strongest predictors of sexual orientation. Do mothers' bodies attempt to cap the number of potential grandchildren? Or are parents somehow subconsciously moulding the sexuality of their children, perhaps to the same effect?

Sociologists think the effect is more likely to be social, not the result of evolution or biology. They also point to a strong link between "childhood gender nonconformity" – tomboys and sissies, to use the old terms – and adult sexual orientation. One researcher found that 80 percent of boys who threw a ball in a "girly" way at school failed to fit in and became sexually oriented towards men. "Throwing like a girl" is about nothing more than practice, and copying your peers, so these boys were evidently identifying with the opposite sex early on. Some think gender noncomformity leads to the "other" gender becoming regarded as the sexual object: a practice known to psychoanalysis as transference.

Others believe that both are effects of some other, as yet undiscovered, evolutionary advantage.

Why it's good to be gay

If homosexuality does have a genetic component, the obvious question is: why? Why would a gene continue to exist that, on the face of it, would seem to predispose its carriers not to have children? What's it for? Biologists have come up with all kinds of speculative theories, among them the "gay uncle" theory – he is supposedly around to help out with the childcare, thus boosting the survival chances of his little prehistoric nieces and nephews.

There's precious little evidence for either this theory, however, or for the "nice guy" theory, which supposes that genes for useful, "feminine" nurturing traits sometimes get over-enthusiastically expressed. At least there is some evidence that gay men tend to be more sensitive and empathetic, but this could just as well have been a cultural development – marking out social distance from the far-end-of-the-autistic-spectrum culture of hetero males.

Perhaps more convincing is the theory that there's actually a gene for attraction to males, which has obvious evolutionary benefits for women. It might just happen to get itself expressed in some males – perhaps because a gene carried by the father didn't "switch off" the male-attraction gene. This theory makes homosexuality sound dangerously like a malfunction – but then maleness itself, put in these terms, could be seen in that way. Certainly, comparison with the gene for sickle-cell, which protects against malaria but can cause incredible pain, is unhelpful.

Ultimately, the extent to which homosexuality is biological is entirely unclear – so speculating about the purpose of the imagined genes which cause it is rather fantastical. It's quite possible that culture is transcending biology, in any case. Homosexuality could just as well be an expression of human creativity. It could be *for* pleasure. Evidence from animals is certainly pointing that way.

Birds do it – homosexuality in animals

Homophobes often justify their prejudices by claiming that homosexuality isn't "natural". In 2007, Oslo's Museum of Natural History put on an extraordinary exhibition which brilliantly countered this argument. It showed male giraffes having anal sex with each other, river dolphins penetrating blowholes, whales rubbing their penises together, orang-utans enjoying a blow job and all kinds of natural-world fornication.

And that was only a few examples. In 1999, Canadian biologist Bruce Bagemihl counted no fewer than 470 animal species which enjoyed same-sex sexual behaviour. Since then, the count has reached the thousands, partly because zoologists have been re-evaluating what they're seeing. In the past, anal intercourse between male giraffes was explained away as "sparring", and female monkeys ignoring males and rubbing their vulvas together were said to be "socializing". No longer.

It's not just physical sex, either. Animals of the same sex pair long-term and share parenting, too. Penguins are famously inclined towards "gay marriages" – as in Roy and Silo, the celebrated pair of chinstrap penguins at New York's Central Park

Zoo, who famously raised a baby together in 2003. In fact, roughly one in five penguins, one in ten male sheep and half the orange-fronted parakeets in zoos get it on with a partner of their own sex. Bighorn rams will mate with ewes in the rutting season, but the rest of the time they prefer their own sex.

One in five penguins are gay: two male Humboldt penguins cuddle up, impervious to the charms of Schumi, a female controversially brought in by the zoo's keepers in order to "turn" them.

The conclusion isn't so much that some animals are "gay", and that homosexuality is therefore "natural". It's more simple: different species behave differently. It's also clear that animal sex is about pleasure as well as procreation. The more social the species, in fact, the greater the rate of homosexual behaviour – arguably because the cleverer the species, the more able it is to act on its own volition, rather than being slave to hormonal urges.

Bisexuality

Bisexuality is perhaps the most misunderstood sexual identity – maybe because it's the least well-defined. It doesn't necessarily mean being equally attracted to men and women, and it may not involve having sex with men and women, still less at the same time. Freud claimed that humans are innately bisexual, and research into fantasies and use of pornography lends his idea some

Deviant, greedy, undecided — or bisexual?

❝ I was born bisexual. And I was aware of my sexuality from a very young age: from something like four years old, I'd say. I was more strongly sexually attracted to women – it was breasts, I was transfixed by breasts. I was always attracted to men as well, but it was with a very different mindset. With men it's more an emotional thing, it's more about them finding me attractive – I like the power dynamic of the male-and-female relationship. With women it's different, it's more physical. When I sleep with women I'm maybe slightly more anxious initially about my body. (I've got quite heavy thighs and if I sleep with a girl who's got skinny legs I actually find myself getting jealous.)

The lovemaking is different. Men are generally more sexually aggressive and, in a lot of situations with men, you've got this golden goal of having an orgasm, and that can be it, over, once the man has come. With women it's much more of an organic process.

I mean, it can be like that with men – getting lost in sensuality, you don't know which way round you are in the bed, that sort of thing – but it does tend to be the thing with women more often. And women are better at fingering, definitely. They have a much better idea of where the G-spot is.

I think being bisexual affects the way I make love, as much as anything. It brings a sensuality: there's not a script, not a menu that you have to pick things off. In terms of how people see me, I think there's something more socially acceptable about gay men than bisexual women. The problem is lack of understanding. Bisexuality is not seen as a sexuality in its own right, it's seen as deviant, greedy or undecided. People always ask "what do you prefer?" because they think you must prefer one sex over the other. And if I am in a relationship with a woman, people see me as a lesbian. As bisexuals we just get lumped in. It's "LGBT" – and I'm "partly lesbian". But actually, as a bisexual woman you share something with other bisexual women. ❞

support. As do population statistics. A significant number of "heterosexual" people have had sexual experiences with someone of their own sex, and many more might do so if there were less social pressure to select one sexual identity.

To explain the "give" built into the system, pioneering sexologist Alfred Kinsey (see p.379) proposed a seven-point scale, with one as exclusively straight and "six" as exclusively gay, and with various degrees of interaction in between. (The seventh point is an "x" for asexuality). "Nature rarely deals with discrete categories", Kinsey said, "the world is not to be divided into sheep and goats". And as a zoologist he would have known.

The Kinsey Scale has passed into legend – some gay men will proudly describe themselves as a "Kinsey Six" – but it still doesn't really account for the nuances of orientation and identity. It doesn't describe a married man who has had sex only with his wife but fantasizes about having sex with men, for example. It isn't much use, either, to a woman who is married for many years before finding a female partner in middle age. Her behavioural history might be predominantly heterosexual, but society would be more likely to call her a lesbian. As feminist biologist Anne Fausto-Sterling has commented, "the act of coming out as a lesbian can negate an entire lifetime of heterosexual activity".

It might be more useful to talk about sexualities. Many people pass through different phases in their life: from casual sex to serial monogamy to marriage, for instance. Or from men and women to just one man, or woman. Sexuality isn't just about identity, it can be about who you happen to fall in love with.

Martians and Venutians – the gender gap

In the West, the prevailing view seems to be that women are less "highly sexed" than men, and much scientific and statistical research seems to end up proving it. So too do the theories of evolutionary biology: women would have to invest much more time and energy in any resulting conception, the argument goes, so they are wired to require much greater investment in the sexual act. Men, meanwhile, will compete for casual sex wherever they can get it.

Yet many cultures around the world and throughout history have characterized women, not men, as sexually voracious. Europeans long perceived women's sexual appetites as a threat, for instance. It was Eve who "brought sin into the world", after all, thanks to her inability to resist that juicy apple. Of course, this belief may reflect cultural misogyny and a justification for controls placed on female sexuality. But it is arguable that if sex is potentially so costly for women, in evolutionary terms, then female desire must be all the stronger; why else would women by driven to risk it?

Perhaps there is no major difference. One 1970s survey of 93 societies around the world found that more than three-quarters believed that both sexes had roughly the same sex drive. And modern surveys into sexual behaviour and beliefs tend to show that the more liberal and equal societies become, the more women's sexual behaviour starts to look like men's. Even if the words first emerged from within gay, male culture, "fuck buddies" or "friends-with-benefits" are now features of heterosexual teen life – for young men and women alike.

What women want

If personal ads are any guide, men and women are attracted to rather different qualities. That is, while they share the same core desires women's "wish lists" mention status-related qualities ten times as often as men, according to one study. Another survey found that women mentioned resources twice as often. Men, by contrast, often emphasize a certain look or visual standard.

What causes the difference is controversial. Men are certainly more sexually sensitive to visual cues. Evolutionary psychology would also have it that, in the deep past, men only needed to seek fertility in a partner: they could inseminate and move on. Primeval women, who would have had to breastfeed children at least beyond early infancy, needed to find a co-parent as well as a sperm donor. Hence the importance of personality, and ability to provide resources.

It sounds persuasive. But evolutionary psychologists often seem to find adaptational explanations for what could simply be cultural norms – justifying their own gender prejudices, even. Male fetishization of physical attractiveness may equally have been shaped by centuries of patriarchy: men have long been able to express blunter desires than women, and may have internalized this relative freedom. People want what they think they're allowed to want, in other words. And in a world where women are still at a huge socio-economic disadvantage, they remain obliged to value partners who can provide resources.

As liberal societies emerge, with improved opportunities for women, sexual behaviour and partner preference is equalling out. Women may still seek potential fathers for their children, but when it comes to casual sex, many are more interested in attractive – if possibly unlikeably over-masculine – partners. Studies even suggest that women are more likely to have sex with good-looking "cads" around the time of ovulation, and "dads" at other times. And relatively wealthy women, studies show, place a higher value on male attractiveness.

How much, how often

Research typically finds that men usually say they want sex much more often than women. In the Richters survey (see p.163), for instance, Australian men ticked the "four to six times a week" box more often than any other, while women most commonly ticked "two to three times". Men also masturbate and use pornography more frequently. But statistics can be misleading. Men tend to want (or be able) to have sex for much shorter periods of time than women, and their orgasms may be less powerful. Their energy investment in each sexual act tends to be lower, therefore. So is it really that they want "less sex" more often?

On average men do seem to be more sociosexual, meaning they are more likely to have multiple partners on the go, and they're typically more interested in less "invested" relationships. In 1989, Russell D. Clark and Elaine Hatfield published the results of a study which starkly illustrates the gender divide. On campus, the two psychology professors instructed attractive men and women to ask strangers, variously, to go on a date, to come back to their apartment, and to have sex right away. Fifty percent of men said "yes" to an attractive woman asking for a date, 69 percent agreed to come back with her and 75 percent were up for sex. Among women, the percentages of those saying "no" to the same offers, posed by attractive men, were 50, 94 and a flat 100 percent.

Perhaps Clark and Hatfield were asking the wrong people. American students, stereotypically, have fairly rigid gender expectations about sexual behaviour. And while younger men are relatively promiscuous, or want to be, sociosexuality in women tends to peak in the 30s when, perhaps, they are conscious of their declining fertility. Interestingly, masculine-looking women, and women rated as "attractive" have relatively high sociosexuality, which may, in the latter case at least, simply reflect a greater number of opportunities.

Ultimately, there's more variation within the sexes than between them. The Clark–Hatfield study doesn't account for personality. It turns out that trusting people, men and women alike, are more monogamously inclined. In fact, the classic promiscuous person scores high on extroversion (they're confident enough to try), low on neuroticism (they can cope with rejection) and low on agreeableness (they don't much mind who they hurt). Promiscuity has also been linked to childhood stress, and to insecurity.

Cruising and networking

Men almost invariably report having had more sexual partners than women – a statistical anomaly which is partly explained by female sex workers being under-represented in surveys but which also arises, as one sociologist put it, from

Desire, arousal and consent

It is entirely possible for both men and women to exhibit physiological signs of arousal without feeling any desire for sex. Female victims of sexual assault, for instance, may experience some internal lubrication. Unless this is understood as a purely physiological reaction, this can be distressing. This is one area where men and women are very similar, in fact, as male rape victims sometimes report experiencing erections or ejaculation. The key issue is very simple: saying yes is the only way in which someone can give consent.

"men's tendency to exaggerate and women's fear of derogatory labelling." Men often make rough estimates to researchers, and round up; women tend to count carefully and maybe drop a few awkward or ambiguous encounters.

Contrary to popular belief, gay and straight men commonly have a similar number of partners over a lifetime. But it's also true that promiscuity is both common and widely accepted in many gay circles, whereas lesbian cultures tend to be characterized by the pursuit of longer-term pairings. Male "cruising" sites like manhunt.net ("get on, get off") and gaydar.co.uk are responsible for millions of "hook-ups"; lesbian equivalents tend to be more like social networking sites – and lesbian user profiles aren't illustrated, on the whole, by a close-up of the owner's genitals.

The obvious conclusion is that, in the absence of a culture of sexual restraint, and in the presence of opportunity, men will sleep around. Of course, gay men don't necessarily represent a pure version of male sexuality. Sexual behaviour is driven by culture as well as biology, and gay men are subject to cultural pressures which encourage promiscuity. They don't encounter the matrimony model in the same way as straight men, for instance, and they tend to form very strong friendship networks. And by coming out, gay men have already questioned and overcome a social practice (heterosexuality) which traditionally disapproves of promiscuity.

Flaring up and cooling down: arousal

If there is a biological difference between men and women, it's probably connected to arousal. As the ancient Chinese classic *I Ching* puts it: "Fire easily flares up, but it is easily extinguished by water; water takes a long time to heat over the fire, but cools down very slowly." It's true that men tend to be more quickly ready for sex, given that their arousal seems to be less dependent on contextual factors (right place, right time, right person, right lighting), and more on visual cues (breasts and bottoms, stockings and sexual display). Men orgasm more quickly, too, and take longer to recover before they're ready to go again.

For a long time, research supported the view that women were "cooler". They weren't thought to initiate sexual encounters, for instance – quite mistakenly – and they didn't respond nearly as enthusiastically to pornography. Then somebody realized that if you show women porn designed to arouse men, it might not work so well. Given a more even-handed stimulus, men and women are about as quickly and easily aroused as each other – physically aroused, at least. In laboratory conditions, some women don't report *feeling* desire even though the equipment may register bodily arousal. It may be that it takes a little time for the internal desire–arousal feedback loop to become established – for a woman to "warm up", to use old-fashioned language. If so, this would explain why women stereotypically prefer longer and more mentally stimulating foreplay. It may be that desire and arousal lie further apart in women than in men (see p.54).

Women may have a slower desire response to pornography, but it seems to be more open to all kinds of pornography, whether straight, gay or lesbian. Male arousal, by contrast is relatively dependent on watching scenes that fit the man's own sexual orientation. As psychologist J. Michael Bailey put it, "arousal is orientation", in men: "that's how gay men learn they are gay".

Is female arousal shaped more strongly by the mind, less rooted in the body? Or is it simply that men are trained to be aware of their own genitalia? Perhaps men are more genitally focused, partly because the evidence of arousal is so much more … pressing. You can miss the first light sweat of vaginal lubrication, but a twitch of the penis is a convincing telltale.

Fantasy

Many people would argue that the true core of their sex life is located in their mind – in fantasy. For those without partners, in fact, fantasy may be the only place where sex regularly occurs, and it is even more popular than masturbation.

Fantasies are not the same as fleeting sexual thoughts, or even romantic daydreams. Fantasies

Le Minotaur (1933) by Pablo Picasso. Sexual fantasies can be as troubling as nightmares.

for meditation, or they may involve elaborate scenarios with well-developed characters and storylines. As often as they are truly "fantastical", however, fantasies may be entirely realistic. Many are straight or tweaked replays of past sexual experiences, almost as if the memory was a pornographic cinema or slideshow. (Men sometimes joke about collecting "material" for later masturbatory use.)

Dream or nightmare?

Everyone has what British psychologist Brett Kahr calls "pub fantasies", the ones they are willing to share or joke about with friends or partners. They often involve celebrities, or re-runs of pornography. Most people, however, have deeply private fantasies as well, ones which they would never discuss, and may feel very guilty about – even as they enjoy the sexual rush. Often this is because they fear the content or style of their fantasy is (or would be seen as) "kinky" or "perverted" – and by public standards, many peoples' fantasies would often be judged in exactly that way. Many would be outright illegal.

Fantasies are also kept private because they are seen as a form of quiet infidelity to a partner. For some, the distinctively repetitive quality of what

are the backing track to sexual activity or the focus of mental concentration during it. They help people achieve arousal, even when it might be difficult. They improve the quality of orgasms. Their familiar nature, and the ability to control them, provide psychological comfort. They can lead the mind out of its daily fears and worries and, perhaps, prepare it for sexual activity – or sleep.

Fantasies stereotypically occur during private, solo sex but they often sit alongside or overlay or underpin partner sex. They may be simple and repetitive thoughts or ideas, almost like mantras

Freudians call their "central masturbatory fantasy" makes them fear that fantasizing in itself is evidence that they are some kind of sexual compulsive.

Fantasies may be as exciting as dreams – to which they are closely related – but they may equally be as troubling as nightmares. They often explore the forbidden: sexual violence or coercion, group sex, anal sex, sex with young people or family members, gender-transgression, domination, sadism, masochism or, for heterosexuals, same-sex activity. For Freud, this was evidence that they fulfill primitive wishes – typically desires born from infantile experiences – which cannot consciously be acknowledged.

Freud also commented that fantasies were "a correction of unsatisfying reality". In a very simple way, he was right. Fantasies often explore the most ordinary of all forbidden territory: sex with someone who's not your partner, or who wouldn't ever actually have sex with you. Even though more than half the adult population fantasize chiefly about having sex with their own partners, the majority will be thinking about someone else for significant stretches of time, even while having sex. The potential for guilt and shame is obvious and yet (almost) everyone does it.

Fantasy material

While having sex with "someone else" is a fantasy shared by billions, the *kind* of sex is a much more personal affair. Highly romantic, intimate, emotional sex is incredibly popular, especially among women. Novelty and transgression is too, especially among men. Men may be more focused on the body itself, women on their lovers' reaction to their own bodies. Men may seek "pure" sexual experiences; women to impose social conditions or emotional scenarios.

Different surveys come up with very different figures for who fantasizes about what, but every conceivable behaviour and "perversion" occurs, in much greater numbers than reflect the things people actually do. Fantasy is, literally, extra-ordinary. That said, romance, or sex attached to loving feelings, is perhaps the number one fantasy – and it's often a fantasy firmly attached to a past, present or (imagined) future lover.

Voyeurism and group sex, however, are also very popular. This could be a way of exploring homosexual desire, it could be a method of rewriting feelings of sexual inadequacy – it could also be about using danger to accelerate sexual tension and arousal. Fantasies of being dominated are hugely common, too. Many people act out scenes of humiliation in their minds, often delighting in a sense of being dirty – either in some abstract way or literally, involving perhaps sweat or excreta.

Displaying body parts, or having them observed, is also common. For Freudians, this is evidence of the mind adapting itself around the trauma originally experienced by an infant discovering its own body, or the bodies of others. It could also be leakage between stress and sexual arousal. The aggressive content of many fantasies is a sign that violence and sex share some common roots, or perhaps pathways. Both serve to get the heart pumping, and both are pointed towards some kind of explosive release. In fantasy, that connection can be safely explored without the terrible consequences of actual violence.

The puzzle of rape fantasies

A few surveys have suggested that "forced sexual encounters" are the most common of all fantasies – a disturbing finding, given that non-consensual sex is one of the cruellest things humans do to each other. That quite so many people have "rape fantasies" should perhaps be comforting, given that few do, in fact, force themselves on people. So too should the fact that many more people fantasize about being forced into sex than the other way round.

Looking beyond the headline, a rape fantasy is not the expression of a desire to rape or be raped, and fantasy rapes bear very little relation to real ones. The person being forced in a fantasy almost invariably enjoys the experience, or starts enjoying it, unlike real life rape. And in their fantasy, they are usually being compelled to do something they "actually" or "secretly" want to do – which, again, is untrue of actual rape situations, however much rapists may persuade themselves otherwise. Nancy Friday, the author and collector of fantasies, wrote that in the few sadistic fantasies reported by men, they were usually seeking the woman's approval: "A man might fantasize using softly padded handcuffs on a woman, so he won't hurt her wrists", she observed, "or make sure that she enjoys the 'rape' and has plenty of orgasms."

Rape-victim fantasies may be a protection against guilt or shame. If you "had no choice" in your fantasy, you're not responsible for it. As Nancy Friday puts it, you can still be a "nice girl". She also believes that sexual violence may "deal with the mix of frustration, love and rage that men feel towards women". Women, she says, are traditionally the gatekeepers of sex: it is they who have the power to accept or refuse the supplicant male. A fantasy of forced sex is a way in which the man can regain his power.

Rape fantasies may also give the fantasizer licence to explore forbidden territory. Someone who might be disgusted or terrified by, say, rough or group sex in real life can freely enjoy the experience in fantasy without having to confront the real-life consequences. Even while being compelled in your fantasy, you are, ultimately, in control of it.

Safety and danger

According to psychoanalysts, fantasies may act as a defence against terrifying or shameful thoughts. By turning the darkest desires or the most traumatic experiences into a kind of theatre in which the fantasizer is the director, those negative or disturbing thoughts and experiences can be managed. The danger is that they may also be used to avoid facing up to issues and actually reinforce patterns of thinking or behaviour which are destructive to the self – or others. For one person, an occasional, private fantasy of forced or underage sex may satisfy the inward urge; for another, the fantasy may take on a life of its own, growing in force and intensity until the desire to attempt to fulfill it becomes an obsession.

Acting out fantasies in real life is risky. Often, the fantasy is only enjoyable as fantasy; the real life experience is not at all the same. Fantasies may not be free of guilt, but they are free of consequences. In real life, the emotional impact of a sexual act – guilt, discomfort, pain, injury, relationship stress or breakdown, loss of trust or respect or self-esteem or just money – may far outweight the sexual or emotional reward of living the fantasy.

2
Bodies

2
Bodies

The deepest human emotions seem to be actually felt *in the body* – and sexual emotions are perhaps expressed there most strongly of all. Confidence and self-esteem are often reflected in the relationship between a person and their genitals – some would argue that they are even produced by it. Relationships between lovers, equally, may be encapsulated in the way they touch or talk about each other's otherwise secret parts.

Most obviously, gender, or the sense of which sex we belong to, is inextricably linked with the sexual parts of the body. After a cultural phase of a few centuries or so in which the distinctions between men and women were rigidly maintained, the West seems to be moving towards a more fluid conception of what and who it's possible to be. Transgender people are presenting notions of masculinity and femininity in new and often creative ways; transsexuals are asserting self-definition, and winning if not acceptance then a degree of respect; and, beyond gender, intersexuals, whose bodies from birth didn't conform to the physical norm, are forcing the medical establishment – and society in general – to rethink what biological sex actually is.

Given the extreme importance of the relationships people have with their own genitals, it's odd how little their workings are understood. Penises and clitorises and the rest are largely tucked away in the dark, brought out only for sanitation, micturation and the odd bit of copulation. Most people know their knuckle from their cuticle but relatively few can identify the fornix or the frenulum. And then there's the whole set of language difficulties that surround the words "vagina" and "clitoris" and their referents – both astonishing structures, as this chapter will reveal.

Hers

Women's bodies are especially subject to name confusion. People often use the word vagina to mean everything "down there", but properly, the whole genital area is the vulva, and vagina refers only to the opening. As for the word clitoris, it turns out that the piece of flesh to which the name is usually given is just the glans or tip of a far larger set of structures – which, amazingly, lacks a proper name of its own, even though it's the powerhouse of female orgasm.

The greater clitoris

The name of the clitoris, whose tip nestles at the top of the vagina's lips, reflects its importance.

It comes from the Greek word *kleitoris*, which originally referred to the female genitals as a whole. There's some truth to this. In diagrams of the female body, the label saying "clitoris" usually points at the piece of flesh at the top of the vestibule, where the lips join. This is, however, like mistaking the helmet for the whole penis.

Connected to the clitoris's glans, but invisible, are a host of deeper structures which play a crucial role in sexual response, from arousal to orgasm. There's the urethral sponge and the so-called G-spot (see p.47) and a wishbone-shaped tissue, which lies beneath the inner lips. This is made of cavernous erectile tissue, and becomes engorged with blood when aroused. Where the lower ends of these twin bulbs press against the sides of the vagina wall, they are sensitive to pressure – one of the reasons penetration may feel satisfying.

What Marie Stopes famously called a "small, vestigial organ" in 1918 is now thought to make up a tissue cluster along with the urethra, vagina and the nerves, blood vessels and muscles of the perineal area. It's this cluster – not just the tip of the clitoris – which is now understood to be responsible for the wide- and deep-rooted phenomenon of female sexual response.

The glans and shaft

The clitoral glans – the so-called "man in a boat" or "pea in a pod" – is typically the most sensitive part of a woman's body, with between 6000 and 8000 nerve receptors. That's more than the lips, the fingertips or anywhere else in the body (and roughly four times the number found on the head of the penis). It becomes engorged on arousal, and may swell or project (or, further down the line of

arousal, retreat), but it doesn't become erect like a penile glans, as there is no rigid "tunica" for the tissue to press against.

Behind the glans, a shaft made of spongy erectile tissue runs up and back for an inch or so (making it at least double the length of the glans), before splitting into two wishbone-like legs (or crura) that there internally deeper in the body. These crura are mirrored (and joined) to the paired bulbs, which are made of a spongy material – much like the shaft of the penis. The crura and bulbs are internal, and their engorgement can't be felt by the hand. But when it's aroused, the ridge-like shaft of the clitoris can be felt above the glans: it's something like the eraser on the end of a pencil in width, but longer – maybe the length of a fingertip.

When masturbating, many women rub this shaft as well as (or instead of) bearing down

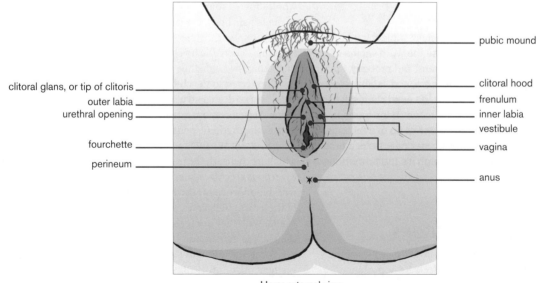

clitoral glans, or tip of clitoris
outer labia
urethral opening

fourchette

perineum

pubic mound

clitoral hood
frenulum
inner labia
vestibule

vagina

anus

Hers: external view

directly on the glans. Others avoid touching the tip directly, but work on top of or alongside the clitoral hood – a fold of skin that's the equivalent of the male foreskin. Like the male foreskin, if you look underneath it you can find smegma, the white, waxy accumulation of shed skin cells and oils which builds up in any healthy adult.

The G-spot or urethral sponge

A finger of spongy erectile tissue extends back from the opening of the urethra, cushioning the urethral tube on its two-inch journey towards the bladder. You could think of it as the equivalent of the penile shaft, which is how the seventeenth-century Danish doctor Thomas Bartholin thought of it. He described a penis-like organ "of a hard

and nervous flesh, and somewhat spongy", and observed how it "becomes longer or shorter, broader or narrower, and swells sundry ways according to the lust of the woman".

The elusive G-spot is in fact just the area within the vagina where the underlying urethral sponge can be felt. To locate it you'll need to start off aroused, as only then does the tissue get engorged with blood and press against the interior wall of the vagina. Put a finger into the vagina, with the knuckles pointing down, and curl it upwards in a beckoning-type motion. Search about a bit on the upper wall of the vagina and the fingertip will eventually come upon a bobbly or ridged area which feels something like the skin of the upper palate just behind the front teeth, only more fleshy.

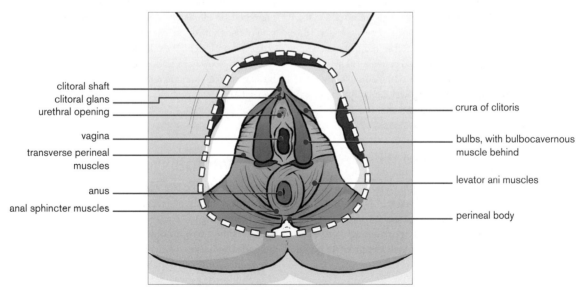

clitoral shaft
clitoral glans
urethral opening
vagina
transverse perineal muscles
anus
anal sphincter muscles

crura of clitoris

bulbs, with bulbocavernous muscle behind

levator ani muscles

perineal body

Hers: internal view

G-spots, X-spots, U-spots

The G-spot was unleashed on the world in 1981 by the sexologists John Perry and Beverly Whipple. They named it in honour of Dr Ernst Gräfenberg, who had been the first modern anatomist to describe the urethral sponge in his 1950 paper *The Role of the Urethra in Female Orgasm*. The press reacted as if someone had invented a second clitoris. Women, on the whole, reacted rather differently. Some were puzzled and disappointed, as they failed to locate any such spot at all. Some found it and thought the sensation vaguely unpleasant, making them feel as if they needed to urinate. Others delightedly reported newer, deeper orgasmic sensations or even hitherto undiscovered talents for female ejaculation (see p.171). A few feminists decried the G-spot on political grounds, seeing it as part of a conspiracy to re-establish the supremacy of penetrative sex and to reinforce the myth of the "vaginal orgasm" (see p.164).

Sexperts weren't slow to see the commercial potential. If the G-spot could cause such a sensation, what other parts of the sexual body could be "discovered"? Sticking with the urethral sponge, there was the U-spot, named after the urethra itself.

Gentle stimulation of the area above and on either side of the opening, it was reported, could result in an "unexpectedly powerful erotic response". Then there was the X-spot, which one sexpert trumpeted as "better than the G-spot and double its thrill", but "X-spot Orgasm" was the result of an "X-tasy spot rub" – which turned out to be a method of directly stimulating the cervix.

The A-spot refers to the snappily named Anterior Fornix Erogenous Zone – which is basically the toe-end of the vagina, a tiny space tucked away behind the mouth of the cervix. When a woman is seriously aroused, this space opens up, allowing access to parts of the female prostate embedded in the vaginal wall. Stimulation of the A-spot is said to ensure speedy lubrication. According to its chief promoter, sex therapist Barbara Keesling, the right kind of penetrative stimulation can "trigger explosive orgasms", and "open the door to a lifetime of sexual fulfillment". You'll have to buy her book to find out how, of course – though nowadays you can buy dedicated vibrator-probes, which should at least help unpick the lock.

This is where the vaginal wall touches against the urethral sponge. Inside is a skein of some thirty-odd tiny prostate-type glands – one reason that the G-spot has been renamed by some as the "female prostate". These area can be sensitive to touch, but the G-spot is no more a magic orgasm button than its male equivalent, the prostate gland (see p.64).

The vagina

If the clitoris is the live wire of the female anatomical family, sensitive, brilliant, moody and always wanting to be at the centre of the action, the vagina is the earth mother: slower to respond, but powerful in her own way. It is usually some four or five inches long, but capable of dramatic expansion – as childbirth proves.

The root of the word vagina is telling. It comes from the Latin for "scabbard", implying that it's purpose is for a sword to be sheathed there. Of course, the vagina is a remarkably active part of the body, and it plays many roles. It features in the birth canal and as the conduit for the outflow of the menstrual cycle. And it also allows penetration.

The upper or inner parts of the vagina are relatively insensitive to touch, but as an organ it's far from being without sexual function. In fact, one survey found that 94 percent of women considered their vaginas to be erotically sensitive. The entrance of the vagina has specialized nerve endings called Merkel receptors. These respond to steady pressure but are not well adapted for sensing other kinds of touch, like friction.

The inner end, or top of the vagina is closed off by the cervix. Properly speaking, the cervix is the neck of the uterus, but it projects out into the vagina for roughly a fingertip's length, ending at the external os, or mouth. Depending on the stage of the menstrual cycle, it is lubricated with mucus which can either help or hinder sperm from getting through. In orgasm, the cervix undergoes a series of miniature convulsions. Some think this the source of the deepest orgasmic sensations of all, though Alfred Kinsey found that 95 percent of women couldn't feel the touch of a metal probe on their cervixes.

Nymphs and tidal pools

Like the mouth, which shares its halfway status of being partly open to the world, the vagina is virtually a living entity. Due to its natural bacteria and its slow but constant secretions, it doesn't really need to be washed, certainly not deodorized.

It is, in fact, one of the cleanest parts of the body, thanks to its acidity, which varies across the course of the menstrual cycle, and the yoghurt-like lactobacilli that keep it fresh.

Vaginal discharge is similar to blood serum, a mix of water, the proteins albumin and mucin (the latter found also in saliva) and a few white blood cells. It combines with secretions of oils, fats and waxes from no less than 51 separate areas which serve to coat and proof and protect. The odd episode of thrush aside (see p.274), if left to its own devices the vagina will manage its own affairs superbly. The science writer Natalie Angier has compared it to a tidal pool: "aqueous, stable, yet in perpetual flux".

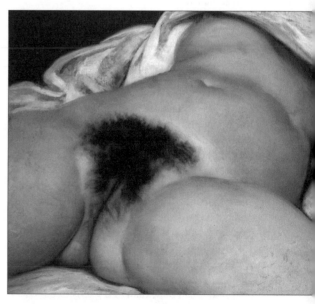

Courbet's *L'Origine du Monde* (1866). Currently hanging in Paris's Musée d'Orsay, many visitors choose not to examine it too closely.

The inner labia, vestibule and hymen

The inner labia frame the vagina like a halo. Medics call them the *labia minora* or small lips, but they're not necessarily any smaller than the outer lips, ranging from a third of an inch to two inches wide. In fact, the inner vaginal lips vary from person to person even more than facial ones: they can be furrowed or smooth, dark or pale, flaring or evenly curved, plump or trim. They can be symmetrical or very different. They can range in colour from pale peach to cocoa-brown via the brightest of pomegranate hues.

In something like a tenth of women, the inner lips are more sexually sensitive than the clitoris. One particularly delicate point is the frenulum or "little bridle", at the point where the inner edge of the inner lips meets like the corner of an eyelid, just below the glans of the clitoris. The outer edges of the inner lips continue up above the clitoris, protectively encircling it with a hood of skin. When masturbating, some women prefer to touch the hood itself rather than the exposed clitoris, as the hood's elasticity and the oils that collect underneath it allow a particularly smooth kind of friction. (Though accumulation of oils can sometimes cause the hood to adhere to the clitoris, making this impossible.)

The area between the inner lips is the vestibule. At its centre, just above the vagina, is the urethral opening. Its main function is to expel urine, but it can be sexually very sensitive, as it forms the visible end of the so-called urethral sponge (see p.47). Just below the vagina, the inner lips meet to form the fourchette or "little fork". In childbirth, this is vulnerable to tearing or being cut in an episiotomy. It's around the fourchette that a skein of tissue known as the hymen is sometimes found.

The hymen

Thanks to the myth that the hymen "breaks" when you lose your virginity, thousands of women must have searched for this mysterious body part – mostly in vain. If it exists at all, the hymen may stretch across the lower part of the vaginal opening like a half-moon on its back. It may partly encircle the vagina like a thin ring. Very rarely, it completely covers the vaginal opening: these "imperforate" hymens give adolescent girls problems with their periods – basically, the blood backs up instead of draining way – and they have to be surgically removed.

Often enough, adult women don't have a hymen at all, either because it stretched or wore away in childhood or because it disappeared in the womb, before birth. (Or, in the US in the 1950s and 1960s, because your family doctor cut or stretched it away at a state-sanctioned "premarital" medical examination.) They're often more obvious in younger children, and some woman do bleed a little when they have sex for the first time – but only a minority. For the few women with thicker or more inflexible hymens, the problem often becomes apparent not when they first have sex but when they start trying to use tampons. Progressive stretching using medical stents or small dildoes is the usual solution.

The outer labia and perineum

When a woman is standing up, the outer labia, or lips, press together over the interior of the vulva, forming a protective cushion and creating the vulva's distinctive heart-shape. In adult women, the labia are hairy on the outside, while the inside secretes sweat and oils which help protect the folds from rubbing and which form a key ingredient of a woman's unique genital perfume. The outer labia aren't as sensitive as the inner ones, partly because they're made from a different kind of tissue – the same, fatty kind that makes up the sac of a man's scrotum. The official medical term, *labia majora*, suggests they're bigger than the labia *minora*, which isn't necessarily the case. Some women's inner lips project or hang down outside the outer ones.

The space between the vagina and anus often gets ignored. It's not in fact a space, but a piece of sexual anatomy in its own right, with its own name: the perineum. The skin there is unusually delicate, but it's what lies beneath that counts sexually. On arousal, the mass of intertwining blood vessels embedded there swells and responds to all kinds of touch, typically with a feeling of stomach-deep excitement or satisfaction. The perineum is often associated with strong emotions, sexual feelings included, and this earthy depth has long been recognized by Eastern systems of esoteric anatomy, in which the perineum is one of the body's most important *chakras* or energy points.

The power of the perineum is underpinned by real muscle – a veritable nexus of the stuff. The muscles of the anal spincter and the bulbocavernosus muscle encircle and support the anus and vagina respectively, and they weave together in a figure-of-eight shape right under the perineum. They're joined there by the superficial transverse perineal muscles, which run from side to side like a band of elastic, attached to the sit bones at either end. All these muscles join at the perineal body, a fibrous ridge that runs right down the middle of the perineum. At a deeper level, fibres of the levator ani muscles, which form the core of the so-called "pelvic floor", also converge on this area. You could say that the muscular core of sexual response is knitted together at this one point. This helps explain why orgasm is – or can be – anything but a localized event, and why keeping the pelvic floor in good muscular shape can improve sexual response (see p.179).

The uterus and ovaries

To follow the track of a hopeful sperm: the mouth of the cervix, or external os, is the gateway to the cervical canal, which leads into the uterus, more traditionally known as the womb. It's usually described as pear-sized and pear-shaped, but in practice, it's basically squidged into the space between the pelvic bones and below the abdomen. It's an incredibly flexible organ, capable of expanding tenfold during pregnancy, and then snapping back to its pre-pregnant size and shape within weeks.

At the top end of the uterus, two tubes extend from each side towards the ovaries, where eggs are stored – thousands of them, each waiting there for their moment of monthly release. Each egg is only the size of the thickness of a baby's hair. The tubes which carry the eggs are called the Fallopian tubes, after the sixteenth-century anatomist who

Venus laid bare

Titian's *Venus of Urbino* (1538) became the archetypal reclining nude, inspiring artists from Goya to Manet.

Nakedness is the simple absence of clothing, but nudity is something much bolder. It is a celebration and an assertion of nakedness, a display of the body to the world. In art, nudes have inspired the deepest eroticism and the most agitated controversy, and no nude subject has been more central than Venus. No subject, either, has been more controversial – especially as the depiction of the goddess of love

has been linked, since the very beginning, with prostitution.

If you ignore the many earthy, prehistoric "Venus" figurines dug up all over Europe, the tradition of depicting a nude goddess began with the greatest of all Greek sculptors, Praxiteles. The ancient Greeks had long created *kouroi, or* images of naked, athletic men, but their *korai*, or sculptures of women, were usually decorously draped in stoney robes. Praxiteles changed all that. He modelled one of his nudes, the Aphrodite (or Venus) of Delphi, on a courtesan who had been tried for corrupting the youth of Athens. In another, he showed the goddess disrobed, a hand half concealing her vulva in the gesture known as *pudica*, or the "modest pose" – though of course her shielding hand only served to draw attention to her nakedness.

Praxiteles inspired generations of Roman copiers but, after the fall of Rome, the nude wasn't properly revived in Europe until the Renaissance took a fresh look at the classical world. In the 1480s, Botticelli's *Birth of Venus*, drawing on descriptions of lost Greek works, showed the goddess emerging from a scallop shell (a symbol of the vulva), while modestly hiding her breasts and genitals with hands and a length of golden hair. The classic pose, however, was established by the Venetian painter Giorgione in his *Sleeping Venus*, which shows the goddess reclining passively, but provocatively, her hand not so much resting on her pubic area as touching it suggestively. Titian followed Giorgione's example with the even more alluringly come-hither *Venus of Urbino*, whose other hand was occupied with the crushing of a rose.

The reclining nude became one of the great erotic themes in art, even if most works were destined for the private cabinets of aristocratic patrons, to be shown to approved and approving visitors only. Often enough, a supposed classical "purity" or a mythological theme provided a fig leaf of respectability. Sometimes, cover was only given by the mere title "Venus". In the 1630s, the elderly Rubens modelled some of his latest and fleshiest nudes – including that orgy of nakedness, the so-called *Feast of Venus* – on his own teenage wife. Velázquez's sensual *Rokeby Venus*, from the 1640s, showed a distinctly earthly-looking goddess regarding herself – or was it the viewer? – in a mirror. The disquieting composition proved that it still had the power to shock almost four hundred years later, when the painting was attacked by an outraged suffragette, in 1914.

Making the goddess human made her seem more attainable, and thus more erotic, but it long remained a risky thing for an artist to do. In around 1800, Francisco de Goya painted a woman in a very Venus-like pose but, far from labelling her a goddess, he entitled her *La Maja* – meaning a powerful, sexual and distinctly unrespectable woman. He also painted her in two versions, one naked and the other clothed, each serving to highlight the eroticism of the other. Somehow, the Inquisition found out. Both versions were confiscated and Goya lost his job as court painter.

By the mid-nineteenth century, French academic painters such as Bouguereau and Cabanel were painting powerfully erotic nudes, including some practically pornographic Venuses, and exhibiting them in the public art Salons. Once again, it was the idealizing or moralizing distance which protected the artists from censure. But in the same period, Courbet and Manet started painting nudes which, quite palpably, were real women. Manet caused a scandal with his *Déjeuner sur l'herbe*, but his *Olympia* was even more shocking – and transformative. With her neck ribbon, bracelet, single slipper and confrontational gaze, she seemed so provocatively available that she had to have her own guards at the Salon of 1865. The art critic John Berger may have reckoned that "the nude is condemned to never being naked" but, by painting what contemporary viewers clearly understood to be a prostitute, Manet recovered her nakedness. Almost at one stroke, the era of Venus had ended and the age of the modern nude had begun.

first dissected them, but they are also known as oviducts ("egg tubes") or uterine tubes. The tubes don't actually lead into the ovaries, but end at a brush-like fringe of tissue called the fimbria, which looks rather like a sea anemone. When the ovary is about to release an egg, these fringes brush against the ovary, gently gathering in the nascent egg before transporting it down towards the uterus.

If a sperm successfully makes it this far, it usually meets the egg as it makes its journey down the oviducts – though a sperm can also swim into an egg once it's already made its way into the uterus. A fertilized egg, or blastocyst, will implant itself into the lining of the uterus, where it's protected by newly released pregnancy hormones. In the absence of a fertilized egg and the hormones released to protect it, this lining is shed during the monthly period (see p.197).

The uterus isn't only concerned with reproduction. It produces prostaglandins, which cause cramps or contractions of smooth muscle, helping expel menstrual tissue – and indeed babies. It also concocts natural opiates such as endorphins and the curious drug anandamide, which has similar properties to cannabinol, the active ingredient in marijuana.

Arousal in women

Female arousal doesn't exactly run a flagpole up the mast, like the male erection, but it's no less dramatic for that – and the vagina responds just as fast, if not so obviously. As a woman gets turned on, or as she is touched in a way her mind interprets as sexual, the nerves of the genital area start sending out signals by means of a neurotransmitting gas, nitric oxide. The pudendal nerve transmits from the clitoris, and the pelvic nerve from the vagina and cervix. The nitric oxide causes increased blood flow into the genitals, making the outer lips darken and expand to around double their normal size, and pushing the stiffening glans of the clitoris, which is engorged with twice as much blood as normal, out from under its hood.

The inner lips expand to two or three times their normal diameter, while the outer labia simultaneously thin and flatten, apparently pulling away from the vagina. All over the body, the skin becomes more sensitive to touch. The nipples may start to pucker, harden and tighten in a kind of erection. For most women, the extra blood flow also causes a "sex flush", in which the nipples, lips, fingernails, toenails, eyes and cheeks redden or darken. (It's no accident that these are exactly the effects – nipples aside – that makeup is designed to simulate.) Sex flushes are more or less visible depending on the woman, the climate and the degree of arousal. Paler women, especially, may experience a rosy blush right across their faces, chests and even all over their skin.

Sexually speaking, the most significant activity takes place out of sight. Blood also rushes into the spongy tissues of the "deep clitoris", while the deeper tissues are pressing in against the walls of the vagina from the inside, making the vaginal opening swell and tighten, rather like the cuff of a blood-pressure monitor. Even deeper inside the vagina, meanwhile, the walls start to balloon or "tent" outwards. The "tenting" phenomenon can be so marked that women having penetrative sex have worried that their partner has gone limp or even slipped out altogether.

The nerve endings of the vagina release another kind of signal chemical, a hormone which pushes a clear serum, formed from the clear, plasma

Pubic hair and pitch-dark shelters

Pubic hair develops only during puberty. Well, technically the hairs are there all along, in their vellus or "peach fuzz" form, but rising levels of androgens (a type of sex hormone) effectively flicks a switch in each follicle, turning the hair into the thicker, curlier, longer, "androgenic" variety. The change in each hair is quite sudden, but it takes some years for all the follicles in the pubic area to switch over, meaning that androgenic hair only spreads gradually across the body. In men, the process can continue for decades, as androgenic hair gradually extends up the belly, down the thighs, across the chest and often into other areas as well, such as the back.

Once upon a time, humans were almost certainly hairy all over, like apes. (Actually, DNA suggests that the human scalp, pubic and body louse split from their common ancestor some 70,000 years ago, which is therefore roughly how long we've been the naked ape.) No one knows why these islands of androgenic hair were evolutionarily stranded when the rest was lost.

Evolutionary biologists have ascribed the powers of cushioning, reduction of friction, insulation and the filtering out of foreign particles to pubic hair, but their arguments are pretty speculative – hardly better than the early anatomists who thought pubic hair existed as a kind of inbuilt modesty. One recent theory would even have you believe that pubic hair survived because it provided "a navigational aid in pitch-dark shelters". The idea of cave people groping about for a bushy triangle in the darkness is appealing, but it does rather assume that early humans couldn't rustle up a pair of warming bearskin pyjamas.

Some scientists think pubic hair exists as a sign of sexual maturity. A preference for pubic hair could thus have become established as an evolutionary trait and, in a process of natural-selection feedback, the gene for growing luxuriant pubic hair would have been reinforced. A related explanation is that pubic hair exists to disseminate sexual scents, or pheromones. There are more sweat glands under the skin in hairy areas, and if sweat gets trapped in hair, it starts to release a distinctive odour as it breaks down. Left to fester, this smell is now widely regarded as offensive, but there's no doubt of the erotic power of fresh sweat, especially when blended with the scent of sexual fluids. Everyone has a signature sexual perfume, and research shows that this plays a hugely important role in attraction. All of which makes the present-day fetish for hair removal (see p.65) somewhat surprising.

component of blood, out through the walls of the arteries and into the vagina. Mixed with smaller quantities of thicker, mucous-like fluids secreted by glands inside the vagina, this creates a kind of lubrication – a sensation that has been vividly described as "creaming your knickers". Levels of lubrication vary hugely, from almost none, despite high levels of arousal, to wet flushes. It's telling that the chemical composition of this lubricant was one of the last of the body's biological mysteries – no scientist thought to investigate it until the 1960s.

Technically, these phases of arousal are known as "excitement" and the "plateau". For more on the last two phases, "orgasm" and "resolution", see Chapter 4.

His

True to its slang name, the penis really is a kind of tool, a delivery device devoted – as far as evolution is concerned – to increasing the chance of a man's sperm successfully fertilizing an egg. Given that women's eggs are produced deep inside their bodies, any head start the sperm can get on their journey is a benefit. The penis is that head start.

The penis's physical prominence, and its astonishing capacity to grow, shrink and apparently summon up two quite different kinds of fluids, is undoubtedly the source of its fascination – a fascination that is, if anything, stronger among men than women, incidentally. It is, you might say, the magic part, and it hogs the limelight. The testicles, tucked away in a discreet (and not altogether appealing) little bag of skin between the legs, are distinctly overshadowed. Yet it is there that the real business of male reproduction is at work, in a kind of marvellous, never-ceasing, air-cooled sperm-production laboratory.

Penile anatomy

The inside of the penis is made up of three strips or cylinders of spongy tissue, laid together a bit like wires in an electric cable. The outside sheath is made up of a tough, skin-covered membrane, the tunica albuginea. The two largest strips, the corpora cavernosa, make up the core of the penis's shaft. They're made of spongy erectile tissue, which, given the right kind of stimulation, gets saturated with blood and swells up to produce an

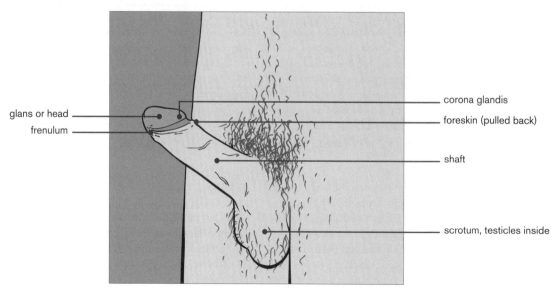

glans or head
frenulum

corona glandis
foreskin (pulled back)
shaft
scrotum, testicles inside

His: external view

erection. Ligaments attach them to the pubic bone at the base.

A third, smaller strip sits between the larger two on the underside of the penis. It is made of a different kind of spongy tissue, corpus spongiosum, and encases the urethra, the tube through which men urinate and ejaculate. At its end, the corpus spongiosum flares out in a kind of bell-shaped helmet that caps the end of the whole penis – this is the glans, better known as the head, helmet or "bell end". It is one of the most sensitive parts of the entire male body, especially around its rim, known technically as the corona glandis, or "acorn's crown".

The shape of the glans neatly echoes the closed, fornix area of the vagina. This is no surprise to biologists, as most mammals have penises and vaginas which form a close fit. A popular theory in evolutionary biology is that the ridge or rim exists to "scoop" out competitor semen. It sounds outlandish, but why else would a natural spermicide be present in the last part of a man's ejaculate? Lab tests have since confirmed that ridges perform better at out-scooping than plain phalluses.

Female first-timers sometimes worry about what it'll feel like. Soft, it's like a little springy puppy-fat sausage. Hard, it's more like flexed muscle – fairly rigid under the soft skin, but with plenty of play in it.

Foreskins

The sensitivity of the glans is one major reason for the existence of the foreskin (also called the prepuce, from the Latin for "before the penis"). Foreskin is a continuation of the skin covering

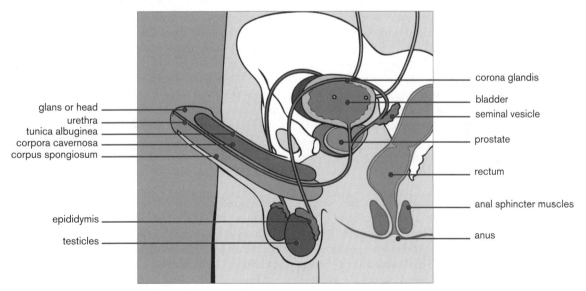

glans or head
urethra
tunica albuginea
corpora cavernosa
corpus spongiosum

epididymis
testicles

corona glandis
bladder
seminal vesicle
prostate
rectum
anal sphincter muscles
anus

His: internal view

Pet names and dirty words

Thanks to their Latin roots, the words "penis" and "vagina" sound a little po-faced and medical. "Vulva" seems even more textbookish, and the old-fashioned medical term, "pudendum", is tainted by the fact that it derives from the Latin for "shame". On the slang side, those hearty old English words, "prick" and "twat", are too often used as terms of disrespect. "Cock" and "pussy" have been taken over by the porn industry. The relatively innocent "willy" and "fanny" are just too childish (and of course "fanny" means "vagina" in the UK and "ass" in the US, which doesn't help).

Many words for body parts start out as unobjectionable but inevitably acquire offensive connotations. "Cunt" is the classic example. Medieval London and Oxford both had a Gropecunt Lane, yet by the eighteenth century a dictionary could describe the word as "a nasty name for a nasty thing" and today it has become so offensive to some people that they refer to the "C-word".

Words for genitalia (which ultimately stems, incidentally, from a Greek word for "birth") are seen as offensive when people have negative feelings about the body parts they refer to. People fear to talk about their "privates" in public. New euphemisms therefore need to be constantly invented to replace the old ones – which results in an extraordinary proliferation of slang. One researcher, who should probably get out more, went through *Partridge's Dictionary of Slang* and counted up 200 expressions for penis and 330 for vagina. Most people find it easier to think up slang words for the male part, however. Mark Morton, author of *The Lover's Tongue*, counted an extraordinary 1300 words for the penis – even if many, from "Aaron's Rod" to "zipperfish", are not so well known. Unfortunately, new slang terms are usually either jocular ("trouser snake") or deliberately offensive ("arse-worm").

So what is the solution? The *Kamasutra*'s translators, despairing, ended up employing the old Sanskrit words: *lingam* for him, *yoni* for her – thus giving their book an exotic (not to mention religious) flavour. They might have done better if they'd been at work not on ancient Indian texts but on Chinese ones, which specialize in pungent euphemisms. Taoist works describe the male "organ" (a word which, by the way, comes from a root meaning "to work", as in an instrument or "tool") as the "Jade Stalk", "Swelling Mushroom", "Turtle Head" and "Dragon Pillar". The female parts are known as the "Jade Gate", "Open Peony", "Golden Lotus" and "Deep Vale". Using these words in a contemporary, English-language guide would be absurd. But it does make "penis" and "vagina" sound woefully prosaic.

the shaft of the penis, but constructed in a subtly different way as a double layer. Crucially, it isn't attached to the tissue of the glans beneath. This allows it to expand and withdraw to accommodate the swelling of the glans during erection. Different men have very different foreskins: some are long and continue beyond the tip of the penis, looking something like a little teat; others sit snugly around the head of the glans; the way they look tends to change anyway, depending how cold (and therefore withdrawn) the penis gets.

Foreskin is sensitive to touch in itself, especially

around the frenulum, the ridge of skin on the underside of the penis that connects the glans to the foreskin. The frenulum is often left intact in circumcised men, although it may be removed altogether (see p.70).

The size question

Given that almost all the sensitive parts of a woman's body are around the entrance of the vagina (or an inch or two inside), men set a surprising amount of store by penis size. One psychologist found that only 55 percent of men were satisfied with their penis's size (45 percent of men wanted more, 0.2 percent less), while 85 percent of women were "very satisfied" with the size of their partner's. Size issues may be about perceived fertility, as if bigger penises could get that bit closer to the ovaries. If fertility were the issue, however, surely men would brag or worry about the weight of their balls. Intriguing research has linked perceived size to self-esteem: broadly speaking, confident men think they have bigger dicks.

So what is normal? Two large-scale studies, The Kinsey Report and Richard Edwards' online "Definitive Penis Size Survey", found that the average erect penis stood at a little over 6 inches. Unfortunately, both these surveys relied on self-measurement, which experts reckon adds an inch. The traditional place to measure is along the top of the penis. If you measure underneath you'll take in the hidden "root" – which may be two thirds as long again as the visible part (and which tends to form a banana-shaped curve). Those extra inches may come in handy if you feel the need to bump up your public statistics.

Responsible modern surveys tend to come up with an average penis length of somewhere around 13cm, or a little over 5 inches. Roughly two-thirds of men are within an inch or so of that figure, it seems, and serious variation is unusual: perhaps one in fifty men have penises longer than seven inches or shorter than three and a half. Flaccid length, however, varies a lot – so much so that giving an average is pretty futile. Three inches or so is fairly common.

Traditional male dress in Irian Jaya, Indonesia, can extend to the sporting of an impressive penis gourd.

The erect circumference is, if anything, even more variable. A Dutch study for the Amsterdam condom manufacturer Het Gulden Vlies found the range, when erect, was anything from 9 to 16cm, or from 3.5 to 6 inches. Somewhere between an inch and an inch and a half less than the erect length seems to be pretty typical. Surveys routinely suggest that women believe "girth is more important than length", but this may be because this has become a modern-day truism. It's what women say when asked a stupid question …

One urban myth that's definitely worth exploding is that of anatomical correspondence. Penis size has nothing whatsoever to do with the size of the nose, the forearm, the foot or any other part of the body. It may run in families to a certain extent, however. As the pioneering seventeenth-century anatomist Regnier de Graaf noted: "there are families which excel mightily in the quality of their venereal armour".

Penis size by race, nationality – and species

Most scientists wouldn't approach the question of racial or national differences with a (very long) bargepole. Spurious figures fill the statistical vacuum and many news stories recycle the same old myths of enormous hyper-masculine African penises and tiny, effeminate Asian ones. Such myths have been circulating since the Greeks contemptuously painted foreigners and slaves with mighty organs (they preferred small, neat ones) and since European imperialists tried to imply that Africans occupied lower rungs of the evolutionary ladder while Asians weren't manly enough to run their own countries.

Kinsey found erect white penises (self-measured) to be marginally smaller than black ones. Richard Edwards' online survey (also self-reported) found black men were longer when flaccid, white men when erect. More recent studies show no significant differences between countries or continents – and genetic research has shown that people in the US may have far more mixed racial origins than previously thought.

As for large penises being associated with "animal" sexual appetites, the strange fact is that humans have far larger penises in proportion to their body size than most mammals. The male silverback gorilla may be four-hundred pounds of chest-pounding, domineering masculinity, but his erect penis is less than two inches long. The record-holder among mammals is the nine-banded armadillo, the "poor man's pig", whose penis is some two-thirds the length of its body. Outside the mammal class, things get crazy: the penis of the humble garden slug is seven times the length of its body, while the superheroic barnacle uses its organ to feel around in the ocean for a mate, and grows a new one every year.

Erections

Men have erections when they're mentally aroused or when their penis is physically stimulated – or, ideally, when they get both kinds of stimulation at the same time. The mechanism is a cascade of reactions. First, the nerves connecting with the base of the spine (the sacral parasympathetic nerves) light up if the penis or pelvic area is touched, or if the brain sends a message to the area – perhaps in response to something the eye has seen or a fantasy that has drifted into the mind.

Once stimulated, these nerves cause messenger chemicals to be released. The "love hormone", oxytocin, is among them, but the key role is played by the innocuous-sounding nitric oxide. It makes the smooth muscle (the type you can't consciously control) in the blood vessels of the penis relax, which allows blood to flow into the spongy tissue that makes up the body of the penis. When this tissue swells, it pushes against the enclosing membrane (the non-stretchy tunica albuginea), shutting off the veins that would normally drain blood away. As the heart pumps in more and more blood, the penis swells and rises up – in much the same way as a balloon expands when you blow air into it.

In a healthy young man, the result is remarkably stiff – the collagen fibres in the membrane are as stiff, weight for weight, as steel. As a whole, of course, the penis is far softer, and erections get naturally gentler with age, even without any erectile dysfunction problems (see p.288). Penises are also much more brittle than steel, too. If you're very unlucky, or extremely sexually acrobatic, it's not impossible to break one in a so-called "penile fracture". There's no actual bone in a boner, it's just the tunica albuginea rupturing. Quick surgery is effective, and the quicker the better.

When the erection isn't needed any more, either after orgasm or distraction, hormonal signals trigger release of an enzyme, phosphodiesterase type 5. This attacks one of the chemicals which helps nitric oxide to allow blood to flow into the penis easily (cyclic guanosine monophosphate, if you must know). The erection ebbs away with the blood.

Anxiety about penis size is part of the male condition – as satirized by Aubrey Beardsley, in his illustrations for *Lysistrata* (1896).

Out of my control

Erections are pretty much involuntary reactions. Erectile pressure can be deliberately increased with a quick clench of the ischiocavernosus muscles – the same ones that can make the penis twitch. If flexed, these muscles compress the base of the penis, further constricting any outward blood flow.

Most men can only hold them for a very short time, however – too short to be of much use – though Kegel exercises (see p.179) can develop strength.

Erections can occur even when a man isn't aroused. They can happen spontaneously four or five times a night during REM sleep (dream sleep), and they often announce themselves with a fanfare first thing in the day, when the bladder is full – a state fondly known as "morning glory" or being "piss proud". During adolescence, they can appear as surprisingly as rabbits popping out of a burrow. Dig a bit, and you'll often find a buried adolescent memory of a sudden, unexplained hard-on which arrived at the most embarrassing of moments.

Most men are Communists

One erection is very different from another. Most make the penis thicker, harder and more veiny, with a darker-coloured and swollen-looking glans but in some penises these effects aren't all that marked, while in others the change is more dramatic. Some jut out at ninety-degrees to the body, some point slightly downwards, some strain up almost to the belly button. In general, the angle and the hardness of an erection usually decreases naturally with age, though any man can have an unusually soft or hard erection, depending on a host of factors. The inability to achieve an erection is covered separately under "Erectile dysfunction" (see p.288).

Many erections also curve slightly to one side or the other, or have a slight bend upwards or downwards. As the Taiwanese urologist Dr Hsu told the writer Mary Roach, "Most men are Communists! Lean to the left! Second most common: bow down, like Japanese gentleman! Number three, to the right. Four, up! Like elephant!" More severe or painful bends can be a sign of Peyronie's disease, or penile induration, in which scar tissue or fibrosis in the tunica algubinea distorts the erection. It's most common in white men over forty and may be associated with erectile dysfunction. There are lots of treatments, including drugs and traction; surgery tends to be a last resort.

The testicles and prostate

If the penis exists to deliver sperm, the testicles exist to manufacture them. At any one time, there are between 2 and 3 billion sperm cells on the go. Heat kills sperm, so the testicles have to hang outside the body where they can be kept cool. They are encased in the scrotum, a bag of loose skin surrounding a strange kind of muscle, the cremaster muscle, that expands and contracts in response to heat and cold, lifting and lowering the testicles towards or away from the body.

Inside the scrotum are two testicles, each about the size and shape of a quail's egg or a queen-sized olive – though they vary a lot in size, and typically one is larger or hangs lower than the other. (The lower one is usually on the left, due to the way blood travels round the body.) Once the testicles have cooked up sperm, it moves into the epididymis, a coiling tube which clings to one side of the testicle. There the sperm matures, waiting to be called upon to pass via the vas deferens into the body, ready to be mixed with the other ingredients of semen and ejaculated at orgasm.

Testicles are miniature factories not just for sperm, but for the hormone testosterone. They're one of the reasons why adult men have roughly

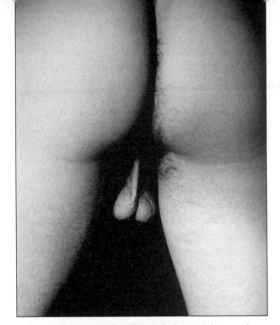

Little discussed and often ignored, the testicles are the very seat and source of masculinity.

ten times as much testosterone as women. Given testosterone's supposed link to aggressive behaviour, saying that someone has "got balls" could be more than a metaphor, although researchers disagree on whether it actually has this effect.

A real pain in the balls

The pain of a blow to the balls is famously indescribable. The medical description of a "nauseating dull ache" just doesn't cover it. The testicles are so exquisitely sensitive largely because there's nothing much in the way of flesh, bone or muscle to protect them. The hypogastric nerve in particular is very exposed.

Testifying

The odd-sounding word "testicle" just means "little testis", but *testis* itself has an even odder legendary origin. Roman witnesses (in Latin, *testes*) supposedly used to take vows while touching their balls (also called *testes* in Latin). Thus to "testify" was to swear an oath on your own bollocks. Unfortunately, there's not much evidence of this actually occurring in Rome. There is, however, a strangely parallel scene in the Bible. Genesis describes an episode in which Abraham's servant puts his hand "under his master's thigh" in order to make a vow. This is allegedly a euphemism for touching his balls – implying that the ancient Hebrews acted rather like witnesses today, who touch a holy book before giving their "testimony", except that the holiest thing to hand was a scrotum.

It's a good yarn, but probably isn't true. A more convincing explanation is that the word *testis* originates in a root that meant "the one standing beside", and thus can refer either to a witness to someone else's action or a pair of testicles hanging alongside each other. But the simplest and best explanation is that the root word "*test*" had a wide range of meanings. One was "witness", another referred to a kind of earthenware pot. By analogy, "pot" became the popular word for testicles, much like we use "sack" today. This kind of slang borrowing happens all the time. The Romans even did the same thing with their word for "head": the technical Latin word may have been *caput*, but on the street they all talked about the *testa*.

Testicular pain can have many causes less traumatic than a sharp kick. Perhaps the commonest is "blue balls" or "lover's nuts". This is a heavy, deep-seated ache that can build up if a man has been repeatedly aroused without ejaculating – if too much blood has been pumped into the area and hasn't had the chance to flow away again. In these circumstances, the extra blood in the veins under the skin can actually lend the balls a bluish tinge. There's only one cure and it isn't found at a doctor's surgery. Ejaculation does the trick, though left alone the fluid will eventually drain away of its own accord anyway – so it's definitely no excuse to pester for sex.

Infections of the epididymis (epididymitis) and of the testicles (orchitis) can cause painful swelling. Often the root cause lies in another infection – chlamydia is commonly to blame. A severe pain with a sudden onset may be the dreaded torsion, where the spermatic cord that carries blood to the testicles twists around, cutting off the blood supply. It can feel like you've been kicked in the balls and is a definite medical emergency. Quick treatment guarantees a good result, but if you leave it for even twelve hours, the chance of saving the testicle diminishes.

Lumps and bumps in the testicles are quite common and can have many causes, but it's well worth checking them out. Testicular cancer is rare – less than 1 percent of male cancers – but it's a particularly nasty type, killing more young men than any other kind of cancer.

The discovery of sperm

The first man ever to see sperm up close – microscopically close, that is – was the seventeenth-century Dutch cloth merchant Antoni van Leeuwenhoek. In Holland, microscopes were used for testing the quality of textiles but as a keen amateur scientist, van Leeuwenhoek soon put his model to other uses, unveiling a whole new microbiological world. One of his most important discoveries, alongside bacteria, was the existence of sperm. Writing up observations made in 1677, he excitedly noted, "I have seen so great a number of living creatures in it, that sometimes more than a thousand were moving about in an amount of material the size of a grain of sand." He described how the spermatozoa were like "a small earth nut with a long tail" and how they "moved forward with a snake-like motion of the tail, as eels do when swimming in water." Fearful that his readers would suspect him of the terrible sin of self-pollution, he hastily added that "What I describe here was not obtained by any sinful contrivance on my part, but the observations were made upon the excess with which nature provided me in my conjugal relations".

The prostate and perineum

The prostate is a curious little walnut-sized gland that wraps around the urethra where it emerges from the bladder. Its day job is to add a sugary, alkali fluid (which looks a bit like egg white) to the semen coming down from the seminal vesicles, thus helping ejaculated sperm stay alive.

The prostate can also have a more exciting role. It's one of the most sexually responsive parts of the male body, and pressing or massaging it can profoundly intensify orgasm. "Milking" it can even cause an ejaculation of prostatic fluid alone. The prostate can either be reached via the anus, or the perineum, the often-ignored area between the anus and the base of the testicles. Pressure applied here doesn't feel as intense, but it's a whole lot easier to reach – and the perineal raphe, the line or faint ridge of skin running down the centre line of the scrotum and on towards the anus – provides a pleasant focal point.

still survive. They prove acceptance into a recognized segment of society.

Not all bodily adornments and alterations need be evolutionary adaptations, of course. Just as sex is *for* pleasure as well as reproduction, conscious self-decoration may be expressions of creativity and joy in the decorative: of the desire to give pleasure, and to feel it in the body.

Adornment and modification

Changing the body for sexual or erotic effect is as old as human culture. Older, even, if you consider how animals do it every time they sprout new feathers in the breeding season, or their bottoms blush bright red. Such changes may advertise evolutionary success. They demonstrate sexual power and erotic potential – much as the peacock's tail advertises how strong he must be to hump around that ludicrous burden and

Bushwhacking and manscaping

If pubic hair has existed for some 70,000 years (see p.55), it has been removed for a good couple of millennia. South Asian and Middle Eastern cultures, in particular, have preferred "clean", depilated skin for centuries. Ancient Indian texts virtually fetishize plucking and threading, ranking it alongside other acts such as bathing and perfuming the skin with sandalwood, and Persian tweezers from the first millennium BC have turned up in archeological digs. In ancient Egypt,

The mysteries of belly-button fluff

Sperm was under the microscope by 1677, and vaginal lubrication had to wait until the twentieth century. But the truth about that most mysterious of human secretions, belly-button fluff, was only revealed in March 2009, when Austrian chemist Georg Steinhauser announced the results of his private research. The suspicious fluff, it seems, is mostly made up of stray pieces of lint, mixed up with

dead skin cells, sweat and dust. Steinhauser's more useful discovery, however, was that abdominal hair has a scaly, barbed structure which scrapes away at clothing, and it tends to grow in a particular circular pattern around the navel – which can gradually move the accumulated fluff towards the centre. Overweight, hairy men are most at risk. Luckily, shaving the belly area cures the "problem" – temporarily, at least.

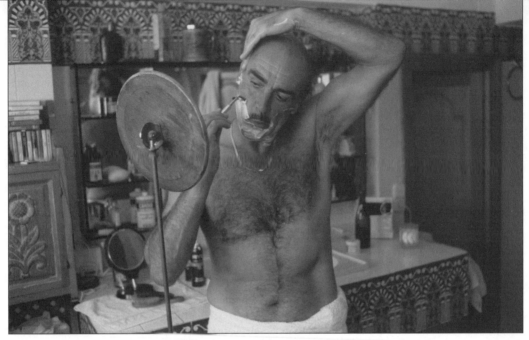

The splendidly hirsute Sean Connery makes some subtle adjustments.

body hair was something seen only on slaves and peasants – and beeswax and razors were used to remove it. Islam has long regarded removing pubic hair as *fitrah*, or virtuously natural.

In ancient India and Egypt, depilation was practiced by men and women alike. In European culture, by contrast, removal of body hair has long been largely restricted to women – though Roman men, unlike the bearded Greeks, were generally clean-shaven. Greek and Roman women are known to have removed body hair, and classical statuary certainly depicts the female pubis – but not usually the male – as hairless. In the Middle Ages, aristocratic woman would even pluck back their entire hairline, in order to create the high forehead which was then regarded as beautiful.

From safety razors to "back, sac and crack"

Modern-day hair removal has gathered pace throughout the twentieth century – largely in line with fashions. Safety razors were marketed at women as early as 1915, just when sleeveless evening dresses began to be worn. The great exception has been the subculture which venerates all things natural – as flowered, particularly, in Germanic countries and across the West in the 1970s. The armpit, said Alex Comfort in his 1972 classic, *The Joy of Sex*, "should on no account be shaved", as it existed to help trap the natural body scent.

From the 1990s, more efficient techniques and better waxes have led to more extreme forms of hair

Furs, fabrics and high heels

The most common way to adorn the body, of course, is to wear clothing. Fashion is as central to human sexuality as the peacock's tail is to his. It not only emphasizes the body, but it advertises the wearer's wealth, status and discrimination. Clothing that's seen as explicitly sexual is often highly textured or brightly coloured. Red has a particularly erotic reputation – and perhaps for good reason. In mammals, it usually signals ovulation or arousal. Fur and leather – two classic "sexy" fabrics – may also stir up evolutionary memories. Fur, according to Freud, recalled pubic hair, and like leather it stores and disseminates scent better than other materials.

But most "sexy" apparel exists to simultaneously conceal and reveal. This double effect may trigger some of the same irresistible interest that the combination of winning and losing causes in addictive gamblers. Lace has this double nature woven into its very fabric. Stockings hide the skin of the legs – but suggest the revelation of the softest, most intimate part. Bras hold the breasts in, but (frequently) lift them up or push them out at the same time.

Bras, like corsets, mould the female torso into a more exaggeratedly feminine shape. High heels do the same job, alongside a whole range of sexualizing effects. They make the gait more unsteady, emphasizing vulnerability and triggering male protectiveness or sexual aggression. They make the bottom sway, calling attention to it. They exaggerate the apparent length of the legs. They may also have a very physical sexual effect: in 2008 Italian urologist (and shoe-lover) Dr Maria Cerruto claimed that wearing heels exercised the pelvic-floor muscles – one of the single best ways to improve sexual response.

removal – and a proliferation of half-humorous terminologies deployed by features journalists. On women, the "Bikini Line" wax is no longer uncommon, and other "styles" leave a "landing strip", "triangle" "Hitler's Moustache" or, in the case of the "full Brazilian" aka the "Hollywood", leave no pubic hair at all. Disconcertingly, this prepubescent style is de rigueur in mainstream pornography.

In the 2000s, hair removal has spread, alongside use of cosmetics, to men – "metrosexual" and otherwise. "Manscaping", and the male "back, sac and crack" wax in particular, is the stuff of magazine legend – though it's far from clear how many men actually do it. It's clear at least that the hairless, youthful look of "chickens" is still popular in sections of the gay community (though big, hairy "bears" have their own admirers), and that some men of Mediterranean and Arab origin feel some pressure to conform to a broadly Nordic standard of beauty which favours hairlessness.

Female Genital Mutilation

The shifting names of Female Genital Mutilation – or Female Genital Cutting, or Female Circumcision as it used to be known – betray the ethical confusion which surrounds the practice. On the one hand, the contemporary, liberal position is

A young Somali girl heals after an operation – and significant cultural rite – known to the West as Female Genital Mutilation.

to respect local cultural traditions as opposed to the imperialist practice of stamping them out (as the British did with widow burning in India). And circumcision of boys is pretty widespread in the West, which further compromises the ethical arguments. On the other hand, FGM deliberately damages young girls' sexual organs with the broad aim of reducing sexual pleasure.

There are three main kinds of FGM. A clitoridectomy removes the clitoral glans, and sometimes the hood as well. Excision also cuts away the inner labia and, sometimes, the outer labia too. Infibulation stitches up the vaginal opening leaving a small hole for urine and menstrual blood. The last, of course, has to be painfully reversed at marriage (and, potentially, before every childbirth).

Around 130 million women have undergone a form of FGM, mostly in West, Central and the northern part of East Africa – though it occurs in pockets in the Middle East as well. In Egypt, more than 95 percent of women are thought to have undergone cutting. Eighty-five percent of girls are still being subjected to it every year, even though it is now illegal. It also exists in migrant communities in the West. And where a practice is not sanctioned by a prevailing culture, the trauma often proves far deeper and longer-lasting.

Why?

Resistance to efforts to stop the practice is largely about cultural identity. In communities

Prince Alberts and ampallangs

Piercings are usually made on parts of the body considered erotic: ears, lips, noses, tongues, navels and beyond. In many cultures, the piercing is made as a rite of passage into adulthood, or upon marriage. In many south Asian cultures, for instance, earrings are often given to a new wife, along with other distinctive jewellery that signifies the married status. In the West, piercings are usually worn by young teenagers – more commonly as an aspect of youth fashion than a mark of adulthood.

The boldest and most intimate piercings date back mainly to the BDSM or "bondage" fashions of the 1980s West Coast gay scene, mixed with the efforts of certain subcultures to ally themselves with "primitive" or "pagan culture". Since the 1970s, many piercings – notably navel studs – have become fairly mainstream, despite healing times of up to a year, and infection rates of a third or more. Rumour – and the efforts of a commercial body-modification scene eager to give itself a gloss of history – has given many piercings impressive-sounding backstories. Take nipple rings, which were supposedly sported in secret by Victorian ladies who would travel to specialist shops in Paris to make their selection. The only evidence for this story is found in 1899 in the letters page of *Society*, an obscure journal known for its erotic, fetishistic and distinctly fictional correspondence.

Among male genital piercings, the usual story about the notorious Prince Albert (a ring passing from the frenulum through the head and out of the urethra) is that it was used to tie back the penis and conceal the telltale bulge in the princely tight trousers, as newly made fashionable by Beau Brummell. Alas, the name almost certainly comes from the fob the prince used to attach his pocket watch to his waistcoat. The "apradavya" (a vertical piercing through the glans) is said to be discussed in the *Kamasutra*. It isn't. The ampallang (the same, but horizontal) is supposedly borrowed from the Dayak men of Borneo. But this story ultimately dates back to tales of Papua New Guinea recounted by the Ukrainian ethnologist Nicholai Miklukho-Maklai who had apparently inspected the pierced "organ" of a Dayak man in the Museum of the Military Hospital in Batavia.

Female genital piercings mostly lack the colourful terminology and backstories of the mens' versions. Even the Christina (a piercing from the point where the outer labia meet through to the pubic mound) is apparently named for the first woman to have it done. And the Nefertiti (the same, but beginning lower, in the clitoral hood) is simply a tribute to the legendarily beautiful Egyptian queen. No one is suggesting Nefertiti actually had it done. Though, oddly enough, her famous bust does appear to reveal an unusual double ear piercing.

where where it is common, it is seen as a sign of belonging, rather like male circumcision within Jewish tradition. Traditionally performed by female elders, it is also a rite of passage into womanhood, and regarded as a mark of beauty. Often referred to in semi-religious terms as "cleanliness", it is said to prevent the clitoris growing into a penis. Religious authority is often cited as justification, and efforts by senior Islamic scholars to deny this often fail to filter down to grass-roots clergy.

FGM is also about controlling female sexuality and it is at least partly designed to safeguard virginity and protect against the likelihood of future infidelity. However, some controversial research suggests that many excised and even infibulated women report experiencing sexual pleasure at greater levels than typically reported in the West. If this reflects a truth, it would suggest that the Western obsession with the clitoris has a cultural as much as an anatomical basis, or at least that sexual pleasure is partly driven by expectation.

Circumcision

Circumcision in the US – and in Nigeria, the Philippines and South Korea, where it's probably even more common – is an embedded cultural practice. (In Japan, curiously, circumcision is more unusual but it's still considered bad form to reveal the penis – at a hot spring, say – *kawakamuri*, or without the foreskin retracted to reveal the glans.) Some half of newborn American boys are circumcised today, and it's the single most common surgical procedure in American medicine. Yet, outside the Jewish and Muslim communities, it isn't a religious practice (see p.326), and it isn't about medicine either. Medical associations now admit that there is absolutely no therapeutic reason for routine circumcision.

Cutting culture

This curious form of elective parental plastic surgery was originally designed to discourage

masturbation by reducing sexual pleasure. Researchers today disagree on whether or not it actually does this, but the early promoters certainly thought so. In 1888 Dr John Harvey Kellogg, of cornflakes fame, pronounced circumcision "almost always successful" in preventing masturbation in small boys. "The operation should be performed by a surgeon without administering an anesthetic, as the brief pain attending the operation will have a salutary effect upon the mind, especially if it be connected with the idea of punishment." (Applying carbolic acid to the clitoris was, he felt, the equivalent operation in women.) Eight years later Dr E.J. Spratling advised that, "one must cut away enough skin … to rather put it on the stretch when erections come later". As late as 1935, a certain R.W. Cockshut (really) was writing in the *British Medical Journal* that "the glans of the circumcised rapidly assumes a leathery texture less sensitive than skin".

Rates of circumcision in the US went up and up, reaching around 50 percent of newborns in the 1920s, 75 percent in the 1950s and maybe 80 or 90 percent in the 1970s. Of course, this wasn't all due to masturbation hysteria. Early in the twentieth century the medical profession started to claim instead that the operation promoted general "hygiene". Besides, it was an easy way to make a fast buck: on newborn babies, the operation takes just seconds and is worth hundreds of millions of dollars each year.

Fighting for foreskins

But the foreskin isn't just a piece of useless tissue, it's part of a man's system of sexual response, as

Circumcision, health and HIV

Until 2005, there was no evidence that circumcision provided any medical benefit. Even the few conditions that are usually treated by the operation have alternatives: phimosis, for instance, in which the foreskin is basically stuck to the glans, almost always cures itself by or during puberty. If not, it responds superbly to stretching and the application of steroids.

Then, in 2005, a trial in Africa found that circumcision reduced the chance of HIV being transmitted from a woman to a man in any single act of vaginal intercourse by 60 percent. That's profoundly more risky than simpy using a condom, but UNAIDS and the World Health Organization were quick to recommend mass-circumcision programmes. Yet the evidence is controversial, and other trials have come up with very different results. Some believe that the common southern-African practice of "dry sex" (see p.140) means that men with circumcised penises may pick up minor lesions through vaginal intercourse – and may actually be more likely to acquire HIV as a result.

Health workers complain that it's hard enough to persuade African men to use condoms anyway, and this story will hardly help – especially as men (apparently) desensitized by circumcision will scarcely be likely to further diminish their own pleasure by donning a condom. Another concern is the spurious linkage of HIV and "female circumcision": some African countries are now defending Female Genital Mutilation as a method of reducing female "promiscuity" and thus HIV transmission. Equally worrying is the prospect that tens of millions of "preventative" circumcisions will result in millions of cases of penile mutilation, death from secondary infection or, with cruel irony, cases of HIV infection due to non-sterile equipment.

rich in nerve endings as any part of the body, on a par with the lips or fingertips. And it may have a function in vaginal intercourse. As an uncircumcised penis moves in and out of the vagina, it can roll backward and forward within its own sheath. (Many uncircumcised men masturbate in this way.) During sex, unless the foreskin is rolled right back below the head (which does happen in many men), there's less actual movement in and out of the vagina and less removal of vaginal lubricant and moisture as a result.

Some men are now fighting what they call foreskin amputation through organizations like Nocirc (www.nocirc.org) and Norm-UK (www. norm-uk.org). They cite the UN Convention on the Rights of the Child, which attacks parents who perform acts of violence on their children, even on grounds of "religion, culture or tradition". One William Stowell, who was circumcised as a baby without proper consent from his mother, even took his case to court – and settled for an undisclosed sum. Shane Peterson, who was left with a deformed penis after a circumcision went wrong, won AUS$360,000 in damages. On a personal level, some men choose to stretch their penile skin using devices like T-Tape, the PUD, the TLC Tugger, and the Your-Skin cone, or resort to reconstructive plastic surgery.

Designer vaginas and plastic penises

It's now possible to ask a plastic surgeon to fix not just your face or belly, but your genitals too – all in the pursuit of an ideal of beauty or, more to the point, uniformity. Labioplasty (or vaginoplasty), which reduces the size of the labia (typically so that the inner labia don't project) is one of the more common procedures. Women who feel that their vulvas are somehow "abnormal" may be relieved – but if images of vulvas were more widespread, then the astonishing variety of their shapes might be better known.

Less common, and less respectable, is so-called vaginal rejuvenation or tightening. Often advertised as a post-childbirth procedure, plastic surgeons sometimes make outrageous claims about its ability to raise sexual pleasure. Pelvic-floor exercises are likely to be far more effective. The so-called "G-shot" involves injecting collagen (typically, tissue from a cow) into the vaginal wall. This might be less dubious if it was backed up by proper research into what or where the G-spot it's supposedly boosting actually is (see p.48). Similar problems beset the so-called hymenoplasty – for that designer virgin look.

Penile enlargement

Most penile enlargement schemes are hogwash. You can tell because they're offered by the same people who post statistics showing that the average penis size is six or seven inches. Pills, pumps and penile weights do not work, and can easily cause damage. Better a short penis than a ruptured one.

Plastic surgery sometimes has results, but it's very problematic. One "technique" involves cutting the suspensory ligament – this is basically the bit of muscle that ties the penis to the pubic bone. Without it, the penis can look up to an inch longer. It may also remain permanently limp. Injecting silicone into the penis to make it thicker is less risky, but the side effects include loss of sensitivity – surely fairly crucial – and deformations or ugly lumps. Use of actual human tissue can increase girth, but you'd better not tell your partner that he or she is touching bits of a corpse. Better results are sometimes had by removing fat from the pubic area, thus revealing more of the penis's base to view. (In fact, simple weight loss works pretty well – it's reckoned a man shedding 35 pounds of excess fat gains a whole inch in apparent length.)

In short, erectile problems are common enough already, and you don't want to go monkeying around down there unless you have to. Most men don't: an Italian study in 2002 study found that every single man among a group of 67 who were seeking penile enlargment had penises which fell within what medics considered a "normal range" of 1.6 to 4.7 flaccid inches. Their problem was false expectations or insecurity, not anatomy.

In the rare cases of men born with a micropenis (one that's under 7cm long when erect), there are now sophisticated techniques which allow an enlarged penis to be built around the existing one while preserving some sensitivity. These techniques have been developed in recent years by highly specialized surgeons, leaders in the field of urology – not people you'll find advertising on the internet.

Eunuchs and castrati

Castrated men were employed as royal servants all over the ancient world. They were "docile and loyal as gelded animals", as a Chinese emperor put it – and, of course, unable to found rival dynasties. They were also less likely to chase after the royal wives and concubines – a particular worry for Hindu Maharajas and Ottoman Sultans, with their extravagant harems and seraglios. And of course their very presence underlined the exceptional power and status of the male monarch.

In China, places at the imperial court were so highly valued that peasant parents would remove their sons' "three jewels" just to compete for a position. Scissors or a silk ligature were used, and the anaesthetic was typically a chilli compress. Survivors of the operation would preserve the dried remains of their genitalia in a jar, since to be mutilated was a sacrilege which might jeopardize a satisfying afterlife; for purposes of bodily resurrection, a eunuch needed to be complete. Eunuchs date back to the eighth century BC in China, but the practice reached its peak in the Ming Dynasty, when the emperors were said to keep a retinue of 20,000 eunuchs. And when the last emperor, Pu Yi, was expelled from the Forbidden City by the warlord Feng Yuxiang, 1500 palace eunuchs went with him. The last to survive, Sun Yaoting, died in 1996, at the age of 93.

In Europe, the eunuchs who once served the imperial Roman court pretty much died out alongside the empire, though the practice persisted for centuries in Byzantium. Visiting crusaders were amazed and horrified to see these hairless, high-voiced men acting as powerful civil servants. In the tenth century, the "vigorous and shrewd" eunuch, Basil the Nothos ("Basil the Bastard"), even led military expeditions for Constantine VII, and became his chamberlain and de facto chief of staff.

Castration had one last European flourishing. From the sixteenth century, a musical fashion emerged for the extraordinary vocal tones produced by men who had been castrated as boys, and whose voices had therefore never "broken" in the usual fashion. In 1600, Pope Clement VIII declared that creating castrati for church choirs was "to the honour of God" – but the real money lay in Baroque opera. At the height of the castrati's fame, in the early eighteenth century, fans were flocking to performances by superstars such as Senesino and Farinelli. The latter had an extraordinary range, extending from full, male-voiced tenor to the highest soprano notes. Adulatory audiences were known to shout "long live the knife", and when the craze was at its peak some 4000 Italian boys were undergoing the operation every year. The last castrato to sing in the Sistine Chapel choir, Alessandro Moreschi, retired in 1913. He died nine years later, having just survived long enough to cut a scratchy, sobbing, wax cylinder recording.

Sex and gender

The idea that humanity is split into two different groups, male and female, runs about as deep as it gets. The Yoruba in Nigeria may prefer to differentiate people by age rather than by using words for "he" and "she" and the Nepali words for "his" and "her" might imply different degrees of respect rather than different sexes. By and large, however, male and female is the first difference anyone picks upon. Thanks to ultrasound, it's now almost the first question anyone puts to a parent-to-be: "so," they ask, "what are you having?"

For millions of people around the world, the question doesn't quite make sense. Some are born intersex, with ambiguous genitalia, or with the chromosomes that drive development and the hormones that shape their body pulling in opposite directions. Some are anatomically unexceptional but prefer to live in the manner more often associated with the opposite sex: they are transgender. Transsexuals feel that their "true" sex is the opposite of the one displayed by their body – and may take medical steps to correct the error.

Anatomy and identity

Such facts suggest that a simple division of the world into two biological sexes is simplistic. Since the 1970s, therefore, the concept of gender has gained currency. Sex is sheer anatomy, but gender is a more nuanced combination of social roles and structures, self-conception and behaviour – including sexual behaviour. Gender is partly a matter of what you've got, partly who you feel you are, and partly who society expects you to be.

Gender is also, crucially, "performed", or created by how an individual reacts to the conditions they find around them. As the philosopher Simone de Beauvoir wrote: "you are not born a woman, you become one". Or, as gender theorist Judith Butler puts it, gender is *doing*, not *being*, it is "a set of repeated acts within a highly rigid regulatory frame that congeals over time to produce the appearance of substance". We perform gender so often, and in the context of such a strongly gender-divided society, that we come to believe our role is us. We start to feel our gender is caused by our biology – *is* our biology, in fact, just like biological sex.

It may not always have been that way. Historian Thomas Laqueur argues that until modern anatomy got going, most Europeans believed that men were basically women inside out (and vice versa): the vagina was an inverted penis, and we were all just one sex, albeit in different forms. As female and male roles became more publicly divided, philosophers and physicians began to focus more and more on the differences between the sexes, even conceptualizing them as polar opposites. With the birth of the "two-sex model" came the belief that sex and gender were inextricably linked. Why? It was the only way to keep male and female apart.

Pinks and blues – children and gender

Children seem to start out with the view that gender is what matters, not sex. Most children learn that they are either a boy or a girl during their second or

No pink, no blue: Victorian parents often dressed little boys and girls the same.

Nature, nurture, dolls and tractors

Many parents insist that biological sex is surely driving their child's behaviour. They were absolutely even-handed, they say, but their little girl just wanted to cuddle her dolly; their boy was simply fascinated by tractors. There may be tendencies based on brain structures – though the differences between male and female brains are usually hugely exaggerated by popular science – but most social scientists say that parents massively underestimate the power of gender. It's not just that parents themselves gender-type their children by, say, unconsciously warming to nurturing play by girls or allowing boys to take relatively unchecked risks; it's the weight and structuring effect of an entire society, combined with a child's own, fast-developing recognition that they must take their own place within it.

third year. They are usually able to label other people accurately by three, or four at the latest, and studies show that they are not deciding on the basis of facial appearance so much as on role. Give a man long hair and make him act in a way that children associate with women, and many preschool children will call the man a woman. It may be another year or two before children realize that they themselves will remain the same sex for life – and until then, many believe that if they behave like the opposite sex they may become it.

Some children, of course, choose not to play the role expected of them. Overwhelmingly, they are boys – though this is surely the result of girls being "allowed" a much wider range of behaviour on the masculine-to-feminine scale. Little girls can be tomboys, to put it crudely, while little boys are more rarely allowed to be effeminate. The Victorian practice of dressing boys and girls alike in long cotton dresses has long since given way to a strictly controlled and even more strictly marketed blue/pink "colour bar". Before the 1950s, however, there was little agreement about which colour was suitable for which. The popular myth that the colours "flipped" at some point around World War II is probably not true, though blue-for-girls was a popular choice in Catholic countries on the grounds that it was the colour associated with the Blessed Virgin.

Those few boys who survive or resist the peer, parental and societal pressure to conform may be diagnosed with having a "gender identity disorder" (though of course the real problem lies with a society that mistrusts people who play a gender role which contrasts with their biological sex). Among children diagnosed with GID, an intriguingly high number – a majority, in fact – grow up to identify as gay.

Transgender, third sex

In the late 1990s, a new letter appeared in what used to be called the gay rights movement. First there were Gay Rights, then Lesbian and Gay rights, then Lesbian, Gay and Bisexual (LGB) – and then came LGBT, incorporating that new coinage, Transgender. Transgender means not conforming to conventional gender roles. It's a very broad term, and can be adopted as an identity or co-opted as a way of talking about behaviour – cross-dressing being the most obvious expression (see box, opposite). Most transgender people would reject a narrow, binary view of gender, and place themselves – or indeed skate around – on a sliding scale of masculinity and femininity.

Uniquely, homosexuality is now too strongly recognized in its own right for it to be regarded as transgender behaviour. A man having male lovers might once have been regarded as effeminate, but that is no longer the case, at least not in the West. In many other parts of the world, however, transgender and homosexuality have a closer relationship, and many transgender people refer to themselves as a third sex. (For more on Thailand's ladyboys, Bangkok's *hijra* and other transgender people, see p.27.)

Intersex exceptional

Gender is clearly a question of degree as well as of binary identity. But even sex isn't always as clear-cut as most people find it comfortable to think. Some one in a hundred babies are born with bodies which do not exactly fit in either of the two categories. They have a disorder of sexual development, as the medics put it; or, as some campaigning groups prefer to say, they are intersex.

For the majority, the variation is fairly insignificant. A fair few infant boys have penises that haven't quite "fused" in the uterus, leaving the urethra open underneath rather than at the end of the penis – a condition known as hypospadias. Some girls have large clitorises and partially fused labia, caused by unusual levels of masculinizing hormones within their own bodies, or congenital adrenal hyperlasia (CAH).

Many parents (and many surgeons) prefer to have minor differences "corrected" in infancy. Exceptions often make people feel uncomfortable, and parents may – with the best of intentions – want to spare their child social problems later in life. There is good evidence, however, that in more ambiguous cases over-hasty surgery can cause as many problems as it's designed to resolve. Some people just don't fall neatly into one sex or the other. And in reality, the two sexes don't divide as simply as is usually assumed.

Cross-dressing, sex and gender

Cross-dressing can mean nothing more than wearing clothes typical of the opposite sex. Some men have long cross-dressed, or worn "drag", for work alone: actors and priests or demiurges, for example. Some stag parties enjoy the taboo-breaking and attention-grabbing that wearing drag brings. In the West, working women have occasionally seen fit to don trousers since the nineteenth century, and after the 1960s "masculine"-styled clothing became so common in "womenswear" that it has become almost impossible for women to cross-dress.

Those women who do cross-dress may find fulfilment in "packing", the wearing of a soft penis-shaped object sometimes matched with a pair of stand-in balls as well. Some women who try packing have reported experiencing surprising rises in confidence or at least swagger, as if they were somehow tapping into the social power that men themselves seem to ascribe to or derive from their penises.

Cross-dressing doesn't necessarily have gender significance, but it often does. Singer Marlene Dietrich and actress Katherine Hepburn both helped popularize trouser suits for women in the 1930s, and it would be wilful to think that Hepburn's feminism and her bisexuality, or Dietrich's gender-play and her (probable) bisexuality wasn't relevant. And if someone describes themselves as "a cross-dresser" or "transvestite", it implies a certain commitment to crossing typical gender boundaries – it is transgender behaviour.

Even if drag is most visibly worn by some gay men ("drag queens"), wanting to wear women's clothing doesn't imply homosexual orientation. In fact, the strongest link between cross-dressing and sexuality is found among straight men. "Fetishistic transvestites," as they are called, are chiefly interested in sex rather than gender play: they are men – typically straight men – turned on by the act of wearing women's clothing. Plenty of men are turned on by other men wearing women's clothing, however. In Brazil, for instance, *travestis* are cross-dressers working as prostitutes. Curiously, a travesti's client may want to be penetrated as well as to penetrate – a case of gender roles being played with at the same time as sexual ones.

Hollywood Street, 1933: Marlene Dietrich looking suave and sexy in a man's suit.

Chromosomes and sex

Intersexuality is entirely natural, just as physical variations in genitalia are pretty much inevitable, given that humans start out on just the one pattern and only gradually diverge towards either male or female as they develop in the womb (see p.191). Human genitalia differ excitingly, but they're rarely entirely ambiguous – and usually match up with a person's karyotype (the pattern of their chromosomes) and their identity.

For a few people, their chromosomes don't fall simply on one side of the fence or the other. People with Klinefelter's or XXY syndrome, for instance, have an extra X chromosome as well as the "male" Y chromosome. Most XXY people live and identify as men: a few may have a faintly boyish or womanly build or appearance, but they have a penis and testes (even if they may not be fertile without medical assistance), which is what counts for most medics. Chromosomes may be what drives sexual division in foetuses but genitalia are more often used to define gender.

A good example of this is complete androgen insensitivity syndrome (CAIS), in which an infant with a male-type XY karyotype lacks the receptors which respond to masculinizing hormones. So in the eighth week of development, the Y chromosome starts building testes, which start to create the hormones which usually turn a body male – but the body never responds. People with CAIS often have internal testes and lack ovaries, but they usually have vaginas (if sometimes shallow ones) – and almost always identify as female. In fact, women with CAIS are stereotypically tall and large-breasted, and have unusually good hair and skin – ideal qualifications for being a model. (Predictably, there is a degree of online speculation about the supposed CAIS-status of various androgynous-looking actresses and models.)

Genitals and gender

In ambiguous cases, doctors have traditionally seen potential fertility as the most important factor in assigning gender. In cases where fertility could never be possible, however, medical decisions have reflected a curious obsession with the penis. Some 90 percent of surgical cases, for instance, have been assigned female identity on the grounds that "you can make a hole but you can't build a pole" – as one member of a surgical team notoriously put it.

Surgeons – a group better known for their pragmatism than for theorizing about gender – have tended to see the penis as the yardstick of masculinity. If an infant had a micropenis (or "oversized" clitoris), it was often simply removed. Never mind sexual response; fitting in was seen as all-important. Scalpels were creating gender conformity. Parents would then be encouraged to raise their child according to the assigned, female gender, and feminizing hormones would be given to encourage development in the decided direction. Treatment might only stop "when the child grows old enough to resist", as Cheryl Chase, founder of the Intersex Society of North America has chillingly put it.

Since the 1990s, however, campaigning groups such as ISNA, and movements within the medical profession have challenged this orthodoxy. Too many people have come forward with tales of their sex being medically interfered with, resulting in

Hermaphroditus

As the son of Aphrodite, goddess of love, and Hermes, the athletic messenger of the gods, Hermaphroditus was extraordinarily handsome. So compelling was his beauty that, when the water nymph Salmacis saw him bathing naked in her pool, she was overcome by lust. Throwing off her clothes, she plunged in, enfolding the youth in her arms like an eagle snatching a snake. Responding to his struggles to free himself, Salmacis implored the gods that they should never be parted. Her prayer was answered, and the two became one.

The story inspired some of the finest and most erotic Hellenistic sculptures, typically of a female figure lifting her skirt to reveal an erect penis, or a depiction of Salmacis' assault and the moment of transformation, or of Hermaphroditus struggling with – and perhaps attempting to rape – a satyr. But the most remarkable portrayal to survive is the Sleeping Hermaphrodite, as represented by a handful of Roman copies of a second-century BC Greek original. It's a strange and brilliant composition, as Hermaphroditus lies half on his/her side, twisting his/her body around to face the other way. He/she reveals a succession of different viewpoints, both apparently male and female – as well as perhaps the loveliest buttocks every portrayed in stone.

The word hermaphrodite isn't used for humans any more, partly because "true hermaphrodites", or people born with both ovaries and testes, are extremely rare. More common are what used to be called male and female pseudohermaphrodites, or people with testicular and ovarian tissue respectively, but whose genitalia are ambiguous or opposite. But the word hermaphrodite, never mind pseudohermaphrodite, is loaded with too much erotic and archaically medical baggage, and "intersexual" is now the usual umbrella term, with different forms of intersexuality each having their own names and definitions.

The celebrated Roman statue of the Sleeping Hermaphrodite has troubled and aroused viewers since the second century.

a genital sexual status which clashed with their own sense of gender identity – not to mention the stories of repeated, painful, and frankly abusive, operations and damaged sexual response. As a result, doctors are more likely than they once were to assign a provisional gender at birth, and hold off on surgery until the child is old enough to decide for themselves who they feel they are: man, woman – or indeed simply themselves.

Transsexual transitions

Having a "sex change operation", for many transsexual people, is exactly what they're not doing. The outside world may think they are changing sex but for them, they are outwardly confirming the sex they are inside. "Transitioning" can offer a cure for the misery of feeling imprisoned in the wrong body. Much more so than for transgender people, transsexuality is rooted in the body: it is about sex, not gender.

Not all transsexuals have, or desire, surgery. Some dress and behave in a transgender way, have regular hair removal and learn to alter their voices. Some take hormones to alter their bodies – which is often experienced as the most profound change. Some pursue sex reassignment surgery (as medics call it) or gender confirmation surgery (as transgender people tend to say), including genital

reconstruction. There are some three to five times as many male-to-female (MtF) "transwomen" as female-to-male (FtM) "transmen".

The people who do have surgery, tellingly, very rarely regret it. Not that it's perfect. Vulvas can be sculpted that even have clitorises preserving the sexual nerve complexes. Lubrication, however, is another matter – and, of course, uterus transplants and fertility are a long way off. For people transitioning from female to male, a neophallus can be constructed from tissue grafts, with sensitive, erogenous clitoral tissue creating the base and a rod or inflatable tube allowing a workable erection. Real erectile function and full sexual responsiveness are, however, another matter.

Debates about the causes of transsexualism are strangely parallel to those about homosexuality. There is a great deal of pressure from within the transsexual community for transsexualism to be shown to have a biological or genetic basis – rather than a potentially stigmatizing psychiatric one. Research has thrown up weak indications of links with both genes and foetal hormones, but the strongest evidence to date is that therapy to treat gender dysphoria (the belief that one's sex is not what it appears outwardly to be) is no more successful than were the "cures" once touted for homosexuality. It seems you can't talk someone out of the sex they know themselves to be.

3
How to do it

3
How to do it

This chapter describes "how to do it". "It", of course, means sex – the whole rich repertoire of things people do to give themselves and others sexual pleasure. It covers everything from touch, kissing and oral sex to that commonest of all sex acts – and most powerful of learning methods – masturbation. And, of course, penetration.

The idea isn't to teach anyone how to be a sexual athlete, but to improve the chance that sex will be "good" – that it will be satisfying, rewarding, pleasurable, considerate, thrilling – and more reliably orgasmic. That goal is the same whether you're having sex with yourself, or with someone of the opposite or the same sex. Exactly what makes sex "good" is a huge question. If it was only about orgasm, or even about the raw pleasure of touch, people would probably be more interested in masturbating alone. Sexual satisfaction is far more complex. It means different things to different people at different times. For some, it's an experience, something that can't be described: like a colour, perhaps.

The quality of the relationship within which sex takes place is hugely important. For someone seeking self-affirming, emotionally uncomplicated pleasure, a one-night stand with an experienced and appreciative partner may do it best. For someone in a committed relationship, sexual satisfaction may be about expressing love and appreciation, or reconjuring the passion they felt when they first formed their bond. Like any kind of fulfilment, the key is to understand what you want. Only then can you recognize it when you get it.

Touching and kissing

Touch lies at the very foundation of sex. Attraction, desire and even arousal may begin in the mind and the emotions, but we express ourselves sexually through touch. India's third-century manual, the *Kamasutra*, even defines sexual pleasure as a kind of touch. A special kind, admittedly – one with positive and aware feelings which results in an orgasm – but a subset nonetheless.

It's said that touch doesn't lie. It communicates emotions very directly – after all, to say something "touched" you means that you responded to it emotionally. The earliest and most powerful human experiences are tactile: being born into someone's hands and being laid skin to skin with a mother; suckling at a breast, being cleaned and coddled as a baby.

Touch is also vital in adult relationships. Just as apes groom and preen, loving couples touch one another in a thousand tiny ways. People in sexual relationships, particularly early on, perform "tie signs" like hugs, little kisses and hand-holding which prove to each other – and show the rest of the world – that they are more than friends. In the UK and the US, where people don't generally touch each other much in public (far less than Latin American or Middle Eastern societies, for instance), intimate touches can become especially important.

Masters and Johnson waxed philosophical on the subject of touch. It is "an end in itself", they wrote in 1976, "a primary form of communication, a silent voice that avoids the pitfall of words while expressing the feelings of the moment. It bridges the physical separateness from which no human being is spared".

How to touch

Touch both relaxes and stimulates – and both are crucial for true sexual satisfaction. Most sex manuals list different ways to stroke or caress a partner, as if these were secret codes for unlocking arousal. The truth is that everyone likes being touched differently, and in different ways with different people – or at different times. Touch is a relationship, not a performance. (Still less is it an opportunity for self-gratification: this is the difference between caressing and groping.) But as long as you touch someone with respect, empathy and a certain amount of attention to detail you can't go too far wrong.

Communication is crucial. All relationship experts stress the importance of letting your partner know what feels good and what doesn't. If murmuring "that feels good!" huskily doesn't come naturally, pleasure can be expressed in sighs and "mmm"s, shudders and little writhings. "Listening" to your partner's body is vital, so as not to miss those tiny signs of pleasure – or boredom. If the signals are getting lost, try touching as you'd like to be touched, then asking your partner to do the same in return.

One popular exercise is to caress your partner from head to toe, touching every inch of skin – except the genitals. Others allow genital touch, but no orgasms. This is really the "sensate focus" training programme (see p.211) in miniature. But it isn't just educational: there's something very sexy about that little restriction.

Confidence is as important as communication. Touching someone as if they might break is rarely sexy. This doesn't mean being overly firm, or rough, or launching at the genitals. Just as in massage, confidence in touch is usually expressed through slowness, repetition and deliberation. Even tentative, flirtatious brushings can be confident if handled in this way.

Techniques from massage

Massage techniques work just as well for sexual touch: be slow; don't break contact; repeat movements several times; don't jump from one thing to another; work in simple circles and lines; think about symmetry on both sides of the body; use oils or lubricants. A massage is only really successful when the person being touched is also an active participant. For the person being massaged, the most useful techniques are breathing, "accepting" the touch, and focusing on your own body while gently pushing aside stray or stressful thoughts.

Imagination and experience are the best massage tutors. Failing that, pay for a massage from a good professional. You'll quickly learn that the key tools are the thumb, the fingers and the heel of the palm, as well as the whole hand. These tools are used to knead, pull, drag, rub, press, stroke and circle. With a partner, you can also use toes, elbows, breasts, the chest – anything. Hair being swept across naked skin can provoke incredible sensations. Long hair evokes feathers or skeins of fine silk, short hair can buzz and prickle. Men can even use beards or stubble.

Water is particularly sensual: you can give a lover a slow sponge bath, trickle from a jug over the shoulders, use jets from the shower (cold jets in a hot bath is sensational), or simply wash your partner's hair lovingly. Breath is an astonishingly subtle and intimate way to touch someone: hot and soft on the belly between kisses, perhaps, or cool and hard on the nape of the neck.

Touching someone using the whole of your body – dragging yourself back and forth on top of them, maybe – is sometimes sarcastically called "Thai-massage-style", after the masseurs who supposedly encourage clients to go for that little extra by going that little bit beyond just "hands-on". It's unlikely to work too well as a first move, but as a preliminary to a spot of "dry humping", where you grind against each other with your clothes on, should do just fine.

Dynamic touch and erogenous zones

Unlike massage, sexual touch has a storyline, and a finale. You might build up pressure and intensity in waves, beginning with tiny strokes of the fingertips or nails and working up to wider, stronger motions. Caressing around the genitals in ever-decreasing circles can be pleasurably tantalizing. Or you might kneel astride a partner and stroke down the sides of their chest and hips, crossing your hands over their stomach in the middle in a figure-of-eight pattern.

The "story" of sexual touch doesn't necessarily end with the genitals – though this narrative can work very well, as Monica demonstrates in an

Outercourse

Sex without penetration is sometimes dubbed "outercourse". The idea originated in the 1980s among abstinence groups anxious about teenage sex, sexual health and pregnancy but has since become popular with people (especially women) who don't see penetration as the be-all and end-all. Outercourse can mean anything from stroking and showering together to mutual masturbation. It's sometimes used to mean sex without taking your clothes off, though most call this "dry humping". Whatever the concept covers, it's certain that sex without penetration can be a brilliant way to get out of a sexual rut in a relationship.

episode of *Friends*. "You could start out with a little one", she instructs Chandler, then: "a two. A one, two, three. A three. A five. A four. A three, two. Two. A two, four, six. Two, four, six. Four. Two. Two. Four, seven! Five, seven! Six, seven! Seven! Seven! Seven! Seven! Seven!"

Erogenous zones – key areas of the body which supposedly tap directly into sexual feeling – are a bit of a 1970s myth. The genitals, or "specific erogenous zones" are obviously "erogenous" in this way, while the "non-specific" zones are pretty much everywhere that is rarely touched in everyday, non-sexual situations, including: the earlobes, neck, nose, hairline and collarbone; the soles and toes of the foot; the small of the back; the back of the knee and inside of the elbow, the belly and navel. But people are remarkably different and results depend as much on emotion and intention as location. Anywhere can be erogenous, if touched in the right way by the right person.

Breast strokes and kisses

According to *The Whole Lesbian Sex Book*, women enjoy "caresses, fluttering kisses, moist lips on nipples. We like squeezing, pinching, kneading, slapping and nibbling. We like having our nipples tugged and bitten, pulled and twisted. We enjoy soft touches around the curves." You might add caressing, stroking, brushing, rubbing, blowing and licking to the list, and note that the underside of the breast is an especially sensitive area, and that a little oil or moisture on the nipples increases sensation.

Contrary to common belief, male nipples and pectorals aren't necessarily any less sensitive than women's but, equally, many women (and many

men) find breast stimulation unarousing or even unpleasant. Pleasure in touch is definitely linked to cultural expectation, and in the West, sexuality and femininity are often measured by the bosom, while men's breasts aren't understood to be erotic. Breast sensitivity often changes dramatically over the course of the menstrual cycle, too (premenstrual syndrome, especially, can cause hyper-sensitivity, a condition some call "atomic tits").

For more playful stimulation, breasts can be bound or wrapped: silk, fur, velvet, and fishnet nylon are popular. They can be stimulated more acutely with melted wax or ice. They can be pierced. Sex shops sell nipple clamps, which are designed to restrict the blood flow so that the nipple goes numb. When the clamp is taken off – which, for safety, should be after no more than twenty minutes – the nerves spring back into glorious life.

How to kiss

If the eyes are the windows of the soul, the mouth is the body's gateway. The lips are uniquely sensual. Their skin is unusually thin, bringing the blood close to the surface and enriching their colour. Arousal may make lips flush deeper still. The lips are unusually tightly packed with nerve endings, making them exquisitely sensitive to touch, pressure, heat and feelings of wetness. One theory in Chinese traditional medicine links the upper lip of a woman to her clitoris and the lower lip of a man to his penis.

The mouth is emotional as well as sensual: sex workers, traditionally, do not kiss their clients. And just as small babies explore the world with their

Kissing: Diana Muldaur shows Charlton Heston how she likes it in the 1969 film *Number One*.

mouths as much as their hands, adults explore new partners with their lips, tongue and teeth. Kissing also brings the most disregarded senses into full play: tongues are the agents of taste (which, of all the senses, is the most grounded in the body), while a kiss brings the nose right up against all the richness of the skin and the breath.

First kisses are popularly supposed to be a test of chemistry and compatibility, and to foreshadow what lovemaking will be like. Author Jane Vandenburgh calls them a "little haiku of how the sex will be". The way you kiss is even said to reveal your character. A

pinched kisser is mean and repressed; a sloppy kisser greedy and graceless; a voracious kisser aggressive – and so on. This puts some pressure on kissing style. In fact, kissing, like any behaviour, is learned – which means that it can be improved.

In surveys, women consistently rate kissing more highly than men, and are more likely to go off someone after kissing them. Men tend to prefer wetter or more tonguing kisses, and to think they're a prelude to sex. Make of that what you will – but it's always worth knowing what the opposition thinks.

French kissing around the world

A French intellectual was once asked if she knew the difference between kissing and "French" kissing. She answered: "it is the presence of the tongue". She might just as well have said "the presence of sex", because when you're kissing, tongues equal sex. A few people kiss their friends on the mouth, but only lovers kiss with the tongue.

The phrase "French kissing" took off in the 1920s, when France was associated with all things sophisticated or a little racy. They call it "English kissing" in south India for similar reasons – because in India, that kind of thing was once restricted to English and American films. Nowadays, Brits tend to call tongue-kissing "snogging", or "getting off with" while Americans say "making out" – though these phrases cover light foreplay too. Germans, Scandinavians and Greeks, very accurately, call it "tongue kissing". Mandarin Chinese, with equal directness, talk about "wet" kisses. Some cultures are more wry about it: Australians call it "pashing", while Afrikaans-speakers are known to refer to "a bit of tong in die long", or "tongue in the lung". The Portuguese call it linguado, which means "tongued" but, disturbingly, is also the name for a sole – as in the flatfish.

The French don't call it French kissing any more than they call condoms French letters, though the people of Quebec may say "frencher". Young French people may occasionally "roll the spade", in slang, but mostly they just call it kissing: tongues are assumed. The real danger in French is whether you use a verb or noun: to give

Auguste Rodin's *The Kiss* is the West's pre-eminent monument to sensuality.

your mother-in-law "un baiser" just means planting a kiss on her cheek; to "baiser" her would be vastly more intimate.

Some cultures view ordinary kissing as pretty disgusting, so adding tongues seems unthinkable. Conservative Hindus frown on the exchange of body fluids (though Sanskrit literature is quite obsessed with kissing). Inuit culture, where people are said to rub noses rather than kiss, actually focuses on bringing the breath of two people close together, rather than lip contact. Traditionally, Mozambique's Chewa and Thonga people, the Trobriand Islanders of the Pacific, Finland's Laplanders, the Lepcha of Sikkim, and the Sirono of Bolivia, would rather not. In fact, a 1951 study of kissing in traditional societies found that 169 out of 190 groups surveyed didn't indulge in kissing with the mouth. One wonders how many have succumbed to the pleasures since the 1950s.

Japan, which banned Rodin's sculpture *The Kiss* from public exhibition in the 1920s, thanks to very negative feelings about kissing, has certainly relaxed its views. Although if they'd known the background of the sculpture they might have let it pass. The original title was *Francesca da Rimini*, as the embracing couple isn't just any old pair of lovers, but Paolo and Francesca from Dante's *Inferno*. According to the story, moments after they began their embrace Francesca's husband (and Paolo's brother), the crippled Gianciotto, burst into the room and ran them both through with his sword. Hardly an advertisement for kissing.

Kissing technique

The best education is undoubtedly to kiss a lot of people. Failing that, the ground rules are basically the same as sex. Think about pacing (start slow – in fact, stay slow), mirroring (do what they do back), exploration (try things) and variety (try different things). Don't even think about copying how they kiss in classic films, where they swerve from side to side in much the same disconcerting way as they drive. Contemporary actors tend to eat each others' faces off, which is fine for ultra-intense moments but otherwise best left to teenagers on park benches. In general, observe good oral hygiene: brush, floss and, if necessary, mouth-wash and tongue-scrape. Beware short stubble, which can produce a tell-tale "pash rash" around the mouth.

Specific kissing skills include swallowing and moistening your own lips with a quick sweep of the tongue before you start – but don't be too obvious about this or you'll just look hungry. If you're going to lunge, be very sure that you're not going to be rejected (the dreaded "turn-away"; you end up hovering in the region of their ear like a vulture poised above a carcass). Unless you're modestly nasally endowed, tilt the head before leaning in.

It's usual to begin with ordinary lip kisses – mixed, perhaps, with soft and melting brushings of the lip. Don't gape and lunge in film actor-hungry-shark-style. Think about keeping the mouth and lips relaxed and mobile. Come up for air regularly. A tiny tip-to-tip touch of tongues is the usual cue for deeper exploration, in which lip-sucking and tonguing can be brought into play – but beware excessively pointy thrusting, which is usually a turn-off.

Many sexperts offer "advanced" tips. Suzi Godson advises circling and sucking your partner's tongue "like an ice lolly". Pam Spurr recommends the "Stretch" manoeuvre, in which the tongue reaches right up to the roof of the mouth. The *Kamasutra* describes an early "throbbing" kiss, where the woman wants to grasp her partner's lower lip but, feeling too shy to do this with her upper lip, gently makes her lower lip throb against his instead. Other manuals advise running the tongue along the teeth and gum lines, lapping like a dog or sucking the tongue back and forth as if you were giving a blow job. Informal canvassing suggests people may react to these "techniques" with horror.

Beyond lips and tongues

Passionate or loving kissing rarely restricts itself to the mouth. Close to hand – or rather close to mouth – lie the neck (try the corner of the jaw, the nape and the hollow of the clavicle), the ears (the lobes, the skin just below and behind the ear) and the hair (the hairline, the sideburns, the temples). According to sex writer Lou Paget, "the man who doesn't like a tongue in his ear is rare, but the woman who does is rarer still".

You don't have to kiss *with* the mouth alone, either. The so-called "butterfly" kiss is the use of a flickering eyelash. The nose can brush and prod and stroke. Breath provides the rhythm and the warmth of a good kiss. An incredibly intimate (if rather tricky) thing to do is to seal mouth to mouth and exhale and inhale as one person. Breath has often been likened to the soul, after all, and kissing with tongues is sometimes called "soul kissing".

Little nibblish bites can always be thrown in. Lovebites, or hickeys – where the lips seal around the skin and suck it up, causing a bruise – are a kind of branding, saying either "you're mine" or "look at me, I'm in a relationship". They're best kept away from the face. You can't cure a lovebite, but you can help it heal by applying ice or the back of a frozen spoon. To cover one up, begin with a base layer of green-tinged concealer, to neutralize the red shading, then apply a second layer of concealer that's slightly lighter than the natural skin shade.

"Advanced" – that is, unusual – techniques mostly involve exchanging fluids other than saliva. Ice is surprising and stimulating. Alcohol is very popular: Champagne for the fizz, Margaritas for the tang, maybe, or a Bloody Mary for a chilli kick. Gourmands might find chocolate kisses enticing. Kissed exchanges of period blood (the "rainbow kiss") and sperm (the "snowball") are probably acquired tastes.

For first-timers, it might be useful to know that in one study 80 out of 124 people turned to the right, not left. As to whether or not you should kiss with the eyes open or closed: people do both. The only conceivable issue here is if one person is a regular open-eyed kisser and the other a devoted, cosy shut-eye. In this scenario, opening a tentative eye and finding the other person already gazing balefully at you might be alarming.

Masturbation, or sex by hand

Masturbation is sometimes talked about as if it was somehow second best to the "real thing", but the art of having sex using the hand is probably the world's most common sexual activity. Animals do it (at least, non-hoofed animals do it). Children do it – often long before they begin sexual relationships. People without partners do it. People with partners do it, on the side. Couples do it, to themselves and to each other. People masturbate to get themselves to sleep, to relax, to pick themselves up, to treat headaches and period pain. They do it to arouse themselves before trying other kinds of sex, to spend some time with their imaginations – and just because they want to give themselves a little pleasure.

In the days when solo masturbation was regarded with deep anxiety, it was blamed for all kinds of ailments, from eye conditions to mental disease (see p.338). It used to be thought that orgasms from masturbation spoiled people for "real" sex. (This notion survives in the theory that men who apply a lot of pressure when masturbating can become desensitized.) It's still relatively taboo: it's harder to talk about on television than couple sex, for instance.

Yet masturbation is the best way to learn about sex. If you want to know how your body responds to pleasure, touch yourself. And if you want to learn how to give a partner an orgasm, begin by touching them – or let them show you exactly how it's done, or guide your hand with theirs. One general tip: the researchers Masters and Johnson found that lesbians treated the clitoris more delicately than straight men, while gay men tended to use a heavier hand on the penis than straight women.

Doing it yourself

Comedians love masturbation. Gay stand-up and actress Lily Tomlin reckons that "man first walked upright to free his hands for masturbation", while for Woody Allen, it is "sex with someone I love". It's not just comedians, either. The Greek philosopher Diogenes, a Cynic who despised the hypocrisies of civilization, once masturbated in the Athens marketplace in order to prove his honest devotion to simple virtues.

Diogenes also told a shaggy dog story about the origins of the art. The god Mercury, he said, taught masturbation to his son, Pan, to console him for the loss of the nymph Echo. Pan loved Echo; she rejected him; he had her torn apart by his followers, the shepherds. In return for the shepherds' help, Pan was said to have taught them how to bring themselves off.

Humans have been wanking very happily ever since. The figures in surveys vary from country to country and depend a lot on age, but, broadly speaking, around half of all people (in the US, roughly 60 percent of men and 40 percent of women) masturbate to orgasm. In the UK, 73 percent of men and 37 percent of women masturbated in the four weeks before a survey of 2007. In the US, according to the 1992 National Health and Social Life Survey, 25 percent of men and 10 percent of women said they masturbated at least once a week.

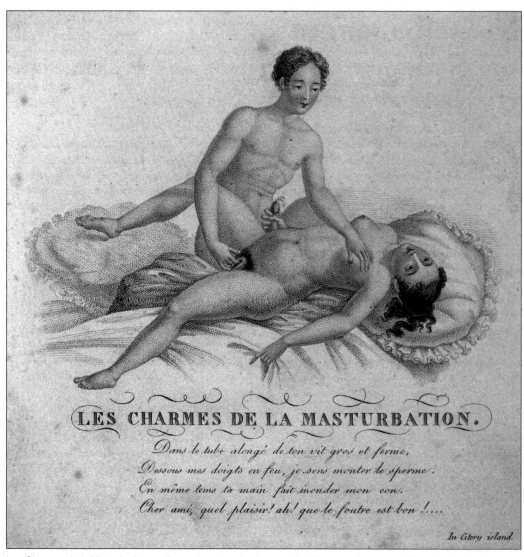

Les Charmes de la Masturbation … "beneath my burning fingers I feel the mounting sperm." From *Invocation à l'amour. Chant philosophique* (c.1825).

Masturbation playlist

Chuck Berry, "My Ding-a-Ling" (1972)
Violent Femmes, "Blister in the Sun" (1982)
Cyndi Lauper, "She Bop" (1984)
The Divinyls, "I Touch Myself" (1991)
Radiohead, "Thinking About You" (1993)
Green Day, "Longview" (1994)
Britney Spears, "Touch of My Hand" (2003)

The difference between male and female frequency is striking. Some say it's evidence that women have lower sex drives. Others reckon it shows how much more publicly acceptable male masturbation is, arguing that many women still feel awkward about acknowledging that they masturbate, while others are put off doing it altogether. Male masturbation is certainly more culturally visible. One slang dictionary, for instance, has twelve whole pages of terms for men ("whacking off", "spanking the bishop", "feeding the ducks", etc) and just one page of obscure terms for women. Does "buffing the squirrel" sound familiar?

The sex activist and writer Betty Dodson has run a lifetime campaign to promote masturbation, especially to women. She calls it "an erotic meditation" and "the ongoing love affair that each of us has with ourselves throughout our lifetime". Denial or prohibition, she argues, is the basis for all other kinds of sexual repression. She may be right: for many people, solo masturbation is their first sexual experience, and it forms the foundation for all other sexual activities. If you don't learn how to enjoy yourself in bed, it's harder to show anyone else how they can please you.

By hand: for her

Knowing how to touch a woman's vulva and clitoris is probably the single most important skill anyone planning on having sex with a woman can learn – and that includes women who plan to have sex with themselves. Elizabeth Blackwell, a pioneering female doctor, had it about right when she wrote in 1902 that women crave not so much intercourse but instead "delight in kisses and caresses". She called this the "love touch", or sex "by hand and by tongue".

The techniques described here are good for partner-sex and solo-sex alike, but because women's genital geography varies so much, what works for one woman won't necessarily work for another. As ever, the answer is to try things out. The exploration is worth it on its own account. It's worth reading up on the fascinating pleasure structures that lie beneath the skin, too: what's usually called "the clitoris", for instance, turns out to be just the tip of a far larger organ (see p.45).

The basic technique is the clitoral strum: a steady rubbing that's applied either directly onto the glans or tip of the clitoris, or just off to one side, or indirectly through clothing or the skin of clitoral hood. The right combination of pressure and rhythm may take time to find or establish – which is one of the reasons why women having one-night stands are much less likely to come than women having sex with a regular partner. The right "beat" can also vary dramatically according to mood, time of the month, and as arousal and orgasm develop. Women's partners sometimes complain that they've hardly found their rhythm when they realize the music has moved on – which is one of the reasons why touching yourself is so wonderfully effective.

Getting started

Penises, by and large, tend to leap into action with boyish enthusiasm. (Though this doesn't mean this is the best way to approach them.) The glans of the clitoris, by contrast, usually demands a more seductive or at least nuanced approach. Many women don't like having their clitorises touched directly until they're very aroused. As John Cleese's sex-education teacher tells the over-hasty schoolboy in Monty Python's *The Meaning of Life* (1983), "What's wrong with a kiss, boy? Why not start her off with a nice kiss? You don't have to go leaping straight for the clitoris like a bull at a gate."

If you're touching yourself, your hand falls naturally into the position that works for most people: the hand approaches either from directly above or slightly from the side, with the fingers pointing down. You can rest your wrist on your pubic bone and just begin by feeling around. If you're touching someone else, maybe copy this angle and approach.

When touching a partner, it's wise to start by being open to ideas: masturbatory preferences can be incredibly detailed and specific. Being committed is also important: it'll help your partner relax and feel comfortable. Getting comfortable is crucial, as you may be in for some hard, manual labour. Lying side by side works, or she might be on her back with you nestled against her, lying on your side. You can also approach her from behind, reaching round her waist or between the legs (though the latter can feel cramped). Sitting face to face, perhaps with one leg crossed over hers, or lying face to face, missionary-style, also forces the hand into a more cramped position, but it's far from impossible.

Many sex writers advise going "round the houses" or "around the neighbourhood" to begin with. Some women find that starting with the knickers on feels sexy, and of course it allows indirect pressure to be applied to the clitoris. You might start by stroking your partner's belly or her inner thighs, by cupping her whole vulva in your hand to feel its heat, or by pulling open the outer lips slightly to stroke them on the inside, tracing the grooves and the crevices with a soft finger. You might press gently on the pubic mound with the heel of the palm.

At around this point, lubrication could be useful. Saliva works very well and, of course, doesn't require a trip to the bathroom or an awkward fumble in the bedside drawer. The drawback is that saliva can run out, especially if you've been drinking. Lick your fingers or gather some spittle into your hand (a bit of subtlety is advised). As your partner becomes aroused, you can shallowly dip your fingers into her vagina, spreading her own juices around with sweeping strokes.

Supplemental lubrication (see p.139) can improve things dramatically, especially for post-menopausal women. Natural oils, moisturizers and the like tend to smell better than commercial lubricants, but perfumed products can disrupt the vagina's chemical balance. It's important not to use oil if you're going to use a condom later, as it damages latex rubber.

Clitoral strokes

As things warm up, the clitoris (or, technically speaking, the clitoral glans; see p.46) usually becomes more responsive – though indirect touch is still best at first. You can rub the lips between thumb and forefinger, or pull them back to stretch the skin of the clitoral hood. You can stroke against the side of the glans of the clitoris, or swirl around it, returning again and again to a particularly sensitive place, slowly extending the edges of what is pleasurable.

If you're touching a partner, be alert to her reactions. When you're on the right track, it's usually pretty obvious. As the poet Ovid put it, in the first century AD, "when you've found / Those places a woman adores to have touched up … go right in. / You'll see that tremulous glint in her eyes, like the dazzle / Of sunlight on a lake; / She'll moan and gasp, murmur words of sweet endearment".

As a woman becomes fully aroused, her clitoris engorges with blood, swelling and stiffening. This "erection" isn't nearly as visible as the penile variety but if you place a fingertip just above the glans of the clitoris you can usually feel the ridge of the erected clitoral shaft as it extends upwards into the body. Rubbing or rolling this shaft through the skin can be very effective: try little circles with the fingertip, or back-and-forward rubbing. For many women, especially those who don't like direct pressure on the glans of the clitoris, it's the stimulation of this shaft which brings them to orgasm.

A popular technique is to place two fingers either side of the clitoris, with the fingers pointing down on the inside of the outer labia and then start rubbing. Betty Dodson, the American queen of masturbation, calls it the scissor stroke; British sex writer Pam Spurr wryly dubs it the "V for Victory" manoeuvre. It certainly touches all the right places in just the right way: the weight of the hand rests on the pubic mound, the edges of the fingers rub against the inner or outer lips, the soft pads at the base of the fingers press on the shaft of the clitoris,

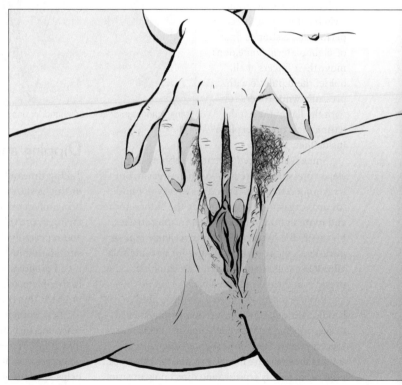

The scissor stroke or "V for Victory" manoeuvre.

while the skin of the hood is dragged to and fro across the clitoral glans.

Many women like to hold the hood or the labia out of the way with a second hand. Most prefer circling, side-to-side or up-and-down motions – or whatever combines the right stimulation with ease of access. Some switch between all three, or perform an elaborate figure-of-eight pattern. Some don't move their fingers at all, but let them pulsate with pressure, while others rub with the flat of the hand, letting their fingers explore inside their vagina.

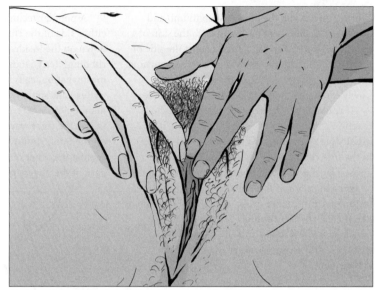

Many women guide a lover's hand, or use it to hold the labia out of the way.

Some women need sustained rubbing at a steady pressure and tempo to reach orgasm, but it's common to get faster and faster as you build towards orgasm, perhaps circling the clitoris more and more tightly. Some like deep, strong strokes, for others the hand ends up in a veritable blur of ultra-light, flicky motion (it's not for nothing that vibrators oscillate so rapidly). Any combination of pressure and rhythm is possible.

If you're touching someone else, you need to handle their orgasm with care. Some women need to keep moving right through orgasm; others find touching has to stop (or be shunted sideways) as soon as the first wave hits. At orgasm, the clitoris can become incredibly sensitive and direct pressure can become suddenly painful.

Dipping and reaching

Taking time out to return to stroking the belly or thighs shows that you're not just trying to bring off an orgasm as quickly as possible, you're trying to provide a bigger sensual experience. If you repeatedly draw back from intense clitoral stimulation just before the orgasm begins to build, it can progressively lift the intensity to higher and higher plateaus, ultimately releasing a massive orgasm. This is called edging.

Few women put their fingers inside themselves when masturbating (Kinsey reckoned it was one in five; still fewer use dildoes). That said, some enjoy an occasional "lucky dip" into the vagina, which helps keep things wet. This is important: you're not rubbing two sticks together to make fire. You can use the fingers of the free hand to push into the sensitive vaginal opening or, more adventurously, curl the fingers round in a beckoning motion in order to stimulate the so-called "G-spot" (see p.47). Sex campaigner Annie Sprinkle says you can stimulate this sponge from the outside, too, by pressing down on the abdomen. She calls this "ringing the doorbell".

A free hand can be used to spread open the outer lips, and to rub, flick and tease the inner ones. It can reach up to caress or pinch the breasts or belly, or to be bitten or sucked upon. Slow rhythmic pressure on the perineum can intensify an orgasm, and you can also tease the anus with a free finger. Bolder lovers may take advantage of all that lubrication to slip a fingertip inside at the crucial moment – though for health reasons the same finger shouldn't penetrate both vagina and anus. (Some reckon you should use latex gloves if you're going anywhere near the back door.)

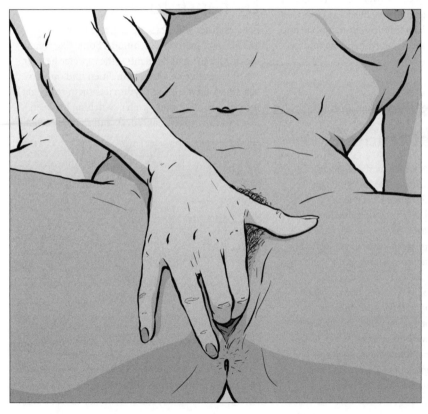

Penetration isn't really the point of sex by hand for her, but fingers can dip inside to help spread natural lubrication around, they can stroke the vaginal opening, and they can reach for the G-spot.

Bedposts and vibrators

The hand is a perfect masturbatory tool but it's not the only option. Women describe bringing into service bedposts, mattress edges, chair arms, pillows placed over a hand, bunched up T-shirts – anything that provides the desired combination of soft and hard. One correspondent to a sex advice site proudly confessed to having experimented in her early teens with: "hairbrush handles (smuggled under my nightie to bed), drawer knobs (removed in the dark and replaced before morning), parts of my brother's toys, Vicks inhalers, douche-bag and enema-bag nozzles, and whatever else I could get hold of."

You can also use your hand as if it was a foreign body, lying on your arm and moving against it. Shower heads are very popular – the water jets they produce, that is, not the head itself – as is the water from the bath tap, which you can allow to pour all over your vulva in a warm, steady and subtly pounding stream. The ultimate add-on, of course, is a vibrator (see p.142).

By hand: for him

Penises differ widely (see p.56), and every man has his own preferred technique. Some like small, quick, vibrating movements, others prefer heavier, more expansive gestures. Some men find only a sustained, unwavering rhythm lets them really get into the groove, others prefer switching between fast and slow speeds, and deep and shallow strokes.

Vaginal fisting – "downright tender"

Vaginal fisting, say the authors of *The Good Vibrations Guide to Sex*, is "downright tender", requiring patience and trust. It produces "sensations ranging from profound passion to meditative tranquillity". It requires the slow insertion of the entire hand – a very well-lubricated hand, probably sheathed in a latex glove – into the vagina, knuckle side down (facing her bottom). The vagina needs to be "coaxed", and you'll need to do deep breathing and consciously relax or bear down on the vaginal muscles. The hand forms not so much a fist as a "duck" – a pursed, beakish sort of shape. Once it's in, you can explore gentle rocking motions, clenching and unclenching or even some light thrusting.

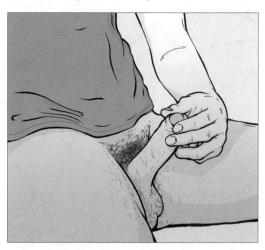

Many uncircumcised men prefer finger pressure to whole-hand action.

Dynamics are important, too: many men like a slow, teasing build, often starting with slow, upward strokes, but culminating with urgent pumping.

A smooth stroke generally works best: more like milking a cow than a piston's rapid shuttling. It's partly about not putting too much stress on the skin at the extremes of the motion. But beginners are sometimes surprised quite how hard and fast men like it. The penis may appear to be a delicate little organ, but it can take some punishment, and getting to the end of a high-tempo handjob may require stamina.

Foreskins and masturbation

Circumcised and uncircumcised men typically fall into two camps. Men with intact foreskins tend to hold their penile skin firmly – often very firmly – with fingers or a hand, making the penis slide back and forth within the sheath of the skin. Circumcised men are more likely to pump their whole penis within the hand – which, for many, is uncomfortable without lubrication: spit or baby oil, for instance.

Of course, it's not quite as simple as that. Some foreskins automatically pull back on erection, exposing the glans, but others, especially longer ones, cover the glans up all the time unless they're actively pulled back. Some men leave their foreskin forward for masturbation (or putting on a condom), others peel it back. Circumcisions vary, too. Tighter cuts tend to lend themselves to rubbing with a lubricant, while men with looser circumcisions may be inclined to the skin-pumping technique.

Circumcised men with a tighter cut often use a pumping hand technique.

Talking and positioning

Just tugging away on a man may well produce ejaculation but, to give real pleasure, hand placement is crucial. Many men position the hand quite precisely so it stimulates the most sensitive areas: the edge of a finger might just drag to and fro against the rim of the glans, for instance, or the grip might be tightest on the responsive underside of the penis, near the frenulum (the sensitive skein of skin that joins the skin to the head of the penis).

To find out what works for him, demand some feedback. If he's not much of a talker, get him to show you how he does it or guide your hand with his. You'll need to find a position which comfortably lets your hand come from the right angle. From the side or from behind often works

The manifold masturbations of Samuel Pepys

The great English diarist, Samuel Pepys, was a Member of Parliament, a respected naval reformer – and an enthusiastic masturbator. He recalled his fantasies with great pleasure in his diaries, describing on one occasion how, before going to sleep, he fancied himself "to sport with Mrs Stewart". Stewart was the king's mistress, a woman considered so beautiful she was the model for the figure of Britannia (as cast on Britain's coins then and since). This fantasy was "the best that ever was dreamed", Pepys wrote.

In November 1666, he masturbated in church while thinking about a friend's teenage daughter (an erotic transgression for which he asked his God to forgive him). He even pulled himself off during High Mass on Christmas Eve, while gazingly longingly at the queen and her ladies-in-waiting, gathered around the altar.

Pepys' proudest masturbatory moment, however, took place in the bottom of a ferry boat on the River Thames. As he lay there, daydreaming on the tide, he called to mind a "pretty wench" he'd seen that morning in Westminster Hall. So vivid was his erotic imagination that he managed to ejaculate without even touching himself. It was "the first time I did make trial of my strength of fancy of that kind", he wrote, with pride.

Samuel Pepys' bookplate: the Latin motto at the top reads "a man's mind is what he is".

best – missionary-position masturbation can be tricky, especially if he likes vigorous jerks. The position can make quite a difference for him, too. On his back is good for relaxation and letting thoughts and fantasies drift. Kneeling or on all fours switches on the abdominal muscles.

Two hands and beyond

Once you've found the way he likes it, stick to that groove. You don't want to rule out experimentation, but beware the baroque advice peddled by many sex writers. Adding in a second hand is the simplest extra (though lubrication will be required). Both hands can be held around the penis with the fingers interlaced, rather like in prayer. For a change (or a rest), the hands can be held still while the penis is thrust to and fro.

You can also throw in a twist. Some sex writers imagine tracing the curves of a corkscrew as you go up and down – but this requires a pretty lengthy penis. So too does stacking the hands à la one-potato, two-potato, then twisting them out and in with a turn of the wrist, as if giving a (gentle!) Chinese burn. (Try ringed fingers instead of the whole hand – more like twisting the cap off a bottle of beer.) The how-to masturbation video, *Fire on the Mountain*, describes an extreme variation called, appropriately, "Twist and Shout": the skin is held taut at the base with one hand, while the other twists and pulls "in a down-grasp, corkscrew motion".

Some writers recommend approaching from above, the fingers reaching out so as to let the head of the penis slide into the palm of the hand. Bizarrely, this move has been compared to the guddlings of an octopus, the juicing of a lemon or the beak-like nibbling of a swan's head. You might begin with the wrist turned over, so that the thumb points down. You might use the palm to rub the frenulum or the head of the penis itself in a "buffing" manoeuvre, perhaps pushing it up against his belly to work the underside. The ever-creative Lou Paget even recommends rubbing the penis between two palms as if starting a fire. Lubrication might help prevent very real friction burns.

Beyond the penis

To lift a handjob above the ordinary, pay attention to other parts of the body: the perineum, for instance. It lies just below the testicles, where the penis is rooted into the body. Pressure applied here as orgasm builds can be like adding in an earthquake as the volcano starts to spew: try pressing, pulsing or vibrating with the fingers or knuckles. You can also stimulate the root of the penis itself, reaching down with the fingers around the ball sack to work on an area that's mostly ignored.

The anus is right alongside the perineum. Even if he doesn't *think* he appreciates anal play, some rubbing or ringing here at the right moment might prove surprisingly acceptable. If he's relaxed about having his anus touched, you could slip in a (well-lubricated) finger and reach the prostate from the other side (see p.136). Men can be anxious about having their testicles touched (see p.63) but gentle handling can be pleasurable. Cup the balls appreciatively as if weighing them. Ring them with a finger. Tug down on them lightly to make the penis "come to attention".

Beyond the genitals, it's worth remembering that as arousal mounts, sensitivity throughout the body tends to increase. Circling or brushing strokes on the stomach, chest and thighs – or beyond – can add love and intensity. Not forgetting kisses and words of tenderness and encouragement, of course.

Hands-free

If you're a woman with larger breasts, you can squeeze his penis in your cleavage, or use the breast to beat against the shaft. The buttocks, lubricated, make an amazing channel for an enthusiastic penis – this could be a way to approach anal sex (see p.132). Then there are the toys: cock rings, penis vibrators and artificial vaginas.

A few men can apparently bring themselves to orgasm without using their hands at all – including the seventeenth-century diarist, Samuel Pepys (see box on p.100). For a rare minority it's a question of sheer concentration, but most need to work their core abdominal muscles in combination with vigorous fantasizing. One Texan correspondent to masturbation site jackinworld.com claims he merely has to "find a chin-up bar, grab it, bring my knees up to my chest and hold the position". Another writer, from the UK, says it's all about tensing and relaxing "the muscle that connects to the penis" – which almost certainly refers to the PC muscle (see p.179).

Many men have had one-off, hands-free orgasms when hyper-aroused. Finding yourself in an unusually hot sexual situation – watching a girlfriend with another man, in one case – seems to be a fairly common trigger. You might argue that this wasn't so much hands-free masturbation, however, as premature ejaculation. Which isn't quite so impressive.

Finishing off

A lot of men find it hard to come if they're being wanked off by someone else. They may require a certain stroke, or their partner just can't keep going, or something about the action is a little bit painful – not enough lubrication, perhaps, or over-stretching of the foreskin. Many men feel self-conscious, or need the erotic stimulation of a partner who's also turned on. You can help this by matching your own breathing to his – it's not exactly faking it, more providing encouragement. Telling him that you want him to "come now" gives him permission and encouragement at the same time. You could also try whispering erotic somethings in his ear (see p.105).

To delay orgasm, try changing the hand position. It'll usually reset his erotic thermostat, and it'll take some time for the temperature to start rising again. Doing this repeatedly can actually raise his boiling point, and by the time he finally comes, the orgasm will be that bit hotter than usual. This technique, as mentioned before, is sometimes called edging.

At the moment of orgasm, some penises become so sensitive that pressure and movement have to slow and lessen dramatically, or stop altogether. Other men like the orgasm to be pushed and pushed, however, even as it hits. When masturbating solo, some men alter their stroke, almost as if milking their ejaculation out of themselves. A lot of men like to feel their come spray or leak onto their own bodies – or onto yours. It's worth having something for mopping up, though men with longer foreskins could try catching the sperm inside the tip, as if in the reservoir teat of a condom.

Oral sex

Oral sex used to be an act that only the most louche lothario or abandoned harlot would perform. During the AIDS crisis, British politician Norman Fowler asked his civil servants: "Oral sex? Do we know how many people *do* this sort of thing?" Today, it is almost universal among young people, and likely seen as a preliminary, even a second-best. President Clinton, famously, did not regard a blow job as amounting to sex, and teens eager to hang onto their "virginity" may agree. Blow jobs are particularly big in the US, in both gay and straight circles alike – perhaps because of Christian anxieties about penetrative sex. According to *The Joy of Gay Sex*, men travel to the States from all over the world "to experience the superb technical prowess of American cocksuckers".

Bringing your face to a lover's genitals is certainly sensual – quite literally, many senses are involved. Tongues and lips also provide the subtlest sexual sensations, and have natural lubrication. While the physical intimacy is profound, it can be an emotionally distant kind of sex: they're working away down there while you're left isolated. Eye contact is broken. Many people rule out kissing afterwards. The neck gets sore, the tongue tired, the jaw locked. There may be pungent fluids to spit out or wipe away, or aggravating pubic hairs stuck between the teeth or in the back of the throat. (Few things are less sexy than hawking or retching to shake loose a pubic hair.)

Then there's the risk of transmitting herpes or another sexually transmitted infection (see p.363). In some cultures, oral sex just isn't acceptable.

In Thailand, for instance, it's popularly supposed to bring bad luck, while orthodox Hindus may have religious doubts about ritual pollution. Some people simply feel it's unpleasant or overly submissive (though the person giving head could be seen as controlling their partner's responses). The US's 1992 National Health and Social Life Survey found that 45 percent of men found receiving fellatio "very appealing" while only 17 percent of women felt that way about doing it. By contrast, 34 percent of men found giving cunnilingus "very appealing" while just 29 percent of women had the same level of enthusiasm for receiving it. Ultimately, if someone really doesn't want to go down, it's their prerogative.

Going down on her

"The tongue", says Ian Kerner, author of the US bestseller, *She Comes First*, "is mightier than the sword". The Australian Richters survey found that cunnilingus, in combination with clitoral stimulation by hand, gave nine out of ten women an orgasm. That's a lot more than the two or three who come during penetrative sex. Lesbians, of course, have known this for years. In one American study, almost half of lesbian women enjoyed oral last time they had sex, and a third had more than one orgasm. Among straight women, the figures were one in five, both ways.

Not everyone's keen on opening themselves up for that kind of close inspection, however. A survey conducted by British lesbian magazine *Diva* found that while nearly half of their readers thought oral sex was the best way to please a partner, only 38 percent liked receiving

When going down, comfort is crucial.

it above all other sexual activities. Common worries include how you smell or taste, whether you've washed or shaved or waxed recently enough, whether your lips or your clitoris are too long or too baggy or just not right, and whether you might have an infection or your period. Many women feel diffident about quite literally thrusting their vulva in someone's face. Reassurance from the partner giving oral sex, then, is pretty crucial.

Not just licking

Oral sex given to a woman is called cunnilingus, a word which supposedly comes from the Latin to tongue (*lingere*) the *cunnus* (which needs no translation) – but it's not real Latin and was only coined in 1897, when the pioneer sexologist Havelock Ellis described it as the "extreme gratification". It's not a great description. Licking is just a part of it.

As with sex by hand, the clitoris is best approached with a bit of respect. And as with French kissing, you don't just go diving in. Little kisses, licks and caresses around the thighs, belly and outer lips make a good start. (You could follow Ian Kerner's advice in *She Comes First*, and savour the first kiss like "the first sip of an expensive bottle of wine that you've been saving for that special occasion". Or you might not.)

A slow approach helps to make everything wet, so that she's protected from irritating frictions and at her most sensually responsive. It also helps you work out what's going on. Most women don't lay themselves open for inspection like an anatomy textbook, and different women have rather different parts. And most of us aren't used to navigating by tongue in the dark, with the map pressed up an inch or two from our noses. Other than starting slow, the best advice is to smooth away any stray pubic hair or flesh, and focus on her reactions.

Talking dirty – the other oral sex

Sex talk, or "talking dirty", is a way to raise the sexual temperature, to show your partner – and indeed yourself – how your inhibitions are melting away under the blowtorch of arousal. It's about letting go. It won't work if you can't, as you've got to mean it – or at least really sound as if you do. A simple sigh or moan – which might become a deliciously sighed "that's good", or "that feels good" – easily breaks the ice.

To heat things up, be more specific: "I love it when you …", for instance, or, more naughtily, "I love it when I …". Communication of this kind can actually improve your sex life, too. Asking questions draws your partner in: less "do you want to fuck me now?", perhaps, and more "tell me what you want me to do".

You don't have to suddenly pretend you're on a porn set. That said, "fuck me" is the all-time favourite, and that same fucking could easily become "now" or "hard", and you might "want" or "need" it. Other classic porn-style lines – most oriented at men, funnily enough – are "fuck me in the pussy/mouth/ass" and "I want your dick inside me". Maybe men need more reassurance.

If you're not sure how your partner will react, you can drop in the odd word or phrase in the heat of the moment and gauge the reaction. Even if you don't end up whispering sweet obscenities in a lover's ear, you can always laugh together. Talking dirty just for a partner's sake could get problematic. Just as with faking orgasm, you risk alienating yourself from your own sexual feelings.

69 = 0/10?

Sixty-niners, or soixante-neuf – as they used to call it when only the French were sexually adventurous – sound like the perfect sexual solution: egalitarian and nicely mutual. In practice, giving and receiving oral sex at the same time is, to quote British columnist Suzi Godson, like trying to pat your head and rub your stomach: not impossible, but definitely distracting. Doing a sixty-nine also presents both penis and clitoris at the wrong angle, with the tongue facing the top side rather then the more sensitive underparts. It also puts the nose where you might not want it to be. And that's leaving aside the problems of height differences.

If you can pull off a good sixty-nine, however, you may have got it made. *The Joy of Gay Sex* reckons that if your excitement and abandonment can feed into a virtuous circle, with "total reciprocity", the result can be "truly terrific, bone-crunching, simultaneous (or nearly so) orgasms". It also points out that a sixty-nine is a great way to encourage a younger or less experienced partner to give as well as receive, as it leaves them "free to decide ... without guilt or the sense of being watched".

If you're determined to make a sixty-nine work, try it on your sides. If one person is lying down on their back, a pillow or two helps avoid neck strain; the person on top should probably kneel, taking their weight on knees and forearms. If you're a male–female couple, it might work best if she goes on top so that she can control how deeply she takes in his penis; this also allows her breasts to hang down or press enticingly against his stomach.

Oral positions

Get comfortable. If there's a "standard" position, it's lying between her legs with your head looking up – imagine you're swimming breaststroke. This can strain the neck, so prop yourself up on your elbows or cradle her bottom in your hands. As long as she opens her legs wide, this position allows for relatively easy access, and you can caress her legs and lower back with your hands. You can also look up to make eye contact (though some women find this unnerving: they'd rather tip their head back and pursue their own fantasies).

A pillow underneath the buttocks or hips presents things at an easier angle, especially if you're approaching from the side, and may put a light strain on all those orgasmic pelvic muscles. Trying to come at her from above – with you on top – is mostly unhelpful. You can't get at the sensitive underside of the clitoris, your tongue is the wrong way up, your chin gets in the way and your nose is virtually burying itself in her anus.

If she's on all fours, however, you can slide under like a mechanic beneath a car, either from above or below. This is sometimes called "sitting on your face", though if she actually sat on you, it'd be hard to contribute much (although she could certainly use your face as a clitoral grinding post, if you were willing). Face-sitting is more about her straddling you while you crane your neck and bury your face into her. This can be incredibly empowering for the woman, allowing her to control the pace while simultaneously turning on all the right pelvic muscles. Standing positions can be sexy for the same reasons – you're like a knight (or page, or lady-in-waiting) kneeling before his (or her) mistress.

Clitoral action

Stimulating the area around the clitoris is a popular early move: circle it with the tongue, and lick the shaft where it disappears into the body under the hood. Some sex writers recommend humming as a way to transmit vibrations; you could try it, though show tunes might be off-putting. Others suggest nibbling at the inner labia, perhaps sucking one into the mouth.

As arousal mounts – and you'll know by wetness, changed breathing, relaxing or tensing of the stomach muscles, or wider opening of the legs – focus on the glans of the clitoris. There are two basic strokes: rapid flicking with the edge or tip of the tongue, and a deeper rubbing with the flat surface. You'll have to discover what she likes. The same is true for the direction of the motion: the authors of the woman-focused sex guide *A Piece of Cake* reckon that "up-and-downsies" are generally most effective but a bit of side-to-side action can certainly give the tongue muscles a break.

You could also try moving your tongue in a circle, going faster or slower. You could lap gently with the top of the tongue's tip, like a kitten taking milk. The underside of the clitoral glans is very sensitive. Later on, you can make deeper, more forceful upward licks – more like a cat grooming itself, maybe, or an ice-cream lick. With this last technique, you can make eye contact at the top of each stroke – assuming her eyes are still open.

Building up intensity generally works, but it's important not to make your partner feel she's being pushed towards some finishing line. Relax and follow her lead. Back off the clitoris for a while; throw in some more sensual sucks or teasing kisses. When she's ready to come it's time to put in the serious tongue work on the clitoris. You may not find the right action immediately, but once you've got it, consistency is the key: keep it steady, keep it continuous, and keep it fairly rapid. This rhythm can be quite hard to achieve, and harder to sustain for long enough, so many people use a hand towards the end.

Going down on him

Men like blow jobs – even if, as is very common, they can't actually come without a helping hand as well. Fellatio, as oral sex perfomed on the penis is technically known, provides a uniquely satisfying mixture of warmth, wetness, titillation and pressure – with, for some men, the added psychological stimulation of having someone apparently worshipping at the altar of their almighty dick.

Kneeling-at-his-feet postures undoubtedly heighten this psychologically dubious effect, but most men find it more comfortable to lie down while you lie between or alongside their legs. You can also kneel or curl up beside one hip, possibly resting a cheek on his belly. This last is probably the most loving posture, if not the best for agility and access.

The basic technique, of course, has nothing to do with blowing. (Although respiration is pretty crucial: concentrate on breathing through your nose.) Even sucking is only a part of it. A blow job is about giving pleasure by stimulating the most sensitive part of a man's body – the glans or head of the penis, and its underside especially – and for that you need the same lightness of touch that he'd use on the clitoris. At first, at least.

Tongue techniques

Light flicks of the tongue and little kisses are probably the best way to get started. (Well, washing and removing stray pubes is probably the very best way for the man receiving a blow job to get started.) As his passion builds, give deeper, longer, harder licks – perhaps up the length of the underside towards the frenulum, where the skin joins to the glans. Alternate with more intense quiverings of the tongue or softer, wetter nibblings: the best and most commonly given advice is to imagine you're French kissing him – preferably with at least a semblance of passion. (Machismo aside, he may be anxious that what you're doing is physically awkward or unpleasant for you. Some kind of reassurance, verbal or otherwise, should help him relax.)

Once his penis is wet with saliva, you might choose to take him inside your mouth, but it's not obligatory. Keep things enticingly soft and gentle at first, and think about keeping your teeth out of

Not called a job for nothing

According to Samantha, the voraciously sexual queen of the hit TV series, *Sex and the City*, "You men have no idea what we're dealing with down there. Teeth placement and jaw stress and suction and gag reflex and all the while bobbing up and down, moaning and trying to breathe through our noses. Easy? Honey, they don't call it a job for nothing!"

Satisfying oral sex isn't about nodding away like a porn star.

the way. To build towards orgasm, you'll need to provide more rhythmic and gradually more intense stimulation. As your lips rub and press against, or drag to and fro across, the rim of his glans, your tongue can continue to work away at the area of the frenulum – which really is about as close as a man gets to having a clitoris, so go cautiously at first. In fact, this area is so sensitive that you don't even need to take him into your mouth. You can lick with the flat of a relaxed tongue, like a cat lapping milk, or tense the tongue and flicker it from side to side with the harder tip.

Oral sex and condoms

Oral sex is not safe sex, so if you're determined to do it with a higher-risk partner, or if you already know your lover has an STI, use a condom or a dental dam. Sex workers have a neat trick which makes using a condom less off-putting. They unroll it a tiny way, then pop it into the mouth so the teat is at the back, and held in place by the tongue against the roof of the mouth. The open ring of the condom is gripped between the lips and teeth in a round "O". Holding the penis firmly, with the skin pulled tight at the base, they then roll the condom on using their lips, all the time holding the teat firmly with the tongue. Some sex workers advise lubricating the inside of the condom or his penis to help it slide on easily – but don't do this if you're going to have penetrative sex, as it could make the condom come off. Ready-lubricated condoms, especially ones with spermicide, taste awful. Flavoured condoms and lubricants don't taste much better but at least they mask that peculiar latex tang.

Finishing off

You'll know a man is about to come from his breathing, but if you're in any doubt – and you might want some warning – keep an eye on his balls. They'll tighten and draw up towards the base of the penis as he gets near. Many men can't come through blow jobs alone, so you may well end up wanking him with your hand while you work the top of his penis with your tongue and lips. For lots of men, this is the most satisfying combination

What's a fantasy blow job for him isn't necessarily one for her. If he thrusts, try tugging on his testicles.

Ejaculation gastronomy

Depending on who you're asking, ejaculate tastes slightly salty, or sweet with a hint of bitterness. It has been likened to cleaning fluid, or almonds, or glue or even caviar. Its smell is weirdly similar to a number of trees during their early summer flowering – notably the Spanish or sweet chestnut, with its musky odour. Warmth and a slightly glutinous texture are probably the most distinctive qualities, as the taste varies from person to person, and is affected by diet.

Meat and dairy products are supposed to make semen taste unpleasantly sharp or acid (though sex writer Candida Royalle quotes a porn actor who thought that heavy yoghurt intake made his come taste delicious, and he must have had plenty of feedback). Unsurprisingly, no in-depth scientific studies have been done in this area, but it seems that bitter flavours may be caused by coffee and alcohol – or urinary infections. Beer can make come taste stale, while garlic, onions and the brassicas (cauliflower, broccoli) may come through as sourness. Asparagus, oddly, makes come smell and taste of … asparagus. To improve flavour, you're supposed to eat lots of fruit (or drink lots of juice), especially pineapple. Mint is said to help, too.

The taste of ejaculate is also affected by things you can't necessarily control: yeast infections and diabetes, which often go together, can affect it profoundly. One reason may be the sugar content: one survey found variation in the level of fructose to occur over a range of 400 percent. This also means that there is no absolute number of calories in a mouthful of come. Even at its sweetest, however, there's no need to worry about putting on weight, as the quantites are so tiny. Even a teaspoon of pure sugar has only about 15 calories, while semen, which typically arrives at under a teaspoon-load is mostly water. It's reckoned that the average ejaculation contains no more than 2–5 calories (kcal).

anyway. Some men like stimulation to continue right through the orgasm, while others very quickly become hypersensitive, especially around the glans. Putting pressure on the underside of the penis or the perineum works well alongside a blow job. You can also tell him that you want him to come … now.

Teenagers waste a lot of time discussing the "spit or swallow" issue. In truth, most men would far rather have a blow job without swallowing than miss out on it because their partner was worried. In gay culture, interestingly, the whole spit or swallow debate arouses relatively little interest. Few people find having come in the mouth particularly appealing, so you could switch to the hand at the last moment (keeping up the ejaculatory momentum), put your tongue over his urethra as a kind of splash guard, or let him come against your lips. In either case, you can let the come dribble away back down his penis. If you want to swallow, try taking him deeper into your mouth when he comes (but beware gagging, see p.113) and swallow hard straight away; that way, the ejaculate may bypass your taste buds.

Refinements

The best blow-job tip of all is to work him with your hand at the same time. This has the brilliant side effect of giving you more control over his movements, too. You could wrap the shaft in your palm and fingers and press his penis back against his belly; this makes it feel warm and enclosed, gives you full access to the frenulum and underside.

Nodding away like a porn star won't do much without some suction. Don't suck away as if getting juice out of a carton but simply seal around his penis with your lips, create a little light suction, then draw your mouth upwards towards the tip. The pressure increases as you move upwards. Then you can run your mouth or tongue over the tip of his penis, take him in again, and slide back down again ready for another upwards, sucking stroke.

The tip of the tongue can explore his urethra or "blow hole" (although proceed with caution, this can hurt), or work around his balls and towards the perineum and anus for a spot of "anilingus" (though there are obvious health and hygiene drawbacks). If he's got a foreskin, you can lick inside it, around the tip of the penis, or draw the skin right down against the base of his penis to increase the sensation – though some men can't tolerate their foreskin being pulled back over the head until they're very wet and very turned on.

Sucking the mango

In third-century India, oral sex was mostly something heterosexual men enjoyed receiving from other men. So said the *Kamasutra*, at least. People who performed oral sex were said to be "of the third nature": either men who dressed and acted like women, and worked as prostitutes, or more masculine types who made a living as masseurs. Promiscuous women and servant girls were also known to give head, but it was relatively frowned upon.

The ancient Indian blow job apparently had eight stages. The first, "casual" stage meant closing the lips around the penis and moving it in and out. Number two, "biting the sides" was nibbling the glans with the lips. The "outer tongs" was a sucking motion, while the "inner tongs" was a deeper suck followed by spitting out the penis. Then there was "kissing", and "polishing" with the tip of the tongue – which also involved inserting its tip into the urethra. The seventh stage, "sucking the mango", seems to have been a kind of intense, deep and possibly bobbing up-and-down suck. It resulted in the eighth and final stage: "swallowing".

Oral sex for women was barely mentioned in the *Kamasutra*. The book rather sniffily admits that some men do it using the same techniques given for kissing a mouth, but doesn't go into any detail. It does admit, however, how incredibly effective cunnilingus could be. Women on the receiving end of cunnilingus, it confesses, were known to "reject virtuous, clever, generous men, and become attached to scoundrels, servants, elephant-drivers and so forth."

As for special effects, hot (well, warm) and cold drinks can provide sensational feelings, mask any unpleasant flavours and sort out the dry-mouth problem. Mints add a certain zing. If you've got long hair you can let it hang around his balls and belly. Among special moves, the classic is to take him deeply into your mouth, then twist your head as you pull back.

You might expect *The Gay Man's Kama Sutra* to have some interesting variations and, true enough, it describes what it calls "reverse fellatio", where you approach from behind, pulling his penis down between his legs. The book admits that this requires "a reasonably long and low-slung penis", but points out that the person being fellated can have attention paid to their balls and anus, "which will be well exposed". "Teabagging" involves taking a whole testicle into your mouth. The point of this isn't so much how it feels, but the intimacy involved in the surrender of such a sensitive part of the body.

Thrusting, deep throating and gagging

Gentlemen don't thrust. (Neither – while we're on etiquette – do they push people's heads down when they fancy oral sex.) The average penis is longer than the average mouth, so you risk provoking the gag reflex or even bruising the sensitive soft tissue at the back of the throat. The rougher things get,

the higher the chances of transmitting any sexually transmitted infections, too.

"Mouth fucking", or irrumation, as it's technically known, turns few men on in any case. If you're both up for trying it, you can apparently train yourself not to gag when something penetrates into the back of the mouth. (If you orgasm yourself, incidentally, this gag reflex is temporarily lost – one of anatomical science's weirder discoveries.) It's easier to limit the depth of penetration by wrapping a hand or a couple of fingers around his shaft. And if you lean on him with the weight of your forearms, it'll limit the effects of any thrusting he might do – as will keeping hold of a testicle. Paul Joannides' *Guide to Getting It On* suggests that if he thrusts you can simply tug harder, "as though you were pulling back on a horse's reins".

Sex guides make a lot of fuss about "deep throating", which is an extreme form of mouth fucking where the penis is actually partly swallowed. It's extremely difficult for anyone to get so far on top of their gag reflex that they can do this at all, and as difficult to imagine why they'd want to try. The idea is basically a circus trick that stems from the darker, sexual humiliation side of pornography, and the notorious 1970s flick *Deep Throat* in particular. One sex manual suggests that if your man is insistent about deep throating, find a vegetable of approximately the right size and ask him to swallow it first.

The ins and outs

Penetrative heterosexual sex – aka penile–vaginal intercourse or PVI, aka sexual intercourse, aka fucking – is an enormously powerful act. For many people, especially heterosexual men, it's "the real thing". If you haven't done that, you haven't done "it". It can be an act of love, reconciliation, forgiveness or delight. It can be an act of possession, hatred or violence. It can, of course, be an act of creation.

Penetrative sex comes with weighty cultural baggage. In Taoist and Tantric philosophies, it was seen as a uniquely powerful vehicle for the exchange of spiritual energy. In the West, mutual orgasm through penetrative sex has long been thought to create a unique spiritual bond between husband and wife, to be the very cement that holds a relationship together. Some feminists have wondered if it isn't the very tool of patriarchy.

Penetration certainly seems less than essential for some women. Statistics vary, but according to Elizabeth Lloyd's meta-analysis of 32 studies, about a quarter of all women come "often" or "very often" without any other stimulation except penetrative sex alone; another 45 percent manage it "sometimes"; for a good third, it's "never". Among men, roughly 90 percent reliably orgasm through penetrative sex. If oral sex or masturbation aren't involved as well, this may mean she's desperately trying to get there while he's just as frantically trying to hold back. This isn't a recipe for emotional fulfilment.

Penetrative sex: making it work for women

No one's quite sure why penetrative sex results in orgasm for some women. The pioneers of laboratory sex research, Masters and Johnson, reckoned it was all thanks to "penile traction on the labia minora": the penis tugs the inner lips, they reckoned, which in turn pull on the clitoris. Since Masters and Johnson, new orgasmic structures have been discovered. There is the "deep clitoris" (see p.45) and the G-spot (see p.47). There is the periurethral glans, the tissues surrounding the urethra whose male equivalent is the head of the penis: sex physiologist Roy Levin found that during intercourse, this glans is pulled in and out

Safer sex

Any activity that brings you into incredibly close contact with another person carries health risks. Throw in sexual fluids – sperm, vaginal lubrication – and the possibility of blood-to-blood contact through invisible little internal nicks and cuts, and you've created the perfect conditions for transmission of infection. Unless you're absolutely sure you know everything about your partner's sexual status – do they have any sexually transmitted infections? are they HIV-negative? – practise safer sex: use a condom. Full details of sexually transmitted infections, including HIV, along with detailed advice on how to put on and use a condom, are given in the dedicated chapter on health. See p.362.

of the vagina, rubbing against the vagina itself as well as the shaft of the penis.

The popularity of the CAT position (see p.122) suggests that orgasmic success for women may be a matter of technique as well as anatomy. The right movement and position can almost always bring pressure to bear on the clitoris. But above all, as Masters and Johnson observed, the biggest obstacle to female orgasm in penetrative sex is "male control of thrusting pattern". When men relax and women start to take charge, the potential for great sex is typically vastly improved.

But orgasm during penetrative sex is surely related to technique: both the women's own and their partner's. And, of course how much they like, love or are attracted to their partner – factors rarely covered in laboratory studies. But the best recipe for female satisfaction is to do other things as well. A mere twenty minutes of sexual kissing or touching can lift the number of women who come in penetrative sex to ninety percent or above. Or so claimed the brilliantly crafted Richters survey (see p.163), conducted in Australia in 2006.

Maria Theresa: so as to conceive a child, doctors advised that "the vulva of Her Most Holy Majesty should be titillated before intercourse". She had 16 children.

Foreplay, after play and sex scripts

When the Austrian Empress Maria Theresa was having trouble conceiving a child, in the 1740s, the royal doctor was urgently consulted. He concluded that "the vulva of Her Most Holy Majesty should be titillated before intercourse." She went on to bear more than a dozen children. The lesson is that foreplay – or mutual arousal and stimulation before intercourse – leads to good, not to mention frequent, sex.

The term "foreplay" suggests that "real sex" is penetration, and everything else is mere "play" beforehand – which is an old-fashioned concept. But it's true that if you're a woman, and you're going to have penetrative sex, you'll need to be aroused, and lubricated. As the sixteenth-century Arab sex manual, *The Perfumed Garden*, put it, "Woman is like a fruit, which will not yield its sweetness until you rub it between your hands".

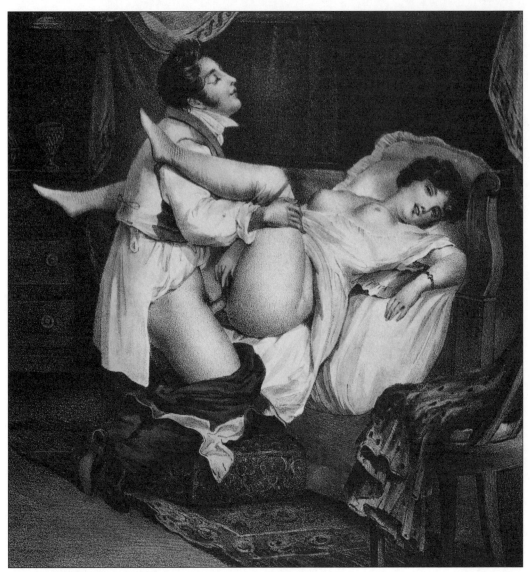

Sexual bliss in the nineteenth century. Mr Darcy never had it so good.

Sex scripts

It begins with a cuddle and a loving kiss. The kissing gets deeper as you become turned on, so you get to stroke and caress each other. You start touching, maybe one of you goes down. Before too long, however, you get down to it: fucking. This is the so-called "heterosexual script". It has worked splendidly for millions of people over thousands of years. Unfortunately, the majority of those millions have undoubtedly been men.

The script is changing, however. One of the bestselling US sex books of the 2000s was Ian Kerner's *She Comes First* – and the title said it all. And in 2003, the Braun–Gavey–McPhillips study found that New Zealand men appreciated sexual reciprocity. One man who took part reckoned that "usually she'll come first; I go down on her and then later I'll come inside her".

The problem with the new script, you might call it the Kerner or Kiwi script, is that it still has the same old happy ending: orgasm. Responding to *She Comes First*, British psychologist Petra Boynton drily observed that "it would have been more radical to call it 'She Comes Last' or 'She Comes When She Happens to Come' or even 'She Doesn't Come This Time'. There needn't be such emphasis on either sex having orgasms all the time", she said, "it just heightens the pressure and imposes a formula." Masters and Johnson would have agreed. They noted that straight men tended to direct sexual encounters with orgasm as the goal, while lesbians and gay men typically took their time, "making each step in tension increment something to be appreciated". They reckoned that committed homosexual couples had the best sex they'd witnessed.

Bonaparte's thumb

In the 1920s, a great-great-niece of Napoleon, Princess Marie Bonaparte was driven (by sexual frustration, it was said – her husband preferred men) to investigate the link between female anatomy and orgasmic proficiency. She measured the position of the clitoris in 243 women, and asked them about their orgasms. She found that those with the shortest distance between clitoris and vagina – a gap of less than an inch – were far more likely to have orgasms than those with a longer gap. The contemporary researcher Kim Wallen thinks Bonaparte was on to something. His "rule of thumb", as recounted to sex writer Mary Roach, is that "if the distance is less than the width of your thumb then you are likely to come". Wallen also pointed out that taller women with big breasts tended to have wider gaps. As Roach drily puts it, "the stereotypical ideal female – Barbie tall with Barbie big breasts – is the one least likely to respond to a manly hammering."

Studies reveal that the male orgasm – and the man's pursuit of it – is still the key to many sexual encounters. The 2003 New Zealand survey also found that vaginal intercourse without any other kind of stimulation made up some 12 percent of reported sexual encounters. You might think of this as sex that's basically focused on the man. Sex that's focused entirely on the woman, that is clitoral masturbation with or without cunnilingus (and without any stimulation of the penis), accounted for fewer than one in two hundred sexual encounters. "When the man is keen to have

Marie Stopes on Foreplay, from Married Love (1918)

> It can ... be readily imagined that when the man tries to enter a woman whom he has not wooed to the point of stimulating her natural physical reactions of preparation, he is endeavoring to force his entry through a dry-walled opening too small for it. He may thus cause the woman actual pain, apart from the mental revolt and loathing she is likely to feel for a man who so regardlessly uses her.

sex but the woman is not, intercourse ensues and the man reaches orgasm," the survey concluded, "but when the woman is keen but the man is not, sex rarely happens." The script, in other words, still needs work.

Afterplay

What you do *after* sex also matters. Orgasm, for most men, is pretty conclusive. Some get incredibly sleepy or retreat into themselves, even if they don't go quite as far as to "roll over and leave her lying in the wet patch". Women, stereotypically, are more likely to want to cuddle or caress, exploring any emotional bonds that have been created or reaffirmed. Partners who follow stereotype might want to meet somewhere in the middle. Sleepers and retreaters might make an effort to stroke and reassure. Talkers and cuddlers, equally, might respect their partner's needs, or at least not read it as rejection or indifference.

Unlike men, who mostly need a "refractory period" to recover from ejaculation, most women are physiologically capable of moving towards a second or third orgasm – a phenomenon known as sequential or multiple orgasm (see p.159). Whether or not they have the energy or are in the mood, is a different question.

If you're not using a condom, and don't want to lie in sheets that rapidly get colder and stickier, mopping up is important. It's easier to wipe come away before it turns runny, which happens after a couple of minutes. The lazy way – and, for some, the sexy way – is to rub it into your skin with your hand. Tissues, a hanky, a spare towel or a pair of pants bound for the wash are probably more effective. Women who ejaculate a lot of fluid (see p.171) might want to have sex on a towel from the outset.

Post-coital peeing isn't a bad idea, as it helps flush away any residue, keeping the tubes good and clean. Some use the opportunity to have a wash – though leaping out of bed and rushing to the bathroom as if you wanted to scrub away the plague doesn't look great. And peeing immediately after sex isn't always easy. In men, the erectile tissue surrounding the urethra may still be pumped up with blood, constricting the tube through which the urine has to pass and creating a sort of bottleneck effect.

Sometimes it's hard to be a man

It wouldn't be hard to argue that women tend to do worse out of sex than men. Even if their orgasms are more powerful, and potentially multiple, they have fewer of them in sexual encounters.

This is not to say that men have it easy. In the bedroom, men are often expected to lead the running, not least by themselves. In *Men in Love*, Nancy Friday writes that men find themselves in the position of someone who suggests going to a new restaurant. It might just pay off – but what if it's no good? "The macho stance", Friday says, "makes the male the star performer. The hidden cost is that it puts the woman in the role of critic."

Even while they're running to keep up with their own and their partner's expectations, men are frequently let down by their equipment. Erectile dysfunction (see p.288) is a huge problem as men get older. Younger men may well be plagued by premature ejaculation (see p.168). And even if the male orgasm comes relatively easily, it's famously a pale imitation of the female variety.

Bernard Apfelbaum, psychotherapist and Director of Berkeley's Sex Therapy Group, believes that sex, for many men, is "a valiant but often failed effort to avoid ejaculation that comes too early, before arousal has had much chance to build".

Veteran sex therapist Betty Dodson gives a group class called "Running A Sexual Encounter". The women have to get on top and pretend they're having sex like a man. Dodson keeps them hard at it by calling out that they're too high up to stay inside, they're crushing their partners and need to straighten their arms, they shouldn't stop moving or they'll go soft, that they're moving too fast and are going to come too quickly – all the things men have to do (or think they have to do) when having sex with a relatively passive partner. After a timed three minutes, the women in the class apparently collapse exhausted. Many say they feel for their men more than before. Many are willing to experiment, just in order to give them a break.

Motions

Vaginal penetrative sex that produces orgasm for both partners generally requires finding a way to stimulate the clitoris. Well, a minority of women can come through intercourse alone, and being in love or feeling very turned on helps a lot, but clitoral stimulation is the golden rule. The easiest methods are the "reach-round", where you have sex from behind and touch her with your hand, and the "reach-down", where either she or you masturbates her when you're face to face. You can also push or hold the clitoris against the penis during sex.

Sex by hand, or masturbation, is covered pretty comprehensively elsewhere in this chapter. This section is all about having sex without using your hands. Like any hands-free endeavour, sex takes practice. Knowing your partner's body well helps a lot. Positions help a bit, but the sexual action or "motion", as you might call it, is more important than any position ever invented.

Rocking, rubbing, riding

Thrusting seems to be a pretty basic male instinct – and surprisingly hard for him to resist – but rocking, rubbing or circling is really where it's at. It makes the woman's clitoris and the man's pubic bone grind together. If you're a man, imagine you're riding a bronco or standing on the heaving deck of a yacht, not driving a piston with a boiler up your backside.

To increase the effect, one or both partners can tilt their pelvis forward – imagine you're lifting the whole pelvis up slightly and then placing it down on a surface that's just higher than you. If you're doing it right, the curve in the small of the back gets flatter, the stomach crunches slightly and the buttocks may clench too. Stronger pelvic floor muscles are very helpful here – and they intensify orgasm too. Failing that, you can always just put a pillow under the hips of whoever's underneath.

This basic pelvic tilt can easily be converted into a back-and-forth rubbing motion. As it happens, this makes the penis slide in and out of the vagina slightly, but the motion isn't led by the penis. As an alternative, the man can slide his whole body up and down while otherwise holding still, using his pubic bone as a sort of rigid edge to grind against the clitoris.

This rub can become a circling motion – not side to side, but in line with the spine. Imagine that you lift your perineum (the point between the penis/vagina and the anus) upwards; you then pull it backwards as if through the belly button towards the spine; next you push it down, imagining you're following the line of the curve of your buttocks; then you lift forward and up again – and so on. You should find the small of your back arches and

then rounds rhythmically as you go, and your head rocks gently forward and back again. If you think of the movement of a rider on horseback, you won't be far off. This probably explains the old euphemisms for her-on-top: *à cheval* (on horseback), or "riding the St George".

You can deepen this circling motion by adding sideways circles of the pelvis, so that the hips move up and round and down and back round – much as if you were riding, or perhaps sitting on one of those big inflatable exercise balls. Alex Comfort,

Victorian screwing, from Ida Craddock's *The Wedding Night* (1900)

❝ As to the bride, I would say: bear in mind that it is part of your wifely duty to perform pelvic movements during the embrace, riding your husband's organ gently, and, at times, passionately, with various movements, up and down, sideways, and with a semi-rotary movement, resembling the movement of the thread of a screw upon a screw. These movements will add greatly to your own passion and your own pleasure, but they should not be dwelt in thought for this purpose. They should be performed for the express purpose of conferring pleasure upon your husband. ❞

in *The Joy of Sex*, memorably referred to it as "the round-and-round and cinder-sifting motions of the woman's hips – what the French call the Lyon mail-coach (*la diligence de Lyon*)".

Making music

Either partner can work away with this motion, but it usually helps if she's the one moving, as only she gets direct feedback from her clitoris. (This is one of the reasons that her-on-top positions work so well for many women.) The man needn't be passive. His hands are free, of course, and it often helps if he tilts his pelvis up while she's on top of him, providing a harder edge of muscle or pubic bone for her to work against. Conveniently, the strain this puts on his pelvic floor muscles may have the side effect of ramping up his orgasm.

Moving in sync – the ultimate goal, surely – can be tricky at first. It takes time to get to know how each other's bodies move, and meanwhile you may end up ineffectually or awkwardly bumping against each other. It's a bit like learning to dance salsa: you can count it through slowly to learn the rhythm but you have to just throw yourself into it to really find your groove. Like salsa, this "bump and grind" is amazingly satisfying once you've got it. And, like salsa, practice is as effective as flair. All the statistics show that sex with a regular partner results in many more orgasms than one-night stands – especially for women.

Different people prefer different rhythms. For some, a steady, grinding motion feels glorious. For others, fast and furious is best – more like masturbation, perhaps. Many people like to start

Learning to dance

66 Years ago, I went on holiday to Cuba. We were in a club, late at night, dancing to a Cuban band – or trying to. My friend was fine. She was being spun round the floor by an endless succession of thoughtful local guys. Things weren't looking so good for me, a wallflower propping up the bar. After a while, one of the musicians took pity on me. He showed me a few basic salsa moves. He didn't look convinced. He tried a different tack, so did I – and I still wasn't getting it. After a frustrating half hour or so in which he just couldn't work out where I was going wrong he suddenly smiled and asked, "Do you know how to make love to a woman?". I thought it was pretty obvious by now that I couldn't do anything much, but I nodded confidently. "Oh yes, definitely", I replied. "So, dance like it!" I had no idea what he meant. Then he took hold of my hips and subtly shifted them forward and upward. Suddenly, I was standing in a more macho, Cuban way. And suddenly I was dancing, as he'd no doubt have seen it, like a man. Inside, though, I was really thinking, so that's how you do it. 🕿

slow and build up the tempo towards orgasm. You'll have to work out your own rhythm together – a guiding hand placed on a buttock is a great way to communicate. Talking is even better, especially if you want to time it so you come together.

Coital alignment – and putting the penis to work

The Coital Alignment Technique, or CAT, isn't snappily named. It works better than it sounds. The man is on top. He enters his partner, then shifts his whole body upwards slightly. The idea is that the upper face of his penis's shaft will thus rub across the clitoris as it moves, rather than thrusting into and out of the vagina from below in a futile, bucket-scuttling kind of way.

She wraps her legs round his, with her ankles resting on his calves. Once in place, a rhythm is set up: on the upstroke the woman pushes her pelvis against the man's, and he responds by pushing forward to meet her. On the downstroke, the woman pulls her pelvis back and down, causing the shaft of the penis to rub firmly against the clitoris. The downside is that the man may well find himself staring at the top of his partner's head, which doesn't feel half as loving as gazing into her eyes.

The penis's head can also rub against the inner labia, or make shallow thrusts into the relatively tactile outer third of the vagina. Teasing of this sort can build up to, or alternate with, deeper thrusts, which may prove psychologically more satisfying. You can also use a penis as a focus for squeezing the pelvic muscles (see box, opposite), or to probe for the G-spot (see p.47).

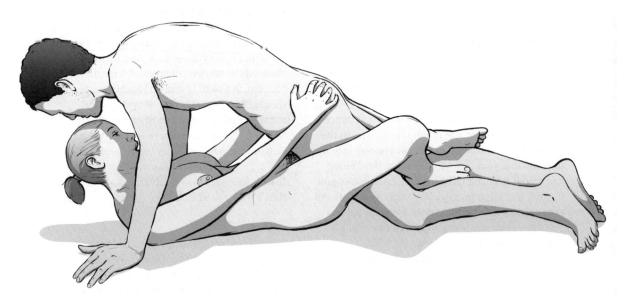

Coital Alignment Technique: not as difficult as it sounds.

Kabbazah, or the lemon squeezer

To his adoring public, the Victorian maverick Richard F. Burton was a daring explorer with a wild side. The scar on his cheek – left by a Somali spear – said it all. Unbeknown to his fans, Burton was also the driving force behind a secret society dedicated to publishing erotic works. Its goal was to both shock and educate Victorian society, and to prove that the West was sexually backward.

Burton wasn't above adding his own material to the society's translations in order to score political points. To the Hindu erotic manual the *Ananga Ranga*, for instance, he added a peculiar footnote: "Amongst some races", he observed, "the constrictor vaginæ muscles are abnormally developed. In Abyssinia, for instance, a woman can so exert them as to cause pain to a man, and, when sitting upon his thighs, she can induce the orgasm without moving any other part of her person. Such an artist is called by the Arabs, 'Kabbazah', literally meaning 'a holder', and it is not surprising that the slave dealers pay large sums for her." Whether or not Burton's wife, the devout Catholic aristocrat Isabel Arundel, was aware of the joys of Kabbazah isn't known.

Today, the technique is usually known as "the lemon-squeezer". The woman squeezes her vaginal walls together around the base of a man's penis, then lifts herself up, holding the squeeze as if drawing the sap up his shaft. At the top, she releases, envelopes him softly – or perhaps flutters and squeezes the rim of her vagina around the head of his penis for a short while – then plunges down again. At the deepest point of the stroke, she can rock her pelvis forward to bring the clitoris hard up against his pubic bone, before beginning the slow upwards draw again.

If he can bear it for long enough – and few men can – it's a brilliant route to a huge orgasm. There are benefits to her, too: it provides a brilliant workout for the pelvic muscles – which in turn improves female orgasm.

No motion – the benefits of stillness

Keeping still is almost as important as moving. Alice B. Stockham's 1896 book, *Karezza: Ethics of Marriage*, advised that couples wishing to experience "an exquisite exaltation" should attempt "the complete but quiet union of the sexual organs". (Eccentrically, she called this union "karezza", from the Italian word carezzare, meaning to treat with affection.) Couples were supposed to maintain "a lengthy period of perfect control" in which "the whole being of each is merged into the other". Thrusting, clearly, was out. So too, unfortunately, was orgasm: karezza was supposed to be more about spiritual than orgasmic union.

Stillness needn't be passive. Women can press together their internal vaginal muscles in a move sometimes called the lemon squeezer (see above). Building up muscle tension is a major part of orgasm, and some women can come simply by squeezing and releasing their pelvic floor muscles rhythmically. (In 2007, French researchers showed that contracting the levator ani, one of the pelvic floor muscles, brings the

Pthhhh – fanny farting

It's hard to put a positive spin on the vaginal fart. It's not actually a fart: it happens when the vagina lengthens or expands then squeezes together again, squirting out a little air – there's no bowel gas involved. Yoga or certain abdominal exercises easily produce the same effect. So too does penetrative intercourse.

There's not much you can do about fanny farts, as the Brits call them, or "queefs", or "varts", as they're sometimes known. You could try a different position or movement – some women find they happen more often if their hips are raised. If penile pushing seems to be the problem, you could try breaking the suction as he withdraws by inserting a finger. Explaining that a fanny fart wasn't, in fact, a "real" fart, might sound even stupider than the fart itself did, but it might just claw back a little poise.

clitoris closer to the front of the vagina, which may assist sexual response during penetration.) If men pull up on their pelvic floor, meanwhile, it makes the penis twitch and briefly throb and may stimulate the perineal area too.

At the right moment, stillness can be an absolute gift to your partner, allowing them to have complete control of their own orgasm, or just to lose themselves in the moment. The sex advice column of *Men's Health* magazine sensibly suggests thinking of yourself "as a rock and a hard place. Or The Rock. In a hard place. Whatever. Just keep still."

How not to do it – the porno pound

Porn films like to show men pistoning themselves in and out of a relatively passive partner. The "porno pound" has nothing to do with pleasure, and everything to do with displaying the vulva and the penis to the camera (there's a strong homoerotic tendency in most mainstream pornography). The move also underlines female submissiveness, thus pandering to the lowest common denominator of male fantasy. The problem – or the joke, maybe – is that millions of men worldwide pick up their early sexual technique from pornography.

"In and out" isn't entirely hopeless, however. In men, it'll produce orgasm in an average of two to five minutes. In women, it can set up satisfying pelvic vibrations, stimulate the G-spot (if approached from the right angle) and the sensitive tissue around the urethra. It may also give some clitoral contact at the top of the in-stroke. A few women like the feeling of their cervix being stimulated with very deep penetration, though most find this uncomfortable or actually painful. And, of course, some women like to play with feelings of being dominated by a powerful male.

Positions

Sex manuals usually make "positions" their gorgeously illustrated centrepiece. The truth is that it's not hard to work out a dozen odd combinations and give them exotic-sounding names. All positions are really just variations on whether you're lying, sitting, kneeling or standing; whether your legs are raised, opened, squeezed together or extended; whether you're facing each other or facing in the same direction; and of course who's on top.

Positions aren't irrelevant, though. They can alter the depth and angle of penetration, the degree of snugness and the area of the penis or vagina which is being stimulated. They can change how you feel. Face-to-face is intimate, for instance, from-behind feels excitingly animalistic, while the person on top may feel more in control. Positions also tap into a rich culture of imaginative sexual variation which goes back thousands of years.

Most longer-term couples find one position which works best for them. (Sometimes, it works best for just one partner; if this is the case, changing position can change the whole dynamic of lovemaking.) Other couples have one or two variations they sometimes throw in for a change of scene, or because they associate different positions

From gibbon grabbing to dragon crouching

When it comes to naming positions, Far Eastern sex manuals seem to have a thing about animals. The two-thousand-year-old Chinese medical texts discovered at Mawangdui, for instance, describe the joys of "tiger roving" (from behind, on all fours), "cicada clinging" (behind, lying down), "gibbon grabbing" (feet over shoulders), "fish gobbling" (her on top) and the hilarious up-and-down cottontail "rabbit bolting" (her on top, facing his feet). Ancient Taoist texts have discussed the "Unicorn's Horn", "Winding Dragon", "Fluttering Butterflies" and "Reversed Flying Ducks". The 1930s Javanese marriage manual, *Serat Candraning Wanita*, mentions the "deer with branched horns" (missionary, with raised legs), and "monkey takes care of its child" (standing).

Indian erotic texts often use dramatic terms, almost like stage directions. The *Kamasutra* lovingly describes the "twining vine", in which, "as a vine twines around a great dammar tree, so she twines around him and bends his face down to her to kiss him". In "climbing the tree", she rests one of her feet on her lover's foot and the other on his thigh, and acts as if she were climbing his body in order to claim a kiss. "Sex in the manner of crows" is a 69 (which only makes sense if you've ever seen crows pecking over a field).

Western sex manuals often use more clinical-sounding or baldly descriptive terms. The 1920s pioneer of "scientific" sex positions, Theodoor van de Velde, went for "medial", "anterior" and "ventral" attitudes, as well as the enticing "Second Extension Attitude: Suspensory (Variation [b])". Positions like "female superior", "the squat", or "from-behind" need little explanation. Even more colourful English terms, like "doggy-style", "spoons", "strip search", "riding St George" or the "wheelbarrow reversed" are self-explanatory. Racier or trashier sex guides, however, like to throw in a touch of oriental spice. Follow the advice in the magazines, and you might well find yourself splitting the whisker, crouching like a tiger, leaping like a lusty frog or making the crab. Whether any of these will do your love life any good, however, is another matter.

Counting to 729

Counting up sexual positions has been a nerdish pastime ever since the third-century *Kamasutra*. Thanks to its detail, the book became known as "The Sixty-Four". To the disappointment of many readers, however, it only recorded eight actual positions – albeit alongside five moves for the woman "playing the man's part" (that is, on top), ten "sexual strokes" and three "unusual sexual acts".

Twenty-six is a respectable total, but later Indian erotic scientists worried that the *Kamasutra* didn't live up to its billing. On the grounds that the *Kamasutra* listed three different kinds of sexual size, endurance and temperament for each of men and women – the "hare", "bull" and "stallion" man, and the "doe", "mare" or "elephant cow" woman, and so on – they worked out that if men and women mated in all possible combinations, the total came to 729.

In Europe, the classical world was almost as enthusiastic about positions. The German atheist philosopher Friedrich-Karl Forberg listed ninety supposedly known to the ancients. But for centuries afterwards the Church clamped down on any sexual position other than the "matrimonial" (see p.324). The Italian Renaissance poet, Pietro Aretino, apparently wrote sixteen erotic sonnets, each accompanied by a drawing of a different sexual position but all known copies of the pictures were destroyed.

Thanks to religious censorship, European erotology only really got going in the nineteenth century. In 1899, *The Horn Book: A Girl's Guide to Good and Evil* listed 62 positions. Dr Josef Weckerle's Viennese *The Golden Book of Love*, of 1907, counted an astonishing 531 positions – with 69 "oragenital postures" added to a later edition. Theodoor van de Velde's 1928 manual, *Ideal Marriage*, included a vast "Systematized Table of Attitudes Possible in Sexual Intercourse" together with "Indications" and "Contra-indications" helpfully prescribed for different men and women.

A more sensible line was adopted by Helena Wright's 1930 *The Sex Factor in Marriage*, which suggested that just five "attitudes" were "sufficiently varied for adoption at the beginning of married life"; thereafter, the couple would apparently "need no further directions". Alex Comfort's era-defining *The Joy of Sex*, first published in 1972, actually dismissed positions as a "human classificatory hobby" and regretted only "the loss of the fancy names, Arabic, Sanskrit or Chinese, which go with them". Despite his wise words, every sex manual on sale today finds the need to list positions – and the more, apparently, the better.

Mughal prince and concubine try an imaginative variation.

with different sexual moods. Few people make love like they're running through the moves in a yoga class – or like the actors in the average porn movie. Both would be a great way to make your lover feel like an exercise bike. Changing position at the wrong moment is also the fastest way to put someone off their stroke, and delay (or defeat) orgasm. That said, a shift or a change can instantly transform the mediocre into the mind-blowing.

The missionary position 1 – Pacific tales

The name of the "missionary position" is supposed to come from Pacific Islanders, who thought it hilarious that missionary settlers would do anything as inept and unimaginative as face-to-face, with the man on top. At least, this is the story recounted by Alfred Kinsey in his 1948 book, *Sexual Behavior in the Human Male*. Kinsey claimed his source was the anthropologist Bronislaw Malinowski, who supposedly said that in the Trobriand Islands of the 1920s, "caricatures of the English-American position are performed around the communal campfires, to the great amusement of the natives who refer to the position as the 'missionary position'".

But Kinsey got it wrong. Malinowski did write that islanders who worked for white settlers sometimes mimicked their bosses' inept lovemaking, and he also recorded that they disapprovingly called public displays of affection "missionary fashion". But the idea of an actual "missionary position" seems to have been Kinsey's own invention.

In the 1960s and 1970s the story grew more elaborate. Missionaries, it was said, actually preached against any other kind of position as sinful. It's true that, for centuries, the Church taught that non-missionary sexual positions were unnatural, unlawful and ultimately punishable with hellfire (see p.324). Many Christians were shocked by the sexual liberalism of Pacific societies, too.

Today, the usual criticism of the missionary position is that it is somehow basic. It's certainly the case that it is culturally dominant. Anthropologist Helen Fisher has concluded that it is the preferred position in most cultures around the world. Kinsey himself found that 91 percent of American married women used it most often. Even today, according to Elliott and Brantley's 1997 survey of college students, 48 percent of women prefer the man to be on top. (Amusingly, a similar percentage of men prefer the woman to be on top; a mere 25 of men and 33 percent of women actually like being on top themselves. Perhaps these were stereotypically lazy students …)

The missionary position is also attacked for being patriarchal. It certainly hands over a degree of control to the man. This doesn't mean that women who enjoy it are letting down their sisters, however. Positions are ultimately about what works for you.

The missionary position 2 – how and why

Missionary-style brings you face to face with your partner, making loving eye contact and deep kissing possible. It brings chests and bellies and breasts and chests together. It allows the legs to intertwine passionately. It makes it easy to lovingly interlock hands or cradle heads. You can reach round to fondle each other's buttocks. In short, it's a truly whole-body position.

The drawback of the missionary position is that it's hard to stimulate the clitoris. Coital Alignment Technique (see p.122) can help, as can shoving a pillow under her hips, or if the man kneels rather than lies between his partner's legs, and draws her legs up his thighs so her hips are raised right up.

The best variations are all about what you do with your legs. If a woman pushes her legs together, it increases the resistance, and switches on the thigh muscles. Splaying your legs apart or lifting them up in the air is like offering yourself up to be devoured: a wonderful act of submission or acceptance. It also brings the maximum area of genital flesh into contact. If you're flexible enough, you can bring your knees to your chest or even hang your legs over his shoulders. This can put delicious pressure on the abdominal muscles and, for women, increases the chances of his penis hitting your G-spot. Rhythmic movements of the legs, meanwhile, are an excellent route to orgasm.

The missionary is also great for two men: if you can work the angles correctly the "spare" penis can rub up against the penetrating partner's belly. Some men find it too deep, but *The Joy of Gay Sex* recommends an incredible variation for "agile" men of the right fit: the man doing the penetrating sits back, pulling his partner onto his lap; "lower his legs", the book advises, "the more direct the pressure against his prostate gland, the more pressure (and thus pleasure) he feels". Once in position, the man doing the penetrating can bend down and suck off his partner – an achievement that heterosexual couples can only dream of.

Apes and doggies – from behind

Of all the positions, "from behind" is the most satisfyingly animal – for the very good reason that this is how mammals do it, hence "doggy style". (There are exceptions: the great apes, especially the hyper-sexual bonobos, are known to indulge in the occasional bit of face-to-face fucking, but it is relatively unusual.)

Some archeologists have argued that sex-from-behind is the "original" sex position. Turkey's Çatalhöyük site, which is sometimes called the "world's oldest city", contains a wealth of ancient murals and figurines which, according to Timothy

Archeologists have argued that sex from behind is the "original" position, as seen in this Pompeian fresco.

Taylor, author of *The Prehistory of Sex*, point to the conclusion that the all-fours, from-behind position was the standard one. Of course this doesn't mean that this was true across the Neolithic world, and Taylor would the first to point out the variety of ancient human sexual cultures. Still, if the apes are anything to go by, at some point in the very distant past, we were probably all at it from behind.

Sex from behind in the classic "doggy" position is ideal for the "reach-round" – which is usually pretty crucial if the receptive partner, man or woman, is to end up with an orgasm. In vaginal sex, it angles the penis for the G-spot better, too (see p.47). Ernst Gräfenberg himself (he who lent the spot its "G") recommended sex *à la vache* for this reason. Weirdly, he thought it necessary to deny that its popularity had anything to do with "the melodious movements of the testicles like a knocker on the clitoris".

Sex from behind also makes deep thrusting much easier. In vaginal penetration, you risk going as deep as the cervix, which can hurt. Going deep in anal sex has its own risks (see p.135) though, as *The Joy of Gay Sex* points out, from-behind "affords the easiest entry". Doggy-style can be quite tiring for the man or woman underneath, as they may end up taking most of their partner's weight on their arms. To help out when you're on top, lean back to take more weight on your own legs, or lean over and sideways to put a hand down on the floor or bed (or sofa or whatever).

Lying down is the relaxing alternative. It may prove difficult to get it in or keep it there, but she can always raise up her hips for better access. Cuddling in the "spoons" position, with both of you on your sides is very fond and very gentle – but again, you may find that he keeps on slipping out, if he can get it in at all. Sitting or kneeling works for some.

A particularly lovely from-behind variation is where both partners lie looking up at the ceiling (or sky), with the receptive partner stretched out on top, probably with their head resting on a convenient shoulder. This position allows them to turn or tilt their head for a kiss (the lack of kissing is otherwise the great drawback of sex from behind) and makes it easy to touch the person on top. If you're into names for positions, you might call it "the cello, recumbent".

Woman on top

Postwar sex scientists, reacting to the old patriarchal ways, thought that the woman-on-top position was the answer. Lab researchers Masters and Johnson said it solved the main problem with penetration because it allowed the woman to control the pace, rhythm and angle of thrusting. Kinsey thought it was sexually liberating, though he admitted that "the female who will assume such a position is already less inhibited".

It's true: lots of women who don't come underneath will reach orgasm if they're on top. Unfortunately, some men find it so sexy –

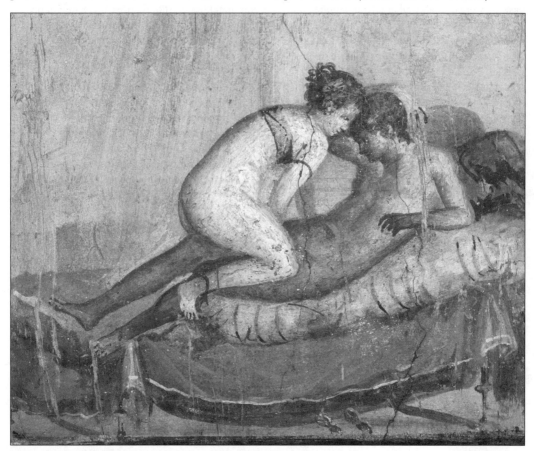

Roman Pompeii celebrated sexual athleticism and variety.

especially if she "milks" his penis as she draws herself upwards, squeezing and engulfing the head before bearing down again – that they're likely to come even faster than any other way. There is another problem with this position. If she gets really carried away, especially if facing away or leaning back, it's possible to bend the penis too far down. This can hurt and, if you're very unlucky, cause a penile fracture (see p.61).

The classic version of "her on top" is where the woman straddles her partner. Sitting or squatting upright, meanwhile – what the Victorians used to call "riding St George" – gives the most control and freedom of movement, but it can feel lonely. Lying stretched out on your partner's body has the face-to-face intimacy of the missionary position, and many woman find that the further they bend their body down towards his, the better the clitoris rubs against the base of his erection and his pubic bone. Two women using a dildo have an advantage over heterosexuals, as the woman on top can, by squeezing her PC muscle (see p.179) around the dildo, press the base into her partner's pelvis.

For heterosexual base-grinding, sliding your whole bodies up and down over each other is the way forward. If you're oiled up or very sweaty, this can give an amazing all-body rub. If the woman on top puts her legs between the man's rather than astride them, it gives a tighter, snugger fit – useful for sex with the smaller man. The woman can also straddle and face away from her partner in the so-called "reverse cowgirl" (which is really "from behind" as much as it is "on top"). It gives her partner an unrivalled view of her backside – unless of course she leans right back for a cuddle.

Tops and bottoms

Gay culture has long embraced the idea of "tops" and "bottoms". Whether you're one or the other isn't really about who's actually on top or underneath. It's sometimes a question of personal style, as in the stereotypical division between "butch" and "femme", and sometimes one of roles – especially in "Sub/Dom" relationships where the "bottom" is the submissive partner and the "top" the dominant one (see p.137). Between men, however, being a "top" or a "bottom" is largely about penetration: who's fucking and who's being fucked.

As rigid categories, the idea of tops and bottoms went out of style for a while. The closeted days when men signalled their preferences by wearing jewellery or a coloured handkerchief on one side or the other are mostly gone. Nowadays, as San Francisco activist Karlyn Lotney, aka "Fairy Butch", pointed out in her agony column, for some people using terms like top and bottom "is deeply expressive of an integral part of themselves; for others, it's a fun way to solicit dates in a personal ad."

The meteoric rise of internet cruising has brought self-definition back into fashion. But for all the guys who wltm dark, uncut bear tops – or whatever takes their fancy – there are many more who would describe themselves as "versatile top" or "versatile bottom". That said, The Joy of Gay Sex states that "it's simply a fact that bottoms out-number tops (some bottoms wail that the ratio is four to one)." It's odd, then, that heterosexuals tend to be more reticent about which positions they prefer. Straight men and women often know very well what works for them and what doesn't, but they're rarely upfront about it in the classified ads.

Sex for more than two

Human culture has invented endless ways in which sex can be about more than two people. Most do not involve all three (or more) in bed at the same time. The illicit affair, or fling, or extramarital relationship is usually all about keeping the other two apart, of course. "Sexual friends" and "fuck buddies" rarely mingle with each other quite as easily as the ordinary kind of buddy. The *ménage à trois*, in which three people share a household and a sexual relationship, is usually a matter of one of the trio (rarely two of them) flitting from one partner to another. The Bloomsbury group of writers and artists famously "lived in squares and loved in triangles" but they kept the points of those triangles rigidly apart. The 83.5 percent of human cultures estimated by anthropologists to allow polygyny (or one husband with multiple wives), do not, on the whole, expect or allow those husbands to have their numerous wives in the same bed. Even in the famed harems of the Turkish and Chinese courts, the sultan or emperor would typically distribute his favours sequentially, not all at once.

And yet the threesome is one of the commonest sexual fantasies of all. It seems to hold out the possibility of truly liberated, abandoned and sexy sex, of total erotic satisfaction at all levels and in all places. (The fact that it goes up against some of the most hard-wired beliefs in Western culture, namely that sex is private, intimate and bonding, is no doubt one reason it is so popular. A broken taboo is a key ingredient of the erotic.) One enthusiastic participant of an organized group session felt as if she "was being massaged by the eight-armed Hindu goddess" – well, the word "orgy" did originally mean an erotico-religious frenzy – "one hand caressing my temples while another kneaded my tummy, another tugging on my nipples, fingers of a different hand on my clitoris, and another lightly tickling my feet. When I felt ready, I reached for my vibrator…"

The reality isn't always quite as divine. Group sex is generally just too complicated to manage in a way that achieves the total abandonment of the fantasy. There are embarrassments to get over, then limbs to negotiate, turns to take and, most importantly, egos and feelings to protect. Seeing a partner with another person, maybe

For sexual gymnasts, there's the "X" position, where she straddles him then leans back to lay her down her head between his feet. This is better for intense, meditative appreciation of the sensation of penetration than for movement. It's no good for affectionate cuddling, and it won't work for men whose penises don't bend forward happily, either. On the plus side, he can usually reach her clitoris with his hands.

Anal sex – and beyond

Strait-laced straights like to imagine that anal sex is something that only gay men do. Far from it. The most common sexual act between gay men is the blow job. Heterosexuals, meanwhile, are moderately keen on anal experimentation, according to the statistics. Various studies, from analsexyes.com (who might just be biased) to the prestigious Kinsey doing things with them that you don't do together, can be a shock. So, too, for those without prior same-sex experience, can being confronted by your own bisexual feelings – or the all-too-glaring lack of them. There's the danger of comparison, too: either of bodies (do they have nicer thighs?) or technique (can I do it like that?).

The deeper issues are relationship insecurity and its evil twin, jealousy. As one one-time-only threesome taster confessed, "What if they were only doing this to get to each other, and I was really an obstacle?" Dossie Easton and Catherine A. Liszt, authors of the 1997 classic, *The Ethical Slut: A Guide to Infinite Sexual Possibilities*, reckon that cutting jealousy out, as if it was a cancer, is impossible. "What you can do", they say, "is learn to deal with it as you learn to deal with any emotion – until it becomes not overwhelming and not exactly pleasant, but tolerable; a mild disturbance, like a rainy day rather than a typhoon".

Even with its attendant difficulties, group sex remains a significant minority pursuit. In the 1960s and 1970s, before HIV-AIDS, it's estimated that between 1 and 2 million pretty ordinary Americans practiced "swinging", "wife-swapping", "co-marital coital sex" or "the lifestyle", as it was known. At the same time, a number of much-less-ordinary communes and communities practiced "free love" "polyamory" or "polyfidelity" – usually until it was realized that the leader was pretty much running the show to gratify his own sexual appetites (and, yes, it was almost always a he).

Post-internet culture has somewhat revived group-sex culture, with chat-rooms, e-lists and the like allowing sexual networking. Singles or couples can stipulate exactly who they want to join them, and for what. Commercial sex-parties and "take-outs" now take place in most major cities and regularly appear as titillation features in lifestyle magazines. At its best, group sex should be what the "ethical sluts" say they want it to be: "an intimacy based on warmth and mutual respect, much freer than desperation, neediness or the blind insanity of falling in love. It's to be hoped that it might just also be that dream lived out, that fantasy fuck come true".

Institute, have come up with figures that suggest around a quarter of people have tried anal sex, and maybe five to eight percent enjoy it regularly.

Those figures do suggest that a good number of people try anal sex and don't like it. Others never look back. In 2004, former New York City Ballet dancer Toni Bentley wrote a whole book, *The Surrender*, about how much she loved it. "Sodomy", she writes, is the ultimate sexual act of trust …

But pushing past that fear, by passing through it, literally, ah the joy that lies on the other side of convention."

Some of that joy is psychological or maybe spiritual: the joy of surrender, of complete intimacy. Some of it is physical: the anus is rich with nerve endings, and gives access to the G-spot, in women. In men, anal sex stimulates the powerful prostate gland as well as the often-

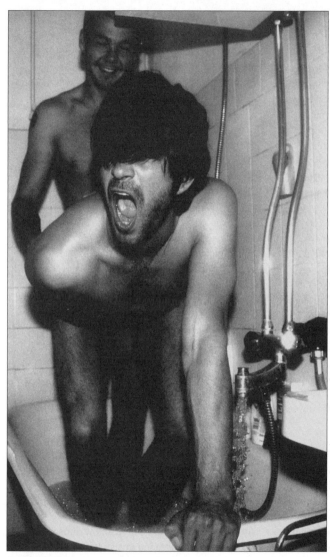

Anal sex: all about cooperation and commitment.

neglected root of the penis. Some people, men and women, reckon they have fuller, deeper orgasms through anal sex.

Toni Bentley believes that anal sex is all about cooperation and commitment. "You can't half-ass butt-fuck", she says, pithily. According to Tristan Taormino, activist, porn-producer and author of *The Ultimate Guide to Anal Sex for Women* – which really is the last word on the subject – "anal sex is my way of saying, 'Here is a delicate part of my body, and I trust you not to hurt me but to make me feel very good.' That power exchange can be very intense."

There's certainly no place for coercion or emotional pressure in anal sex. It will only work if the receiving partner really, really wants it to, and it may not work the first few times. The best advice for anyone feeling pressured into trying it must be to suggest a quid pro quo: if he won't try it, neither will you. The advice for eager men is the same: you shouldn't ask anyone to do anything that you wouldn't do yourself. Luckily, it's not just gay men that enjoy receiving. The phenomenon of the (straight) "bend-over boyfriend" is well-established enough to have a name.

Warming up

Anal expert Tristan Taormino warns that "it's not going to happen in one night"; "everyone must go at their own pace". Relaxation is essential, but not necessarily easy, as "the ass can be a place where we store much of our stress and tension". Mixed-up feelings about bottoms and cleanliness put off a lot of people, too.

The Joy of Gay Sex sensibly suggests bathtime self-exploration is the best place to start. Baths are warm, relaxing, clean and private, too, and there are plenty of lubricants on hand. The authors of the guide recommend deliberately tightening the sphincter around a finger, then just as deliberately relaxing it. Get to know the different areas of the rectum, breathing deeply, relaxing, and complimenting yourself on how well you're doing.

If you're with a partner, washing is a good place to begin, for obvious reasons. Some prefer to give themselves a full enema, maybe some hours beforehand. (Most pharmacists sell kits on either the rubber bulb-and-tube or shower-head-attachment principles.) You could warm up by massaging the buttocks, crack and, especially, the perineum. This is a good time to introduce lubrication – and keep it coming, as the anus has no natural lubrication of its own.

Kissing or licking around your partner's anus can be a beautifully intimate act, an expression of complete acceptance of their body, right down to the most secret part. Obviously, you'll want to ensure things are pretty clean down there, especially as "rimming", as it's known, is a remarkably efficient way of transmitting infections, and not just the sexually transmitted ones like hepatitis A or gonorrohoea, either; there's always dysentery to consider.

Going in

To help the anus relax, gently touch or stroke the opening. When the sphincter "winks", and when you both feel ready, you can slip in the tip of an extremely well-lubricated finger – or it might make more sense for the person being touched to move onto the finger when they feel ready. The anus will inevitably and hastily tighten; at this point, discomfort or burning sensations are common, along with urges to have a bowel movement, but these feelings should quickly subside if all's well.

The person being penetrated, Taormino suggests, should focus on relaxing the sphincter muscles by "bearing down" on them. There is more than one anal sphincter, so it may take a while. The giver should concentrate on turning their partner on as hotly as they know how – and on listening to them, and asking lots of questions. "To get one finger in and bring your partner to an orgasm", she says, "is a good goal for an evening".

Safer anal sex

Anal is riskier than any other kind of sex – a woman is some five times more likely to catch HIV through receptive anal sex than vaginal, for instance (see p.283). It follows, then, that you should use a condom – unless you and your partner know everything about each other's HIV status. Condom-free sexual encounters with strangers, or "barebacking", is, of course, riskiest of all.

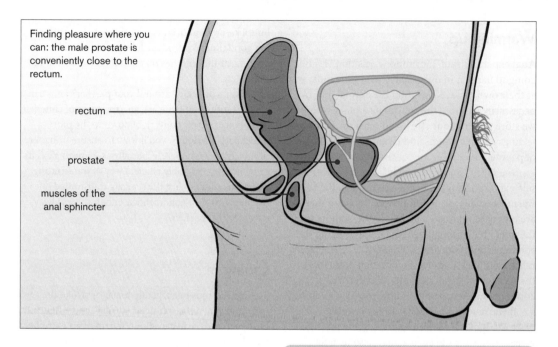

Finding pleasure where you can: the male prostate is conveniently close to the rectum.

rectum

prostate

muscles of the anal sphincter

As things progress, you could introduce a second finger, crossed over the first one, maybe. You could use an ass-plug, which dilates the anal opening and has a flared base to stop it being pulled inside. (The anus possesses an extraordinary sucking power; ask any emergency department medic if using other foreign objects is a good idea.) Anything that goes in should go in, and come out, very slowly. Penises, with their wide heads, need especial care.

As for positions, doggie-style is probably the easiest and gentlest, but it does depend on how you're both configured. Others find missionary, with the legs held up high over the shoulders, is more comfortable.

Prostatic touch

The prostate gland lies just inside the anus – about 5cm or slightly under 2 inches inside, to be precise, on the side facing the penis. The prostate has been called the male G-spot (or P-spot), and not just because it's hard to find. Once a finger is inside (see p.135), use a beckoning gesture (assuming he's facing you), feeling for a smallish, softish swelling about the size of the end of a thumb. If you hit the right spot, he's likely to think he needs to urinate, but persist. Steady or pulsing pressure, alongside masturbation, can help produce an overpowering orgasm.

Masters and slaves – BDSM for beginners

Lots of couples enjoy a bit of light bondage (tying up or restraining) or Sub/Dom (submission and domination) play without ever thinking they're getting into anything "kinky". Holding someone's hands while you make love is only a few newtons of pressure away from pinioning them by the wrists, and a finger placed across the lips could so easily become a handkerchief used as a whisper-light gag.

The joy of restraint is that it takes away all performance anxiety for one partner, and allows the other to wholly concentrate on giving. Or taking, depending on your taste. The English, in particular, have traditionally enjoyed a bit of spanking, and in fact the buttocks do seem to respond sexually to relatively vigorous pressure. More serious sadomasochism (S&M, or pleasure in giving or receiving pain or humiliation) tends to involve implements – whips or paddles are particularly common, along with nipple clamps – and sustained Sub/Dom role play, perhaps with exotic leather or rubber costumes (see p.357). People who play these games usually prefer one role rather than the other: "bottoms", or masochists, or submissives, like being punished or dominated; "tops", or sadists, or dominatrixes, prefer doing the punishing and the dominating. Some prefer "switching".

At the committed end, BDSM (bondage, domination, sadism, masochism) is a whole subculture. There are books, magazines, networks, websites, shops and clubs. There's also a wealth of equipment, costumes and the like – a lot of it pretty cheap or silly, but then the whole point about bondage is that it's a game. It's not about cruelty or actual harm – that would be officially "perverted". The mantra of BDSM culture, in fact, is "safe, sane and consensual". A 2008 Australian study found BDSM appealed to around 2 percent of people, and they were typically just as well-adjusted about sex as the other 98 percent. The researchers also concluded that BDSM wasn't related to sexual anxiousness, a history of past abuse or any difficulty in having sex in a "normal" way.

If you get into tying up, gagging or any kind of "punishment", get into safety rules too. Never get tied up by anyone you don't know or trust. Never use anything that could cut off blood flow or air supply. Agree boundaries. Use equipment that's designed for the purpose – or have a strong pair of scissors handy in case you need to get undone in a hurry. If you inflict actual cuts or bruises, make sure they're treated properly. And always agree on a code or "safeword" that stops the game – probably not "no" or "stop" as that'll spoil the fun. For further exploration, see the books and websites listed under Resources on p.385.

Anal fisting

Anal fisting, or the insertion of the entire hand into the rectum, doesn't seem to have even existed as a sexual practice before the late 1950s. It is a pretty odd thing to do: "dangerous and could result in complications that lead to death", according to *The Joy of Gay Sex*. The risk of damaging your insides is fairly high: in certain areas, the rectum has the incredibly delicate consistency of a wet tissue. Internal bleeding can't be felt, and you could end up with a colostomy bag – or worse.

Despite, or perhaps partly because of these risks, there used to be a big fisting subculture, especially among gay sadomasochists. But the men involved tended to be very experienced and well aware of the need for nail trimming, enemas, plentiful lubrication and so on. If you're going to try it, beware novices and don't mix fisting with drugs or alcohol.

Access all areas

If there's an orifice, someone will have penetrated it. Leaving aside Chinese bound feet, ears and maybe crooked knees, the other obvious hole in the body is the urethra. It's so small that this is a case of using some kind of implement as a stimulus, rather than penetration with fingers or a penis. (One gay man did tell Kinsey's researchers that he had gradually stretched his urethra over time, however, in order to receive his partner's penis.) Kinsey himself filmed a masturbatory session, with himself as subject, bringing on an orgasm using the working end of a toothbrush inserted in his own

Popping nitrites

Since the 1970s, amyl nitrite and its slightly less potent sister, butyl nitrite, have been a legal part of sex culture, especially on the gay leather scene. The drugs used to be called poppers, as they were originally supplied in little vials that made a pop or snap when opened. Today, they usually come in little bottles. Either way, the point is to sniff, not to swallow: nitrites are corrosive and highly flammable.

Nitrites cause a brief rush by increasing the heart rate and reducing blood pressure, but that was never the point. They relax smooth muscle – which, not incidentally, helps relax the muscles of the anus. Many men report feeling less inhibited and having intensified or prolonged orgasms, as well – though they have to time the inhalation right, as the effects only last a couple of minutes or so. Nitrites are relatively safe, though as with all drugs your main concern should be with who's selling them and whether or not they're pure. Even pure nitrites can cause headaches and vomiting, and you really don't want to combine them with Viagra, or any kind of heart condition – not if you want to avoid having a heart attack.

urethra. Whether this was scientific thoroughness or evidence of masochistic tendencies is still debated today (see p.379). If you want to explore or "sound" urethras, either male or female, take great care. They're easily irritated and make excellent conduits for infection.

Lubes, vibrators and plastic parts

Sex toys are sometimes treated as optional extras but for many satisfied customers they're an integral part of their sex lives. In the US, somewhere between 46 and 60 percent of women (depending on which study you trust) are said to use a vibrator – and three-quarters of them are in a relationship. Statistics on lubricant use are harder to come by, but more people should probably be using "lube" than actually do, especially if they're also using condoms. Compared to the almighty vibrator, dildoes and "artificial vaginas" are minority tastes, but for the sake of inclusiveness they're also discussed below. As for sex toys and other add-ons, clothing is discussed elsewhere (see p.67), while bondage and sadomasochism gets its own section (see p.355 and the box on p.137).

Lubrication

Vaginal sex without lubrication isn't much fun for women (see the box on p.140). And anal sex without lubrication is just stupid. Far and away the best vaginal lubricant is the one naturally supplied by a woman's body in response to arousal, which is a kind of distillation of blood plasma mixed with oils and glandular secretions. This lubrication may be natural but unfortunately it isn't always as copious as it might be. The menstrual cycle, childbirth, ageing and menopause can all interfere with the hormonal switches that produce it, leaving the vagina dry and literally unreceptive.

Lubricants don't have to be used to solve dryness. Along with the vibrator, they're probably the most enjoyable and effective sex toy of all, and trying out different degrees of wetness can make more difference than any new position. Wet sex can be a huge turn-on, too: lubricate each other's entire bodies and slip and slide together to orgasm.

Natural lubricants

The best solution to a lack of female lubrication is to focus on arousal, but you may need extra help. Saliva is a useful, free and perfectly organic booster. Don't grab whatever moisturizer or lotion is to hand, as

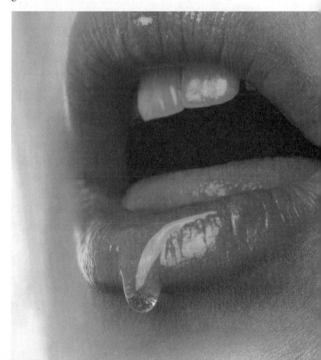

many are petroleum-based and perfumed, and can mess up the vagina's chemical balance. Improvised lubrication can also cause condoms to fail, even days after you've used it.

Dry sex in Africa

In the West, a wet vagina is the true sign of sexual satisfaction. In sub-Saharan Africa, however, the opposite may be true. Wetness is traditionally associated with disease and infidelity, and dryness with good health and fertility. As a consequence, millions of women regularly insert herbal pessaries or wads of cotton and newspaper to dry out their vaginas so that they will be as hot, tight and dry as possible. Some even use salt, detergent or antiseptics, while traditional folk remedies – also considered aphrodisiacs – include soil urinated on by a baboon and a crushed stone agent known as "wankie".

A study in South Africa in 1999 found that almost half of all the women surveyed practised dry sex, while in Zambia the figure was 86 percent. One sex worker in Kwazulu-Natal told a researcher that "men do not like loose vaginas. If sex is wet the man thinks I have had sex with someone else and then he won't pay me". Providing male satisfaction comes at a cost. The pessaries themselves can be painful to apply. During sex, dryness is closely associated with painful friction, along with lesions and lacerations of the skin, and, consequently, the easier transmission of sexually transmitted diseases, including HIV. Dry sex also dramatically reduces the reliability of condoms.

If you're going for natural oils, choose the lighter kinds, such as almond and apricot-kernel oils, as used in massage. These are more quickly absorbed. Fractionated coconut oil is also light, and has the benefit of not staining sheets. Jojoba oil is actually a wax, more akin to skin's natural sebum than many oils – this makes it feel very silky; it is, however, relatively pricey. At a pinch, ordinary sunflower oil as used for cooking is kind to skin – much kinder than olive oil. In the US, sex shops sell oil- or shea-butter-based creams specifically designed for use in masturbation. Or you could try soaking a tablespoon of linseeds in about 5 tablespoons of water, producing a perfect and totally natural kind of gel.

Commercial "lubes"

Commercial lubricants, or "lubes", are pretty effective – too effective, some say, as they can rob you of some useful friction. You can buy lubes from "adult" shops and, of course, over the internet. Many are based on combinations of water and starch – including the famous KY Jelly, which is commonly used for medical examinations and remains the best-known brand. Other, dedicated brands of water-based lube include: the creamy, glycerin-free Liquid Silk; Sylk, which is based on a kiwi-fruit extract; the relatively thick Probe, which uses grapefruit seed extract as a preservative; TLC; Slick and Slide; Durex's Sensilube; and ID Pleasure.

Some water-based lubes have had strange routes to market. Astroglide was supposedly inspired by a lubricant used on NASA's space shuttle (not for sex), even though its ingredients are actually fairly standard for a water-based lube. Slippery Stuff began

Granville's Hammer

The first vibrators were sold not to women but to British and American doctors who provided laborious "pelvic massage" to "hysterical" women (see p.182). The treatment – which, admittedly, was a minority practice – could apparently last as long as an hour before it brought on the relieving "paroxysm" or "crisis", so inventors came up with all kinds of water jets, rocking chairs, wind-up tools and even a kind of giant steam-powered ironing board which provided rhythmical massage. Incredibly, the medical establishment largely failed to associate this treatment with masturbation or orgasm.

The electrical vibrator, therefore, came as a huge relief. To doctors. It was invented in the 1880s by Joseph Granville, who insisted that his "percussor" or "Granville's Hammer" was only designed to treat insanity or muscular tension. Before long, women began discovering the joys of personal "invigoration" for themselves. Adverts for "massagers" appeared in needlecraft magazines and catalogues of general household electrical appliances – as they do to this day. The "Vibratile", of 1899, claimed it treated neuralgia and wrinkles.

By the 1930s, psychotherapy had replaced masturbation as a cure for hysteria. Vibrators appeared in early "stag films", which rather blew their therapeutic cover and led to laws restricting their sale. The re-emergence of vibrators in the 1960s, then, was a key victory for women's liberation. Women were taking pleasure into their own hands, taking control of their own orgasms. As Betty Dodson, the "godmother of masturbation", told her fans, "independent orgasms, I guarantee, will lead you to independent thought."

In the US, this was seen as a threat. Many states openly banned the sale or display of "sex toys" – or, as the Alabama legislature called them (as recently as 1999) "any device designed or marketed as useful primarily for the stimulation of human genital organs". Orgasms were to be achieved in the marital bed only. In the 2000s, bans or restrictions on the sale of vibrators were still in force in Alabama, Georgia, Kansas, Louisiana, Mississippi and Texas. As more than one feminist pointed out, the massive sales of Viagra made this look like something of a double standard. After 2006, states gave way one by one. A federal appeal court ruling against Texas's ban, in February 2008, left Alabama as the last bastion of this particular kind of sexual repression.

---

life as a diver's lubricant for getting wetsuits on and off. The big drawback of most water-based lubricants is that they thicken or become "gummy" during use, so you may need to keep on reapplying – or just add a little water to reactivate.

Many lubes contain unpleasant additives: colourings, flavourings, sweeteners and even chemicals which heat up on contact with the skin. They usually contain preservatives called parabens, too, which have been linked to allergic reactions and are environmentally harmful in a relatively modest way. Another common ingredient, glycerin, is sticky-sweet, and may increase the chance of developing a yeast infection. Lubricants

Cock rings

Cock rings are designed to fit tightly round the base of the penis and the scrotum, stopping the blood flowing out and thus maintaining a firmer, longer-lasting erection. Some men find their penis feels more sensitive. Others just like the look of their penis dressed up in its little dog collar. Before you don a cock ring, it's worth thinking about how they work. They restrict blood flow. Restrict for too long – longer than twenty minutes, say – and you could end up in penile casualty. There's also the problem of removal. The much-admired firemen of San Francisco are apparently so bedevilled by cock-ring emergencies that they now carry an alarming-sounding miniature circular saw.

Some cock rings come as vibrators, perhaps with a quivering anal plug, a scrotal pouch or a clitoral stimulator attached. The last is either a bullet-type vibrator or a bit of textured latex, and it usually sits up at one end of the ring like the raised head of a rubber duck. The idea is to restore some clitoral satisfaction to penetrative intercourse. If you can get past the silliness, it might just work.

which include spermicides like nonoxynol-9 should probably be avoided: they taste awful – the active ingredient is a kind of detergent – and have recently been shown to actually increase the chance of passing on a sexually transmitted infection, probably by irritating any tiny cuts or grazes.

Silicone-based lubes have some big advantages over water-based ones. They're slippery rather than sticky, you can use them with condoms, they don't taste of anything in particular, and you don't have to keep on reapplying. The chief drawbacks are the cost and the fact that you have to wash with soap to clean them off.

Vibrators

In his bestselling 1970s guide, *The Joy of Sex*, Dr Alex Comfort warned that vibrators were "no substitute for a penis". He was right. Dildoes (see p.145) are the penis substitute, and a poor one at that. Vibrators do something completely different and, as millions of women have discovered, they do it much better.

Vibrators are not "toys" any more than they are penis substitutes. They can be amazingly efficient orgasm-producers, even for women who have previously struggled to reach orgasm. Many are sold as "personal" or "hand-held" massagers. The high-grade electrical appliance manufacturer Wahl, for instance, makes a 4120 Pro series 2-speed massager. Only if you look closely at the seven extraordinary attachments does it become clear that one of them is a boomerang-shaped, G-spot-targetting, miniature dildo.

Vibrators can also give pleasure to men. They can be held against the base, shaft or head of the penis, or pressed into the perineum or anus to accompany masturbation. G-spot-style miniature dildoes can be perfect for accessing that hard-to-reach prostate gland, just inside the anus. Some stores offer dedicated vibrators for men, some in the shape of a masturbatory "sleeve", others in the form of a cock ring (see box, above). And, of course, vibrators can always be used as massagers, taking their historical journey full circle. Some

Something for everybody: dildoes and vibrators come in a bewildering variety of textures, shapes and sizes.

breastfeeding women have even found them useful for releasing blocked milk ducts.

Using a vibrator is pretty much a matter of exploration, but San Francisco's long-running Good Vibrations sex store offers some useful tips – as published in 1977 (and revised in 2000) in a dedicated vibrator's manual by Joani Blank called, appropriately, *Good Vibrations*. Blank suggests trying different positions and touching different areas, varying pressure and speed, and perhaps using clothing or a towel between you and the vibrator if it's too intense. Lubrication can make a huge difference, too.

Choosing a vibrator

You tend to get what you pay for – and if you're concerned about having electrics near your private parts, you might want to pay for a product that has been properly tested and carries the regulatory mark to prove it. The best vibrators are often the ones that look least sexual, like Wahl's, which is designed on the coil-operated "cake-mixer" principle, or Philips "Intimate Massager", which comes in a male/female two-part set and is designed to fit easily into the shape of the hand. The renowned Hitachi "Magic Wand" looks like a karaoke microphone, but its soft, ball-like rubber vibrating tip is famously effective. As for the BetterSex Synergy Pleasure System, it closely resembles an electric toothbrush.

Probably less reliable, but perhaps less intimidating too, are the tiny, battery-powered "eggs", "pearls" or "bullets", which you can either insert or press up against the clitoris with the fingertips, though some come attached to a finger- or cock ring. All fit handily in a handbag. Vibrators packaged up as dildoes are often novelty toys, but some are elaborately produced, covered in soft-feeling silicone or "cyberskin", maybe, or attached to strap-ons.

The best dildoes designed for insertion are probably the so-called "dual vibrators". The most famous brand is the Rabbit, which began life in Japan. (It used to be illegal to make "realistic", ie penis-shaped sex toys there. Curiously, when the Rabbit was first offered to "novelty" distributors in the US, it was rejected on the grounds that people would only want flesh-coloured, veiny "realistic" dildoes.) The Rabbit's dildo part is inserted into the vagina – where it twirls around, ineffectually – while the vibrating ears of the offshoot "rabbit" section rest against the clitoris.

Less whimsical dildo-type vibrators have become available since the Rabbit bounded onto the scene. Some have elegant, ergonomic shapes which allow them to be used as both dildoes and for the advertised "intimate massage" of the clitoris.

A key choice is whether to go for mains or battery-powered. Some people don't like feeling they're plugged into the grid, and batteries are the only solution if you want a waterproof vibrator for use in the bath. Battery power is often noisier, less reliable and lower-powered, however – and you run the risk of running out of juice at the wrong time. Batteries have improved hugely in the last few years, but it's still an infuriating possibility. The other technological improvement is the microchip. It came late to vibrators, but you can now select from various programmes of speeds and actions. Few people like changing the tempo mid-session, but fine-tuning your vibe so that it gives you exactly what you want is worthwhile.

An innovation of recent years is the Eroscillator, which was developed by the inventor of the electric toothbrush. Its key innovation is that the motor isn't attached to the part you hold, so it doesn't vibrate your hand as well. (You wouldn't want to develop vibration white finger...) Technology of a different kind is employed by the rather brilliant Vielle Stimulator, which is a simple but effective finger sleeve with rubber dimples – you could think of it as an all-natural, electricity-free vibrator. The big market of the future, meanwhile, is online or gaming vibrators for use by couples – or, indeed, horny strangers.

Plastic parts – dildoes and vaginas

Most ancient sex practices are missing from the great, censored book of human history, but evidence of dildo use has survived. Few cultures engraved their sex manuals in tablets of stone but plenty of them carved artificial penises in the stuff. The British Museum has entire drawers of Egyptian dildoes, while a dig in Bulgaria turned up one with a golden tip, and Japan's artfully crafted tortoiseshell models have become collectors' items. Greek women apparently wielded *olisboi* in leather, wood or ivory while the Chinese used silk, bean curd and a plant which swelled when wetted.

Dildoes

Dildoes today are often *objets d'art* or gift novelties as much as real sex toys, but some women like to use a dildo in combination with a vibrator, and of course they're vital if you want to use a strap-on harness.

They range from bargain-bucket lurid acrylics to "realistic" casts of porn actors' mega-penises, complete with moulded veins, testicular suction-cup bases and flesh tones in shades of anything from Icelandic to Congolese. At the top end of the scale come the "handcrafted" wooden or glass dildoes, and those with warm-to-the-touch "cyberskin".

Some dildoes are designed for exercising the vaginal muscles, or have double heads for use by two women, or a man and a woman together, or curve round on themselves for vaginal-anal solo action or G-spot stimulation. If you're buying a dildo for anal use, don't buy anything that doesn't have a flared end: the unappealingly named "butt plugs" are the answer. In terms of texture, softness may be appealing, but can make a dildo hard to clean – silicone or hard materials are handier. Size is, inevitably, a matter of taste.

You don't have to buy a dildo of course. Inserting something breakable is a bad idea, given the strength of the pelvic muscles. Vegetables are justifiably popular, being completely natural and, apparently, responsive to light warming in a microwave or steamer – though you've got to worry about the possibility for burns and explosions.

One insertable device that keeps cropping up in sex shops are "geisha" or "Ben Wa" balls – little marble-like devices that you insert for, allegedly, all-day pleasure and/or vaginal exercise. Few women report any satisfaction whatsoever.

Dildoes in harness

Donning a dildo in a harness can provoke surprisingly deep feelings. Love it or hate it, the penis has plentiful totemic power in most cultures.

Some women feel self-conscious or just silly. Either way, harnesses open up all kinds of new possibilities for lovemaking.

Strap-on harnesses come in just as many varieties as dildoes, but the basic division is between single-strap models (like a thong) and double-strap versions which attach round both thighs (like a jock strap). The latter often sit lower down, allowing better pressure for the wearer on their own pubic mound. Cheaper harnesses are worth avoiding: strap-ons are hard to control at the best of times, and you want to be able to rely on a snug fit and buckles and straps that won't fail. It's also worth buying a dildo that's designed for use with a harness; most have flared bases.

Artificial vaginas

At some point in human history, men have tried fucking just about anything with a hole in it. The ancient Chinese stitched little, heart-shaped leather cushions, stuffing them with cotton before stuffing them with something else entirely. Japanese men are said to have used the splendidly named Devil's tongue plant; tongues had nothing to do with it, nor its spectacularly phallic flower: when boiled, its tubers produce a stiff edible jelly, konnyaku, into which a soft hole can be easily shaped.

American men seem to be unusually inventive manufacturers and finders of artificial vaginas. In 2007, a man in Lakeland Florida got his penis stuck in the filtration pump of a motel swimming pool. Neighbours of another Florida man, alerted by the unceasing noise of a vacuum cleaner, found their friend slumped dead over his machine, with burns to "areas in direct contact with the beater bar" – as the report put it. Hollywood Frat-boy flicks, meanwhile, extol the virtues of socks filled with warm pasta, condoms packed with foam rubber, microwaved marrows (which apparently need a vent to prevent excessive suction, and sound dangerous), watermelons and even grapefruit. You wouldn't want to have any little nicks or abrasions when enjoying a grapefruit.

Sex-store vaginas may be electrically heated, vibrating or fillable with warm water. They may be made of "cyberskin". They may come with a bulb for suction. In Japan, pre-lubricated Onacups are a new entry to the market, and the company is apparently developing larger sizes for export. One of the most ubiquitously advertised artificial vaginas, the Fleshlight, is disguised as an electric torch. The drawback of this cunning disguise, customers have complained, is that you can't squeeze the outside of the tube. On the plus side, you can swap inserts – mouths, butts and signature porn-star vaginas are all available.

It's probably best not to consider the ethical implications of manufacturing a woman shorn of legs, abdomen, head, ears, eyes, everything, but it's surely no more or less worrying than a blow-up doll (some of which come complete with pubic hair and up to three orifices). Perhaps the same principle should apply to artificial vaginas as to dildoes: they're not substitutes, they're an independent source of pleasure.

4

Orgasm

4 Orgasm

Orgasm is sometimes said to be the "point" of sex. But people don't have lovers simply because they want orgasms. Masturbation would be a far simpler method. Sex may be much bigger than orgasm but this doesn't mean orgasm doesn't play a hugely important role in sex. Orgasm isn't just one of the most remarkable things that the human body can do, it's also one of the most mysterious. Thinkers from Aristotle to Freud have puzzled over its nature and purpose.

Recently – astonishingly recently – scientists and researchers have started investigating its causes and function. Orgasm makes a hard target. It is deeply subjective and incredibly various. People can enjoy multiple orgasms, sequential orgasms and simultaneous orgasms. Men can have dry orgasms and orgasms without erections. Women can have orgasms with ejaculation, and some believe they can experience "clitoral" and "vaginal" orgasms – a much-disputed notion.

Some lose their orgasms or never once find them, others have orgasms while sleeping or, in rare cases, without meaning to. According to the latest research, a lucky few can bring on orgasms by thought alone, or by stimulating parts of the body other than the genitals.

What, where, how – and why

The first "Kinsey Report", Alfred Kinsey's 1948 *Sexual Behavior in the Human Male*, defined "sexual climax", as "the explosive discharge of neuromuscular tensions at the peak of sexual response". Studying orgasm at all was a major leap forward, but the definition didn't say much – other than locating orgasm in the nerves and muscles.

The sex researchers William Masters and Virginia Johnson were the first to examine orgasm in detail. They defined it as "a brief episode of physical release from the vasocongestion and myotonic increment developed in response to sexual stimuli". Again, this definition was less than revealing: "vasocongestion" simply meant the tissues were swollen with blood, while "myotonic increment" refers to increasing muscular tension. There is much more to orgasm than this.

Orgasm in the body

In their 1966 book, *Human Sexual Response*, Masters and Johnson revealed that orgasm affects the whole body. The heart rate soars – up to 180 beats per minute in some cases – while the speed of breathing doubles. Sensitivity to pain drops dramatically even while every touch is exquisitely felt: the classic example is a stray pubic hair being infuriatingly apparent on the tongue even while unnoticed fingernails dig deep into the back. Peripheral vision drops away and hearing seems to temporarily drop out. Bizarrely, stutterers may lose their stutters, pains in phantom limbs may disappear and sufferers from cerebral palsy may have spasticity temporarily calmed.

In women, the inner lips sometimes turn a dark red colour; the outer third of the vagina may throb subtly and rhythmically while the inner part expands and the uterus pulses irregularly. In men, the balls are pulled upwards towards the body. In both sexes, the rectum may twitch or contract while shuddering waves roll up and down the spine between the head and the genitals.

Muscles throughout the body stiffen, especially in the face, which may be screwed up as if in pain. (Fascinatingly, neurologists say the emotions behind pain and orgasm alike seem to be generated in the same region of the brain – in the anterior cingulate cortex, to be exact.) The big toes may stretch out while the other toes curl in and the feet arch or quiver. The pupils of the eyes dilate to their pool-like maximum. Veins may stand out against the skin, and a blush or "sex flush" spreads across many fair-skinned women and some men. Most dramatically, people tend to gasp, moan, grunt, squeal or cry out involuntarily when orgasm hits.

Individual orgasms vary hugely, but most women experience a powerful muscle contraction in the outer (or lower) third of the vagina, which lasts for a good two to four seconds. The pubococcygeal or "PC" muscle group of the pelvic floor (the one which wraps around the rectum and genitals) contracts at 0.8 second intervals – though as orgasm continues, the contractions are further spaced apart. The uterus also contracts powerfully. Men experience three or four ejaculatory contractions – also at intervals of 0.8 of a second – followed by less regular "aftershock" pulses.

Orgasm in the mind

People describe their orgasms in such different ways that it's clear that there's a very large cognitive element to orgasm. The leading scientists of orgasm, Barry Komisaruk and Beverly Whipple, claim that orgasm isn't so much an event as a process – and a perception of that process. It's a chain reaction begun not just by stretch receptors but by events in the brain as well. It's a cycle that spins off into a cascade in both body and mind.

Just before the physical contractions of orgasm begin, many people describe a sudden feeling of suspended time, often accompanied by intense sensual awareness. After this existential moment – but still before the orgasmic contractions – women told Masters and Johnson of a second state, in which a "suffusion of warmth" spread through the body. Only afterwards were the actual contractions felt.

In the lead-up to orgasm, as tension builds in the core of the body, the mind becomes more and more frantic – until the moment where both seem to break out of themselves in an explosive self-release which spends its pent-up energy in a series of waves or aftershocks. Of course, orgasms aren't always as grand as this. Some are more like sneezes than volcanic eruptions, more like sighs than hurricanes.

The perceived epicentre of orgasm varies just as much as the scale of the quake. Some feel very "pelvic", or radiate outwards, or are whole body, or are focused in just the very tip of the penis or clitoris. Others seem more mental than physical. At their most extreme, orgasms can result in out-of-body-type experiences, or what one therapist's client described as "the psychedelic jackpot that lights up the universe".

Many orgasms are profoundly emotional. They may produce warm feelings of comfort or intimacy. Orgasms for partners in the throes of romantic love are often said to be peculiarly intense, as if orgasm dissolved them and reconstituted them as one person. Orgasms can also access pain and distress, either to release it or, more troublingly, to recall it. At orgasm, it can feel as if deep feelings are being torn up by their roots from within, and weeping in its aftermath is not uncommon.

Masters and Johnson found that orgasms reached through lovemaking were felt more acutely by the participants in their study than those achieved by masturbation – even if masturbation was a more efficient method. And men often rate orgasms on the basis not of how they feel but how they're obtained. At the top of the pecking order is the orgasm procured through vaginal intercourse, then oral sex, then masturbation. The sleeping orgasm, or wet dream, comes a distant last.

The causes of orgasm

Most sex researchers see orgasm as a reflex, a physical reaction to arousal rather like that produced when a doctor taps your knee with a hammer – though of course in a more extreme, not to mention more enjoyable, form. The basic idea is that muscle tension builds and builds while blood flow increases and increases until eventually a spinal reflex is triggered which in turn causes the orgasmic muscles to rhythmically contract.

No one knows, however, why increased tension and blood flow should trigger a spinal reflex. While a doctor's hammer is very obviously a single, causal blow, there isn't a single event immediately *before* orgasm which sets the sexual reaction going. Some researchers believe orgasm is "like an overloaded electrical circuit shorting out", or that when arousal reaches a certain level it triggers another higher-threshold system. Muscular tension seems to play an important role – and yet some people have been shown to have orgasms without any muscle tension at all.

The feminist psychiatrist Mary Jane Sherfey reckoned that orgasm was ultimately caused by blood flow, not muscular tension. When this vasocongestion in the pelvic muscles reaches a certain threshold point, it fires the stretch receptors – a kind of neuron in the muscle that responds to mechanical stimuli – and this in turn triggers the spinal reflex.

This triggering seems to be done by neurotransmitters, the chemicals which carry messages around the brain and nervous system. Dopamine (a chemical relative of adrenaline) builds during arousal, making the brain more responsive to sexual stimulation. At the same time, the action of serotonin is progressively inhibited, thus overcoming the blocking effect that this neurotransmitter seems to have on orgasm.

The famous "love hormone", oxytocin, is released into the bloodstream in significant quantities during and after orgasm. In its role as a neurotransmitter, oxytocin seems to link sensations in the genitals – via the pelvic nerve and spinal chord – to the area of the brain where oxytocin is produced. Tests show an area called the paraventricular nucleus of the hypothalamus "lighting up" during orgasm. It may be here, then, deep in the brain, that orgasm is ultimately "switched on".

What's the point?

Ancient medical authorities were in little doubt that female orgasm was absolutely necessary to guarantee conception. Galen, following his master, Hippocrates, thought that because men and women both contributed "seed" to help form the foetus, mutual orgasm was clearly necessary. Aristotle, as ever, was more perspicacious, arguing that orgasm and ejaculation weren't exactly the same thing – but even he thought conception without orgasm was unusual.

Western medicine – which long preferred classical wisdom over lived experience, especially that of women – remained largely convinced of the relation between orgasm and conception right up until the Enlightenment. Even the observations of the twelfth-century philosopher Averroes, who described the (dubious) case of a woman who got pregnant from semen in her bath, did nothing to change medical minds. As anatomical knowledge

grew, however, doubts crept in. And when one Lazzaro Spallanzani artificially inseminated a spaniel in the 1770s, the game was up. Female orgasm, it was concluded, had nothing to do with conception.

But if so, then what, in evolutionary terms, is the female orgasm *for*? The point of the male orgasm seems obvious: it promotes ejaculation, which enables conception. Women, on the other hand, can just as easily get pregnant without an orgasm as with one.

Evolutionary theories

Biologists (most of them men) have been amazingly reluctant to accept the idea that female orgasms might just be "for pleasure", meaning that they have no specific "adaptation", or role in improving a woman's ability to reproduce. It's often assumed that orgasms encourage women to seek more sex, thereby increasing the number of children they're likely to have. But it's the itch of desire that makes people have sex, not the desire to have an orgasm. And no one has found any link between women's orgasmic potential and the number of children they end up having.

Human zoologist Desmond Morris reckoned that orgasm encourages woman to bond with their partners, thus increasing the chance of their children's survival. The elusive nature of female orgasm, he thought, makes women seek out partners patient and intelligent enough to be able to produce them. But Morris rather assumed that the "naked apes" of our distant evolutionary past behaved like people in modern, monogamous societies. He also thought orgasms might encourage

How was it for you? Zoologists debate whether or not all primates have orgasms.

women to lie back after sex, thus giving sperm a better chance of staying inside: the so-called "poleaxe hypothesis". But lying back probably makes no difference anyway; and who said women were lying down to start with?

Theories since have become more refined. Primatologist Sarah Blaffer Hrdy thought that orgasms prompted female chimps and macaques to seek multiple partners – because they had to keep on mating for longer than any single male could manage in order to elicit an orgasm for themselves. And multiple partners confuse paternity; and when a monkey thinks a child might just be his, he's less likely to kill it to "weed out" the offspring of hated male rivals.

An evolutionary predisposition to multiple partners may lie behind another theory: that women are unconsciously engaging in sperm selection, using their own orgasm to help retain or reject greater or lesser quantities of semen from different lovers. Evolutionary biologist Randy Thornhill and psychologist Steve Gangestad also found that women had copulatory orgasms more often with more symmetrical partners – and symmetry equates with attractiveness and "good genes" (see p.18).

Dr Hrdy has a theory for why female orgasm is relatively unreliable. Perhaps it is "phasing out", she says; "our descendants on the starships may well wonder what all the fuss was about". Until then, and unless someone comes up with better evidence, the most likely theory is that female orgasms have no biological function whatsoever – any more than male nipples do. They're simply "artifacts", glorious by-products of the fact that the core nerves and tissues are created during the first eight or nine weeks of an embryo's development, in the period before boys will be boys and girls, girls.

Sucking up – female orgasm and fertility

In 1872, an American doctor, Joseph Beck, reported examining a female patient who warned him she was hyper-orgasmic. As he inspected her, she duly orgasmed, whereupon he saw her cervix apparently dip down into her vagina with every orgasmic contraction. He interpreted the movement as the cervix trying to suck up any sperm that might have been waiting there, but when sex researchers William Masters and Virginia Johnson got out their measuring equipment in the 1960s, they thought it was an expulsive movement rather than an "upsucking" one.

They did find, however, a "tenting" of the uterus that seemed to help it act as a kind of reservoir for semen. And later studies suggested that while the cervix may push out fluid around the time of menstruation, it changes direction and sucks it up around ovulation. Certainly, women who have had multiple orgasms have been known to suck up air into their uterus and fallopian tubes – a painful condition that some gynaecologists dub "bonkers belly". The "upsuck" theory also had a boost from Drs Baker and Bellis, who claimed in 1993 that if a woman had an orgasm within a certain window – namely, from one minute before the man's ejaculation to up to 45 minutes afterwards – she retained more sperm than if she hadn't come at all, thanks to muscular contractions of the uterus. The difference could be as much as two times the volume of sperm. They also reckoned that women who had sex with men who weren't their regular partner had more orgasms in the critical window – though critics dismissed the study as too small to be significant.

In 1998, a German study discovered that women actually have uterine contractions all day long, with or without orgasm, thus casting doubt on the whole idea of a chain of influence from orgasm to conception via contractions and upsuck. But it's possible that the oxytocin released at orgasm intensifies any uterine contractions, creating negative pressure which hoovers semen up through the cervix.

There's some evidence from animals, too. Stump-tailed macaques have been shown to have enormous uterine contractions during sex at exactly the moment when their mouths widen in a joyous "oh!" shape. And Danish sows, when stimulated by farmworkers doing artificial insemination, have improved rates of fertilization. It's only a six-percent difference, but worth it if you're a pig farmer – and worth trying if you're a woman trying to get pregnant, with orgasm as the only cost.

William Masters and Virginia Johnson holding copies of their book *Human Sexual Response*.

Earthquakes and anchovies – orgasm described

When people describe their orgasms they reach for very similar words and images. Top of the list are "relief", "release", "explosion" and "expulsion" – often matched with their opposites, "tension", "control", "pressure", "tightness" "strain" and the like. Orgasms are explosive and energetic: likened to the eruption of a volcano or the unleashing of an earthquake, to "lightning bolts", "electric shocks" or, more mildly, "pulses" and "golden glows".

Most commonly of all, orgasms are compared to waves. There's all that power building from underneath, the inevitability of the impact ahead and the wonderful sensation of floating or surfing towards the end. Some arrive with an almighty crash: the freak wave that leaves chaotic swirlings in its wake. Others break regularly in smaller wavelets. Others still feature a single big swell followed – or preceded – by other waves, with moments of rocking withdrawal between each.

Some people sense vibrant colours at orgasm, apparently in some non-visual way. Gold and white are particularly popular, while some people see whole rainbows. Metaphysical adjectives are popular: the experience may be "ecstatic", "euphoric", "liberating" or simply "wonderful", it may feel like "floating", or even taking the orgasmic person some way towards "heaven", "bliss" or an apparently welcome "oblivion".

Some orgasms are more unusual – and maybe more enviable. One woman, quoted in the Indian magazine *The Week*, described hers as feeling as if a hot chocolate egg were breaking inside her.

The language of orgasm

The roots of the word orgasm lie in the Greek *orgon*, meaning to swell up or be ripe. But an "orgasm" in English once meant any kind of climactic movement or convulsion, or a violent outburst. A sexual orgasm was known as a "crisis" or a "spasm". Victorian pornographers preferred the euphemism "spend", as in "I felt her crack deluged with a warm, creamy spend whilst my own juice spurted over her hand and dress in loving sympathy" – a fairly typical sentence from the magazine *The Pearl* of 1879–80.

By the end of the nineteenth century, doctors were starting to talk about sexual "orgasms". The non-sexual meanings of the word quickly – very quickly – died away. "Climax" first appeared in print in Marie Stopes' 1918 sex manual, *Married Love*. Stopes warned that "In many cases the man's climax comes so swiftly that the woman's reactions are not nearly ready." The word soon became a verb, as in Shirley Conran's multi-million-selling porno-romance *Lace*, from 1982: "After he climaxed, he kissed her gently on the lips."

The word "come" has been around for a very long time indeed. Latin speakers used *pervenio*, meaning "I arrive". Shakespeare has Cressida entreat her lover, Troilus, to "come again into my chamber", pausing before continuing: "You smile and mock me, as if I meant naughtily." But using "come" as a noun, to refer to ejaculatory fluids, is a

Petite mort

The highbrow phrase *petite mort*, or little death, originally referred to blackouts, fainting fits or nervous tremblings. Thomas Hardy could write in 1891, for instance, that his heroine, Tess of the d'Urbevilles, "felt the petite mort" at some "unexpectedly gruesome information." She wasn't coming. While orgasm was considered to be related to these kinds of hysterical symptoms (see p.182) *petite mort* only began to be used as a synonym for orgasm in the mid-twentieth century. It was a way of describing the depersonalization of the experience. This might either progress to a sense of merging or re-constitution with a beloved partner, or to a hollow, lonesome, post-orgasmic melancholy – a sensation also known as *tristesse*, French for sadness. Some relate the feeling of *petite mort* to the idea that ejaculate is a kind of life essence (see p.170). Others say that it's a neurological reaction to an orgasmic high, and chemically very similar to coming down from opiates like heroin.

Orgasms are often compared to extreme natural phenomena: earthquakes, volcanoes, tidal waves.

modern phenomenon. The expression only arrived in print in the late 1960s, in Richard Brautigan's 1967 novel *Trout Fishing in America* (which wasn't really about trout fishing – as one might imagine from a novel which includes the sentence "The walls, the floor and even the roof of the hut were coated with your sperm and her come".) More recent still is the porno-spelling "cum" – which has quickly become fairly mainstream.

Was it better for you, dear?

Whether men or women experience more pleasure in sex is a millennia-old question. There's even a Greek myth entirely devoted to the problem. For the crime of separating two copulating snakes with his staff, the goddess Hera turned Tiresias into a woman. After

Literary orgasms

One of the world's most ancient orgasms was described by the ancient Greek poet Sappho – who loved women and lived on the island of Lesbos, hence the word "lesbian". At the crucial moment, she wrote, "my tongue is struck silent, a delicate fire / suddenly races underneath my skin, / my eyes see nothing, my ears whistle like / the whirling of a top and sweat pours down me and a trembling creeps over / my whole body".

Renaissance poets loved to compare orgasm to death: "dying in your arms" was very much a double entendre. In *Come Again*, by the Elizabethan composer John Dowland, the lover wants "to see, to hear, to touch, to kiss, to DIE … with thee again in sweetest sympathy". If the listener was in any doubt as to the double meaning, the song's melody swells and pulses upwards to a soaring high note on "die".

Orgasms vanished from mainstream (if not pornographic) literature in the nineteenth century, and even struggled to reappear in the twentieth. In James Joyce's banned novel of 1922, *Ulysses*, Bloom and Gerty watch a firework display as they fool around together – but what with all the rockets banging and gushing, the rapturous sighs of "O! O!" and the sparks fading afterwards, it's pretty clear what's actually going on.

D.H. Lawrence's *Lady Chatterley's Lover*, written in 1928 and also banned, was even more direct. Lady Chatterley has sex with gamekeeper Oliver Mellors, in a young fir wood, in spring. Mellors comes first – and then,

"... she felt the soft bud of him within her stirring, and strange rhythms flushing up into her with a strange rhythmic growing motion, swelling and swelling till it filled all her cleaving consciousness, and then began again the unspeakable motion that was not really motion, but pure deepening whirlpools of sensation swirling deeper and deeper through all her tissue and consciousness, till she was one perfect concentric fluid of feeling, and she lay there crying in unconscious inarticulate cries."

Today, orgasms are found in books everywhere. A poem by Scottish writer Alison Fell, "In Confidence", is based entirely on descriptions of orgasms overheard at a women's group meeting. "An orgasm is like an anchovy," one woman says, "little, long, and very salty." Another calls it a caterpillar, "undulating, fat and sweet." A third says it's a sunburst, or "an exploding watermelon" – adding, drily, "I had one at Christmas."

seven years – in which he became a renowned courtesan – he was turned back into a man, and questioned by Hera and her husband, Zeus. Who, they demanded, experiences greater pleasure in sex, a man or a woman? He replied that women's pleasure was nine times that of men. Hera took away his sight.

"Nine times as great" is exactly what 'Ali ibn Abi Talib reckoned. He was the prophet Muhammad's son-in-law, the first Imam in the Shi'ah tradition, and no enthusiast for sex: a companion overheard him addressing God in the night, imploring him to protect him from the temptations of pleasure. "One who rushes madly

Babbling like a partridge – sex cries

The third-century *Kamasutra* devotes an entire chapter to "slapping and moaning". The latter comes in eight varieties: "whimpering, groaning, babbling, crying, panting, shrieking or sobbing". Shrieking was "a sound like a bamboo splitting" while sobbing was more "like a berry falling into water". Woman also apparently shouted things like "Stop!" or "Let me go!" or "Mother!" – this was centuries before anyone pointed out that "no" does, in fact, mean no. When orgasm arrived, it made women "babble fast like a partridge or a goose".

The sounds of orgasm – the ohs and ahs, the grunts and screeches, the gasps and whimpers – can be strangely similar to those of pain. Many lovers find the sounds of sex cries – either their own or their partners' – very arousing. And while no one would argue for faking (see p.184), a few well-placed yelps can provide that little bit of extra encouragement.

The vocabulary of sex lurches from tendernesses such as "darling", "baby", "I love you" and gasps of the partner's name, to obscenities: "God" and "Jesus" are strangely popular. "Fuck" is less surprising. "Fuck me" is also wildly popular – some people like to be very specific about what they want. "Now" and "yes" are similarly encouraging.

Some sex cries have deeper meaning. For the philosopher of eroticism, Georges Bataille, they can be "an immense alleluia, flung into endless silence, and lost there". Some link the sacred seed-syllable of Hinduism, "om" or "aum", to the sensation of release or disconnection that can characterize orgasm. Om represents the audible vibration of the universe; according to Patanjali's Yoga Sutras, om is the voice of God itself. An orgasm that ended in om would be one worth having.

after inordinate desire", Ali said, "runs the risk of encountering destruction and death."

A thousand years later, Jonathan Margolis, author of *O: the Intimate History of the Orgasm*, could compare women's "satisfying" orgasms with meagre male ejaculations: "a fleeting feeling not dissimilar, when the emotion is stripped out of it, to common-or-garden urination from an overfull bladder, a sneeze or an urgently needed bowel movement". It doesn't have to be like that, Jonathan (see p.167).

Physical differences

In 1976 the psychologists Ellen Belle Vance and Nathaniel N. Wagner asked students to write down how their own orgasms felt. They then edited out all references to gender and asked experts to guess which descriptions were by men and which by women. None were able do so. A survey conducted by William Hartman and Marilyn Fithian, of Long Beach, California's Center for Marital and Sexual Studies, backed up this view. They found that while there were plenty of differences between people's orgasms, none of these could be separated into distinctively male or female characteristics. What made the biggest difference, they said, was cardiovascular fitness.

Other researchers disagree. Woman have been measured experiencing anything between five and eight major, rhythmic pelvic contractions followed by a sequence of up to a dozen or so more minor and often irregular spasms. Measured in a laboratory, a woman's orgasm can last anything from thirteen seconds to almost a minute.

Men seem, very broadly, to have shorter and less variable orgasms. Most undergo ten to fifteen contractions, not all of which are easily felt, and the entire orgasmic experience lasts a sorry ten to seventeen seconds. Some have irregular contractions after the main series – these orgasms seem to be the longest-lasting – while others have smaller, preliminary contractions. Most simply have different kinds of orgasm on different occasions – they're just not quite as different from each other as women's orgasms are.

The perception of orgasm may make a big difference. The first contractions of orgasm, for many men, feel far and away the biggest and most intense. This may be an effect of ejaculation, which tends to begin on the second contraction and continues for only a few contractions. Women's orgasms, by contrast, may build up in power, or move quickly onto a plateau and then fall off, and the feeling may not be quite as clearly tied to the physical contraction.

As to who has *better* orgasms, only someone who'd enjoyed both could answer. In the early 2000s, an internet message board in the US received a posting from a female-to-male transexual who claimed to experience two different kinds of orgasm. One was felt in his testosterone-stimulated penis (or "neo-phallus"), the other in his vagina. The two, he claimed, were definitely different in "the polarity of the

contractions". His vagina, he felt, contracted from outside to inside, his penis from base to tip.

Of course, a female-to-male transexual does not have exactly the same anatomy as a man born with male genitalia. Underlying the more visible differences between men and women are some remarkable variations. Women have a whole network of linked tissue, blood vessels, muscles and nerves under the skin (see p.47); in men, these tissues are concentrated in the penis. Much of a woman's "orgasmic crescent" would persist even after sex-reassignment surgery – and so, arguably, would the "female"-type orgasm.

Multiple orgasm

According to the feminist psychiatrist, Mary Jane Sherfey, woman have better orgasms for three indisputable biological reasons: their pelvic region and genitals are better supplied with blood, their pelvic muscles are stronger, and they are able to experience multiple orgasms. This last capacity hasn't long been recognized. A 1929 survey found that just five in 100 women were "repeaters", while Kinsey's *Sexual Behavior in the Human Female*, which came out in 1953, reckoned that just one in seven regularly had multiple orgasms. Of course, there's a big difference between being able to have multiple orgasms and actually having them. A society which barely recognized the existence of multiple orgasm and downgraded female sexual pleasure generally was hardly likely to produce women – or indeed men – who pursued multiple orgasms as a matter of habit.

In 1966, Masters and Johnson wrote, in *Human Sexual Response,* that "if a woman is immediately

The orgasmic saint: Teresa of Avila

The Catholic saint Teresa of Avila was highly passionate from an early age. Born in Ávila, Spain, in 1515, she tried to run away with her brother to seek martyrdom at the hands of the local Moorish population – at the age of seven. As she grew up, she began, as a Carmelite website puts it, "to take an interest in the development of her natural attractions and in books of chivalry". This sorry conduct led her father to pack her off to a nunnery.

Once ensconced in a convent, she began to have intense mental experiences. These seemed to rise in levels of intensity from "recollections" and "devotions of peace" to more ecstatic "devotions of union". She interpreted these as evidence of her own mortal sinfulness, and began chastising herself in intense and savage bouts of mortification of the flesh.

On St Peter's Day, 1559, however, she saw a new kind of vision. Seeing "not with the eyes of the body

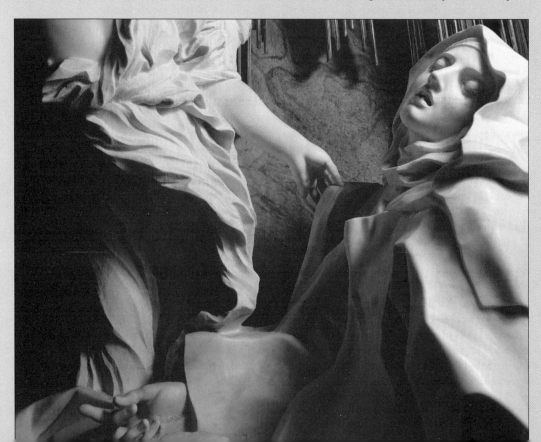

but the eyes of the soul", she perceived Christ standing in front of her "in the full beauty and majesty of his resurrected body". These ecstatic visions continued for two years, during which she repeatedly saw an angel, "not tall, but short, and very beautiful", who held in his hands a spear with a fiery tip. Repeatedly, he pierced her heart with it so that it penetrated to her "very entrails", drawing it out again and leaving Teresa burning with the love of God.

"The pain was so great", she recalled, "that it made me moan; and yet so surpassing was the sweetness of this excessive pain that I could not wish to be rid of it … The pain is not bodily but spiritual; though the body has its share in it. It is a caressing of love so sweet which now takes place between the soul and God." Was this redirected sexuality? Catholic scholars mildly suggest Teresa's earthly words for heavenly union may have been shaped by what she knew of ecstasy. If so, she would not have been the first nor would she be the last to interpret orgasm as a microcosm of divine joy.

The notoriety of Teresa's visions was ensured by Gian Lorenzo Bernini's glorious Baroque sculpture (pictured left), a virtuoso white marble group which stands in the church of Santa Maria della Vittoria, in Rome. The *Ecstasy of St Teresa* shows the beautiful angel with the fiery spear, and an expression on Teresa's face which, for all that it may attempt to show heavenly joy, looks deliriously orgasmic to modern eyes.

stimulated following orgasm, she is likely to experience several orgasms in rapid succession. This is not an exceptional occurrence, but one of which most women are capable." The iconic feminist historian and sex educator Shere Hite pointed out that what they were talking about was really a "sequential orgasm" rather than a "multiple" one. Research by William Hartman and Marilyn Fithian has backed her up. They have shown that the most common multi-orgasmic pattern is for the woman to pause for a minute or two after orgasm – the clitoris can become too tender to touch during this time – and then continue stimulation towards a second orgasm, and often a third, and occasionally a fourth or fifth, or beyond.

Repeat orgasms are, typically, more intense than the first. They're also reached much more quickly – often within one or two minutes, though some women have repeat orgasms as little as thirty seconds apart, or even less. At this point, sequential orgasm shades off into what is best described as "continual orgasm": a much-less common experience in which a woman has orgasm after orgasm with just a few seconds' gap between each. The laboratory record, incidentally, stands at an exhausting 134 orgasms in an hour.

Women who claim to be "multiple" are more likely to have examined their own clitorises, to regularly enjoy oral sex, masturbation and erotic fantasies, or to be in the habit of using thigh pressure to help build up muscular tension towards orgasm. In short, women who are more comfortable with their sexuality are more likely to pursue – and therefore have – multiple orgasms. If you don't try, you'll never know.

Multiple orgasm in men

Some men have extended "aftershock" contractions following orgasm, and can in some cases spin them out by limiting stimulation or stopping it altogether. But to have another full, ejaculatory orgasm, the vast majority of men need an extended "refractory period". The exact time a man needs to pool his resources varies hugely, probably due to the release of widely differing levels of oxytocin and dopamine, chemicals which are capable of killing both desire and erectile function. But many men need an hour or more, unless they're exceptionally aroused.

In fact, men are clinically recognized as multi-orgasmic if they can have two orgasms inside an hour. This feat is apparently achieved by roughly one in ten adult men. And lots of pre-adolescent boys, many of whom are capable of orgasm without ejaculation, and multiple orgasm, to boot. Sadly, this ability either fades gradually through early adolescence, or is lost outright with the arrival of ejaculation.

Men who want to "re-learn" how to have multiple orgasms need to hold back some or all of their ejaculate. This technique – as taught by Tantrists, Taoists (see p.314) and Barbara Keesling in *How to Make Love All Night* – only works for men with a healthy, well-controlled PC muscle (the same muscle that can cut off urine mid-stream). Sexologists Hartman and Fithian recommend clenching this muscle hard just before the moment of ejaculatory inevitability and holding it tightly right through the period when the urge to ejaculate is strongest.

Some experts say that this isn't true multiple orgasm, but merely delayed gratification. A "real", male, multiple orgasm, in which a man has orgasms one after the other, all with ejaculation, is rare indeed. Masters and Johnson witnessed one man ejaculating three times inside ten minutes, but this was exceptional. If not weird.

Frequency and timing

Women may have bigger orgasms, but they have fewer of them. Women, on average, masturbate less frequently, and they're less able to come on demand – even on their own demand. (They're also much more likely to give "freebies", aka the "mercy fuck", where they let their partner orgasm without trying to get off themselves.) The orgasmic deficit is also the result of vaginal intercourse's sheer orgasmic ineffectiveness – matched with its extraordinary persistence as the sexual gold standard in most cultures.

As for the widespread belief that women take much longer to come than men, surveys show that men and women alike are physically capable of giving themselves an orgasm in around four minutes, given the right conditions. Under laboratory conditions the averages for women soar to around twenty minutes, but that probably says more about women and science labs than women and orgasm. Women are often said to prefer an emotional or romantic context, while men may be more inclined to shut their eyes and let fantasy lead them on.

Speed may get you more orgasms, but they may be less intense as a result. And orgasms that arrive way too fast, as with premature ejaculation (see p.168), can be deeply disappointing.

Going down under

In 2001 and 2002, almost twenty thousand Australians aged between 16 and 59 were telephoned and asked detailed questions about their last heterosexual encounter. The result, known as the Australian Study of Health and Relationships or "Richters survey", is a fascinating snapshot of sexual repertoires. The headline figure is that 95 percent of men had an orgasm at their last sexual encounter, an experience enjoyed by just 69 percent of women. (This was a better score rate for women than in Finland, however, where just 56 percent of women in a 1991 national survey reported having had an orgasm the last time they had sex.)

Almost all the "encounters" reported in the Australian study included vaginal intercourse – perhaps because the respondents didn't count the experiences as "sex" if they didn't. But only half the women surveyed had orgasms through vaginal intercourse on its own. Perhaps unsurprisingly, women were much more likely to have had an orgasm if their partner also touched them. This was, in fact, the most common practice of all and it enabled 70 percent of women to come. The rarer combination of touching and cunnilingus with vaginal intercourse was even more effective: it enabled over 85 percent of women to come. Unfortunately, this triple combination was enjoyed by just 20 percent of the women surveyed.

But the most effective sexual act was when women had manual and oral stimulation without vaginal intercourse. When attended to in this considerate way, a triumphant nine out of ten women had an orgasm. You'd think this would recommend it to their partners. In fact, less than 1 percent of women found themselves in this happy situation. To quote the original survey, "it is hard to escape the conclusion that when the man is keen to have sex but the woman is not, intercourse ensues and the man reaches orgasm, but when the woman is keen but the man is not, sex rarely happens."

Moving beyond sexual repertoire, some revealing facts about the contexts of orgasm emerged. Women were significantly less likely to have orgasms in casual sex (50 percent) than in sex with a regular partner (70 percent), while the women most likely to have had an orgasm the last time they had sex were those in relationships between one and two years old (80 percent). The figures for men reflected the same variations, but rose and fell in a much more limited range – around the 95 percent mark. The only exception to this exceptionally high score rate was when men had sex with non-regular partners: a mere 88 percent of Australian men had an orgasm the last time they had casual sex.

Clitoris versus vagina

Whether or not women experience separate "clitoral" and "vaginal" orgasms – and which is best – is the single greatest orgasmic controversy. The pro-vagina campaign has very deep roots. Christianity frowned on sexual pleasure unless it was for the "legitimate" purpose of procreation, so it was always going to value the vagina over the clitoris. Then there was the great masturbatory panic of the eighteenth and nineteenth centuries (see p.339): orgasms produced by hand were tainted by association. Male hubris is another factor: if women can have better orgasms without the penis, where is the sexual role for men?

Ida Craddock's 1900 pamphlet, *The Wedding Night*, was one of the first to recognize that the vagina was, relatively speaking, a "duller tract". But even Craddock, a proto-feminist and free thinker wasn't free of the prejudices of her time. She warned bridegrooms that "There is but one lawful finger of love", and that using the hand would "pervert the act of intercourse". "The clitoris," she continued, "should be simply saluted, at most, in passing, and afterwards ignored as far as possible". She reasoned that it was "a rudimentary male organ" and aroused male-type feelings, thus "sensualizing and coarsening" the woman.

Freud's phallic phase

Sigmund Freud gave the old prejudices about the superiority of the vagina a new rationale. In his 1905 *Three Essays on the Theory of Sexuality*, he speculated that "the leading erotogenic zone in female children is located at the clitoris". At puberty, however, sensitivity was supposed to somehow move from the clitoris to the vagina. If a woman failed to "successfully transfer" her erotic feeling it meant that she was trapped in an immature, "phallic phase".

If vaginal orgasm was the test of sexual maturity, more than half of all women were sexually immature. Freud's fantasies, needless to say, were incredibly influential. In 1928, psychologist Estelle Cole even claimed that clitoral-focused women were frigid: "the vaginal sensations, so necessary for normal and satisfactory intercourse are absent", she claimed. "She has probably been a masturbator and may be unable to rid herself of the habit." Freud was also partly responsible for the pervasive notion that clitoral foreplay is a kind of starter to the main course of penetration. Or, as Freud put it, the clitoris is "like a pile of pine shavings" whose only use is to "set a log of harder wood on fire".

The clitoris emerges

One of the first serious assaults on Freud's thinking was led by Alfred Kinsey. On the evidence of his exhaustive interviews with American women, he asserted that for the vagina to be "the center of sensory stimulation" was physically and psychologically impossibile for "nearly all females." He hailed the clitoris, instead, as the most nerve-rich part of the body – which indeed it was.

From now on, all attention would be focused on the clitoris. Survey after survey showed

Three American women ponder the implications of Kinsey's startling report on female sexuality.

touching it to be far and away the most effective way to produce an orgasm (see p.177). Historians of sex began to find mentions of the clitoris in old medical manuals, references which had previously been misinterpreted, ignored or even suppressed. Magazines everywhere instructed men to track down "the man in the boat" – and men who tried, learned that their partners could come just as easily as them. Women, meanwhile, could begin to value their own, masturbatory orgasms just as highly as orgasms achieved through penetration.

The shift of sexual attention from the vagina to the clitoris was a key victory for feminism – and

for women. The vagina efficiently gives orgasms to men, after all; for women, the clitoris is far better. Shere Hite even called vaginal orgasms "emotional" ones, as opposed to the "real", clitoral ones. But a backlash was coming – from feminists themselves.

The vagina resurgent

Germaine Greer's 1970 polemic, *The Female Eunuch*, claims orgasm is "qualitatively different when the vagina can undulate around the penis instead of a vacancy". In Doris Lessing's 1962 feminist classic, *The Golden Notebook*, the heroine, Ella, asserts that a vaginal orgasm is pure emotion, "a dissolving in a vague, dark generalised sensation like being swirled in a warm whirlpool." Clitoral orgasms may be more various, more thrilling and more powerful, but "there is only one real female orgasm, and that is when a man, from the whole of his need and desire, takes a woman and wants all her response."

Laboratory studies show that direct stimulation of the vagina or cervix without attention to the clitoris *can* generate orgasms which many women describe as "deeper" or more intense. Some women attribute the intensity to a sense of "completeness" – which may be culturally determined. Others believe that orgasmic contractions take place more strongly in the uterine muscles, whereas "clitoral orgasms" set off the PC muscle more strongly.

It may be that in the great rush to the clitoris, the deeper-lying sexually responsive parts of women's body, such as the uterus, the "deep clitoris" and the famed G-spot – the area on the anterior or front wall of the vagina which some believe is the chief driver of vaginal orgasm – have been unfairly neglected.

Convincing circumstantial evidence for the sexual importance of the vagina is provided by the existence of the dildo. Not all the millions sold each year are misguided presents or joke gifts. The reports of high levels of orgasmic sexual encounters among African women who have had their clitorises excised in "circumcision" rites (see p.67), meanwhile, are possible evidence that the clitoris is not necessarily the be-all and end-all of female sexual responsiveness.

Multiple centres

In the early 1970s, Josephine and Irving Singer renamed the clitoral and vaginal orgasms as "vulval" and "uterine". The former was said to centre on the clitoris and PC muscle, the latter to be caused by deep stimulation. Their most convincing argument, however, was that many orgasms are in fact "blended". Evidence increasingly suggests that dividing women's orgasms into "clitoral" and "vaginal" is a grotesque over-simplification.

Today, the scientific emphasis is on the stunning array of possible locations for sexual pleasure, including the clitoris, G-spot, vagina, labia – and indeed the whole body. Research now focuses on the nerves that convey sexual pleasure to the brain, and the brain's activity during orgasm – which can be measured using fMRI scans, or magnetic resonance imaging.

The vagina (along with the cervix and anus) has been found to rely mainly on the pelvic nerve, while the clitoris and labia depend on the pudendal nerve, but still, there's plenty of common ground. One nerve, the vagus or "wandering" nerve, even travels right through the body: fMRI studies done in the 2000s suggest that the vagus may lie behind the extraordinary fact that some women with severe spinal chord injuries have still been able to have orgasms.

Perhaps the only thing it's possible to say with any certainty is that many women perceive differences in the location and the qualitative sensation of their orgasms, and that the huge variation in their perceptions suggests that there's a significant cognitive element to orgasm. In a nutshell: everyone's different.

Ejaculation

For many men, ejaculation lies at the centre of their sexuality. It's not just that part of the pleasure of orgasm lies in the ejaculation, thanks to the fluid pressing down on the urethral tube as it passes through. The key issue is psychological. From puberty onwards, ejaculation is the visible, salty proof of manhood. Yet men can have orgasms without ejaculating. Some learn to do it, while hundreds of thousands of men stop producing semen (but carry on coming) after prostate surgery.

Female ejaculation is more controversial. Some scientists deny it exists; many women tell a very different story. The truth is that it's relatively uncommon, compared to the male version, and relatively poorly understood.

Ejaculatory hydraulics

Male ejaculation is a two-part process. The first, "emission" phase begins at the moment of ejaculatory inevitability or "point of no return", when the body draws itself together like the compression of a spring. Fluid reserves start to pool. Sperm are released from the testicles – anything from 20 to 1000 million of them – and carried by contractions of the vas deferens tubes into the body as far as the ampullae, which lie close against the bladder.

At the same time, seminal plasma is produced. The seminal vesicles, also up near the bladder, secrete a fructose-rich fluid which makes up some three-quarters of semen. (This contains, incidentally, some 6 percent of the vitamin C that the US government recommends as a daily intake.) The prostate gland secretes its own prostatic fluid, making up around fifteen percent of the total. The bulbourethral glands, near the base of the penis, contribute a few extra drops – in fact, this pre-ejaculate or "pre-come" leaks into the urethra as sexual arousal mounts, helping to clean and lubricate the tubes prior to ejaculation.

At orgasm, the sperm moves through the ejaculatory ducts, where it's mixed with the seminal plasma to form semen – aka ejaculate, or come. As the pelvic muscles contract orgasmically, semen is forced along the urethra in pulsing waves – distending the urethral tube as it goes in an intensely pleasurable fashion – and out of the tip of the penis.

How much, how far, how sticky

The speed of semen at this point has been measured at 28mph. Mysteriously, the contractions of the bulbocavernosus muscle are not actually powerful enough to produce such violent spurts. No one's quite sure how it happens, but one convincing theory is that semen builds up pressure behind a sphincter valve whose release is coordinated with the muscular contractions of orgasm.

The force of ejaculation varies dramatically. Men are known to boast of how they once came so hard they hit themselves in the eye. At other times, ejaculate barely leaks out. The sexologist pioneer Alfred Kinsey, who measured it, concluded that macho spurts were pretty rare, coming up with typical figures of anything from inches to, at most, a foot or two – though one man pulled off an eight-foot ejaculation.

Come is typically pearly white, or tinged with grey or yellow. In adolescence, it's often a clear fluid, but for adults it's usually slightly sticky and globular immediately after ejaculation, like a weak gluey paste. (For detail on its taste and smell, see p.111). Within a few minutes, however, enzymes decoagulate the fluid (this serves to liberate sperm from the semen for purposes of conception) and it turns clear and runny, before drying.

In pornography, absolute torrents of ejaculate are produced – stand-in fluids are used for many supposed "come-shots". Real ejaculations fill between half a teaspoon and a teaspoon (2–5cc or 2–5ml). Note that these are official teaspoon measures; actual domestic teaspoons can hold anything from 2.5ml to a whacking 8ml – and a man who could fill one of the latter would be a prodigious ejaculator indeed. That said, it's not impossible. A study by Chen et al in 2003 found upper and lower limits of 8ml and 0.1ml.

Premature ejaculation

Athens must be the only capital city founded on a premature ejaculation. According to Greek myth, the lame blacksmith god Hephaestus tried to rape the virginal Athena, but only managed to ejaculate on her thigh. The disgusted goddess wiped herself with a piece of wool which fell on the ground, thus causing the earth goddess, Gaia, to become pregnant with Athens' future founder king, Erichthonius.

Clinically speaking, premature ejaculation depends on what doctors call ejaculatory latency, meaning the time it takes between a man beginning vaginal intercourse and his ejaculation. Anything under around two minutes, say some doctors, may lead to a diagnosis of "PE". But by these standards, anything between one in ten and a third of men are premature ejaculators. (Which, rather conveniently, turns millions of men into potential customers for drug therapies.) Other doctors set the bar at one minute.

The truth is that almost every man will be a premature ejaculator if his sexual technique centres on vigorous thrusting. Wide definitions of premature ejaculation don't help that minority of men who find themselves in a genuine "hair-trigger" scenario – where he comes off before his clothes do. It doesn't help partners left feeling isolated or unsatisfied, couples who are trying to become pregnant, or young men whose sexual self-confidence is low.

Trigger treatments

The causes of premature ejaculation are hotly disputed but there's little doubt that anxiety is a significant factor. Many boys find greater control over their orgasm as their confidence and experience grows, while many men find themselves coming too quickly in problematic or stressful relationships. Learning to relax during stimulation can be hugely beneficial, therefore – though of course it's easier said than done.

The squeeze technique

The squeeze technique to avoid premature ejaculation requires a particular grip. The thumb sits on the underside of the erect penis (placed just on the frenulum, the small ridge of skin underneath the glans), while the index and middle fingers are placed on the upper side of the glans (the index finger on the head of the penis, the middle finger below it). As the man feels excitement mounting, he (or his partner) squeezes for fifteen to twenty seconds, thus halting ejaculation.

All too often, the squeeze squeezes out the erection. But the technique, properly, is part of a whole programme of behavioural therapy, devised by Masters and Johnson. The man pays close attention to his levels of arousal and re-trains himself to hold back from ejaculation before approaching the "point of no return". The idea is to repeat the start–stop process a number of times before allowing orgasm to take place.

Try breathing slowly and refocusing awareness throughout the body.

The classic treatment is self-distraction. As the medieval Indian manual, the *Ratirahasya*, puts it, "Direct your thoughts to rivers, woods, caves, mountains or other pleasant places, and imagine proceeding through them gently and slowly." It adds, bizarrely, "If you imagine a particularly nimble monkey swinging on the branch of a tree, you will not ejaculate, even though your semen is already at the tip of your penis." Thinking sexually negative thoughts – the "imagine you're

Ejaculate as life force

The idea that semen represents life force is one of the world's most widespread cultural beliefs. Quite where women's vital energy is supposed to reside is usually skated over, though it's often said – by Aristotle, among others – that women have their own mysterious "seed". But for men, the combination of *knowing* that sperm is a key part of conception and *feeling* the lethargy after ejaculation makes it seem like common sense.

The early church father, Tertullian, asked himself "whether we do not, in that very heat of extreme gratification when the generative fluid is ejected, feel that somewhat of our soul has gone from us?" Following this line of thought, the medieval tract, the *Malleus Maleficarum* (or "Witches' Hammer"), reckoned that alluring female dream demons called succubi seduced men as they slept, feeding on their semen as a vampire feeds on human blood. (Vampires may, in fact, be descendants of succubi and their male equivalents, incubi.) The draining of a man's energy could lead to fatigue, exhaustion and, if left unchecked by prayer, death.

Ancient Hindus were convinced of semen's vital power. It was thought to be a kind of distilled version of blood. No less than forty drops of blood were said to be needed to produce one of semen – a ratio that would make a man nervous about excessive expenditure. Retaining semen, by contrast, was considered to be a powerful tonic. Hindu myths are full of gods and renowned ascetics performing marathon stints of austerities to build up their *tapas*, a kind of heat or spiritual energy that one spilled drop of semen would destroy.

In the first millennium AD, Taoist thinkers came up with the idea of *qi* (or *chi*), a life force underpinning the universe. Semen was said to represent its most concentrated form, so Taoist men would go to incredible lengths to preserve it – especially as each man was said only to have a finite amount. Some men stayed celibate, others "pressed the 'P'ing-I' point" on the perineum just before ejaculation, thereby either stopping it entirely, reducing its force, or diverting it into the bladder in a painless process now called retrograde ejaculation. At the same time, men having sex would "harvest" the *qi* lost by their female partners in order to prolong their lives.

Similar beliefs persist in Asia today. In Indonesia, men reportedly justified having sex with other men because their powers were diminished by having sex with women. Doctors and sex therapists throughout India and Pakistan report cases of *dhat* syndrome, a kind of depression characterized by fear of premature ejaculation and the draining away of semen during urination.

In the West, lost semen is often linked to lost potency or creativity. "I've just lost another novel", Balzac is supposed to have said after leaving his mistress's bed, while sportsmen are routinely put on no-sex bans before important matches (despite a complete lack of evidence that it makes any difference to levels of energy or aggression). After the 1982 World Cup, Peruvian football fans actually blamed their team's defeat on players who wouldn't save themselves for the match.

having sex with your grandmother" line – is very common.

The obvious drawback with psychological distraction is that it detracts from pleasure. Simple physical distractions like pinching the skin, biting the lower lip, changing position or thrusting pattern or even gripping the base of the penis may help. So too does a precautionary ejaculation a few hours before an expected encounter – "taking the edge off", as it's called. Or use of more than one condom to reduce sensation. Strengthening the pelvic floor muscles (see p.179) is likely to be more useful over time, as is Masters and Johnson's celebrated squeeze technique.

The most radical solution is to relearn patterns of sexual behaviour. Men don't *have* to come inside their partners, after all. A man can come some time before his partner, too, as long as he's willing to devote themselves to giving oral sex or masturbation afterwards. He may even have enough time to recover and come again. The great thing about having one orgasm is that it gives a man much more control over a second.

For a few men, ejaculation is too premature for any of these behavioural or cultural treatments to work. A leading drug-based treatment is off-label use of selective serotonin reuptake inhibitors (SSRIs) like Prozac. These capitalize on their side effect of increasing levels of serotonin and thus help block ejaculation. Some recommend applying anaesthetic gels to the penis (sometimes pre-coated on the inside of a condom), but these aren't very effective, can cause unpleasant skin reactions and doesn't address the psychological root-causes of PE.

If nothing else works, there's always Giovanni Marinello's 1563 Italian tract, *Medicine Pertinent to the Infirmities of Women*. It recommends tying a string around the testicles so sperm cannot escape. "When the wife feels ready to orgasm," Marinello advises, "she can untie the knot." Cutting off the bloodstream and killing the testicles didn't seem to be a problem in those days.

Female ejaculation

In 1950, the German-born gynaecologist Ernst Gräfenberg – he of the G-spot – watched a woman masturbating to orgasm in his clinic. "Large quantities of a clear, transparent fluid are expelled not from the vulva, but out of the urethra in gushes", he observed, the fluid having "no urinary character".

His observation was largely ignored by sexologists until very recently, even though many women have always known about ejaculation – in the lesbian community, especially. One scientific paper has claimed that slightly more than half of a sample of around 200 women had experienced at least one ejaculation in the course of their sexual lives. Regular ejaculators are thought to be more unusual, though a 1990 survey of 1292 women found that 40 percent expelled some kind of fluid during orgasm.

What's in it?

The quantity typically varies hugely – far more than with men. Anything from a few drops to about 50ml seems typical, though a gushing half litre has been reported. What the fluid is made from is controversial. Out of six lab tests conducted

Seed and spending – the strange history of female ejaculation

Before ovaries were discovered in the seventeenth century, most people believed that human embryos were created by a combination of men's and women's "seed" – the so-called pangenesist theory. Sexual desire was thought to be caused by heat causing blood to froth up in the form of semen, so there was all the more reason to suppose that women had semen. Women felt sexual desire, after all.

The Greek philosopher Aristotle famously observed that the pleasure a woman experiences in sex "is sometimes similar to that of the male, and also is attended by a liquid discharge". He pointed out that it "occurs in some women but not in others" and "when it occurs, is sometimes on a different scale from the emission of semen and far exceeds it."

The second-century anatomist Galen agreed that semen "manifestly flows from women when they experience the greatest pleasure in coitus". The influential eleventh-century Arab physician, Avicenna, went further. He reasoned that sexual desire was an itch engendered by excessive semen, and that sexual intercourse was a scratching of that itch, which was finally relieved by emission of seminal fluid – in men and women alike.

Ancient Chinese and Indian authorities apparently held similar views. The treatise *Secret Methods of the Plain Girl*, which may date back to the third century,

describes how, when the woman's "Jade Gate becomes moist and slippery", the man "should plunge into her very deeply" until, "finally, copious emissions from her Inner Heart begin to exude outward." *Secret Instructions Concerning the Jade Chamber* divides arousal into five states, of which the first is "reddened face", the fourth is "slippery vagina" and the fifth "genitals transmit fluid".

The third-century masterwork of Indian erotic science, the *Kamasutra*, was long thought to hold similar views. It said, "the semen of the female falls in the same way as that of the male". That, at least, was the way the 1883 edition rendered it. A recent translation, however, says instead that "the sensual experience of a woman is manifested just like that of a man" – a reading based on a key medieval commentary which very specifically explains that "a man experiences sensual pleasure when he ejaculates, but a woman does not have that kind of sensual pleasure, because she does not have semen".

Whatever the ancients thought, a surprising number of modern men have believed that female ejaculation was typical of female orgasm. One of the first was the seventeenth-century Dutch anatomist Regnier de Graaf (he who discovered the ovarian follicles – though he himself called them "kleine bollekens", or little testicles). He also wrote about female fluids pouring out "in one gush" and noted the source of this fluid as the female prostate.

By the time the Victorians were writing pornography, it seems to have been widely assumed – by pornographers, at least – that women "spent", as they put it, when they came. In the magazine *The Pearl* (1879), for instance, the young heroine grapples with "a jolly bedfellow ... a beautiful, fair girl, with a plump figure, large sensuous eyes, and flesh as firm and smooth as ivory." The girls' adolescent gropings soon come to a climax; as the heroine describes it: "'Ah! Oh! Rub harder, harder – quicker', she gasped, as she stiffened her limbs out with a kind of spasmodic shudder, and I felt my finger all wet with something warm and creamy.'"

It wasn't just male pornographers who believed that most women ejaculated. One of the biggest-selling marriage manuals of the pre-war era, the Dutch gynaecologist Theodoor van de Velde's *Ideal Marriage*, observed that "the majority of laymen believe that something is forcibly squirted (or propelled or extruded), or expelled from the woman's body orgasm, and should so happen normally, as in the man's case". He also pointed out that this doesn't happen as often as people thought it did. The situation today, ninety-odd years later, is a strange reversal. Most sex manuals strive to point out that female ejaculation is more common than is usually thought.

to date, four found it wasn't the same as urine, with substantially lower levels of urea and creatine, while two labs reckoned there was little difference.

Most women who investigate say it doesn't smell acrid, like urine. One sex researcher's student drank a kind of blue dye before masturbating to orgasm, ejaculating and then urinating. While her urine came out a deep blue, her ejaculate only had a hint of colour. Women who have ejaculated in a relatively modest way often describe a mucous-like fluid which can be clear, milky or have a yellow tinge. More prolific gushers report producing a more watery liquid.

Vaginal lubricants seem to play a part, as does a milky fluid secreted from the paraurethral (aka Skene's) glands, which are embedded in the prostate. In fact, some of the same proteins and enzymes produced by the male prostate, and present in semen, have also been found in female ejaculate – and in post-orgasmic female urine as well, which suggests that prostatic fluid may backwash into the bladder on orgasm. This in turn opens the remarkable possibility that most or all women ejaculate, but only some know that they do.

Until more research is done, exactly where female ejaculate comes from, and exactly what it is, will remain controversial. Framing the debate are, on the one hand, the British Board of Film Classification, which bans female ejaculation on the grounds that urination during sex cannot be shown on UK screens. On the other side of the debate, the last word can be left to the porn actress Cytherea: "I'm a grown fucking woman", she told Xtreme magazine. "I know what it feels like when I'm fucking peeing ... I know what it's like when I'm fucking orgasming! ... At least do some fucking research."

How to do it – and whether to try

Since the 1980s, a spate of assertive books and videos have promoted the cause. At the moment of orgasm, women are advised to fight the urge to control their bladders, instead letting go: "Press out and relax your pelvic muscles," says the-clitoris.com, and "welcome the feeling of the liquid escaping from your bladder". (The website also suggests that women empty their bladders before beginning to explore their ejaculatory function.)

Many ejaculatory experts recommend stimulating the G-spot (if you're looking for it, see p.47). Whether or not this influences ejaculation directly or just intensifies the orgasm isn't clear. The usual methods are with the beckoning or "come-hither" gesture or a dildo – up-curved ones more efficiently reach the prostatic area. Without assuming success, having towels handy would be a good idea.

Some women who achieve ejaculation find it empowering. Fanny Fatale, a self-described sex activist who produces a video called *How to (Female) Ejaculate*" even claims that it's unhealthy *not* to. Other women are suspicious of this kind of approach. Ejaculation is a quintessentially male obsession, so why should women feel the need to compete? Is ejaculation yet another sexual standard that women will feel obliged to live up to – and will be liable to fail against? Are women trying to piss higher up the wall?

Finding, losing and improving orgasm

In very broad terms, if you believe the surveys, something like a third of women have them sometimes, a third have them more often than not, and another third have them rarely. Yet almost all women can come, physiologically speaking. When they don't, it may be because they don't know how to or haven't had enough opportunity to practice.

The picture in men is almost the reverse. If a man can have an orgasm, he will. On the whole, it's only when serious health problems occur – erectile dysfunction (see p.288), diabetes, prostate cancer – that orgasm is lost. And even lack of erection need be no bar to orgasm. Whether or not men have *good* orgasms, of course, is another issue.

Anorgasmia

Shere Hite's survey of 3000 American women painted a bleak picture: 12 percent of the women who replied to her said they never had orgasms. This isn't quite the same thing as saying they *have* never had an orgasm. One German study found that 99 percent of women had experienced at least one orgasm by the age of 27.

True or "primary" anorgasmia, or the complete absence of orgasm, is rare – and not to be confused with lack of desire, problems with arousal or problems achieving orgasm with a partner. It's only diagnosed when sexual response and excitement follow the usual patterns but orgasm, frustratingly, doesn't follow.

The Canadian hypno-psychotherapist Bryan M. Knight claims that if a woman isn't having orgasms then, setting aside biological considerations, she "was sexually abused as a child. She has a need to feel in control. She's having sex with an inconsiderate or unknowledgeable person. She'd be responsive to a woman". This puts it rather baldly – and leaves out the potential role of traumas such as sexual assaults – but there's some truth to it. Many women who enter lesbian relationships for the first time describe discovering orgasm – or dramatically improved ones, anyway. And many women who seek therapy or help finding orgasm have histories of sexual violence. (For more on this topic, including resources and support organizations, see p.346).

Knight's idea that women need to relinquish control to have orgasms is controversial. Relaxation is important, and orgasm itself is, physologically speaking, a release of tension. But many sex therapists reckon that a woman needs to *take* control of her own orgasm, not give it up. The widespread cultural belief that people "give" each other orgasms may even be a significant barrier to orgasmic success in women. It would be more accurate – and far more useful – to say that women give orgasms to themselves.

For heterosexual women, the problem is potentially particularly acute. According to Jane Roy, psychosexual training coordinator for Relate, the UK's respected sex and relationship therapy organization, "women are still holding back because they imagine that in order to fully enjoy sex and reach orgasm the man has to be in control and the woman has to lose control. Whereas an orgasm is something you choose, when you are ready." A man who thrusts in and out of a woman's vagina is basically awarding himself an orgasm; if women want to have orgasms during vaginal intercourse they need to pursue them with similar dedication.

The Hite Report, first published in 1976, revealed that many women never had orgasms.

Sexual awareness

Poor sexual awareness also causes anorgasmia. A 1990 study of poor field workers in Brazil found that anorgasmia was fairly common – but then a third of the women in the study did not even know that sexual intercourse was normal in marriage. Even in liberal, developed countries, orgasm itself is relatively rarely discussed. Children can go through years of biology and sex education classes in which it is barely mentioned. Parents who will happily explain the mechanics of conception and contraception, and even lovemaking techniques, may shrink from discussion of what keeps the whole merry-go-round turning.

The sex therapists Hartman and Fithian reported that of twenty women clients who came to them for help because they couldn't experience orgasm, fifteen were in fact having orgasms. They simply weren't aware of it. Hartman and Fithian commented, "It is as if the modern mythology and cult of orgasm has placed the sensation on such a pedestal – created such an aspirational 'super-brand' of it' – that women perfectly capable of orgasm refuse to believe they are having a legitimate one and must instead be experiencing an inferior imitation brand."

The other kind of sexual awareness is more literal: body-awareness. "Sensate focus" is a therapy technique for improving sexual satisfaction, including orgasm. The name explains itself: it's all about focusing on the body, and driving out anxious or distracting thoughts. Similarly, urologists who have prescribed low, "off-label" doses of the "hyperactivity" drug, Ritalin, have found it seems to improve orgasmic response. This would be no surprise to the users of marijuana and other perception-altering drugs who have found that it can ramp up the intensity of orgasmic experiences as much as musical or other ones.

Physical problems

Some orgasms are lost – or never-found – for biological reasons. Depressed levels of sex hormones such as testosterone (in men and women) and oestrogen can result in loss of libido and, eventually, loss of orgasm. Lower levels of oxytocin seem to relate to the perception of how intense an orgasm is – which makes it quite possible for gentle orgasms to come in below the radar. Recent research on twins suggests that anorgasmia may even be genetically influenced.

Drugs and disease, however, are probably the commonest causes of orgasmic problems. Diabetes can cause loss of erectile function for men, and loss of desire in both sexes. Multiple sclerosis can have similar effects, with the added complication that many men and women with MS, perhaps the majority, experience numbness or lack of sensation – which can seriously affect the possibility of reaching orgasm. Parkinson's Disease, similarly, often affects the ability to sense differences in textures.

Like a canary in a mine, libido is often one of the first things to be hit by the side effects of drugs. Few seem to specifically affect orgasmic ability, but there is a major exception: SSRIs such as Prozac (a trade name for fluoxetine). These antipsychotic and antidepressant drugs effectively act by increasing the amount of serotonin in the brain. (They block the amount of serotonin that is re-absorbed by pre-synaptic neurons after it has done its work; that is, after it has transmitted a neural impulse. This in turn means that serotonin is maintained at higher levels in the brain.) But serotonin seems to depress sexual arousal and, at high enough levels, can block orgasm.

Finders keepers – masturbation and orgasm for women

Most men discover orgasm through masturbation, a topic which is relatively freely discussed among boys, in most Western countries at least. The same may not be true among girls, where parental prohibitions, negative sexual feelings and sexual anxiety have tended to keep a stronger grip. And women who don't masturbate are probably less likely to be able to achieve orgasm with another person.

There are other gender-specific barriers to orgasm. Unlike boys, who hold their penises many times a day when they urinate, girls tend to be less familiar with their own genitals. And female masturbation is a far less visible part of general culture. The "wanker" gesture, for instance, is a staple of street life; the "shaky fingers" sign for female masturbation, however, is rarely seen. The result is that some women don't know enough about masturbation to do it successfully – or are afraid, or feel too guilty, to persist long or hard enough to get over the cultural barriers.

Getting in training

In Rebecca Chalker's *The Clitoral Truth*, a woman who had never had an orgasm describes how she finally discovered the experience in her mid-thirties. She ran a hot bath, put on some music, lay back and began slowly massaging herself. As she experimented with different strokes (for which, see p.94), she began feeling a change; she was becoming aroused. "Then, quite by accident", she recalled, "I found the one that worked. I put my index and middle fingers into my vagina curving them around the pubic bone and used hard, fast strokes pulling the glans down and the inner lips in. I visualized the clitoral muscles and could feel them getting tighter."

She had her first orgasm. She didn't feel spasms, but felt "this sort of golden glow in the clitoris that spread through my pelvis and down my legs like warm honey. My legs felt weightless and for maybe twenty seconds – who can tell time in this situation – my feet sort of went spastic. Then, without warning, I burst into tears."

Encouragingly, once orgasm is learned, it's rarely forgotten. The bathtime experience described above combines a number of the key techniques. Masturbation comes first, often combined with use of a vibrator (see p.142) – which can provide intense and accurate stimulation. Relaxation and the cultivation of a sense of self-reward are important too. Then there's the "sensate focus" technique taught by Masters and Johnson (see p.176), in which a woman moves from non-sexual to sexual touch, concentrating on the sensations all the way through. Finally, there's training of the PC muscle, which can be in the form of Kegel exercises and visualization techniques. All of these techniques can be used to improve or intensify orgasm, as well as to find it in the first place.

Improving orgasm

Orgasms tend to be bigger if they're delayed. For men, especially, there's a huge difference between the casual, "quick wank" orgasm and the one which finally steams in after hours of expectation, seduction and maddening rises and falls in stimulation.

The sex writer Barbara Keesling recommends monitoring arousal levels. "Let them rise in a set of peaks from one to ten", she says, "pausing as each level is achieved". This method works on a key orgasmic principle: the juxtaposition of tension and relaxation. It's almost as if the threshold of orgasm can be deliberately lifted by increasing stimulation until it's almost reached, and then letting arousal drop away again. You could call it two steps forward, one step back. Some refer to this as "edging" – a technique also used by men to improve sexual stamina.

Clenching or tensing muscles in the rectum, thighs and stomach can drive a more intense orgasm. Many people stiffen right through the body as they enter orgasm, but relaxing the body at this point can produce intense results. As Rebecca Chalker points out in *The Clitoral Truth*, a relentlessly stiff posture can be limiting; "try dancing like that", she says.

The scientists of orgasm, Barry R. Komisaruk and Beverly Whipple, reckon that orgasm works best if stimulation follows, or is echoed by, a strong rhythmic cycle. This could be the thrusting of vaginal intercourse, the buzz of a vibrator, or the alternate stretching and relaxing of the legs. Spreading the legs wide then pressing them tight together again can be very effective. So can pushing them out – like a ballet dancer going up onto *pointe* – then bringing them in again towards the chest.

The orgasmic potential of rocking chairs and swings has been known for centuries. Another incredibly powerful rhythm is set by the squeezing and releasing of the PC muscle. Some women with a strong PC muscle can orgasm without clitoral stimulation simply by clenching and releasing – and this is a useful technique for women who want to come during vaginal intercourse.

Many people hold their breath as they come, which can sometimes seem to "cap" the orgasm. Try holding and releasing rhythmically, breathing deeply, or consciously panting instead. Sounds or moans can help deepen the breathing and intensify the orgasmic experience – and they can have the very useful side benefit of providing much-needed encouragement to a partner who's working hard for your pleasure.

One experiment worth trying is watching yourself have an orgasm in a mirror. It may not intensify orgasm, but it might deepen understanding of what it does.

Kegeling to orgasm

A powerful pelvic floor makes for a powerful orgasm, so strengthening the PC muscle is probably the single most useful way to improve orgasm. The PC or pubococcygeus muscle is the same one that allows men and women to cut off urination mid-flow – in men, it also makes the erect penis twitch. It stretches from the pubic bone, at the front of the body, right through to the coccyx, at the base of the spine, forming a kind of supportive tent for everything inside the pelvis, and encircling the rectum and genitals.

In the 1940s and 1950s, gynaecologist Arnold Kegel worked out a way for women who had become incontinent after childbirth to recover urinary control. He invented an instrument which could provide them with feedback on their own internal vaginal pressure – a rubber hose with a pressure meter on one end and a dildo-like sensor on the other – so that they could exercise their pelvic floor muscles and at the same time see how hard they were working. It wasn't long before clients using his "Perineometer" began reporting having orgasms – some of them for the first time.

Betty's barbells

Modern perineometers have names like Gyneflex, FeminX and KegelMaster. Some are spring-loaded devices, others are weights, others still, squeezable rubber bulbs. The "Barbell", as sold by veteran sex writer Betty Dodson on bettydodson. com, is stainless steel, just under seven inches long and weighs a little under one pound (450g). It is "sturdy enough to become a family heirloom", says Dodson, "that can be passed down from grandmother to granddaughter". In Dodson's early 1970s orgasm workshops, women apparently took turns using a metered perineometer (hygienically supplied with a condom), egging each other on to greater feats of pelvic floor strength like men swinging mallets to ring a bell at the circus.

Nowadays, people doing Kegel excercises – or "kegels" – usually tense, hold and relax their PC (pubococcygeus) muscle repeatedly without working against the resistance of a perineometer – though you can still buy them (see box on p.179). This makes it possible to exercise anywhere, but some people find it hard to locate the muscle to start with, or don't squeeze hard or long enough. The easiest way to find the PC muscle is to cut off the flow of urine in midstream. The resulting backwash can theoretically cause infections but a few exploratory squeezes shouldn't hurt. Alternatively, women can put a finger in their vagina and men can insert a (well-lubricated) finger into their anus.

The right kind of squeeze will put considerable pressure on the finger. It's usually described as a lifting motion, rather than a bearing down. The trick is to keep other muscles in the legs, buttocks and stomach relaxed. A typical exercise session might involve holding the PC muscle squeezed for ten seconds, then relaxing, and repeating this action ten times – and doing this anything from two to four times a day. Other therapists recommend repeated squeezes and relaxations – say two sets of twenty, morning and evening.

Orgasm and health

Mae West reckoned that an orgasm a day kept the doctor away. It's more true than she could have known. A 1997 survey in the UK by the Bristol-based epidemiologists George Davey Smith, Stephen Frankel and John Yarnell showed that men who have frequent orgasms – which they defined as two or more a week – have half the risk of death from heart attack or stroke than men who had orgasms only once a month. The risk of "death in the saddle" (see box, opposite) is much exaggerated.

Some of the health benefits of orgasm are connected to emotional satisfaction. One headline survey, for instance, asserted that regular sex could make people look "ten years younger" – though this basically reflects the fact that people who are in positive, stable relationships are happy. A 1982 study of elderly Americans found masturbators were less depressed. Kinsey even reckoned people

Sex headaches

The only known health problem associated with coming is orgasmic cephalalgia, a condition where orgasm triggers an explosively intense headache, often behind the eyes. It usually lasts fifteen or twenty minutes, but can linger for hours. These headaches are often experienced by migraine sufferers, and are most common in men in their early twenties or late thirties and early forties. They're probably caused by increased blood pressure, and can sometimes be treated with beta blockers or anti-migraine drugs – taken beforehand. Another kind of sex headache is sometimes called coital cephalgia. It seems to be caused by tension in the head and neck muscles, and the treatment is simpler: relaxation after orgasm.

Death in the saddle

"Death in the saddle" or "la mort d'amour", is rarer than folk wisdom would have it, causing just 3 in 1000 sudden deaths, according to one survey, and 3 out of 500 deaths among people with heart disease, according to a third.

It may be rare, but it follows a typical pattern: in the words of one medical examiner, "the deceased is usually married" and "he is with a nonspouse in unfamiliar surroundings after a big meal with alcohol". A German team which reviewed 21,000 autopsy reports found 39 cases of sex-related coronaries, and found that most occurred "during the sexual act with a prostitute".

Ageing men with a taste for high-living, experimentation and commercial sex should beware, then, but the rest can relax. Or can they? Sex-researcher Leonard Derogatis suggests that autopsies are misleading as they may only take place when a death is suspicious or puzzling. If non-adulterous sex is, say, three times as frequent as the autopsy-provoking kind then, he estimates, there are more than 11,000 sex-related deaths in the US every year – roughly the same number as killed by food poisoning or brain cancer.

If the statistics are true, then surprisingly few famous people have died in the saddle – or perhaps the exact circumstances tend to be covered up. Attila the Hun is often said to have died while having sex. In fact, the Greek historian Priscus of Panium recounts how, after a feast celebrating his marriage to a nubile young spouse, he retired to bed reeling from drink and died in his sleep by choking on his own nosebleed. Which is a less heroic way to go.

The death of French president Félix Faure, in 1899, is perhaps the most notorious. He is said to have been finished off by a blow job, and his society mistress was quickly dubbed "pompe funèbre", a word that means "undertaker" in French but could be rendered "funeral cocksucker". Society gossips circulated other double entendres. When a priest arrived at the scene he supposedly asked a servant whether Faure still had his *connaissance*, meaning was he still conscious; the servant, thinking the priest was using a slang word for a mistress, replied: "no, we showed her out by the back door". The statesman Georges Clemenceau, meanwhile, claimed Faure wanted to be Caesar but only ended up Pompey (*pompée* meaning "sucked off").

One of the few women alleged to have died of orgasm was Catherine the Great of Russia – supposedly while having sex with a stallion. Catherine had taken many lovers during her reign, and was known for her delight in exotic animals, but in reality the two pleasures remained separate. She was, after all, 67 years old at the time of her death in 1796, and rival factions at home and abroad were quick to try to smear her and thus undermine her political successors. The less extravagant truth is that she had a stroke in a closet adjoining her bathroom and never recovered consciousness.

who came frequently were less hostile and less violent – an idea developed by Alex Comfort, author of 1970s classic *The Joy of Sex*, who reckoned that sexual play provided a safe discharge of aggression. Making Love, for Dr Comfort, really was the cure for Making War.

Other orgasmic benefits can actually be proven. The endorphins released at orgasm are known to boost immunoglobulin A, which plays a key role in the immune system. The hormone, dehydroepiandrosterone (DHEA), which promotes coronary health, surges at orgasm. Higher levels of oxytocin and DHEA, meanwhile, seem to protect against cancer.

Oxytocin is a key chemical link between sex and health. It is released into the bloodstream at orgasm, washing away stress. Along with the endorphins released, it's also hugely beneficial in helping people fall asleep. In fact, sleep is probably orgasm's single greatest contribution to physical and mental health. And people know it: survey after survey has shown that significant numbers of men and women masturbate in order to relax and get to sleep – 39 percent of women, according to Carol Ellison's 2000 study.

Orgasm also relieves pain – as anyone who has hurt themselves in the throes of ecstasy and only noticed afterwards is well aware. It effectively targets migraine and menstrual cramps – Ellison found that 9 percent of women masturbated to relieve period pain. Women who orgasm during their period are also less likely to develop endometriosis (where the tissues that line the uterus grow in the wrong areas and become inflamed). And women who have orgasms while pregnant have a greater likelihood of the pregnancy going to full term.

Ejaculation may have its own benefits. Research from the Cancer Epidemiology Centre in Melbourne, Australia, found in 2003 that men in their twenties who ejaculated more than five times a week were a third less likely to suffer from aggressive prostate cancers later in life. The likely explanation was that "cleaning the tubes" regularly prevented carcinogens from building up in prostate fluid. Dr Gordon Gallup of the State University of New York has even claimed that semen has health benefits for women: at least, his 2002 survey found that women whose partners didn't use contraception were measurably happier.

Perhaps the most obvious benefit of orgasm is cardiovascular, as doubling the pulse rate is undoubtedly very good for the heart. The challenge for fitness experts is to develop orgasm into a programme of three twenty-minute sessions a week.

Hysterical paroxysms

Doctors have prescribed orgasm for centuries, chiefly as a cure for the mysterious condition called "hysteria". The word means "womb disease", but it doesn't refer to gynaecology. According to the venerable Hippocratic tradition of ancient Greece, hysteria was "suffocation of the womb", and caused by lack of sexual expression.

One prevalent view, shared by Plato, was that the womb was a kind of roving creature, half-independent of the woman who bore it. It was thought to move around the body seeking moisture. According to the *Timaeus*, "The animal within them is desirous of procreating children, and when remaining unfruitful gets discontented and angry, and wandering in every direction through the body drives them to extremity, causing all varieties of disease."

Some physicians made their patients sniff foul scents, to drive the womb away from the head, while introducing sweet, aromatic herbs to the vagina, to attract it back to its proper place. Others instructed virgins to get themselves married. The second-century Roman physician Galen, more practically, advised fellow physicians to rub the hysterical woman until she felt "the pain and at the same time the pleasure".

In the Middle Ages, the theory of hysteria found its way back to Europe via Arab medics. In the middle of the fifteenth century, the Pavian physician Giovanni Matteo Ferrari da Gradi advised midwives to "use sweet-smelling oil on

French neurologist Jean-Martin Charcot demonstrates female "hysteria" with a hypnotized patient at La Salpêtrière hospital in Paris.

Faking it

Faking orgasm is nothing new. Ovid's licentious Latin poem, *The Art of Love*, suggests putting on an act if you can't do it for real. But "take care that you make your performance convincing," he warned: "thrash about in a frenzy, roll your eyes, let your cries and gasping breath suggest what pleasure you're getting".

Things haven't changed much in two thousand years. The Hollywood star Candice Bergen once confessed "I may not be a great actress but I've become the greatest at screen orgasms." Asked to elaborate on the niceties of her technique, she suggested "Ten seconds of heavy breathing, roll your head from side to side, simulate a slight asthma attack and die a little." Off-screen fakers may need a little more finesse. Few cinematic orgasms would pass muster in the real world – a fact that's remarkable in itself.

Feminists are none too keen on faking orgasm. *Cosmopolitan* magazine once asked "who has two spare hours to make him feel better about not making you feel great?" It's true that women who admit faking in surveys also tend to say that they do it in order to prevent their lovers – especially their male lovers – feeling inadequate. A 1985 survey of women in Puerto Rico, where male culture is famously macho, found that more than half of the women in the study said they put on a show in order "to avoid a vanity-fuelled interrogation from their male partner".

Faking is decried by relationship experts on the grounds that it is habit-forming – as if one too many fake orgasms will make the real one disappear. Lies in relationships can be dangerous, but pulling the odd fast one can be very handy. And in an age of condom-use, a convincing male fake is now possible. Sometimes you just don't want to go through all the effort of getting there – and you don't want to get into a debate with your lover about why you haven't, either.

her finger and move it well in a circle inside the vulva" in order to procure "pleasure and pain" combined, and a cure. In the 1680s, the medic Thomas Sydenham diagnosed hysteria, after fever, as "the most common disease, especially among women". It was thought responsible for fainting and epileptic fits, nervous twitches and all kinds of sleeping and eating disorders. Some doctors applied tight bandages. Others prescribed orgasms.

Treating hysteria

Nineteenth-century doctors no longer believed in wandering wombs, but they still believed in hysteria. French neurologist Jean-Martin Charcot linked it to the nervous system, and produced women displaying "grand hysteria" to enthusiastic lecture audiences. Their symptoms were described in a book by his colleague, Desiré Magloire Bourneville, alongside some remarkably orgasmic photographs. "Her body curves into an arc and holds this position for several seconds", he wrote, noting "movements of the pelvis" in which "she raises herself, lies flat again, utters cries of pleasure, laughs, makes several lubricious movements and sinks down onto the vulva and right hip."

The nineteenth-century cure was marital sex – preferably followed by childbirth, but where this wasn't available, other outlets were recommended, from riding to the use of swings, rocking chairs and hammocks. Another common treatment was pelvic massage or "vulvular stimulation", performed by either a doctor or a midwife. Doctors became expert at masturbating women to induce a "convulsive crisis" or "hysterical paroxysm". Strangely, these paroxysms were seen as quite distinct from sexual orgasms.

Yet many doctors found pelvic massage tedious, distasteful or hard to master. They were saved first by electric vibrators, which arrived in the 1880s, and then by psychology. Charcot's work in Paris influenced Sigmund Freud, whose seminal 1895 essay on hysteria claimed that it was caused by repression of sexual trauma. The original emotional reaction, he said, was seeking outlet in the wrong channels – a process very similar to the age-old wandering womb theory. Freud dubbed this process "conversion" (though he later came to believe that sexual fantasies lay behind all symptoms). Its result was that instead of lying on a bed and being treated with health-giving orgasms, women were now supposed to lie on a couch and talk their way to sanity.

Unusual orgasms

The Surrealist self-publicist Salvador Dalí claimed to have experienced his first orgasm while scrambling up a tree. But then, he also claimed to have fallen in love with the tree afterwards, so perhaps he shouldn't be trusted. Women have occasionally reported experiencing spontaneous orgasms in response to critical moments of acute stress or anxiety. Epileptics, meanwhile, have described feeling orgasmic sensations during the "aura" moment before a seizure comes on. Neither phenomenon has yet been explained.

Thought orgasms

Despite the near-ubiquity of the "wet dream" in adolescent boys (and a very few girls), no one knows how orgasm can be produced by the brain alone, during sleep – if this is indeed what is happening. Some put wet dreams down to half-accidental self-stimulation of the erections that men have during sleep, by rubbing against bedclothes for instance.

Non-mechanical orgasms in waking life are far more rare. Kinsey's 1948 report claimed to have tracked down just three or four men – out of some 5000 – who could ejaculate without any bodily stimulation at all. This feat was famously achieved by the diarist Samuel Pepys (see box on p.100). The playwright Tennessee Williams recalled in a 1973 interview with *Playboy* magazine how he

The cult of simultaneous orgasm

In her classic 1918 manual, *Married Love*, Marie Stopes described the "mutual climax" as the great goal of sex. It could change marriage from being "brutalized and hopeless and sodden" to "rapturous, spiritual and vital". It was "a mutual, not a selfish, pleasure," she said, "more calculated than anything else to draw out an unspeakable tenderness and understanding in both partakers of this sacrament".

Stopes was speaking with the whole weight of Victorian values behind her. The Victorians had elevated marriage above all other sacraments, and made sex the key ritual within it. The high moment of that ritual was the mutual and simultaneous orgasm. D.H. Lawrence – no upholder of Victorian values – even turned these same mystical ideas into the grounding theory of his fiction. For him, simultaneous orgasm was the "only evidence of a perfect union". It was the bread and wine of love, the unique provider of spiritual health.

Simultaneous orgasm was also thought to be health-inducing. In a world where men and women were thought to have vital, energizing fluids, and these were present at their most concentrated in the man's and woman's "seed", the only safe act involved the equal exchange of these precious commodities. Some – including Stopes – even took the view that mutuality was the way to ensure conception. If having sex without the goal of bearing children was morally dubious, this made double-handed orgasm even more important: it proved the lovers' good intentions.

Unfortunately, the cult of simultaneous orgasm was at its height at the same time as the cult of vaginal intercourse. And the two do not, on the whole, go well together – a fact which must have led thousands, perhaps millions, of couples to feel that they were not just failing in their sex lives but proving with each act of failure that they were not spiritually bound together. Still, who's to say that simultaneous orgasm, if it can be achieved, doesn't strengthen the loving bond? It's certainly enjoyable. As the Latin poet Ovid put it: "both should pass the winning-post neck and neck – that's the height of pleasure, when man and woman lie knocked out at once."

was in love with his college roommate. "I was so puritanical", he remembered, "I wouldn't permit him to kiss me. But he could just touch my arm and I'd come. Nothing planned, just spontaneous orgasms." (Williams also recorded orgasms meticulously in his notebooks, describing sex as when "the nightingales sang" and masturbation as "the desecration of the little god".)

As for women, if you believe the responses to an appeal by myth-busting syndicated newspaper column, "The Straight Dope", they're more readily capable of hands-free orgasm. Respondents claimed to have come, variously, as a result of: phone sex, oral sex, cyber sex, kissing, while talking to a boyfriend, while sleeping, while lying on the beach fantasizing and while reading erotic stories.

The "hypersexual" subject of a 1950 study – on blood pressure, and the effect of orgasm upon it – was able to bring herself to orgasm five times in succession merely by thinking about it. (Interestingly, the lack of "physical interference" was one reason the experiment was able to take place in such a conservative era.) Kim Airs, who learned her techniques from the feminist sex activist Annie Sprinkle, has managed to convince sexologists in a modern lab that she can come by thought alone – or rather, in her own words, by using chakras and energy waves. One witness described her taking long slow breaths for a minute then "her face flushed pink and she shuddered". It doesn't sound earth-moving, but heart rate, blood-pressure and contractions don't lie.

Accidental orgasms

Accidental orgasms are rarely welcomed. A mother from Saudi Arabia complained to her doctor of "repeated uncontrolled orgasms" – as many as thirty of them in a day, and they were tormenting her. A Taiwanese woman was no happier about the orgasms that happened every time she brushed her teeth. She started using mouthwash.

Orgasms are known to take place during breastfeeding – which certainly surprises the women who experience it. The trigger is probably the neurohormone oxytocin, which plays a double role in activating the milk reflex in the breast, and being secreted into the bloodstream and spinal cord at the moment of orgasm. Somewhere along

the line – possibly in the brain region known as the paraventricular nucleus of the hypothalamus – the two actions can cross-talk. (Nursing mothers who have conventional orgasms, meanwhile, have sometimes noticed milk leaking or spurting from their nipples with each contraction.)

Still more cross-referencing goes on at childbirth. During labour, some women have reported having orgasmic sensations – albeit mixed in with pain – which may be due to the hypogastric nerve sharing responsibility for feeling in both the uterus and cervix.

Non-genital orgasms

Shared nerve pathways are probably behind other non-genital orgasms, though prostate tissue seems to be emerging as an orgasmic source in its own right – whether accessed through anal sex, stimulation of the cervical sponge in women or prostate massage in men. A few people are able to have orgasms courtesy of the nerve-rich mouth or nipples.

Other locations are also possible. Women who wrote in to "The Straight Dope" said they'd had orgasms from having their earlobes, fingers, or necks touched, from using a back scratcher, from having their hair tugged and simply from having an over-full bladder. Other surveys have unearthed a man who claimed to have come thanks to applying a vibrator to his knee (though admittedly, he was high on marijuana at the time.) Most weirdly, another man experienced phantom orgasms where his amputated foot used to be.

There's better-documented evidence of non-genital orgasm in cases of people with severe spinal-cord injuries – where it can be proved that the usual nerve pathways from the genitals to the brain have been blocked. Forty to fifty percent of people supposedly without feeling below a certain point on the spine have experienced distinctively orgasmic feelings when the skin on the area near their original injury, or the skin on nerve-rich areas higher up the body, has been given the right kind of stimulation. Even if there were no contractions, the sensation produced orgasmic-type sensations of "warmth" and "tingling", with energies apparently "releasing" and "merging" in the genital region.

Sex/Life

5
Sex/Life

Sex is sometimes said to be one of the only ways in which adults still play. Real play, that is, as children play: lost in the game and the moment. At its best, sex really can be like that, but it is otherwise powerfully linked with the wider context of a life. How sex works – and how well it works – depends hugely on when it's happening, and who to, and who with. First-time sex isn't at all the same thing as sex between older people in a forty-year relationship, even if it has plenty of similarities.

The human lifespan is often measured by key moments in social and professional development: the first day at school or at work, graduation day, marriages and anniversaries, promotions and house-moves. These are the photographs put on public display, the red-letter days talked about in wedding or retirement speeches. Most people have another set of markers, however, more personal or more intimate, but easily as powerful. It's made up of memories (but rarely photographs) of the key sexual events: first crush, first period, first wank, first time; coming out, getting together, splitting up; that one-night stand; that time in the back of the car; that day we made the baby; that argument and make-up session. These events create the sexual lifespan.

Infancy and childhood

The path to being either female or male is not quite as unwavering as it's often assumed to be: intersexuality is far more common than the world acknowledges with its either/or tick-boxes and toilets (see p.74). But sex, meaning maleness or femaleness, does begin at the very beginning: with the fertilization of a woman's ovum, or egg, by a man's sperm. Sexuality, however, meaning sexual feelings and responses, is very much a process. Childhood is the very womb of sexuality, nurturing it and protecting it as it grows. Every human has a different sexual development, created by different experiences and conditions even though certain developmental stages are shared.

Girls will be girls and boys, boys

This meeting of the two gametes brings together genetic information from both parents, carried on chromosomes, which have been described as microscopic shoe trees for genes. Each gamete – each parent – contributes twenty-three. You could also think of chromosomes as massive decks of cards, with each card representing a gene. When they meet at fertilization, the genes combine and cross over in a sort of mega-shuffle. The result is a unique being with its own set of chromosomes: a zygote. Just two chromosomes are responsible for determining a zygote's future sex: X and Y. (They get their names because that's roughly how their protein structures look when they're flattened out and examined under a microscope.) During the shuffle, some zygotes inherit two X chromosomes: one from the father and one from the mother.

Other zygotes inherit an X from the mother and a Y from the father. The first, XX group are on their way to becoming female; the second, XY group will become male. *Usually* (see p.78).

The way it's currently understood, femaleness is the default human setting and to be male requires an added something – a gene found only on the Y chromosome. The gene that creates maleness is imaginatively dubbed SRY, for Sex-determining Region Y. It sparks off a series of chemical reactions and cellular transformations that, step by step, lead to the formation of functioning testicles when an embryo is about eight weeks old – when it starts being called a foetus, in other words.

The testicles start to produce androgens, or male-type hormones. (Women have androgens too, but they're known as male hormones precisely because of the way they help create a male body.) Two androgens, testosterone and

Boys turned inside-out

From classical times right through to the Enlightenment, woman were thought to be basically boys turned inside-out. In some circumstances, such as taking excessive exercise, sexual or otherwise, it was even thought that the genitals could re-invert – that a penis could "fall out" of the vagina, in other words. Nowadays, thanks to the discovery of X and Y chromosomes, it's reckoned that if there was a "default" human sex, it would be female. This doesn't mean that boys are girls turned outside-in, although the genitals in both sexes do have amazingly similar structures (see Chapter 2).

dihydrotestosterone, start to sculpt the genitals. Under their influence, the folds that would otherwise become a woman's outer lips swell up and fuse together, forming a scrotum, and the tiny protuberance that would otherwise become part of the clitoris comes together as a nascent penis. At the same time, the testes produce anti-Müllerian hormone, which effectively shuts down the opposite process of developing ovaries and a uterus. Another thirty-odd weeks down the line, and out comes the foetus, as boy or girl.

Wags and prudes – pre-pubescent sexuality

In 1987, ultrasound specialist Israel Meizner reported seeing a seven-month-old foetus touching his penis "in a fashion resembling masturbation movements" over a period of some fifteen minutes. In September 1996, several doctors and a mother observed a 32-week-old female foetus touching her own vulva in the clitoral region. The "light touches" of this "caressing movement" were repeated,

"associated with short, rigid movements of the pelvis and legs, and resulted in a climax of muscle contractions, followed by rest and relaxation".

Neither report should be particularly surprising. Genital touch often appears to give even tiny infants comfort, probably in the way that thumb-sucking does. In some cultures, nursing mothers use gentle genital touch as a way of soothing their babies, just as they'd use back rubbing or cheek kisses. Of course, this kind of touch is about soothing, not sexuality in any adult sense.

The first dim stirrings of what will eventually become adult sexuality usually occur at around three or four years old, when a part of the brain's hypothalamus gland, the snappily named gonadotropin-releasing hormone pulse generator, starts doing its work: generating pulses of gonadotropin hormones. These minuscule bursts happen roughly once every ninety minutes. You could say that a tiny sexual clock in the brain starts ticking. In response to the hormones, children may start to explore their own bodies and those of others, typically friends or siblings.

Freud described this stage as "phallic", observing that boys become sexually aware of their own penises. (He also imagined that they began to desire their mothers and resent their fathers – the so-called Oedipus complex; girls, meanwhile, were supposed to be envious of the male penis, and to start desiring their fathers.) In fact, both boys and girls at around three or four seem to become aware of their genitals in much the same way.

The scientist Nathalie Angier has described the hormone burst as being enough to make children "waggish and slightly erotic", but not enough for puberty to begin. It can be difficult for adults to interpret or handle this behaviour if it's directed at them. Clearly, children are in no way capable of fully sexual experiences, and yet they may be tentatively testing their sexual selves against the world. Their vulnerability at this time is one of the reasons why inappropriate sexual contact with adults can be so intensely damaging (see p.348).

According to Freud, early proto-sexual experiences are the foundation of full adult sexuality. They may well be reinterpreted as such in later life. Certainly, they allow children to begin learning who they are, and how the rules work. Sexuality, they come to understand, is regarded as uniquely private in the adult world. They're taught to cover their genitals and even their underwear in public, and only to touch themselves when alone – if at all. They also learn to make an association between the genitals and hygiene.

By the time the pre-school years have passed, the pulse generator stops generating and children drop their physical self-consciousness as if shedding a skin. Many become little prudes, and stay that way until puberty. Sexual awareness doesn't entirely stop there, however. Children usually know what gender they are by about two or three years old, and by five or six they're fully aware that they're going to remain either male or female for life. At this time, boys may become increasingly reluctant to take part in activities they perceive as "girlish", and they may learn that masculinity means rejecting touch, except in the form of rough play, and doing without overt expressions of affection. Girls, meanwhile, tend to receive a thorough education in romantic culture, and are well-schooled in the importance of physical appearance.

Puberty

For many children, especially later developers, puberty is eagerly awaited. For others, particularly those who start earlier than their peers, it's regarded with a mixture of anxiety and curiosity. No wonder: it's the only bodily change rapid enough for humans to really notice it as it happens. Puberty also signifies the start of the single most important change in status most humans ever experience: from child to adult.

The word "puberty" comes from the Latin, *pubertas*, from a root word meaning "ripe" or "mature". Boys and girls often have a growth spurt a year or so before puberty proper begins. It's part of the slow process of transformation of child to adult, but it may not be interpreted as such by children themselves: children are used to getting taller. Pubic hair, meaning hair around the pubis, or genitals, is different. It's a clear sign – often the first sign – that a significant, sexual change is beginning.

It's not entirely clear what kicks off puberty, but it works rather like one of those water clocks, where each cup fills up before running over and falling into the next cup down – except that in the body the active ingredients are different hormones or neurotransmitters (the body's messenger chemicals) each time. The adrenal glands, on the kidneys, play a part by secreting adrenaline along with small doses of sex hormones. But the most influential events take place in the child's developing brain. The hypothalamus gland, nestled in the heart of the brain, sends signals to the adjacent pituitary gland, which releases gonadotropins into the bloodstream. When these hormones reach the gonads (testicles in boys,

ovaries in girls) they make them start producing greatly increased levels of sex hormones: the testicles manufacture testosterone (a type of androgen), the ovaries make oestrogen.

Basically, sex hormones make males more male and females more female: they turn boys into men and girls into women. In a way, this is a completion of the process of sex differentiation which starts when the initially sexless embryo begins to develop as either a male or a female.

When does puberty begin?

When puberty begins depends on what you call puberty, and also on where you live and who you are. Individual differences have a greater effect than any overall ethnic variations, and diet seems to have more impact than genetics, especially in girls (see p.200). Taking broad averages in the developed world, levels of gonadotropins – the first trigger – start rising from the age of about nine or ten. It's around this time that some children start playing with sexual roles, or playing games of bodily investigation.

Girls start their growth spurts earlier than boys, at roughly ten years old rather than twelve, because oestrogen is more efficient at stimulating growth of this kind than testosterone. Menarche, or first menstruation, typically occurs at around twelve-and-a-half or thirteen, though some start earlier and some later.

First ejaculation for boys often occurs at around the same as menarche in girls. At first, it's often clear or pale grey in colour; sperm tends to appear in the ejaculate a year later, at about fourteen, making it more pearly or creamy white.

Sex education best practice

*"If mothers don't tell their children everything,
they hear it in bits and pieces, and that can't be right."*
Anne Frank, 18 March 1944

Most schools are good at providing the biological basics, and those free from religious control generally provide advice on sexual health and contraception too. Good schools put it in context as "sex and relationship education", and use techniques like inviting anonymous questions from the class. Few, however, offer sex education anything like as early as they almost certainly should, which means that, if you're an early developer, puberty will have got going before your school did.

It is even rarer for schools to offer any information on how or why people enjoy sex, or how to be a more skilful or considerate lover. The words "pleasure" and "orgasm" don't even occur once in the UK government's 48-page paper on Sex and Relationship Education, for example. In fact, "the promotion of sexual orientation or sexual activity" – whatever promotion might mean – is explicitly described as "inappropriate teaching". Worldwide, the emphasis is on children delaying sexual activity as long as possible, as if it will inevitably harm them, alongside a strong promotion of the (statistically unrealistic) notion that sexual activity should be restricted to loving, long-term relationships.

The limitations of school-based sex education mean that parents have to take charge – unless they plan to entrust their child's sexual welfare to playground rumour and magazines. (Arguably, teen zines tend to provide a more honest picture of sex in contemporary culture than any schoolbook.) Parental sex education needn't mean sitting down one day for an all-encompassing talk. The usual advice is to answer children's questions simply and honestly as and when they ask them, gearing the level of information to the child's level of interest.

The problem with this on-demand method is that children may well not ask at all, they may not ask the right questions, or they may appear less interested than they actually are. And the risk of abuse means that children probably need to know enough about sex to recognize sexual danger well before they're likely to become interested. One in three women in the UK started their periods before their parents mentioned menstruation; one in ten had no information from anyone at all before they started.

In terms of what to say, the easiest mistake to make is to be idealistic, as in telling a child that sex is only something which happens within marriage in order to have babies. This is not necessarily true, and children may know it. Idealism also risks presenting sex as something which will only enter a child's life in the unimaginably distant future, not in the next few years. Phrasing sex in terms of the child's own experience – their pleasure in touch, their flirtations and friendships, the role of attractiveness in the playground pecking order – may better help them understand it.

Fearing early pregnancy, parents often advise girls, in particular, not to let boys get too close – thus helping set up an attitude of female sexual passivity from the word go, and shoring up the famous sexual double standard, in which a boy who sleeps around is a stud, whereas a girl doing the same is a slut. This kind of advice may also inhibit girls from actively seeking out contraception. The romantic myth often peddled to young women is that sex is something that happens to you when you're carried away by passion – which doesn't sit very easily with taking sensible precautions and making a trip to the pharmacist.

(Some sperm can be present from the start, however, so young boys having penetrative sex should assume they're fertile.)

The changing body

For girls, the breasts may start "budding" before any other signs are noticed. A hardening may be felt, then the areola (the circle around the nipple) starts to swell, followed by the nipple. Eventually, the fatty tissue of the breast itself begins to build up – one breast often growing at a different rate from the other. Some boys experience slight breast swelling too; it's a perfectly normal reaction to puberty's hormonal rush, and usually subsides within months.

As the body reaches puberty it starts to produce androgen-type hormones, which effectively send a message to the hair follicles in the genital area. In response, they start growing hairs that are darker, thicker, longer and curlier: pubic hairs. These often slowly spread up the pubic mound into the classic upside-down V-shape, a process that takes place

At fifteen, Mexican girls from Michoacan celebrate the Quinceanera, a festival of the transition to womanhood.

over a couple of years or so. Soon other parts of the body join in – the armpits, around the nipples and the legs. In men, the changes continue for years, as the upper lip and chin and chest (and face and nose and arms and back) slowly get hairier too. When this happens, and to what extent, varies widely.

A year or so into puberty, the genitals start to develop, swelling and slightly darkening. In boys, the penis lengthens and becomes wider, especially at the head. The testicles get bigger and may hang down more, and they start producing semen and sperm. This fluid can appear as a surprise, in the form of a wet (ejaculatory) dream, or it may be coaxed out by experimental masturbation. It often starts out fairly clear or filmy in consistency, and gets more milky as puberty develops.

In girls, the labia thicken, lengthen and darken, the fatty tissue responding to increased levels of oestrogen. What was once a neat little "front bottom" becomes a more elaborate organ. Some women describe it as being as if their vagina has "fallen out", though the change isn't half as dramatic as that sounds. Inside, the vaginal walls thicken, the pelvis widens, the uterus gets bigger and more muscular. The vagina starts producing secretions which change the internal pH from alkaline to acidic, and can make knickers feel damp and leave creamy or yellowish stains – all entirely natural. Meanwhile, ovulation and menstruation begin – an important and sometimes dramatic event in any woman's life which is worthy of its own section (see below).

Aside from changes to the genitals, boys' backs broaden, and the nose, jaw and cheekbones start to protude more, lengthening the face; boys' voices lower in pitch, too, sometimes going through an awkward period of "breaking", with squeaks and rumbles. Girls' hips become more pronounced, more "womanly", and their eyes grow further apart. Both sexes start to sweat more – which can cause body odour. The increased activity in the sweat glands is matched by the sebaceous or oil-producing glands in the skin. Sometimes, this increased oiliness causes spots or acne – just at the time of an increased self-consciousness about attractiveness and sexual presence.

Menstruation

The monthly shedding of the lining of the uterus, or menstrual "period", is a powerful symbol of womanhood. It's a reminder of the body's connection to its deep mammalian origins, and an indicator of health and continued fertility – and lack of pregnancy, of course. The feminist Gloria Steinem reckoned that if men had periods, they'd boast about how much they bled and how long for.

The Greek father-of-physicians, Hippocrates, thought menstruation was blood fermenting thanks to women's inability to cleanse their system through sweating. His student, Galen, thought it was a kind of digestive residue. guessed it was the body getting rid of excess blood which wasn't incorporated into a foetus. More recently, it was thought that a period was a kind of self-cleansing exercise, though microbe levels are actually at their lowest just before a period starts, not afterwards.

Probably the best guess today is that periods are a cost-saving evolutionary adaptation: maintaining the lining of the womb at peak condition to accept a fertilized egg would use up more energy than periodically getting rid of it and

Falling to the Communists

Many euphemisms for menstruating reflect the anxiety that periods once evoked. Once upon a time, women suffered from "the illness" or "the curse" – the latter referring to the notion that periods were a punishment for eating the forbidden fruit in the Garden of Eden. More jokey terms were polite euphemisms for blood flow – "on the dot", for instance, or "having your flowers" or your "courses". More elaborately, the "crimson tide" might have come in, you might have "fallen to the Communists", or "Auntie Flo" had come to stay. "On the rag" was derived from the sanitary pads once made out of old clothing. From the Latin *menooo*, meaning "months", came "menstruation" and "menstrual". Nowadays, women generally talk about their "time of the month", or simply their "period".

menstruating women can make meat go bad, turn wine sour, blunt knives, make dough fall and even tarnish mirrors – just with a touch.

Popular myth would still have women withdraw from certain activities – swimming and hair-washing crop up surprisingly often – even though there's no evidence whatsoever that periods prevent women doing anything exactly as well as they do it in any other phase of their cycles. That said, periods are a pain. They can bring mess, expense, bloating, pain, nausea and changes of mood. If you're trying to get pregnant, of course, a period can also bring terrible disappointment.

Cycling through the months

The period, or menstrual cycle, officially lasts for twenty-eight days, though plenty of women have longer or shorter cycles, and lots of factors – illness, stress, travel – can interrupt it altogether. "Day one" of the cycle is counted from when blood first appears. It's not really bleeding as a wound bleeds, but a natural shedding of the lining of the uterus, or endometrium, accompanied by blood: about a fluid ounce and a half of each, on average.

The mechanism is clever. In the lead up to the period, the spiral-shaped arteries that feed the endometrium get longer and more tightly coiled, constricting blood flow slightly. Twenty-four hours before the period begins, they cut off the flow altogether, killing the endometrial tissue. They then open up again, allowing new blood to pool beneath the dead endometrium and push it away. The loss of the uterus's lining washes away an unfertilized egg (if the egg got fertilized, the period doesn't come). This "period", or menstrual phase of the

starting again. The reason that women have periods and animals generally don't (except a few apes and monkeys) is that their uteruses have to be capable of supporting the huge placenta that can feed the relatively giant brain of a human foetus.

Many traditional societies and the majority of religions treat menstruation with great seriousness. Women may live wholly or partially apart for as long as their period lasts, and they're typically excluded or excused from religious ceremonies, sex and perhaps the preparation of family meals – as in the Jewish orthodox *niddah*. According to various misogynistic myths from around the world,

Moonstruation and the McClintock Effect

The lunar and menstrual cycles both last 28 days. Many people find this too strange to be a mere coincidence – and it may not be. Women who work night shifts often have their periods disrupted, and it's often said that if women lived without electric light, their periods would naturally settle to a 28-day rhythm. In the 1970s, Louise Lacey and two dozen of her friends actually tried it – and found that they really did settle into a lunar cycle. Today, women with a pagan bent sometimes like to call their periods their "moontime", and practice "lunaception", where they try to tune their menstrual cycles to the rhythm of the universe.

Sceptics and scientists are insistent, however, that the existence of two 28-day cycles is just a coincidence. The few animals with menstrual cycles have very different rhythms, after all, and there's no reason why the moon should only affect the human animal. And in any case, neither cycle is actually 28 days. The gap between two full moons is closer to 29 and a half days, while the moon actually goes round the earth in closer to 27 days than 28. And while many women have neat 28-day cycles, many do not.

As for Louise Lacey and her friends, they may have been experiencing the "McClintock Effect", named after psychologist Martha McClintock, who, in 1971, finally investigated what women had been saying for years: that if they lived with other women, their periods started to arrive in synch. More precisely, she found that after seven months of cohabitation, the dates of women students living in a college dorm without men were 33 percent closer than they were at the start. The finding became world-famous, and menstrual synchrony became widely accepted as fact. Recent research has cast doubt on both the original study and the whole theory, however. Undeterred, McClintock has gone on to collect samples of underarm perspiration and to show how these can be used – by wiping them under the noses of other women, no less – to influence the duration of menstrual cycles.

cycle, usually lasts from three to five days, though anything from two to seven is regarded as normal.

From around day six, a new egg grows in a woman's ovary. The process begins with a chain-reaction of hormones in the brain, which ends in the pituitary gland setting off twenty or so of the ovary's follicles towards maturation. The main hormone involved is called follicle-stimulating hormone (FSH), and this part of the cycle is called the follicular stage. The mature follicles release the hormone oestrogen, which thickens the lining of the uterus, readying it to receive an egg. The raised oestrogen levels feed back to the pituitary gland, making it trigger the release of luteinizing hormone (LH), which triggers the release of an egg from the best-developed follicle.

Egg release, or ovulation, theoretically happens at day fourteen of the cycle (or, in real life, anytime from day ten to day fourteen). Surrounded by a rich jelly, the egg or ovum, which is about the size of a full stop on this page, squeezes out of a tiny blister forming on the side of its follicle.

Tiny, feathery, seaweed-like brushes, called fimbriae, pick up the egg and sweep it gently into the Fallopian tube, where it passes along into the uterus. It's during the days around ovulation – specifically, three days before it and 24 hours afterwards – that a woman is at her most fertile. (For knowing when ovulation occurs; see p.249.)

After ovulation, in the luteal or postovulatory phase, the used follicle collapses, turning into a cluster of cells called the corpus luteum. This produces two hormones, oestrogen and progesterone, which help keep the uterus's lining rich and nutritive, ready to feed a fertilized egg. If the egg isn't fertilized, however, the hormone levels start to drop and, after roughly eight days, the lining of the uterus starts to degrade. With the first bleed, day one of the cycle begins all over again.

Menarche

All women know where they were when they had their first period – a life-changing event usually known simply as "starting", though it's properly called menarche. In the West, the average age is around twelve or thirteen; few girls start much earlier than eleven or much later than fourteen, though anything between nine and sixteen is possible. And as recently as the mid-nineteenth century, European women were experiencing menarche at between fifteen and seventeen – much the same as in some parts of the developing world today. (Diet is thought to be the chief cause.)

In many parts of the world, menarche is celebrated with initiation ceremonies, sometimes linked with the phases of the moon. In some rural parts of India and Sri Lanka, young women

are given a ritual bath, then jewellery and new clothing, and their horoscope is prepared. In certain Jewish traditions, the mother may administer a slap in the face – gentle, but loaded with symbolism. Some Aboriginal Australian groups take girls aside to teach them about

To mark her first menstruation, a Newar girl from Nepal eats a ritual meal, watched over by symbols of fertility and prosperity.

sexuality at this time. In Japan, where menarche is called "the year of the cleavage of the melon", families may prepare a tray of *sekihan*, rice with azuki beans which dye the rice pink. Among the Khoisan of Southern Africa, a pubescent girl dances as a male bull while the older women mime mating with her.

Whether menarche is exciting or traumatic depends a lot on information, education and mental preparation. Bleeding can be very distressing if it's a surprise and even if it isn't, it can still stir up deep feelings and provoke serious questions. Surprisingly few families in the West celebrate menarche, though a proud hug from the parents and a serious-but-joyful conversation is probably less embarrassing than throwing a party. But pretending menarche hasn't happened is certainly neither kind nor wise. It's a hugely significant moment, even though it doesn't necessarily mean a girl has become fertile. Ovulation may be a few months behind, and it can take two years for periods to settle down into a regular, monthly pattern. (For roughly one in five women, menstruation remains irregular right through to menopause.)

Premenstrual syndrome

Period pain, or dysmenorrhea, is caused by contractions of the uterus. Premenstrual syndrome is much harder to pin down. It was only named in 1931, when gynaecologist Robert T. Frank observed that some of his female patients, shortly before their period began, exhibited "unrest, irritability (like jumping out of their skin), and a desire to find relief by foolish and ill-considered actions".

Since Dr Robert Frank's day, the list of symptoms has grown and grown. Women now blame "PMS", or premenstrual syndrome as it's now known, for tender breasts, fluid retention, bloating, spots, carbohydrate-cravings, headaches, tiredness, weepiness, depression, self-deprecation, hypersensitivity, irritation, sleep problems and a subjective sense of difficulty in concentration. The syndrome has even been renamed a disorder – Late Luteal Phase Dysphoric Disorder, or LLPDD. The American College of Obstetricians and Gynecologists estimates 40 percent of all women suffer, and 8 percent are debilitated by it.

Most women blame their hormones for the symptoms, but tests don't reveal significant differences in levels – though some reckon that serotonin, the brain's mood-making chemical, may be involved. It's likely that PMS is partly a cultural phenomenon. In countries where it's associated with emotional volatility, that's what women are more likely to experience. Women with histories of sexual abuse, or low self-esteem, are more likely to suffer from it, as are women prone to stress, or simply women under a lot of stress.

All that said, many women experience some negative symptoms in the days before their period starts. The discomfort of water retention can be helped by cutting down on caffeine and salt (or cutting them out altogether), and eating healthily. Orgasm can efficiently push fluids out of the uterus and relieve cramps and aching joints. Mood issues are harder to address. Some woman actually report positive symptoms as much as negative ones: sunniness, energy, elation, clarity of thought and, not least in importance, heightened sex drive.

Turning on the heat

Women are pretty rare in having a menstrual cycle. Among the animals, only monkeys and apes menstruate, suggesting that this is a relatively recent evolutionary development. Women are even rarer in not having an obvious period of oestrus: a time of the week or month or year when they're both fertile and up for it – or "on heat", as it's known.

When on heat, most mammals, including apes and monkeys, advertise their fertile status as blatantly as they can. Typically, the vulva swells, reddens – an effect at its most obvious in female baboons – and starts sending out chemical signals to any male nose in the vicinity. At the same time, female animals usually become more restless, and more physical – sniffing, licking, rubbing or riding other animals or, in the case of pets, their owners.

Women are the only animals that don't advertise their fertile period at all. At least, not visibly. Hormones may prompt changes in behaviour, however. The picture from the few academic studies is confused, but desire seems broadly to increase steadily in the lead-up to ovulation, and to drop off after it. Which is what you'd expect, from an evolutionary standpoint. Studies have found, variously, that women initiate sex more often around the time of ovulation, they have more orgasms, go on more dates, wear more jewellery and tighter, sexier clothing, have more flings, and are attracted to men who are more facially symmetrical (an indicator of good genes) or masculine-looking (an indicator of plentiful testosterone). Lap dancers even earn more tips when they're ovulating.

Other aspects of the menstrual dynamic are harder to pin down. Some surveys have found that sexual thoughts and fantasies peak in the first days of the period, others have found minor peaks just before and just after menstruation. It could be that the body draws attention to the sexual self during a woman's period, or that women who don't want to get pregnant – arguably the majority – relax about having sex when they can't get pregnant. It could be that hormonal processes have an influence on libido: when levels of the wet-blanket hormone progesterone dip, they are less able to block the influence of androgens – which have an important role in stimulating sexual desire. Most bizarrely, one study found that women in the least fertile part of their cycle were rated by men as having the sexiest walks. It was suggested that fertile women might be withholding sending the longer-range kind of sexual signal, so as not to interest potentially aggressive strangers who might view them at a distance.

Sex and the menstrual cycle

Many women prefer not to have sex during their period. Their breasts are tender, they feel bloated, they're worried about the mess, their religion bans it – there are many reasons. Plenty enjoy it, however, and there's no medical reason not to (although it is still possible to get pregnant, because sperm can stay alive long enough to encounter an early-ovulated egg). Greater blood flow to the whole pelvic area can increase sensitivity and lubrication, and a towel placed underneath, or a diaphragm inside sorts out the problem of mess.

Coming out

Because people generally assume you're straight unless you tell them otherwise, heterosexual men and women rarely have to make public, or even private, announcements about their sexuality. It may seem as if they have it easy, but, arguably, they're also missing out on a powerful rite of passage. After "self-identifying", "disclosing" or "coming out of the closet", many lesbian, gay and bisexual people feel relieved, liberated or even euphoric. Some feel as if they have graduated or been reborn. Some throw themselves into sexual experiences: the sexual grandiosity of the just-out young man is legendary.

Like most rites of passage, however, coming out can be difficult and painful. It's a rare gay man or woman who doesn't experience a single negative reaction. Bisexual and transgender people in particular may have their feelings dismissed or not taken seriously. Even people from supportive backgrounds can experience depression as the reality of being gay in a heterosexist world bites.

That said, gay men and women are coming out at younger ages than ever before – which is surely a sign that the process is less risky, or at least less fraught, than it used to be. In the 1980s or 1990s, people tended to come out in their late teens or early twenties, once they'd achieved a measure of independence or had left the family home. In 2006, however, one US study reported that the most common age for "self-identifying" was 13.4, with the parents hearing about it maybe a year later.

Starting over

❝ I never thought about sex overmuch until the children were beginning to move out. I looked around and realized I was interested in men. At least, I became aware of it in a way I hadn't before. I would have liked to have come round more quickly to understand.

When my wife died, it made the search much easier. I didn't have to do any explaining. I got in touch with a confidence-raising organization, a self-help group for people who are all gay. There's not much sex in it but a lot of mutual backslapping and encouragement. For a long, long time I was very afraid of disease and of getting hurt. I believed that if somebody was to have anal intercourse with me that it would be very painful. I never actually had any gay sexual experiences until I came across this man who's now my boyfriend. That was the first time I really relaxed bodily.

I was determined I wasn't going to have this relationship in secret. I'd got my pride locked into it in some way. I made it clear to my family that there was no choice: they had to put up with me and him together. I came straight out with it. I've learnt to be more open as a result, and it's a very great transition for me. I'm able to talk about inner feelings, which I wasn't able to do before. I don't think there would have been such a change in me if I'd been straight. ❞

How to do it

The first stage in coming out is self-acknowledgement, or coming out to yourself. Plenty of gay men and women would testify that they were strongly attracted to their own sex from the outset, and knew and accepted it early. Others find they have had fantasies about both men and women, and sexual preferences may only resolve themselves over time, perhaps coming into focus only after a number of actual sexual experiences.

Some young gay people spend months or even years hoping that the attraction they feel towards their own sex is "just a phase". They struggle against their own internalized homophobia or they worry about anti-homosexual prejudice, which is rife in many schools. Anonymous helplines or online forums, often provided by gay youth organizations, can provide a vital bridge between coming out to yourself and coming out to others. But eventually, you're going to want to tell people who you really are.

The usual advice is to start outside the family with a trusted friend – perhaps a gay friend – who will maintain confidentiality until you're ready to tell other people. Schoolfriends may find the temptation to share the hot news too much to bear. Ask yourself why you want to tell a particular person. What, exactly, do you want to say? When and where is a good time and place for them? What questions might they ask? What would you do, and who would you turn to, if they reacted badly? Practice the opening line, maybe "I need to tell you something because our friendship is important to me", and prepare answers to hostile or unthinking questions such as: "are you sure?", "what did we do wrong?", "have you got AIDS?" or "do you fancy me?". And have an exit: "I'm sorry this news upsets you; I think it's best if I leave now" is graceful and compassionate.

Imagining the worst-case scenario is important with parents, especially if you're sharing the same house. How well have they dealt with pain or surprise in the past? How comfortable are they talking about sex? What attitudes towards gay and lesbian people have they expressed? What would happen if you felt forced to leave the family home? Beware of mind reading, however, or assuming your fears will become realities. The parents who smile and say "we know, we were just waiting for you to tell us" are legendary, as are the homophobes who announce they'll support their child through thick and thin. Initial reactions may not be the best gauge of future behaviour, either.

One loving and liberal mother confessed that her first thought on hearing that her son was gay was that he wouldn't be able to have children. Her second was that he would disappear into "a netherworld of promiscuity and leather" whose rules she didn't understand, and where she would be unable to provide guidance. Her third was protective: that her son "had no inkling of how difficult this was going to be". Many parents are also terrified they'll lose their child to HIV-AIDS.

British journalist Simon Fanshawe advises not bouncing people into it. "Don't sit at Christmas lunch with all the family", he advises, "and say loudly: 'Can you pass the salt ... to a homosexual?' " Starting with a letter gives a parent time to absorb the information, to talk through their own feelings with friends and to answer some of their own questions. Most crucially, it allows them to get used to thinking of their little baby as a sexual person – gay, straight or whatever.

First time

Aspirations for first-time sex are often high. And yet sex is an activity which generally takes a lot of practice before it goes well – and many people find it pretty disappointing at first. For sheer orgasmic efficiency, kissing and touching and maybe oral sex is likely to have the best results. Slowly discovering

Just add alcohol

Alcohol is often a lubricating factor in first-time sexual experiences. It strips away inhibitions and supercharges the sex drive. Unfortunately, even as drink increases desire, it famously undermines performance. It's not just that it makes erections softer, it blunts the body's physical responses and creates clumsiness. Alcohol blurs all kinds of social and physical signals, including sexual ones, meaning that it's much harder to "read" what your partner is enjoying and what he or she is not. It also interferes with judgement, meaning that people who are drunk may end up with sexual partners they would think twice about in the light of day – a well-documented phenomenon known as wearing "beer goggles" (see box on p.17). Most dangerously, alcohol dramatically increases risk taking: it's easy to forget or stop caring about safer sex or contraception when you're off your head. It's also easy to find yourself in a vulnerable situation with someone you don't know as well as you should – and easy to find yourself engaging in more aggressive or coercive behaviour than you might when sober. Alcohol is a major factor in a huge number of sexual assaults.

The cult of virginity

"Virginity" is a pretty odd concept. You can't see it or touch it, and somehow it's magically taken away by penile–vaginal penetrative sex. Kissing doesn't do it, and neither does masturbation, or oral sex, or gay sex. Or indeed rape: the early Christian thinker Augustine took the view that the spirit was more important than the body, and the spirit remained intact even if the body was assaulted; sex was only really sex, in other words, if it was willing sex.

Nowadays, both men and women can be said to be virgins, but traditionally, it was a women-only affair.

Virginity was all about being intact and unpenetrated – so much so that until the 1990s, some tampon manufacturers felt the need to reassure users that tampons wouldn't take away their virginity. Virginity was also about the possibility of conceiving a child. When women were effectively the sexual property of their fathers or husbands, and when the whole system of paternity and property inheritance hinged on men being sure that only they had had sexual access to their wives, virginity was the ultimate guarantee.

The penalties for sexual carelessness could be brutal. Athenian women who had premarital sex could be enslaved. Roman fathers were allowed to kill their daughters if they erred, along with their lovers. Throughout much of European history, women who "slipped" – and even those who were raped – became unmarriageable. Many were thrown out by their families, and forced into prostitution to stay alive.

People became so hysterical about the idea of virginity that they even invented a part of the body to prove it. The hymen (see p.50) is a flap of skin said to stretch over the opening

The Purity Ball, Colorado Springs: a father watches his daughter take the pledge, and commit to pre-marital chastity.

of the vagina, and to break bloodily and perhaps painfully at first intercourse. Many infant girls do have a partial membrane here, as do many animals. (Guinea pigs have magic hymens which dissolve away when they're on heat, then close up again once they come off to stop male guinea pigs getting at them, but they're pretty unusual.) A few women still have vestigial hymens well into adolescence or even adulthood, but bleeding at first intercourse isn't all that common, especially since the advent of tampons and good lubricants.

In countries which still place a high price on virginity – where literally, a woman who isn't a virgin would need a huge dowry or bride-price to find a husband at all – bloodied bedsheets are sometimes displayed as "proof" of virginity after the wedding night. In fact, the blood often belonged to an unlucky chicken. Some plastic surgeons do offer a dubious operation to "restore" lost hymens, often by simply putting a few stitches across the labia – an operation known in 1950s America as creating a "lover's knot".

Few in the West would now be horrified if their spouse had enjoyed a previous sexual relationship. (Although the notorious sexual double standard still exists: many men are troubled if their girlfriends have had more partners than them.) And penile–vaginal intercourse is no longer the gold standard. It's absurd to say that a gay man who has never slept with a woman and a woman with a rich but exclusively lesbian sexual back-history have not lost their virginity. If there has to be some kind of virginal arch through which people pass, sharing orgasm with another person would surely be the more meaningful gateway.

each other's bodies and responses, and talking honestly and frankly as you go along, is also the best route to sex that's satisfying on all levels. One theory holds that it's best to have first-time sex with a relatively experienced partner. But in truth, sexual satisfaction usually grows with your own experience, not your partner's.

For many young people, "losing their virginity" – which generally refers to penetrative heterosexual sex – gets in the way of broader sexual discovery. It's an awkward badge of inexperience or childishness that has to be "lost" before sex can be enjoyed in a more relaxed way. For gay men and women, the first time may be even more intense, as any doubts or drawbacks collide with emotions such as relief, liberation or self-discovery.

Other young people feel that virginity is something to be hoarded and "given" only to someone who really deserves it – maybe someone you've just married. Being in a relationship with someone you trust definitely helps, as does being in love, or being able to laugh about mistakes or embarrassments together – and there are likely to be plenty of both to come. Love can make the strange mechanics of sex seem less important, and on the first time, that can be a very useful thing. Then again, as Woody Allen quipped, "sex without love is an empty experience, but as empty experiences go, it's one of the best."

Saying yes, and saying no

A national survey in the UK found that only one in a hundred people couldn't remember their first time. So it's worth taking steps to ensure that the first time is a safe and enjoyable experience which happens in the right way for you. This may mean saying "no", or avoiding certain situations until the conditions are right. (Or almost right. One thing experience teaches is that sex is rarely perfect.)

When you do want to have sex, find somewhere private and safe. Consider being sober (see box on p.205). And if you don't want to acquire a child or a sexually transmitted infection, use and know how to use a condom (see box on p.264). If you're too shy to buy contraceptives or too embarrassed to talk about using them with your partner, it's a pretty good indication that sex isn't likely to be very enjoyable.

According to a study published in the *British Medical Journal*, half of British women wished they'd waited longer, and young people often feel pressure to have sex before they feel ready. Pressure from within is particularly powerful – the feeling that you won't really become a full person until you've had sex (which is, of course, nonsense). Pressure from peers can also be intense. If everyone else is doing it (or saying they are), and you're not, is there something wrong with you?

Pressure from a boyfriend (or, less commonly, a girlfriend) can and probably should be confronted. The old lines have some pretty straight answers. "If you don't have sex with me, you're dumped" invites the response; "if you say that again, *you're* dumped". "If you loved me you'd have sex with me" has the obvious answer: "if you loved me, you wouldn't lay on that kind of emotional pressure". Being called "frigid" or "gay" or a "cocktease" (or whatever) is just stupid. Not wanting to have sex with someone *right now* has nothing to do with whether or not you'll want to have sex with them

(or someone else) later – and nothing to do with your sexuality. Wanting to kiss or touch someone doesn't give them the right to have sex with you.

Putting it in, and it popping out again

In Hollywood sex, people start kissing then, with one easy motion, he's inside her and grinding away and she looks as if she's about to come. Clearly, there's a missing moment or two here. To get a penis into a vagina, unless both are well lubricated and are very familiar with each other, one person usually has to put it in with their hand.

The question of who does it is age-old. Good etiquette would be for her to guide it in when she's ready, though men might put themselves in place while their fingers are down there touching her. You could do it together. If you're a first-timer, this may not go smoothly. And once it's in, there's no guarantee it'll stay there. Some positions and some people (or combinations of people) are worse than others for the pop-out – sex from behind or from any extreme angle is relatively problematic. Reaching down to re-dock eventually stops being sexy. Still, it's better to carry on guiding it with a hand rather than knocking away at the gates futilely. No one likes feeling like they're being headbutted by a blind worm.

How you put it in is another question. Both men and women often say that the feeling as it goes in is one of the best moments of penetrative sex. Some people like it teasingly slow. Others prefer a powerful, affirming, enveloping entry. First-time round, slow is probably best – and, ideally, she should control the motion.

In for the long term

Expectations of marriage and life partnerships are extraordinarily high in the West – including sexual expectations. Sex over the longer term can't always be fantastic, obviously. Every relationship has emotional peaks and troughs, often mirrored by sexual highs and lows. And over a lifetime, there's plenty to get in the way: work stress, money worries, relationship strain, illness, bereavement, having children and simply being tired out. There's even a slang name for the modern celibate couple, DINS (Double Income No Sex), and an apocryphal dinner party game where the winner is the pair who haven't had sex for the longest.

Long-term relationships are good for orgasm, however. A 1994 survey found that for women, 62 percent usually had an orgasm with partners they were dating, but the figure went up to 68 percent if they lived with their partner and 75 percent if they were married. That said, studies of people in partnerships and marriages also show that sexual satisfaction tends to wear off, as does frequency.

There are some simple ways to recharge the sex in a long-term relationship. You can start by wooing your partner all over again. You can just do new things together – proven to reinvigorate many relationships. Getting fit boosts libido very effectively, as does getting enough sleep. And in a busy life, sex may require scheduling, prioritizing or at least a little forethought. But the most useful thing anyone can do is to talk, and listen.

How often is often enough?

Statistics on how often people have sex are perhaps even less reliable than those on how many people they've had sex with. It's harder to keep count, and it *really* depends who you're asking. But one authoritative UK study from the 1990s found that British people under 40 had sex, on average, roughly six times a month. The *Sex in America* survey, also from the 1990s, found that Americans aged 18–29 had sex, on average, 112 times a year, or a little over twice a week; thirty-somethings got theirs 86 times a year, and forty-somethings 69 times a year. Among married American couples, the greatest number of respondents (almost 50 percent) reported having sex "a few times in the past month", and the next most common choice (ticked by roughly a third) was "2–3 times a week". But perhaps the most telling statistic is that men and women alike tend to agree that they're not having as much sex as they'd like to be having.

The thrill is gone

The first flush of sexual desire wears off in time – the peak in divorces at the four-year mark is thought to mirror the trough in the chemicals that drive love (see p.10). While monogamy needn't equal monotony, to quote a phrase, it can sometimes be boring.

The joke goes that the arrival of Viagra and other erectile drugs really made women moan: just as they were catching up with their reading, now this … Fallow patches are normal. But sexless relationships cause discord and resentment. What

"How would you feel if I woke you up every morning wanting sex?"

Marriage Art, "most couples try a dozen different sex positions in their first year, settle on two or three for the next five years, and thereafter find themselves using one particular position almost all the time. Precisely the opposite course makes a great deal more sense."

How to talk

The silent, supercharged "zipless fuck" with a stranger may be a common sexual fantasy, but in real life, the best sex usually happens between couples who communicate well. Unfortunately, couples who will happily argue for hours about where to go on holiday may remain tight-lipped about what they prefer in bed. Talking too frankly supposedly "spoils the romance".

In his studies of the success and failure of long-term relationships, psychologist John Gottman identified two key predictors of stability and happiness: women who initiate discussions in kind and diplomatic ways, and men who listen to and act on their partners' concerns. (His "four horseman of the apocalypse", by contrast, were criticism, contempt, defensiveness and stonewalling.) The same tactics surely work the other way round, and within same-sex couples. Gottman also found that couples who argued early on in their relationship were happier than couples who didn't. People can be remarkably honest when they're angry, and problems aired don't tend to fester.

If you're trying to get a conversation going with a reluctant partner, pick your moment. Avoid bringing up difficult issues when either of you is tired, stressed out, distracted or drunk. Asking

could or should be a bond of intimacy at the core can become a dark little vortex sucking in all the good feelings and spitting them back out in hard words or harder silences.

Even if a couple has sex frequently and satisfyingly, issues may lurk beneath the surface. One partner – stereotypically the woman – may be less inclined to initiate sex than the other. Gradually, the couple settles into a routine in which he becomes "responsible" for creating the conditions for sex. He may start to feel resentful, unwanted or undesirable – a situation in which someone outside the relationship expressing desire for him can become dangerously emotionally attractive. The woman may feel harassed or even used, and perhaps increasingly unwilling to have sex at all. Over time, some women (and a few men) become used to getting aroused only when approached and touched – a situation clinicians call responsive desire, in contrast to spontaneous desire.

Just as couples can get stuck in one dynamic, they can get stuck in one position. As John Eichenlaub put it in his 1961 classic, *The* questions is an excellent start, but beware inviting yes/no answers, or presenting either/or alternatives – this can close things down. A tactical approach is to begin by sharing your own feelings on a certain issue, or voice a positive preference, or at least finish on a positive note: "I'm not so keen on that, but I really like it when we do this …" Be as clear as you can: it's far less stressful to hear a reasonable request than to try to work out what someone might mean, all the time fearing the worst. Stick to the topic in hand without generalizing.

Once you're done, allow time for your partner to respond; listen to what they say, absorb it (deep breath) and show that you understand. Listening is just as important as talking. Behavioural therapists recommend "active listening", using nods, facial expressions, eye contact and noises of agreement or encouragement to show your partner that they're not talking to a wall of indifference or hostility. Ask questions to clarify what your partner is saying, share relevant experiences; show not only that you understand what they're saying but what they're feeling.

Where communication has really broken down, talking to – or simply in front of – a therapist can provide what they call "safe time". If that's awkward, create other safety barriers: call a truce on saying hurtful things, and limit the initial discussion to ten minutes or so at first. Focus on the present and future, and be realistic about what you can change. Coming prepared with one or two things you both want to talk about also stops a conversation spiralling into an argument. Give each other equal time to talk and, if a row does break out, end the session.

Sensate focus

Talking is one approach to rekindling the fire. The other trick is not to talk at all. Therapists teach a form of relationship therapy called sensate focus. Originally devised by the researchers Masters and Johnson in 1970, it seeks to retrain couples in the art of touching and being touched. The person being caressed is supposed to remain still and focused on the physical sensations – hence the phrase "sensate focus". This can be amazingly beneficial. A 2000 study by Natalie Dove and Michael Wiederman showed that women who found themselves distracted by worries about performance or appearance were less sexually satisfied. Push aside or block out those negative thoughts – stop "spectatoring", as they called it – and orgasm is supposed to come more easily.

Sensate focus is intended to run alongside other forms of counselling or therapy, but in 1985, Dagmar O'Connor's bestseller, *How to Make Love to the Same Person for the Rest of Your Life*, provided a step-by-step self-help programme. (O'Connor herself is a respected sex therapist who trained under Masters and Johnson.) For the first week, any form of genital or explicitly sexual touching is forbidden. In the second week, couples can start to be more proactive, adding in kissing and licking, for instance. Week three brings masturbating in front of each other. It can be a hard step. In week four you're allowed to touch each other's breasts. Week five is mutual genital exploration. Week six focusing on expressing needs and controlling feelings in order to liberate them. At week seven, you're allowed to make love to each other. By then, it's hoped, you'll really want to.

Relate, the UK's leading relationship counselling organization, recommends three sessions a week of an hour each – avoiding doing your homework last thing at night when you're tired. Each person puts in half an hour being touched and half an hour touching. You spend one week getting used to each task, then another enjoying it before moving on to the next. Task one is "non-sexual touching". The point is not to be turned on, but to concentrate on how your partner looks, feels and tastes – on what feels nice and what doesn't. Task two is "genital touching". You might begin a session with a bath and gentle, non-aroused exploration. At this stage, the person being caressed is allowed to say or show what feels good. Couples can bring each other close to orgasm as often as they like, but they're supposed to avoid coming until the end of the session, or as long as the experiment lasts.

Sensate focus isn't easy. It requires both commitment and a willingness to expose yourself intimately and emotionally – which can actually be harder in a long-standing relationship, where habits have hardened, than for people who know each other less well. It can also expose anxieties or unacknowledged problems. Facing these together, however, can strengthen relationships and ultimately improve sex.

Procreation

Couples who decide to have a baby often find their sex life suddenly improves. It may be that they've decided to have a child because they're particularly close, or that making this decision has brought them together. Some enjoy the feeling of risk or liberation in having unprotected sex. Some feel connected to their biology or their humanity in a new and sexy way. If the man is used to using condoms, the experience of the subtler physical sensations can be a revelation, too.

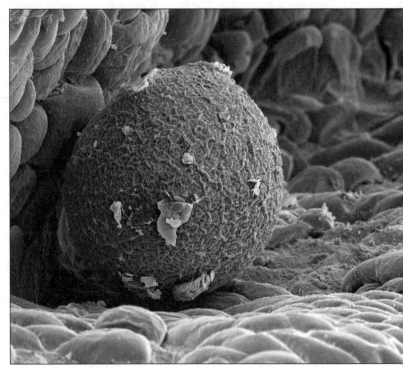

A fertilized ovum, travelling down the Fallopian tube towards the uterus.

How it works

Procreation, or the continuation of the species, requires conception, or the creation of an embryo. The exact point at which life begins is a matter of furious debate, but the process begins with the fertilization of a woman's egg by a man's sperm. In sperm terms, getting from him to her is a marathon journey. When a man ejaculates, he deposits his sperm along with a pool of semen, from which the sperm are released slowly over a period of several days. As the sperm are released, they're brought into contact with the woman's cervical mucus. This mucus capacitates them – effectively switching them on by triggering creation of the enzymes they'll need to get through the outer layers of the egg. Once capacitated, they can only survive for a few hours.

The journey of the sperms is usually described as a kind of torpedo mission, their tails waggling furiously as they swim up the vagina, through the cervix and into the uterus. But it's the woman's body that does most of the work: sperm can get to the Fallopian tubes, at the top of the uterus, in under a minute, a record-breaking time which can't be explained by even the most furiously thrashing microscopic tail. How this happens isn't entirely known, but orgasmic contractions may play a role, as may hormones: during the fertile period, they make cervical mucus stringy, so it can act as a kind of fish ladder for the sperm to climb.

Hormones also ensure that only one Fallopian tube is dilated, so that most of the semen finds its way to the tube on the side where the egg is waiting, and as little as possible wastes its energies in a blind corner. As the egg travels down the Fallopian tube towards the uterus, it finally meets the bold sperm that have made it this far – a mere one percent or so of the 150 million that started out on the journey. The sperms surround it, wiggling their tails like a pack of excited dogs around a dinner bowl. Explosive electrical-chemical reactions occur between the wall of the egg and the enzymes on the sperms' heads. These detonate like tiny depth charges on the hull of a ship until, eventually, the barrier is weak enough for one sperm to push through; the same reaction then closes off the egg to any potential competitors.

Once inside the egg, the incredible process of genetic fusion begins. First, the cell membranes fuse, binding the head of the sperm and the now-mature egg together and leaving them free to exchange their chromosomes, or "shoe trees" of genetic information. At this point, the sperm contributes either an X or Y chromosome, which determines whether the zygote, as the fertilized egg is now called, will develop as either a male or female (see p.191).

The zygote divides and redivides, continuing to move down the Fallopian tubes towards the uterus as it does so, and taking on a new name: the blastocyst. If all is well, after eight to ten days of slow movement and incredibly rapid cell division, the blastocyst embeds itself into the soft, welcoming tissue of uterine wall, using its outer wall to create the placenta and umbilical cord while the inner mass of cells becomes the embryo. At this point, pregnancy is said to begin.

The boggling complexity of conception means that it doesn't always happen like this. Sometimes, two eggs get fertilized, or the fertilized egg divides into more than one embryo (result: twins). Sometimes the egg gets fertilized in the uterus itself, or it doesn't travel beyond the Fallopian tube (result:

ectopic pregancy). Plenty of eggs never get fertilized at all. Many blastocysts fail to implant. Many embryos are lost after implantation, often because they weren't viable: they then miscarry, causing the early end of the pregnancy. Recent studies suggest that as many as half of all fertilized eggs may be miscarried, though frequently (perhaps half the time), it happens so early that women may not even be aware that they briefly became pregnant.

When to do it

Conceiving a child doesn't mean going at it hammer and tongs. Sperm live for up to seven days in the vagina and uterus, so having sex two or three times a week will ensure that plenty of sperm are always lying in wait, ready to fertilize an egg after it is released at ovulation.

Couples trying for a baby, especially if it's not happening as quickly as they'd hoped, can be under a lot of emotional stress. Many try to work out the most fertile moment in the woman's menstrual cycle, and then plan frequent sex at that time. Getting the timing right does indeed boost the chance of conceiving, but scheduling sex isn't necessarily as helpful as it might sound. If sex becomes a chore, there's a risk that you'll actually end up having it less often in the longer term. And certain kinds of stress – including stress about how and when to have sex – can hinder conception. The urban legend of the couple that gave up IVF and almost immediately conceived naturally probably has a basis in fact.

Scheduling sex, if you decide to do it, is all about working out when ovulation happens, because a woman is at her most fertile from three days before ovulation to 24 hours after it. That's the

window you want to aim for. In theory, ovulation occurs at day fourteen of the menstrual cycle, but not all women and all cycles are the same. To work out exactly when you ovulate, you take your temperature, check the clarity and slipperiness of your cervical mucus and monitor the feel of your cervix over the course of the month. By plotting the results on a fertility calendar, or a sympto-thermal chart, you can work out when to make sure you have sex. For full details of fertility awareness techniques, see p.251.

Conceiving a child may take time, and the older you are the longer it may take. Fertility drops with age, especially for women, and so does the chance of a fertilized egg failing to implant, or a foetus miscarrying. Thirty-five years old is often taken to be a watershed: at that age, there's roughly a one in ten chance of conceiving in any given menstrual cycle, and thereafter the steady drop in fertility which began in the teens starts to accelerate. But on average, among 100 couples having unprotected sex two or three times a week, 85 to 90 will conceive within the first year. (Among those 85 women, 60 will conceive within six months, and 30 in the first month.) Within two years, as long as they continue having regular sex, around 95 percent of women will conceive. If you feel under time pressure, however, it might be worth taking the first steps towards exploring fertility treatments after a year.

How to help it happen

Various ancient authorities thought passionate sex was the most fruitful of all kinds – and arguments over the "upsuck" effect of female orgasm continue

Food and fertility

Fertility experts and self-appointed nutritionists often like to advocate special fertility-boosting diets, packed with so-called "superfoods" such as almonds, avocado, alfalfa and goji berries. But food isn't medicine – no matter how hard it's sold as such – and the key thing with diet is balance. With a balanced diet, there's probably no need for vitamin or mineral supplements, except that women are advised to take folic acid supplements – from as much as twelve months before conception, ideally. Folic acid both assists conception and is very good for the developing baby.

In general, women should try to eat a good range of foods containing iron (red meat, green leafy veg, including broccoli, dried fruit, pulses, lentils and dried beans), calcium (dairy products, especially full-fat ones, and wholegrain cereals, including wholemeal bread), folate (bread, oranges and green leafy veg) and fatty acids (so-called omega-3 and omega-6 oils, found in oily fish, certain kinds of nuts and nut oil, sunflower and pumpkin seeds, and leafy vegetables). A healthy amount of zinc in the diet is useful for men; good sources are pulses (beans, lentils, chickpeas), nuts and seeds, wholegrain cereals, meat and shellfish. Selenium is another mineral linked to male fertility, and brazil nuts are packed with it.

As for food villains, the usual suspects are fat, salt and sugar. Processed foods and ready-made meals are typically high in all three, so cutting down may help boost fertility. Some studies have found that artificial sweeteners (except xylitol), rhubarb and peas have a negative impact on female fertility, while soya may reduce fertility for both men and women, thanks to its ability to mimic hormones. But it's arguable that becoming anxious about food could have just as big an effect.

Drinking more than moderate amounts of either booze or coffee (or cola, energy drinks, and so on) probably does reduce the chances of getting pregnant. If you're drinking more than three cups of coffee a day, cutting down would be a sensible move. The alcohol limit is harder to pinpoint, but the damage you can do to an unborn foetus by drinking in early pregnancy is a good enough reason to abstain altogether, or drink only very lightly. (The controversial evidence that moderate drinking actually helps conception is probably only because alcohol helps some people relax, and when they're relaxed they're more likely to have sex.) If you do get pregnant, of course, alcohol, caffeine and, of course, smoking, are toxic for the foetus.

to this day (see box on p.154). Popular wisdom has it that missionary-style is the most effective, on the grounds that gravity helps sperm along, but positioning is almost certainly irrelevant. Having sex in the way that encourages you to have sex regularly is a far better bet.

How often to have sex is a moot point. Every two to three days is probably plenty, and a man's sperm-load drops slightly every time he ejaculates, so if you're having sex very frequently the rule of diminishing returns will apply. Technically, for the greatest number of sperm per load, you should keep

Sex during pregnancy: where there's a will there's a way.

Pregnancy positions

As the pregnancy progresses, positions that involve deep penetration can become uncomfortable – or it may prove impossible to get it in there at all, or not without very creative use of pillows or perhaps the edge of the bed. The best positions (arguably) are her-on-top and from behind – though carrying that extra weight can be a strain. Side-by-side positions, either facing or spooning, provide a gentler alternative, though you may need to do more fancy leg- or pillow-work. But perhaps the most effective position of all involves the woman lying back, taking some well-earned rest and pleasure while her partner strokes and massages her, helping her explore that newly expanded orgasmic capacity.

them in the holding tank for a good five days. That said, repeated shots at goal are almost certainly more important, and a regular turnover of sperm keeps them healthy. And an Australian survey of 2007 found that men could actually increase their sperm count (the number of sperm in any one ejaculation) in the longer term by coming on a daily basis.

Keeping reasonably fit and eating healthily are important ways to boost fertility. Fitness is especially important for women, as being significantly over- or underweight can really interfere with ovulation. The basic medical requirement is to get your heart pumping for thirty minutes three times a week. If you can't manage to swim, run or play sport, try walking quickly to the shops or the office, or even enjoying some vigorous sex followed by an orgasm.

Men can help protect their fertility by avoiding hot baths, which kill off sperm in the testicles. Long sessions on bike saddles or with a laptop rested on the lap can have the same effect. It's said that tight underwear causes the same problems – but it would have to be a very tight pair of pants, or perhaps very warm and woolly long johns.

Where a couple has problems conceiving, it's mostly because one partner (or both, in about a third of cases) is what medics call subfertile. They can have children, but the odds are longer than on average, for one reason or another. Full infertility is more rare. If getting pregnant is taking an unacceptably long time for you, then a consultation with a fertility specialist is the best course of action. Roughly one in ten couples seek medical help in conceiving.

As for "methods" to encourage conceiving a girl or boy: none of them work (or not outside ethically questionable and sometimes illegal sperm-sorting during IVF procedures, anyway.) Some books gossip about creating acid or alkali environments (for girls and boys respectively), using horrors like vinegar douches. These "tips" are based on a long-since discredited study which lacked any theoretical support, and they're more likely to upset the vagina's balance – and therefore get in the way of conception – than anything else.

Parenthood

Parenthood isn't a steady state when it comes to its impact on your sex life. Leaving aside the act of procreation, there's pregnant sex, post-partum sex, then years of demanding parenthood running alongside all the usual challenges of long-term relationships. Having children puts many people in touch with a deep-rooted part of themselves – a mammalian part of the psyche, perhaps. Sex and reproduction are reconnected in the mind, tapping into a rich and satisfying layer of sexual awareness. It almost makes up for all the times you're interrupted, or too tired even to try.

Sex during pregnancy

Pregnancy can switch on surprising feelings about sex. The rush of having successfully conceived, and excitement for the future, can bring couples together both emotionally and physically. And worries about contraception – or indeed conception – can be utterly forgotten, perhaps for the first time ever.

Some women find their new shape puts them more in contact with their bodies than ever before: they feel sexy, maybe in an earthy, powerful way – or, as Angelina Jolie put it, "as a woman you're just so round and full". Women may take charge during sex more than before – which usually makes it work better anyway. Many men respond to their partner's new shape with equal enthusiasm, and are willing to try new, gentler or slower approaches – also very effective.

As long as there are no complications there's no reason why you can't have sex right through pregnancy. One survey of 2001 suggested that sexual activity may even protect against preterm delivery. Popular legend has it that women feel horny in the second trimester (months four to six). Studies don't bear this out, but women may feel less sick, or worried, or exhausted than they did in the first trimester, and correspondingly more up for it. Some women respond to the clitoris and vulva becoming more engorged with blood, too, which potentially heightens sexual response.

Orgasm may change in quality, subtly or dramatically. Some women discover multiple orgasm for the first time, or get into masturbation in a new way. At the very end of pregnancy, when the cervix is starting to ripen and dilate, orgasm can actually help bring on labour. In fact, it's one of the few genuinely effective home remedies, so women with a history of preterm birth are usually advised to avoid sex and orgasm, especially in the final trimester.

Not all the changes of pregnancy make you want to rush into bed. Many couples worry about the vulnerability of the foetus, or feel it's somehow inappropriate to have sex so close to it, as if they were being watched, or felt, by their unborn child. In the first trimester, many women find they're too nauseous, or tired, or their breasts feel too tender. In the third and final trimester, fatigue, water-retention and backache may act as brakes on desire, or performance. And right the way through pregnancy, men and women alike may be getting used to the idea that a child is now part of the emotional mix, and that the woman's body is changing. Starting to identify as a mother can displace sexual thoughts for some women or their partners. So too can new worries about future responsibilities.

Sex as a parent

"No woman", says contraception expert John Guillebaud, "has ever been reported as having conceived within four weeks of having a baby". Staggeringly, this means some women have conceived at five weeks – and it means you'll need to start using contraception pretty much straight away if you plan on having penetrative sex.

You may not be: most parents would agree that looking after a newborn is not conducive to erotic behaviour, and most take six months to a year to get back to pre-pregnancy patterns of sexual activity. Exhaustion, pain, stitches and scarring, and negative feelings about body image all militate against wanting to make love in the aftermath of giving birth – not to mention the loss of privacy in the bedroom for those who sleep with their baby in the same bed or room.

Men may struggle to reconcile all the new emotions they feel with the sexual feelings they had before the birth. Some find their partner's new maternal image and behaviour puts them off. Others find themselves unwillingly resentful of the sudden intense attention placed on the new arrival – and they may retreat from sexual contact as a result. Some men need time to recover from the effect of witnessing the birth. And men with daughters may find themselves rethinking their thoughts about women in general.

Breastfeeding has an anti-erotic effect for some. (It also has a contraceptive effect; see p.252.) It stimulates production of the hormones oestrogen, which can have the effect of lowering desire, and oxytocin, which is known as the love hormone – but for its affectionate, nurturing, cuddling qualities, not its erotic ones. While feeding a child, the breasts can become a sexual no-go zone for many new parents, although others find their newly bountiful size, and sweet stickiness – orgasm and arousal can stimulate milk flow – a huge turn-on.

As the baby grows into a child, many of these issues fade away or resolve themselves. Instead, time and energy become the biggest barriers to satisfying sex: the day is absorbed with relentless work, and by bedtime, sex is the last thing anyone feels like doing. Creating space to renew and reaffirm the sexual bond is important, though. Sex, after all, is one of the key things that distinguishes you from a couple of irritable friends who share chores and a place for sleeping. Children draw great strength from the emotional bond between their parents, and that bond needs cherishing if it's to survive.

Sex and ageing

It's often said that women "peak" in their thirties and men as teenagers, which is true if you're counting orgasmic capacity, but then orgasm isn't everything. Reported sexual satisfaction is broadly just as high for people in later life as it is for younger men and women. The years of awkward mistakes and experiments may be over, and work and young children may no longer be driving stress and exhaustion. Older people may know better what they want, how to ask for it – and, crucially, how to get it for themselves.

So much for the positives – which are widely trumpeted by sex experts eager to disprove the old-fashioned notion that sex is a game for the young. The actual experience of many older people, however, frequently involves decreasing desire (which may be a good or a bad thing), diminishing performance (which can erode self-belief and relationships alike), and steadily dropping frequency. One reliable survey of American seniors found half of 45–59 year-olds were having sex at least once a week, but among people aged 60–74 the figure was less than a third.

People in long-standing relationships undoubtedly get bored, or tired, or lazy. Their partner looks old, they feel old, they've put on weight – they just feel less sexy. They get ill, or have chronic pain, and the drugs they take for heart problems, ulcers, cholesterol, depression and any number of other conditions – especially in combination – undermine their sex drive. But loss of opportunity is perhaps the most potentially damaging of all the sexual consequences of age. Divorce or widowhood is a great wrecking ball smashing right through your sex life, as well as practically every other aspect of your existence,

and many older people don't want to begin again with someone new, or not yet.

Menopause and hormones

Technically, the menopause means the end of ovulation, and it's defined as not having had a period for a year. One survey came up with 51 as the average age at which this marker falls, but it can happen at any time from the mid-forties to the late fifties (and, for one percent of women, it happens before forty). When people talk about

Culturopause and "andropause"

The age around menopause is famously a stressful time in a woman's life. There's increased responsibility at work. Children may be growing up or leaving home, and declining parents may require care – a task which typically devolves principally onto women. Women may put on weight and feel unattractive – and be treated as such. So some feminists and doctors argue that symptoms of "menopause" such as fatigue or depression are cultural as well as medical: or "biosocial".

In Japan, where, broadly, older women occupy a more respected place in society, the symptoms of menopause appear to be less severe. And research has shown that Western women in relatively important positions, either at home or at work, tend to suffer fewer or less troubling symptoms. In Europe and America, where hormones are popularly supposed to govern emotions, women are often most worried about experiencing emotional or mental imbalance around menopause. And Western women do indeed experience irritability, anxiety or depression in greater numbers than in other parts of the world.

Men, of course, don't have a menopause equivalent in that they don't stop being fertile. But they are known to have midlife crises. If the (female) menopause might be partly a cultural phenomenon, could the male midlife crisis be partly a hormonal one? The idea of a male menopause or "andropause" has been supported by some pharmaceutical companies and campaigners. They point out that androgens such as DHEA halve between the ages of 20 and 60, and the drop is linked to a heightened risk of heart attack and stroke (and possibly to lower libido). Few official bodies go as far as to talk about an "andropause" (which means "the end of being male", in Greek), suggesting instead the more modest acronym ADAM, for Androgen Decline in the Ageing Male.

"the menopause", however, they usually mean the hormonal changes which women experience in the years before and after the last period – a time of life that doctors call the perimenopause, being the Greek for "around the menopause".

Menopause is caused by a natural decline in levels of the "female hormones", or oestrogens, specifically estradiol and estrone. This decline is caused in turn by the natural reduction in the number of eggs in the ovaries which produce the hormones. (Except in the case of "surgical menopause", which happens after a hysterectomy in which the ovaries are also removed – an oophorectomy or ovariectomy.) Sexist popular wisdom has it that as the oestrogens decline, the relative amount of "male" testosterone goes up, making women in their fifties aggressive "like men". In fact, androgen hormones like androstenedione and testosterone also decline: testosterone by as much as 30 percent.

Women may notice symptoms of hormonal changes anything from two to ten years before they actually stop having periods. Palpitations, joint pain, night sweats and disturbed sleep can

Sex in your eighties

❝ Many people don't want to do anything when they're older. They retire and sit in front of the TV. That's not for me: I have a porno film! It's a question of "use it or lose it", like anything else. The problem comes when I know I want to have sex and I can't ... I can't get a hard-on without Viagra, or much more stimulation, or more pauses in between. And the amount of sensation decreases if there's no erection. If I eat food now it doesn't taste the same: I need more spices, and with sex it's the same. I also have difficulty ejaculating. It takes a long time – it might take an hour. It means my partner has to be understanding. And with age, you become less mobile. What positions to take, how to stand, how to lie – that all has to be thought about a bit. I don't know of any benefits that come with age, really. Except maybe experience. My performance would have been better when I was younger if I'd been able to speak about it more openly, or if I'd had a partner or partners who also made an effort to do that. I don't know. It has taken me a while to do a little better sexually than I used to, but I'm getting there... **❞**

make life uncomfortable for maybe half of all women undergoing "the change", and hot flushes or flashes are experienced by more like two-thirds. The symptoms can last for two to five years. Unsurprisingly, many women suffer from fatigue, irritability or depression.

Whether or not the symptoms of menopause should be treated is a matter of fierce debate. For some, menopause is a natural part of ageing, and to attempt to remedy it is to devalue post-menopausal women. For others, the symptoms can be unpleasant and distressing, and lowered hormonal levels can have an actual effect on women's health: so why suffer needlessly? Illness, after all, is also "natural".

This was the thinking behind Hormone Replacement Therapy, or HRT, which was widely used until evidence emerged in 2002 that linked it to a slightly heightened risk of heart attacks, strokes, and certain kinds of cancer, including breast cancer. Hormones are now used in safer, lower doses for relief from menopausal symptoms, but the treatment period is normally limited to two to five years. The hormones given are oestrogen, often with a progestogen (rather like the Combined Pill – see p.234), and sometimes with testosterone, too if symptoms include low libido. Whether or not taking added testosterone can boost sex drive, however, is somewhat controversial (see p.11).

Grapes and raisins – sex and ageing for women

The end of fertility is often experienced as a loss, but it can also be a liberation: no more period pains; no more menstrual products; no more contraception. For some women, menopause also coincides with finding they care less about what other people think; their partners, meanwhile, may become more interested in exploring non-penetrative sex. For all these reasons, menopause can often bring increased sexual satisfaction.

Shere Hite's 2000 report even claimed that women experience a mid-life and later-life "sexual renaissance". Many older women, she said, discover multiple orgasm. A 2002 study from the University of Chicago at least confirmed that ageing women experience sexual dysfunction at half the rate of ageing men. This may be one reason why it's not that unusual for women in later life to find female partners, even though they wouldn't call themselves lesbian. Increased confidence may be another, powerful motivation.

The physical changes that typically accompany menopause, however, are rarely welcomed. A minority of women experience a reduction in libido, which may be caused by the fall in levels of testosterone. They say that they have fewer sexual thoughts and fantasies, that they're slower to become aroused, and feel less turned on once they are. Declining oestrogen, meanwhile, causes decreased blood flow to the genitals, making the vagina shallower, less flexible and less well-lubricated, while the tissue of the lips and clitoris becomes thinner and more delicate. It's sometimes said that "the grape becomes a raisin", though this colourful analogy makes the change sound much more extreme than it really is.

The changes to the vagina almost seem to militate against penetrative sex. It's not just the vagina's reduced size and increased tissue fragility – which may result in spotting or bleeding after sex. On arousal, the inner lips may not open, while vaginal secretions may not lubricate sufficiently for penetration to happen without help. It's easy enough to use a lubricant (see p.138), however, and some women also turn to some kind of dilator, perhaps along with an exercise regime

for the muscles of the vagina and pelvic floor, which has the useful side effect of combating the incontinence which plagues many post-menopausal women.

Another common solution is to explore other, non-penetrative kinds of sex. This may be one of the reasons that sexual satisfaction doesn't dip with age in the way one might fear. And there's no doubt that masturbation and orgasm help keep the vagina healthy, as well as the rest of the body (see p.180), by stimulating blood flow. Sex also provides a natural lift to levels of testosterone. Taking replacement hormones is the other alternative. Full-on Hormone Replacement Therapy carries certain health warnings, but it is possible to take low doses of oestrogen by means of vaginal creams or gels.

Using it and losing it – sex and ageing for men

Men remain fertile until the end, albeit at a declining rate. Potency – the ability to sustain an erection – is a different matter, however. Staying hard gets harder. Roughly half of men between forty and seventy have some degree of difficulty getting or keeping an erection. The most common effect of age is that stimulation needs to be continuous: you need to keep it up to keep it up. But spontaneous erections become rarer and rarer, too. And for roughly a third of men from their late fifties onward, erections are unreliable enough to seriously get in the way of sexual satisfaction.

Erectile dysfunction and its drug treatments are covered in the chapter on health (see p.288) but there's always an effective and pleasurable home remedy for the ageing effect. A 2008 Finnish study discovered that having sex once a week roughly halves a man's chance of developing erectile dysfunction; having sex more often further protects potency. Exercise, it seems, works for the penis just as well as it does for the heart and lungs. The Finns didn't examine whether solo sex was as effective, but it seems likely.

Some physical changes are chiefly significant on a psychological level. An erection's angle declines naturally as you get older, thanks to stretching of the suspensory ligaments that hold it up, so from around the sixties onward, most men's erections point outwards or downwards. The penis shrinks slightly with age, too, and ejaculations tend to get gentler. None of this affects sexual function, or sensitivity, or enjoyment. Some men keenly feel the loss of the skyward erections and leaping ejaculations of youth but in truth the smaller, softer erection of the older man is probably better adapted to the smaller, drier vagina of the post-menopausal woman.

Many men find that as the penis becomes less vigorous, sex actually improves – as if their dick had been getting in the way of good sex. As men age, they often find that they have more time and more inclination for cuddling, stroking and non-penetrative sex. They start to relax and enjoy themselves more. Perhaps men get less hung-up on their masculinity. Perhaps they're less worried about what people might think – less anxious about performance. A 2006 Norwegian–US joint study found that men in their fifties were just as satisfied with their sex lives as men in their twenties. One reason may be the reduced importance of penetration, and the discovery of pleasurable alternatives. Certainly, mutual masturbation and oral sex often become increasingly valuable parts of the sexual repertoire.

6

Contraception

6
Contraception

For thousands of years, people sought desperately for a contraceptive that actually worked. The ancient Romans thought the mysterious herb silphium so wonderful that it was worth its weight in silver – and was hunted to extinction. Luckily, innovations such as condoms, diaphragms and, of course, the Pill have effectively changed the world since then. Women can now control if or when they become pregnant – and who by. Relationships can now be unlimited in their sexual possibilities, without the attendant fear of pregnancy and without a commitment to the possibility of raising a child. Recreation and procreation got divorced, as it were, and most people thought they were much happier as a result.

Yet there are still cultural barriers. Information isn't widespread in countries with strong religious traditions, and even relatively liberal societies contain doctors who think sex outside marriage is a problem, or that young people shouldn't be having sex – and shouldn't, therefore, be having contraceptives. Condoms, especially, have stigmatized associations with illicit, casual, paid-for or teenage sex that are hard to shift. Many countries choose to limit how, when and where contraceptives can be advertised or sold. And, astonishingly, among the thousands of sexual encounters projected every day on air and online, almost none ever shows a contraceptive being used.

Condoms

Condoms don't just stop sperm getting to an egg, they also protect against most sexually transmitted infections (see p.263), which makes them unique among contraceptive devices. In the hands of experienced users, they also have fairly low failure rates: if 100 women restrict themselves to sex with condoms over the course of a year, just two will become pregnant. As a result, condoms are often said to be 98 percent effective.

Among younger people, however, the failure rate rises dramatically – condoms may be as little as 85 percent effective. The difference is partly about higher fertility but mostly about inexperience. Young men may put one on after penetration has begun, or unroll one hurriedly or carelessly; they may plunge in before their partner's vagina is adequately lubricated, causing the condom to tear; they may apply an oily lubricant which damages the rubber. They may have carried a condom around long enough for it to become damaged by age and wear. To avoid these pitfalls, see the box on p.264.

Some people feel embarrassed buying condoms, perhaps because of historic associations with venereal disease and sex workers. Attitudes take a long time to change. Acceptance only really began after troops in both World Wars were lectured about "putting it on before they put it in". Many soldiers took the habit home with them along with any surplus military-issue condoms. After the HIV-awareness campaigns of the 1980s, condoms became standard issue, and today it's

Contraceptive choice and sexual health

Which contraceptive to use is a deeply personal choice dependent on a combination of sexual preferences, menstrual patterns, medical history, age, weighing of risks and ethical outlook. There's no "typical user" but there are tendencies: young people often go for condoms, women with children may favour IUDs (formerly known as "the Coil"). And choice may be limited by what's on offer. Family doctors, in particular, may have their own areas of expertise and many are happier giving out a pill than a condom or a diaphragm. In Japan, condoms are king, while in the US, they're slightly less common than the Pill or sterilization. In the UK, the Pill, condoms and sterilization are equally popular choices. In future, the less-commonly used methods look set to grow in popularity, especially as the technology of delivery improves all the time.

Being "responsible" or careful about contraception is not at all the same thing as "safer sex" – which means not running the risk of catching a sexually transmitted infection. The only ways to be sure you won't pick up an sexually transmitted infection are to abstain altogether, to know absolutely everything about your partner's health or sexual history – or to use a condom. No other contraceptive device protects against infection. Sexual health is covered separately, in chapter 7 (see p.261).

Methods that don't protect against STIs

	Pros	Cons	Who uses it?
Diaphragms and caps	Can be inserted hours before use.	Fiddly at first. Messy. Only moderately effective.	Women who don't want to get pregnant just yet.
Combined Pill	Very effective. Can reduce PMS and heavy periods. Daily use can make women feel "in touch".	Remembering to take it. The wrong type may cause a number of side-effects (see p.238).	All women, but especially those with troublesome periods.
POP or Progestogen-only Pill	Effective. Probably fewer side effects than the Combined Pill.	Not quite as effective as the Combined Pill. Has to be taken with "obsessional" regularity. Progestogens can cause irregular bleeding and other side effects (see p.238).	All women, but especially those with regular lifestyles and who are past their mid-20s.
Intrauterine Device (IUD)	Highly effective.	Insertion needs medical supervision and can be painful. Can bring on heavy, painful or or unpredictable periods.	Relatively few women, given how reliable it is. Often – but not exclusively – women who have had children. Women with light periods.
IUS (IUD with a progestogen)	Incredibly effective. Lasts 5 years. Can relieve heavy periods.	Insertion needs medical supervision and can be painful. Expensive (if you're paying).	Women who want minimal risk of pregnancy. Women with problematic periods.
Injections	Extremely effective. One shot lasts 3 months.	You have to live with any side effects for three months. Can take a few extra months to wear off fully. See POP (Cons) regarding progestogens.	Women who don't want to worry about taking a pill.

	Pros	Cons	Who uses it?
Implants	Extremely effective. Can be removed if you don't like it.	See POP (Cons) regarding progestogens.	Women who don't want to worry about taking a pill – but might want to change their minds about getting pregnant soon.
The Patch	Very effective. You only think about it once a week.	Side effects slightly more likely than with the Combined Pill. May cause worries about it working loose.	Women who don't want to take a daily Pill.
The Ring	Very effective. Discreet. Stays in for 3 weeks.	Can cause vaginal irritation.	Women who don't want to take a daily Pill.
Fertility awareness method	"Connection" to cycle. No side effects. No going to hell, according to some.	To be effective, requires training and rigorous self-discipline. No sex some days.	Women who want to be in close touch with their bodies. Followers of certain religions.
Outercourse	No fuss. More orgasms for women.	Requires self-control.	People who've had enough of contraceptives and who aren't hung up on vaginal penetration.
Douching	Feels satisfying.	Doesn't work.	Nineteenth-century prostitutes and misinformed teens.
Vasectomy	The most effective method of all. Safe. No side effects.	It can't always be reversed. Makes some men feel emasculated. Takes three months to work.	Older men in very stable relationships with more than enough children.
Female sterilization	Less often regretted than vasectomy. Immediately effective.	Often needs a general anaesthetic. Slightly less safe than vasectomy.	Women who can't risk getting pregnant. Women in very stable relationships who don't and won't want (more) children.

Methods that protect against STIs

	Pros	Cons	Who uses it?
Condoms	Simple and effective contraception. The only method that protects against sexually transmitted infections. For some men, the blunted sensation can mean more staying power.	Careless or inexpert use can lead to splitting or leaking. Some find the pause in proceedings unsexy. Reduces sensation for some men, or causes softness or loss of erection.	Everyone, but especially young people and those without a regular partner. People concerned about STIs or HIV. People who don't like the "mess" of sex.
Female condom	Can be inserted hours before use. Good for men whose erections can be soft.	Ungainly looking. Expensive. Relatively unreliable.	Women who want to take on the responsibility themselves.

possible for one women's magazine columnist to write that "for many of us thirty and under, heterosexual sex without a condom is nearly impossible to imagine."

Kinds of condoms

A cave painting in the Dordogne dating from 10–15,000 BC supposedly shows an early model being put to good use, while the unfortunate wife of Minos of Crete legendarily employed a goat's bladder as an early kind of female condom. (Her husband ejaculated scorpions and snakes.) The ancient Egyptians wore delicate sheaths made of linen, the Chinese used oiled silk paper, the Japanese had little helmets of tortoiseshell and horn. In the West, the great sixteenth-century physician Fallopius recommended soaking linen sheaths in herbs and salts.

Before the patenting of vulcanized rubber in the 1840s, most condoms were made from animal guts. One 1828 recipe describes how a sheep's intestine would be soaked, macerated, scraped, exposed to burning brimstone, washed, blown up, dried, cut to length and provided with a fetching little ribbon to tie around the base. You can still buy reusable "skins" via specialist mail-order companies – and even condoms made from the air bladders of sturgeons, for the aristocratically minded – but latex rubber is now king.

To make a modern condom, a glass mould is repeatedly dipped in latex until thin layers are built up, and the condom is then heated to vulcanize the rubber. Despite being only 0.7mm thick (on average; in practice they range from the thin ice of 0.3mm to a mighty 0.9mm), they can stretch to well over a metre in length, and hold over 25 litres of air. Special forces troops even use them as emergency water carriers.

Carnival condoms

Some condoms used to come ready-lubricated with a spermicide, nonoxynol-9, but it was found that N9 could cause tiny abrasions on the skin which might increase the chance of an infection being transmitted. Petroleum jellies like vaseline and other oil-based products – including sun lotion and baby and massage oils – actually attack rubber, so mustn't be used. The only safe lubricants for use with normal condoms are water- or silicone-based ones (see p.139). Polyurethane condoms like Durex's (relatively expensive) Avanti model can be used with oil-based lubricants but they are hard to use correctly, possibly because they may be slightly looser fitting. Some men prefer them for exactly this reason, and, of course, for people with latex allergies they're a godsend.

One size fits most but not all, so if slippage or breakage is a problem – and either entirely invalidates the use of the condom – it's important to find alternatives. Look for names such as "Conform" and "Close Fit" or, alternatively, "Magnum" and "Comfort". Avoid the novelty types with "ticklers" or possibly glow-in-the-

Korean men dressed as sperm hand out free Durex condoms on the streets of Seoul.

Quondams, skins and overcoats

No one's quite sure where the word "condom" came from, but it probably stems from the Latin *condus*, meaning "receptacle". The first recorded use is, arguably, by Shakespeare, who, in *Troilus and Cressida*, has Hector mockingly accusing Menelaus's "quondam wife" of still swearing by "Venus' glove". There's a pun buried in there somewhere. In the eighteenth century, there was much talk of a Dr Condom or Cundum, supposedly physician to Charles II and inventor of a fine sheep-gut prophylactic, but it seems the good doctor never actually existed.

Today, condoms have spawned almost as many slang terms as penises. Some are fairly obvious: rubbers or skins in the US; "preservatives" in France and Germany; "lifesavers" in Australia; "things" or "gloves" in Italy; "shirts" in Portugal; Durexes or "rubber johnnies" in Britain. Some are political: the French used to call them *capotes anglaises*, or "English overcoats", while the English and Germans dubbed them French letters and *Parisers* respectively. In Thailand, condoms have taken on the name of the politician Mechai Viravaidya, who has heroically promoted condom use in his country since the 1970s. Thailand became the first country in the world to see a drop in rates of HIV infection in the 1990s, and the *mechai* became Thai slang for condom. Luckily, the Condom King was open-minded enough to take this as a compliment.

dark coatings, but without a government seal of approval. Reputable manufacturers do produce "ribbed" or "textured" condoms but despite brand names like "Mutual Pleasure" or "Rough Riders" they'll do nothing for most women – though they may marginally increase sensation for the man wearing them. Other models try to decrease male pleasure. "Performax" or "Extended Pleasure" are coated with benzocaine, to provide a degree of happy numbness for premature ejaculators (see p.168). The trick here is to put the condom on the right way round – but beware introducing strong chemicals to such a sensitive environment, right-way-round or not.

Condom colours are more adventurous than they once were, though conservative Britain still favours pinky tones. Black condoms – which are about as black as thin black stockings – are obviously marketed at black men, but curiously enough they're also relatively popular in Scandinavia and among gay men. In Japan, where 75 percent of couples use condoms – thanks to a long-standing ban on the Pill that was only overturned in 1999 – they can be found in a boggling range of colours, shapes and smells.

The female condom

The female condom is basically a kind of plastic sock that's held in place inside the vagina by rings at either end. You squeeze the smaller, enclosed ring together and push it inside the vagina and up against the cervix, where it springs into place (in the right place, you hope) and sits securely, much like a diaphragm. The open outer ring sits around the entrance to the vagina.

A Cambodian prostitute demonstrates how to use a female condom in a brothel in Phnom Penh.

The female condom puts women in charge, and can be inserted hours before having sex – no more fumbling around in the dark. They can also be a blessing for men who find it hard to maintain a full erection. Yet female condoms, much like female urinals, have never really caught on. Brand names like Femidom and Dominique may not have helped, and the first polyurethane models made an off-putting crinkling sound during sex. Newer models made of latex solve this problem, but you can still see the outer ring outside the vagina once the condom is in place – which can be disconcerting until you get used to it. The biggest drawback is that they're not quite as effective as the male version: one survey found that 21 out of 100 women who exclusively used a female condom for a year became pregnant, though the failure rate improves with experience.

The anti-rape condom

In South Africa, an estimated 1.7 million women are raped every year. In 2005, the campaigner Sonette Ehlers launched the fight back – or rather, the bite-back. She unveiled the Rapex: a latex sheath designed to be worn inside the vagina, just like a female condom. Where it sharply differs from the condom is in its lining. It has 25 tiny, inward-pointing barbs that spike into an attacker's penis. The idea is to give the woman time to escape while her would-be rapist "processes his surprise", in Ehlers' own words. And to discourage rape in the first place, of course. Responding to the inevitable storm of controversy – she had actually manufactured that figment of male nightmare, the *vagina dentata* – Ehlers commented that it was "a medieval device for a medieval deed."

From the Pill to the Patch

The "Pill" is a tiny dose of hormones that tricks the body into thinking it is already pregnant. Taken carefully, it effectively ensures you don't get pregnant. Failure rates are between 1 and 3 percent – that is, anywhere between one and three in a hundred women who take the Pill for a year will become pregnant. And that's usually because they forgot a Pill or because a bad stomach upset stopped it being absorbed. Among perfectly careful users, the failure rate drops to about three in a thousand women.

Worldwide, some 100 million women now swallow a Pill every day. The biggest downside is remembering to take it (and the fact that it doesn't provide any protection from sexually transmitted infections, of course). Side effects are an issue, too. Until they find the right pill for them, some women experience problems which can range from the upsetting (depression, loss of libido) and the unpleasant (acne, headaches, thrush) to the alarming (raised blood pressure, nausea, even deep-vein thrombosis in rare cases). Temporary weight gain can be a problem (see p.238). For many other women, the Pill solves more problems than it causes. Release from the exhausting cycle of heavy periods and premenstrual syndrome (or premenopausal symptoms) are other, major reasons why many women choose to "go on the Pill".

There are two main types of Pill. The original version, known as the Combined Pill, contains the "female hormone", oestrogen, as well as the "pregnancy hormone", progesterone (or, technically, the synthetic version of it called progestogen or progestin). The other type of Pill, known as the minipill, the progestogen-only Pill, or POP, isn't actually any smaller, and doesn't have a lower dose of hormones – it simply contains progestogen only, without oestrogen. There are fewer side effects, on the whole.

Many women worry about putting "chemicals" into their bodies. If the thought of imbibing human hormones sounds alarming, even in general terms, be reassured. Both hormones are synthetically derived from plants. In fact, the Pill only become possible when maverick chemist Russell Marker discovered he could create hormones from steroids he found – bizarrely enough – in a variety of wild Mexican yam.

The Combined Pill

The Combined Pill – sometimes called the COC or Combined Oral Pill – essentially mimics the hormonal levels of a pregnant woman. Women who take it, in short, don't have full periods (though they do have a monthly bleed). For many, this is a blessed relief, even leaving aside not having to worry about pregnancy.

Two hormones are at work: oestrogen and progesterone – hence the name "combined" Pill. Both hormones rise and fall naturally in the menstrual cycle. The oestrogen in the Pill prevents ovulation, and without an egg being produced there can't be a baby. Put more precisely, the oestrogen fools the brain's pituitary gland into thinking it doesn't need to produce follicle-stimulating hormone, or FSH; without FSH, the follicles in the ovary don't produce a surge of luteinizing hormone, or LH; without that LH surge, the ripened follicle doesn't release an egg. The synthetic progestogen in the Pill plays the part of progesterone, which naturally surges in the second half of the menstrual cycle; they thicken the mucus in the cervix, which stops sperm getting through with remarkable effectiveness.

The monthly "hormone-withdrawal bleed" that occurs with most Pills is not actually a true period at all, but a lighter shedding of the uterus's lining. This isn't actually necessary, but when the Pill was first designed it was felt that women would be reassured by a continuing monthly cycle and the body might benefit from a kind of hormonal week off. Lots of pills still allow for a week-long break every month, though most Pills can actually be taken right through. One recently developed Pill, Lybrel (aka Anya), is actually designed for continuous use, with a week's break at the end of every year. Others officially sanction what women call tricycling – taking three packets in a row before having a break (see box on p.236). The brands Seasonale and Seasonique are designed to be taken in this way, with just four week-long breaks a year, rather than twelve.

Health risks and benefits of the Combined Pill

If someone sat you down and talked you through all the possible side effects of taking the Pill, you might never go near it. But the benefits and drawbacks seem to balance out – especially if you take the numerous medical dangers of being pregnant into account.

Take the various cancer scares. It's true that the Pill increases your risk of getting both cervical and breast cancer. But not by much. Among under-35s, two women in a thousand will get breast cancer; one extra woman in that thousand may get it because of the Pill. For cervical cancer, the chance rises from 3.8 to 4 in 1000 because of the Pill. Set against the stark fact that one in three people develop cancer in their lifetime, these are long odds. Given that taking the Pill actually reduces the risk of getting cancers of the ovary or womb, some surveys suggest that, overall, the Pill protects against cancer.

In the 1960s, it was feared that the oestrogen in the combined Pill increased a woman's chance of developing cardiovascular disease. But the early researchers hadn't factored in smoking – and trend

Developed during the 1950s, the Combined Oral Contraceptive Pill became widely available from the mid-1960s onwards. It is now used by an estimated one hundred million women worldwide.

How to take the Pill

Read the instructions on your own packet carefully. Very carefully. And if you have any doubts or concerns, or if you miss a pill and don't know what to do, contact a doctor or a specialist advisory service.

Currently, almost all types of the Pill ask you to start on the first day of your period – so if it's a Tuesday, pick any pill marked "Tuesday" then go along day by day until, after three weeks, you've finished all 21 Pills in the pack. After that comes the week off, which allows a mini-period. Some brands require you to count off the seven Pill-free days in your head and start again on the eighth day (the same day of the week you always begin a new packet). Packs in ED or "everyday format" include seven dummy Pills.

You don't *have* to take a week off with any kind of Pill. Some women "tricycle" by taking three packets in a row before having a seven-day break. (To do this on a "triphasic" Pill, which varies the amount of hormones over the course of 21 days, you need to stick to the last rows of the packet only.) It's also possible to take the Pill uninterrupted, though most brands aren't designed for this. Contact a doctor or contraception expert if you're thinking of tricycling, or varying the way you take the Pill in any way, as brands vary.

It's best to take the Pill at the same time every day. With the Combined Pill, up to twelve hours late is OK, but less than ideal. Most brands of Progestogen-only Pill, however, have a narrow three-hour window, so even a late start at the weekend can throw this out. If you miss a Pill, start again the next day, but use additional protection – condoms, say – for seven days afterwards. (Technically, you'll need backup for only 48 hours on the Progestogen-only Pill but it's best to play safe.) Missing a Pill either side of the week-off is more risky than around the middle of the 21-day phase, when you've got a good dose of hormones in you already. Vomiting can also interfere with absorption: consider it a missed day. Some drugs also get in the way, including broad-spectrum antibiotics and the herbal remedy St John's Wort. If you're on anything else at the same time as the Pill, check it out. Theoretically, illegal drugs don't interact but then you never know what's actually in them.

If you're on the Pill, you're supposed to have a smear test, preferably with an internal examination, every three years. In fact, it's a good idea to have one if you're sexually active, no matter what kind of contraception you're using.

setting young women on the Pill were more likely than average to be on the gaspers as well, which meant they were having more strokes, heart attacks and the like. Still, to be on the safe side, a second generation of Pills was developed, supplying a lower dose of oestrogen. Even so, heavy smokers over 35 may still be advised not to take the Pill.

A second "Pill scare" arrived in 1995, when the desogestrel (a new kind of progestogen) in the "third generation" Pill was linked to venous thromboses, or blood clots in the legs. Women stopped taking their Pills in droves. Again, the link was quickly shown to be not quite as frightening as was first thought. Among 1000

Margaret Sanger and the Pill

It's easy to blame the mothers, but Margaret Sanger's undoubtedly had a lot to do with her daughter's extraordinary career. Anne Higgins, a devout Irish-American Catholic, was pregnant eighteen times. She gave birth to eleven children and died, broken by childbirth and tuberculosis, at the age of fifty. Her sixth child, Margaret, was determined to save women from similar fates.

Born in Corning, New York, in 1879, Margaret Higgins trained as a nurse before marrying William Sanger and moving to New York City, where she was drawn into the radical bohemian circles of Greenwich Village. She began writing a newspaper column under the provocative title of "What Every Girl Should Know". Unfortunately, what every girl needed to know was exactly what the censors insisted she shouldn't – methods of birth-control – and under threat of a prison sentence, Sanger fled to Europe. There, she visited Dutch birth-control clinics and had a brief affair with the father of sexology, Havelock Ellis.

Her belief in contraception reaffirmed, she returned to the US in 1915 and opened America's first birth-control clinic, which supplied Dutch-style spring-loaded diaphragms, an activity that briefly landed her in jail. She began lobbying vociferously for legalized contraception and, within just five years, more than a million women had written to her to ask for advice. Sanger also began funding scientists, backing the hormonal researches of Gregory Pincus and Min Chueh Chang and persuading a friend, Katharine McCormick, to provide help. McCormick was a biologist, a feminist and, crucially, the heir to a $35 million-dollar fortune. After meeting Pincus and Chang, she pumped $2 million into the project.

The result – the Pill – came within just a couple of years. Clinical trials, which began in 1954, were conducted by an utterly respectable Catholic gynaecologist, John Rock, who argued that the Pill was a natural form of contraception, not dissimilar to the Church-approved rhythm method. This vision was hugely influential in the design of Pill packets: in order to mimic a natural menstrual cycle as well as possible, women would be required to have a Pill-free week, even though it wasn't strictly necessary.

The Pill was launched onto the US market in 1960 but contraception wasn't legalized until 1966, and even then for married couples only. Margaret Sanger died a few months after the landmark judgement, and never saw the sexual revolution that the Pill inspired in the closing years of the 1960s. She never saw the counter-revolutionary strike, either – the 1968 papal encyclical *Humanae Vitae*, which declared that "artificial" birth control caused "a general lowering of moral standards" and made women "a mere instrument for the satisfaction of their own desires".

Margaret Sanger outside the Court of Special Sessions in 1917.

women taking the Pill for a year, just one more woman on a third-generation Pill would develop a blood clot than women taking a second-generation Pill.

The Pill also has health benefits. It halves the risk of pelvic inflammatory disease, and cuts a woman's chance of developing fibroids, duodenal ulcers and rheumatoid arthritis. Most importantly, perhaps, for most women, monophasic Pills (those which provide the same dose every time – which is the majority) greatly relieve PMS. Recent research has shown that having an endless succession of periods isn't necessarily "natural" anyway. One study from Mali, in West Africa, found that, because of later-onset menstruation and years spent pregnant or breastfeeding, Dogon women averaged just two periods between the ages of 20 and 24 and might have only 110 periods in their entire lives. A New Yorker, by contrast, might have up to 400.

Side effects of the Combined Pill

In terms of side effects, you can think of oestrogen as a broadly female hormone, and progesterone as a broadly male one – although both are naturally present in all women. Oestrogen can cause "feminine" effects, such as breast enlargement and tenderness, water retention (with weight gain and headaches) and increased vaginal discharge, along with nausea, brownish patches on the face and proneness to sunburn. Progesterone can cause spots or acne, greasy hair, increased appetite and weight gain – as well as vaginal dryness, spotting or (harmless) breakthrough bleeding. It can also cause depression and loss of desire, probably because it reduces levels of free testosterone.

Weight gain and the Pill

It's true: some women gain a few pounds when they go on the Pill. Water retention might amount to a kilogram of extra weight and can cause a bloated feeling, like in the week before your period. (Or it might just be that going on the Pill coincides with other lifestyle changes.) The newer, lower-dose Pill seems to have a smaller effect than the older formulations, however. One study of the brands Femodette and Mercilon found that over two-thirds of women stayed within 2kg of the same weight after a year on the Pill. Yes, fifteen percent of women did put on more than 2kg, but another fifteen percent lost 2kg or more.

These side effects are, medically speaking, minor. They won't kill you, or anything like it. But to take loss of desire or depression alone, there's little point in being on the Pill if you don't feel like having sex. And loss of desire may not be counted as a "medical" side effect but as a "behavioural" one – and therefore not subject to as stringent regulation. Fortunately, the body often adjusts to the Pill, and side effects tend to disappear within three months. If they don't, however, it's worth trying a Pill with a different balance of oestrogen and progestogen before giving up entirely.

A couple of brands use a type of progestogen that has particularly strong anti-androgenic effects – it actually blocks some more masculine-type side effects of the Combined Pill. Yasmin and Dianette, for instance, help clear up acne, and don't seem to cause the loss of libido that, it's increasingly clear, affects many women.

What happened to the male Pill?

The burden of contraception, like that of childbearing, seems unfairly loaded onto women. The Pill was developed in the 1950s. Where, women ask, is the male version? It's true that less than 10 percent of research money is spent on developing male alternatives, but it's not a misogynist conspiracy. The female reproductive system makes one egg every month. Men produce millions of sperm day and night. To make an effective contraception you've got to stop the vast majority getting through – and also guard against damaged sperm getting to the egg instead. You've also got to persuade men to remember to take it, even though they don't bear anything like the same level of risk or responsibility for a pregnancy.

Another major obstacle to the male Pill is the interdependency of the hormone for sperm production, follicle stimulating hormone (FSH), and the hormone for sex drive, luteinizing hormone (LH). Meddle with the first and you risk taking out the other. One promising possibility is the hormone inhibin, which apparently affects FSH without knocking out LH. Perfect. Except that inhibin can't yet be synthesized. It still awaits the magic Mexican yam that made artificial progestogens and the original Pill possible. Progestogens also turn off FSH production – but would have to be balanced by bump-up treatments of testosterone to stop

"Would you be more careful if it was you that got pregnant?" reads the caption of this famous birth-control poster of the 1970s.

feminizing side effects. In recent years, researchers have developed a number of combined hormone regimes, either as implants supplemented by injections, or as a pill and a patch. To date, however, drug companies haven't thought that there was enough of a market to spend the necessary millions developing a real-world drug regime.

The Progestogen-only Pill

As its name suggests, the Progestogen-only Pill (POP) only has the one hormone in it. (It's sometimes confusingly called the minipill, for this reason, but each individual pill isn't any smaller.) Unlike the Combined Pill, the POP only prevents roughly half of all ovulations. Rather cleverly, it prevents conception simply by causing the cervical mucus to thicken, meaning that sperm can't get to an egg, even if it has been produced. For the sperm, it's like trying to swim in jelly: too much like hard work. The POP also makes it slightly harder for an embryo to embed in the lining of the uterus.

The chief drawback of the way it works is that most brands are slightly less effective than the Combined Pill. Among young women, the risk of getting pregnant starts moving in the direction of unacceptable. If 100 women under 25 take the POP for a year, for example, four of them are likely to get pregnant. It's too many, so most specialists advise that only women over 30 take it, and those who cannot tolerate or otherwise shouldn't take the oestrogen in the Combined Pill – including breast-feeding mothers.

That said, a newly developed kind of POP has a slightly different kind of progestogen (desogestrel) that *does* stop eggs being released almost all the time – just 3 percent get through, and even those ones are just as safe from sperm thanks to the barrier of cervical mucus. At the time of writing, the desogestrel brand Cerazette/Organon was proving increasingly popular; new research had suggested that desogestrel was associated with a slightly higher risk of blood clots, but this Pill was still declared safe.

Pros and cons of the Progestogen-only Pill

Without the additional oestrogen, the body is more likely to continue its natural monthly cycle, and only one in five women on the Progestogen-only Pill stop having periods altogether. That's either a pro or a con, depending on your point of view. In other women, it causes an erratic pattern of bleeding, especially in the first couple of months. Periods can be longer, shorter, more or less frequent, unending or absent altogether. Leaving aside physical inconvenience, if you're inclined to worry about getting pregnant while on the Pill, even though your chances are small, this can be a pretty big psychological drawback.

In practical terms, the chief downside is that you have to take the POP at the same time every day, or within three hours of that time (see box on p.236). On the upside, the lack of oestrogen means that the Progestogen-only Pill has fewer side effects and health risks than the Combined Pill. It doesn't cause clotting, for instance, and can be used by diabetics. Women do report problems like weight gain, lack of desire, headaches and acne, but fewer seem to suffer from them than women on the Combined Pill.

Shots, Rods, Patches and Rings

Taking hormones by mouth has its disadvantages: the gut and the liver get in the way of absorption, plus you have to remember to take a Pill every day. Injections and implants are popular for their long-lasting effect, while patches and rings have the advantage that women can apply them on their own. Pharmaceutical companies are currently vigorously pursuing other methods of delivery, too.

The Shot – injected hormones

"The Shot" is basically the same as the Progestogen-only Pill, only at a higher dose which gradually runs down over time. It has a lower failure rate than the Pill partly because you can't forget to take it – though of course you do have to remember to get a repeat shot. This makes injections about as effective as it gets. Over the course of a year, between one and five in a thousand women will get pregnant.

There are currently two main brands available: Depo-Provera (or DPMA) and Noristerat. The former is more widespread, and has been used by more than 30 million women worldwide. It comes in the form of an injection in the bum or upper arm every twelve weeks. Noristerat is a more painful injection (because it's oil-based), and has to be repeated every eight weeks.

The main downsides are the same as for the POP, with the added drawback that you've got to live with any side effects for three months. Commonly reported problems include mood swings or depression, breast tenderness and irregular periods – though a little under half of women will have no periods at all within a year. Weight gain has been reported too: "marked and unpredictable" weight gain in some cases, to quote an expert. It's not an enticing prospect. If you want to get pregnant again, it does take a while for the effects to wear off. Women who have come off

Depo-Provera seem to take four months longer to get pregnant, on average. To be on the safe side, if you might be trying to conceive even within a couple of years, it's advisable to switch from injections to a shorter-acting method.

The Rod – implants

Implants allow an ultra-slow trickle of progestogen into the bloodstream. They work much like the Progestogen-only Pill or injections. Unlike the Pill, you don't have to remember to take an implant, however; unlike the Shot, if you don't feel good on an implant you can get a doctor to take it out again.

Putting in an implant is slightly more complicated than giving a shot, though. One of the most popular brands, Implanon, is about the size of a matchstick, but flatter. It takes about a minute to insert, under local anaesthetic, and leaves a tiny dot of a scar on the inside of the upper arm. There's no need for stitches. You can feel it under the skin, but you can't see it unless you're very skinny. Removal is much easier than it was with an earlier brand (Norplant), and it takes just a couple of minutes. Another brand, Jadelle, consists of two little rods.

Implants beat injections on their failure rates, too. If a thousand women have an Implanon capsule implanted for a year, just one will become pregnant. (Technically speaking, less than one woman will become pregnant, but that sounds odd.) It doesn't need to be topped up nearly as often, either, and can last for three years. Just like Depo-Provera and the Progestogen-only Pill, however, implants can cause irregular bleeding, and, for perhaps one in five women, this means frequent and prolonged bleeding. Otherwise the potential side effects are much the same as for other progestogen-only contraceptives.

The Patch

The Patch is the nickname for Ortho Evra, a thin sheet of sticky plastic less than 5cm square. Stick it on your bum, stomach, arm or back every week (with a week off after every third week), and it stops you getting pregnant. It sounds brilliant, and it's definitely worth considering as an alternative to the Combined Pill. It releases oestrogen and a progestogen in much the same way but is thought to be slightly more reliable, if only because you're less likely to forget about it.

One downside with the Patch is that it gives a significantly larger dose of oestrogen, meaning that some of the associated risks and side effects are greater, including the chance of developing a blood clot. It can, of course, fall off or become too loose to work properly, but you can be sure that the manufacturers have made it pretty damn sticky. It's not as effective on women who weigh over 90kg, and some women find it irritates their skin. It's also pretty visible, especially if you're not white or pale-skinned – at the time of writing it only came in a Caucasian "flesh" colour.

The Ring

NuvaRing – already known as "the Ring" – is splendidly discreet. It's thin, small (a woman with a tiny hand would struggle to get it on her wrist),

flexible, transparent and doesn't smell. It goes deep into the vagina where it's naturally held in place; there are very few nerve endings up there, so not many women can feel it. Every three weeks you hook a finger round it and pull it out. Then you wait a week (during which time most women have a period-like bleed) and insert a new ring at the end of the fourth week.

The Ring is basically a Combined Pill delivered in a clever new form. It would have much the same failure rate as the Pill except that you can't forget to take it, so it's likely to be slightly more reliable. It seems it can fall out – either during sex, while taking out a tampon or when really straining on the toilet – but this is quite rare. Internal irritation seems to be the main side effect, along with the usual drawbacks of the Combined Pill (see p.238) – though it does give a lower dose of oestrogen, which may work better for some women.

At the time of writing, a progestogen-only ring was undergoing clinical trials. It uses the synthetic progestogen nestorone, apparently to much the same effect as the Progestogen-only Pill.

Emergency contraception

The name of the "morning after pill" paints a vivid but misleading picture. In fact, you can take emergency contraception up to 72 hours after you had sex, which is enough time for anyone to get to a doctor or a clinic. That said, the quicker you take an emergency

Emergency Pill politics

An air of shame still lurks around emergency contraception. It can hint at a wild night of carefree and perhaps casual sex, which makes some people feel uncomfortable or censorious. In fact, women who take the emergency pill are just as likely to have suffered failed contraception: pills can be missed, condoms can burst or come off.

The furtiveness that clings to getting hold of an emergency pill is also the direct result of the obstacles that many governments irrationally put in the way of women getting hold of it. The emergency pill does no harm (although there is a very small risk of an ectopic pregnancy; if you miss a period see a doctor). Even taking it repeatedly doesn't seem to have any bad effects on health, though no one wants to monkey with their hormonal balance too much.

The slippery arguments of religious groups opposed to abortion – if not contraception in general, if not sex itself – don't help. Emergency contraception is not equivalent to abortion. Even if an egg has already been fertilized, a woman isn't considered to be pregnant until the blastocyst (the cells developing from the fertilized egg) is actually implanted in the wall of the uterus. This happens roughly seven days after fertilization. Until then, there's no embryo, no pregnancy – and no abortion. In fact, use of emergency contraception prevents many abortions from ever having to happen.

The truth is that supplying yourself with an emergency contraceptive is just as responsible as fixing yourself up with regular contraception. Some argue that women should have an emergency supply in the house as standard. The jury is out on whether or not this makes women more likely to have unprotected sex, and whether or not this matters. The only drawback is exactly the same as the normal Pill: taking it doesn't protect you against sexually transmitted infections, or HIV.

contraceptive the more likely it is to work. Within 24 hours is best: fewer than one woman in twenty will become pregnant if they take it within this time frame. Within twelve hours is possibly better still. Which means taking it … the morning after.

The emergency contraceptive (ECP) or post-coital (PCP) pill – also called "Plan B" in the US – is basically a bigger dose of the normal daily pill. It used to be a big enough dose to make women who took it feel very sick, and need anti-nausea pills to take alongside it. These days, the more advanced progestogen-only emergency Pills contain no oestrogen. While they still make some women feel a bit queasy, only about one woman in sixty will actually vomit – and, therefore, need another pill.

No one's absolutely sure how the emergency pill works, but it seems to have two main effects. If you haven't yet ovulated, it stops the ovary releasing an egg – which of course stops the sperm getting to it. (In a vaguely sinister way, sperm can hang about inside you for anything from two to seven days, just waiting to fertilize that egg. Trying to wash them out won't work, as they're well beyond reach; see p.213). If you have ovulated, the emergency pill changes the lining of the uterus, preventing a fertilized egg from implanting itself.

The chief alternative to the emergency pill is to have an IUD fitted (see p.246); this is effective for up to five days after unprotected sex, but the sooner it's done, the better. There is also a second kind of emergency contraceptive pill, the French-designed RU486, or mifepristone. It's currently licensed and chiefly used for early terminations, but is also very effective as an emergency contraceptive in that it prevents implantation. Whether or not political controversy will ever allow it to be licensed for that use is uncertain.

Diaphragms

The invention of vulcanized rubber in the mid-nineteenth century improved women's lot dramatically. It brought modern diaphragms, which remained hugely popular right up until the invention of the Pill. Nowadays, however, only about 2 percent of women choose to use diaphragms. The good thing about them is that you can put them in hours before having sex. The downside is that they're not all that efficient at preventing conception. Failure rates are slightly higher than condoms at 4–15 percent, and diaphragms don't provide any protection against sexually transmitted infections.

Diaphragms, caps and sponges

The celebrated eighteenth-century philanderer, Casanova, claimed to have invented the first effective diaphragm. He would cut a lemon in half, partly squeeze it, and place it in his lover's vagina so that it cupped over the cervix. In fact, women have used all kinds of internal barriers to sperm over the centuries, making pessaries from beeswax, sponges, pulped figs, empty pomegranate halves, honey, seedpods, salt, wool and even opium. In China, women inserted discs of oiled bamboo paper; in Easter Island, they used clots of seaweed and algae. Casanova's recipe hardly sounds enticing but it would actually have been one of the more effective, thanks to lemon's sperm-killing acidity.

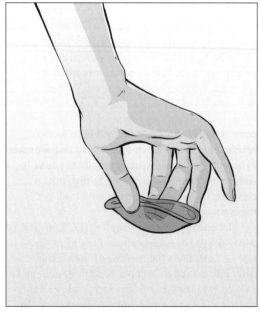

Inserting a diaphragm, step 1: bend the ring flat.

Diaphragms are sometimes called "caps" but work slightly differently from the cervical cap. The diaphragm is tricky to fit at first. It's basically a disc of rubber with a sprung edge that makes it fit snugly against the walls at the upper end of the vagina. You have to bend the ring flat then slide the cap into place – rather like a tampon, only more fiddly. You then need to check that the disc is actually sitting over the cervix by prodding it with a finger. To remove it you need to hook it with a finger and dislodge it from its place before pulling it out. Different kinds of diaphragms have different kinds of springs and slightly different methods of insertion, so it's important to learn the right method from a qualified health professional.

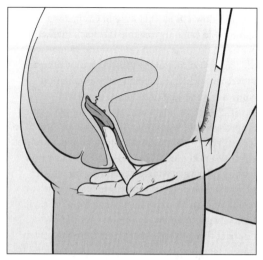

Inserting a diaphragm, step 2: insert so it sits over the cervix.

Cervical caps

Women who can't seem to hold onto their diaphragms or who are prone to cystitis can sometimes use a cervical cap instead. They're sometimes called "Dutch caps" in the English-speaking world, in tribute to their popularity in Holland and Germany in the late nineteenth and early twentieth centuries – and because diaphragms, confusingly enough, are sometimes colloquially called "caps". Cervical caps are about as effective as diaphragms but they're usually even harder to work with – especially the so-called "honey cap", which is soaked in sticky beeswax. Caps stay put by means of suction between the cap and the cervix, so they have to fit very closely, and don't work for all women. The contraceptive experts Szareweski and Guillebaud observe that to use the Prentif cavity-rim cap (one of the three main types), "you must have a reasonably long,

straight-sided, symmetrical cervix and must also be able to reach it properly". It sounds daunting. "Short fingers and a long vagina", they observe, po-faced, "are not a good combination here."

The sponge

One of the least effective contraceptives of them all – leaving aside crisp packets and crossed fingers – has one of the most distinguished histories. The ancient Hebrews used the *mokh*, a sea sponge soaked in vinegar. Some rabbis disapproved, but it was usually allowed for very young girls and nursing women. Sea sponges remained popular for a long time. One of the lesser-known disasters of the American Civil War was the terrible shortage of contraceptive sponges experienced by the North. All the sponge fisheries down in Florida were in Confederate hands. One can only imagine the black market prices. In the nineteenth century, the sponge was the (soggy) banner of the radical, neo-Malthusian movement, which campaigned for population control as a method of reducing poverty.

In the 1920s, the feminist campaigner Marie Stopes was still recommending a sponge dipped in olive oil but, in a modern context, sponges are not effective enough to use as regular contraception. Failure rates vary widely depending on which study you look at, but something like one or two women in ten who use the sponge for a year will typically get pregnant. Some surveys put the figure at three in ten. Apart from being relatively unreliable, sponges offer no protection from STIs. Some users also find the spermicidal foam they produce alarming. And rightly so: the chemicals in spermicides can cause allergic reactions, yeast infections and even (rarely) toxic shock; they can also make transmission of infections easier by causing minute abrasions on the skin.

Intrauterine Devices and Systems

Women have long put contraceptive pessaries inside their vaginas (see p.244), but placing a device actually inside the uterus is an achievement of modern medicine. Well, a ninth-century Persian authority did recommend inserting a twist of paper soaked in ginger water into the cervix, but it never seemed to catch on. It may have stung a little.

An effective Intrauterine Device had to wait for Ernst Gräfenberg, the German doctor who also "discovered" the G-spot (see p.47). He first experimented with devices made of silk, but the string that allowed them to be removed acted as a conduit for disease. In 1929, Gräfenberg came up with the silver "G-ring", which was taken out using a hook. It proved remarkably effective. The nickname "the Coil" came from the first plastic IUD, the Marguiles Coil, which had a spiral shape. Unfortunately, it also had a rigid plastic tail projecting into the vagina, which made it none too popular with men.

IUDs were very popular in the 1960s, but their reputation was hugely dented by the Dalkon Shield scandal of the mid-1970s. Poorly designed and inadequately tested, the Shield's tail had the same old problem: it acted as a conduit for infection. Thousands of women using it suffered from pelvic inflammatory disease: many became infertile; some lost babies; a few died. Since then, rigorously tested IUDs have crept slowly back into widespread use in the West, though they have always remained hugely popular in China, where it's the most common type of contraception.

Copper, T-shaped IUDs have largely replaced plastic, and provide safe, excellent protection against conception. Launched in 1990, the Mirena Coil is the one exception. This "Intrauterine System" acts as a normal IUD but also releases a progestogen, providing Pill-type protection as well.

Contraceptive futures

The "male pill" remains where it has been for a good decade, just a few years away (see box on p.239), but meanwhile non-hormonal technologies are starting to make pharmaceutical companies sit up and listen. One technique stops sperm developing by breaking their link with the Sertoli "nurse cells" which help them grow. Another system, based on cutting-edge genetic science, is aimed at women. A gene called ZP3 is switched on in eggs just before they are ovulated; if this gene is knocked out using a technique called RNAi interference, an egg will be made without an outer membrane – and without that, a sperm can't bind on and fertilize it. Unfortunately, the Sertoli-cell technique has so far only been shown to work in rats, and the RNAi method in mice. The "biotec patch", then, is a long way off.

As for hormonal contraceptives, it will all be about delivery in the future. Already, they don't just come in a Pill any more, they come in a Coil, a Jab, a Rod, a Patch and a Ring. Nasal sprays have been touted as another possibility and other systems, be sure of it, are on their way. Some devices may use different kinds of hormones, like anti-progestins, which counteract the effects of progesterone and thus suppress ovulation.

Fertility awareness is the other big hope. Fertility monitors can become far more sophisticated than they are currently. Research into artificial fertilization is leading the way in this area, and a little creative crossover could put "natural family planning" back on the agenda for millions.

IUDs

On one level, Intrauterine Devices (or IUDs, sometimes known as "the Coil") act as a kind of irritant. Responding to a foreign presence, the body attacks it with white blood cells, to protect against infection. As a side effect, the cells also clean up any foreign sperm they encounter, and will even deal with an egg released by the woman herself. They also make the uterus's lining an inhospitable place for a fertilized egg, and the copper content of most IUDs also acts as a spermicide on its own account. The result is a highly effective contraceptive device – if 200 women use them for a year, between one and four will get pregnant by accident. The higher figure refers only to younger and thus more fertile women.

Most copper IUDs can stay in for five years. Which is just as well, as having one fitted is one of the main drawbacks. Women who haven't had children, especially, may find it painful enough to need a local anaesthetic – which, being injected around the cervix, isn't that much fun. Maintenance is pretty much only a matter of checking that the threads that stick out of the cervix are still in place after every period. For an IUD to disappear into the uterus is a rare problem, but not one you'd want to have.

Some women just won't ever be happy with the thought of something artificial being placed that deep inside their bodies. Physically, the chief drawback of IUDs is that most women's periods become heavier, longer and sometimes more

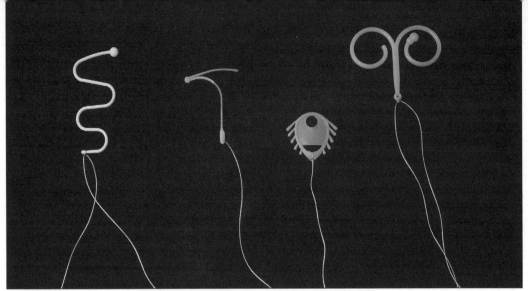

A slightly alarming display of intrauterine contraceptive devices.

painful. This has pretty much restricted their use to women with relatively light periods, though a fairly new kind of IUD has reduced some of these problems by reducing the size of the device. Instead of having a "T" shape, with the top bar holding the IUD in place, the frameless GyneFix is attached to the top of the uterus with a nylon thread. Fitting, clearly, is more fiddly.

The chief medical risk of IUDs is that fitting them can cause an infection. (This has nothing to do with sexually transmitted infections.) Infections, rarely, can cause infertility, so many doctors prefer not to fit IUDs to women who haven't had children. It's very rare, but there's also a chance of perforating the uterus when an IUD is inserted. If you're one of the unlucky few who actually gets pregnant while an IUD is inside you, there are added dangers for the foetus. To avoid a higher chance of miscarriage

or premature birth, doctors usually try to gingerly remove the IUD, but it isn't always possible. The other risk is having an ectopic pregnancy – where the embryo starts growing in a Fallopian tube rather than in the uterus.

Hormone-releasing IUDs – the IUS

Intrauterine Systems are a combination of a normal IUD and the Progestogen-only Pill. A tiny capsule on the device releases the progestogen levonorgestrel very slowly, so that it lasts the full five years that the IUD is carried. The Mirena IUS, which is the only brand currently available (though others are in development) has an extraordinarily low failure rate of around two women in a thousand using it for a year. It also causes fewer problems with menstruation in that, unlike the copper IUD, most women using it have lighter and less painful periods.

Alongside the usual benefits of progestogens, the Mirena does have the familiar side effects as well (see p.238). It often causes breakthrough bleeding, for instance, especially in the first few months, and roughly a fifth of women won't have periods at all after a year, which some women find nerve-wracking. The Mirena IUS is also larger than other IUDs, so trickier and more painful to fit, especially if you haven't had children. If you're paying for your contraception yourself, there's another drawback. It costs about ten times as much as a copper IUD.

Counting, rhythm – and fertility awareness

At some point in their lives, most women will probably do some urgent, rough mathematics to work out whether or not they were "safe" the night before. As a regular approach to contraception, however, rough won't cut it. You need to know all the details of your menstrual cycle, plus how that tallies with your fertile and infertile phases. A number of "rhythm" or "calendar" methods can help with the calculations, but they're not reliable. Some even call them "Vatican roulette", thanks to the Catholic Church's support for this approach.

To have a decent chance of avoiding conception, you need to identify the fertile period around the time of ovulation. Some women feel pain in the 24 to 48 hours around ovulation – a pain known as *mittelschmerz* or "middle-pain" becomes it comes roughly in the middle of the menstrual cycle – but it's not a reliable guide, and most women have no idea when their ovaries release an egg. As a result sophisticated "fertility awareness" or "sympto-thermal" methods have been developed. Using three combined techniques of measuring temperature, the consistency of cervical secretions (also known as mucus) and cervical position, the fertile and infertile times can be plotted on a chart. Recent research has found that if people know the rules backwards, and stick religiously to them, fertility awareness can be as effective a method of contraception as the Pill: roughly one woman in 200 will become pregnant over the course of a year.

It does require commitment. Unfortunately, most people aren't all that tough-minded, and they're not all superb diary-keepers or temperature-takers either. Typical failure rates in fertility awareness can be anything from 1 to 25 percent – that is, if 100 women use this method for a year, anything between one and twenty-five of them will get pregnant. The wide range shows the importance of being taught the method by a specialist health professional; if you "go it alone", you could get pregnant very quickly. The other drawback should be obvious. You'll need a back-up method for those fertile days – or not have penetrative sex at all for at least ten days per cycle, on average.

Counting methods, and the Standard Days

The main method of birth control based on counting days is known as the Standard Days. It's relatively simple to follow, and gives a fixed formula for women whose cycles range between 26 and 32 days. Basically, you're considered to be infertile for seven days from the onset of menstruation; days 8 to 19 of the cycle are the fertile danger period; then, from day 20 onwards, you're infertile again.

Unfortunately, this ready reckoner is not particularly reliable, especially if your cycle is less than regular, or you mistake spotting or other kinds of bleeding for a period. You can buy sets of beads to help you keep count. Ideally, you'd develop a personalized calendar based on previous cycle lengths with the help of a trained professional.

The Knaus-Ogino method (or variation) still sometimes crops up. It is based on a more sophisticated method of counting than the Standard Days, but it's not a reliable method – though its calculations still play a role in fertility awareness calendars.

Fertility awareness methods

Relying on mental arithmetic for contraception is a worry. The joy of fertility awareness methods is that they allow you to find out exactly when you are fertile. There are essentially three techniques: you take your temperature, check the consistency of your cervical mucus and monitor the condition of your cervix. You then plot the results of all three "fertility indicators" on a kind of calendar, or chart. Some women don't use all three techniques at once, but the more indicators you have, the more reliable the method.

Taking readings – the three techniques

After an egg is released at ovulation, the ovary produces more progesterone. This makes the body slightly warmer. The basal body temperature technique (BBT), therefore, involves taking your waking temperature – which means first thing in the morning using a specially accurate thermometer. This can go under the tongue (slower) or in the vagina (faster). After three days of a consistent rise in temperature, you can be sure you've ovulated, and it's safe to have sex. Unless, that is, you've had a cold or a fever …

In the lead-up to ovulation, oestrogen levels in the body rise, causing cervical secretions (or mucus) to become whiter at first, then clearer and more and more slippery – or stretchy, like raw egg white. After ovulation, the secretions quickly become drier, thicker and stickier. With some training in the so-called "Billings method", women can learn to identify the different stages. Unless, that is, the secretions are confused with left over semen or lubricant, or their consistency is changed by a dose of thrush …

The third method involves some careful internal exploration. As ovulation approaches, the cervix withdraws higher into the vagina. It's only a slight movement, but it becomes softer, more

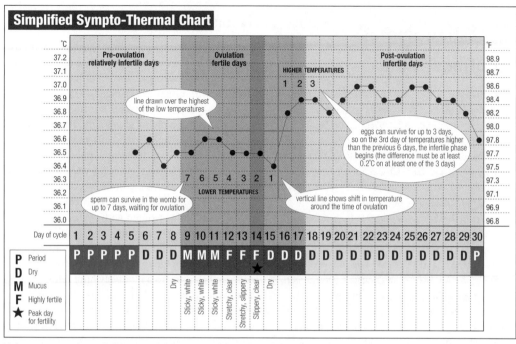

Simplified Sympto-Thermal Chart

Pre-ovulation relatively infertile days | Ovulation fertile days | Post-ovulation infertile days

HIGHER TEMPERATURES

line drawn over the highest of the low temperatures

eggs can survive for up to 3 days, so on the 3rd day of temperatures higher than the previous 6 days, the infertile phase begins (the difference must be at least 0.2°C on at least one of the 3 days)

7 6 5 4 3 2 1

LOWER TEMPERATURES

sperm can survive in the womb for up to 7 days, waiting for ovulation

vertical line shows shift in temperature around the time of ovulation

	Period
P	Period
D	Dry
M	Mucus
F	Highly fertile
★	Peak day for fertility

Using a sympto-thermal chart correctly requires training from a qualified professional.

open and wetter, too – something like a moist lip. After ovulation, the cervix moves down into the vagina again, and becomes drier, firmer and more closed – more like the tip of a nose. Some women find it hard to find their cervix, and hard to feel the difference, so this third technique isn't always used.

Charting fertility

To get any kind of accuracy, you need to plot at least two of these indicators, and preferably three, on a dedicated chart. You can find these free online (and for an example chart, see above) but you really need to be taught how to use one, and how to work out the fertile period – which is up to three days after the temperature rise signalling ovulation (during which time the ovum may still be alive) and up to seven days before it (which is how long sperm can survive in the womb). The rest of the time you can go wild (although depending on the length of your cycle, this may only allow for a little well-timed wildness).

Unfortunately, the phase before ovulation is not *entirely* infertile. The other drawback is that lots of external factors can affect the readings. You have to know how to recognize them. Having a cold or thrush, as mentioned above, is only part

Breastfeeding as contraception

Breastfeeding is a natural contraceptive. (This is just as well, as you can't take the Combined Pill while you're doing it.) A baby's suckling action makes its mother's pituitary gland produce prolactin. This hormone makes the breast produce more milk but also blocks the release of hormones that tell the ovaries to produce more eggs. In theory, the "Lactational Amenorrhea Method" is highly effective (up to 99 percent) for as long as six months after childbirth, or up to the first sign of a bleed. In practice, however, few women can rely solely on it, and it's usually advised for older women who will want another child. It pretty much works if you're feeding using the breast only: no solids, no breast pump, no occasional bottle. This is because you have to be feeding regularly and often, which generally means offering the breast on demand even through the night (or at least with gaps between feeds of no more than six hours). Otherwise, the levels of prolactin drop and the ovaries become active again.

of the picture. Stress, travel, shifts in time zones or sleeping patterns, alcohol – all can mess up your chart. In larger life terms, breastfeeding, approaching menopause and having just come off the Pill can dramatically alter the readings, too.

Testing kits

Technology is making fertility awareness methods easier and less stressful. The Persona device looks like a big personal organizer but is actually a laboratory in miniature. Using test sticks (very like a pregnancy test), it measures hormonal levels and gives you either a red or green light. Red means you could conceive; green means go for it. After the initial, three-month learning phase, where the machine gets to know your cycle, you only need to do the test eight times a month.

If women use Persona perfectly (and it's only recommended for women with cycles consistently between 23 and 35 days long, and who haven't come off the Pill and aren't breastfeeding), six in 100 will get pregnant after a year's use, the company claims. It's a relatively high failure rate compared to, say, the Pill, and it doesn't allow for misuse or mistakes. Other companies are bringing out rival products all the time, but at the time of writing they tended to be marketed as devices for women who are actually trying to conceive: the reason seems to be that they're even less accurate.

Withdrawing and withholding

The book of Genesis tells the story of Onan, who was told to marry his dead brother's wife. Knowing that any children wouldn't legally be counted as his own, and not feeling altogether delighted about this, "when he went in unto his brother's wife", he "spilled his seed" on the ground. Bible commentators concluded that withdrawing before ejaculation to prevent conception was a sin. A later group of moralists – nineteenth-century doctors, this time – insisted that withdrawal had terrible effects on the health. Marie Stopes thought it put such a strain on the nervous system that men became "thoroughly nervous and run-down".

Of course, withdrawal does no harm – unless you count psychosexual frustration, or pregnancy. Even assuming that the man is iron willed enough to withdraw every time, sperm may leak through before ejaculation in pre-come or in the residue in the tubes from a previous ejaculation (so pee first to flush them out). Experienced, older couples can achieve success rates of 90 percent – that is, 10 women in 100 using withdrawal for a year will get pregnant. The chances for younger, more fertile women with more inexperienced partners, however, don't bear thinking about.

Withholding – coitus reservatus and obstructus

If you thought withdrawal required steely control, coitus reservatus is the highly tempered version. To achieve it, the man has to hold back his ejaculation altogether – while still, ideally, having an orgasm, though this takes considerable practice. In ancient China, reservatus was designed to preserve the precious *qi* or life-force otherwise wasted in ejaculation (see p.170). In medieval Europe, it allowed a man to have sex with his wife – thus protecting her from the mysterious disease of

Natural contraception?

Fertility awareness used to be called the "rhythm" or "calendar" method, because sex had to be restricted to an estimated "safe period" within the rhythm of the menstrual cycle. This method of avoiding pregnancy has been authorized by the Catholic Church since 1930 – although the Vatican only got round to telling its followers as much in 1945.

Today, the Vatican prefers the term "Natural Family Planning", or NFP – presumably in order to emphasize that other methods are somehow "unnatural". Sceptics counter that measuring your body temperature and the stickiness of your cervical mucus hardly amounts to communing with nature. Fertility awareness doesn't involve taking pills or putting anything on or in your body, however, so it could be said to be a "natural" method of contraception. For some people, including many religious believers, this makes it the only choice.

Others disagree. In 1923, birth-control campaigner Marie Stopes tartly observed that the rhythm method was "a cold, calculating, pseudo-restraint which tends to debase the true sex relation and reacts unfavourably on the character of both participating parties". It was, moreover, she added with a snort, "quite unnatural". Her preferred method was the judicious application of a sponge. A natural sea sponge, of course.

A proud Irish father with his brood. The influence of the Catholic Church in Ireland meant that contraception was officially banned until the 1970s.

hysteria (see p.182) – while avoiding experiencing any sinful pleasure.

The masturbation anxieties of the nineteenth and twentieth centuries (see p.338) brought reservatus back into fashion. In the communalist utopia of Oneida, New York, it was supposedly a sign of grace – and had the useful side benefit of allowing free love without endless pregnancies. In the 1890s, the pioneering gynaecologist and feminist Alice Stockham advocated a kind of coitus reservatus she called "karezza" (see p.123), from the Italian word for a caress.

The more sophisticated version of reservatus is known as coitus obstructus. In origin, it's an ancient eastern practice, particularly beloved of Taoism and Indian Tantrism. You have to press firmly on the perineum (between bum and balls; see p.51) just before orgasm, so that the urethra is temporarily blocked. Positioning and timing are crucial – and very hard to get right. According to the ancient Chinese texts, concentration, controlled breathing, pressing the tongue against the roof of the mouth and gnashing the teeth may help. Anatomically, the ejaculate diverts into the bladder, and is lost later at urination. As with withdrawal, however, this doesn't solve the problem of stray sperms sneaking out before or after orgasm, so it's not a reliable method.

Outercourse

Traditionally speaking, outercourse meant rubbing without penetration – or what later generations would call "dry humping". In colonial New England, courting couples were actually bundled up in bed together, either tightly clothed or with a "bundling board" separating them. Oddly, the practice fell out of fashion. Today, outercourse can cover anything from massage and mutual masturbation to the various kinds of quasi-penetrative sex – that is, using the thighs, breasts, an armpit or even the soles of the feet or the back of the knee to stimulate a penis. For women, especially, this may well lead to more orgasms than penetration.

Oral and anal sex, of course, allow penetration without conception – though you do still need to be careful about where the semen gets to. Archaeologists have sometimes assumed that anal sex was a particularly widespread type of contraceptive, based on its frequent depiction on, say, Peruvian and Greek pottery decorations. The thought that it might just have been fun doesn't seem to have occurred to them.

Sterilization

Sterilization is hugely popular among older couples. It's simple – especially in men – and very effective. For couples who have had children already, who don't want more and aren't worried about sexually transmitted infections, it seems a strong candidate. The obvious drawback is permanency. Relationships may break down or end in bereavement; more rarely, losing a child makes some couples think again about having more children. One problem that many couples don't envisage is that risk-free sex can dampen some people's desire.

The snip – vasectomy

Vasectomy means putting a snip in the vas deferens – the tube which carries sperm from the testes into the body. It's also called tubal sterilization. It's a simple operation done under local anaesthetic, and requires just a day of bed rest followed by a week's strategic use of supportive underpants. Failure rates are as low as 1 in 2000 men, though it does take a couple of months before the operation takes full effect. Afterwards, men still ejaculate in exactly the same way as before. At least, it looks the same, it's just that the active but microscopic sperm content isn't getting through.

Vasectomy reversal, which is requested by ever-increasing numbers of men, isn't quite as straightforward. If you're paying, it's also expensive. A newer technique of using clips rather than a scalpel to sever the tubes does get better results than the older, less kind type of cut, which could be successfully reversed in just 50 percent of men, though a long delay between the vasectomy and reversal can increase the chances of a man having built up antibodies to his own sperm.

Better figures may yet be achieved if research on blocking rather than cutting the tubes bears fruit. One technique involves inserting silicone plugs. Another envisages injecting the tubes with a mixture of polyurethane and silicone rubber.

A family planning sign in Bombay offering payment (and gratitude) both for sterilization and for encouraging others to be sterilized.

Promising results have also been achieved with methlycyanoacrylate – a substance better known as Superglue. Heat-based treatments, where the testicles are subjected to a short burst of high energy, aren't working out quite so well. Few men like the thought of boiling up their bollocks.

Female sterilization

Sterilizing women means cutting, tying, blocking or removing the Fallopian tubes, which carry the egg into the uterus. Laparoscopic sterilization is the most common technique. Under either a local or general anaesthetic, a microscopic tool is inserted through the navel along with a tiny camera on the end of a fibre-optic cable. A surgeon then cuts,

electrically burns, clips or ties the tubes, and ties the ends up. For some reason, Fallopian tubes just love to come together again, and this is the main reason that between one and five in 1000 female sterilizations fail.

A salpingectomy, in which the tubes are removed altogether, is a more serious operation and rarely done just for the purposes of sterilization. Hysterectomy, which means taking out the uterus altogether, and salpingo-oophorectomy, in which the ovaries and Fallopian tubes are excised as well, are bigger operations still. Nowadays, they're only done for medical reasons, and as a last resort. Even then, the procedures are increasingly controversial. Leaving aside medical risks and complications, they can have unpredictable effects on hormone levels and the

The Real Thing

For some men, the very act of getting out a condom makes them lose their erection – which of course makes it impossible to put it on. As Martin Amis puts it in his teen-confessional novel, *The Rachel Papers*, "after thirty seconds my cock was a baby's pinkie and I was trying to put toothpaste back in the tube." The sudden halt in physical stimulation, the break in the mood, self-consciousness, performance anxiety, the thought of pregnancy or disease – these are just some of the reasons a condom can ruin the moment.

And then there's sensation. As one man put it, "sometimes I just want to feel the real thing." The popularity of "bare-backing" – anal sex without using condoms – in some gay circles proves just how powerful this desire can be. Among heterosexual couples, the focus may be on the feeling of potency. Couples who start "trying for a baby" may find that sex suddenly acquires a new erotic dimension. Some love the earthy, free, "natural" feeling of "letting nothing stand in the way". Some feel a deeper intimacy and a stronger emotional bond, perhaps born of the sense that each act of lovemaking represents a commitment to a shared future.

For one man, tragically, his vasectomy had the opposite effect. "After I had it done", he recounted to his doctor, morosely, "she completely went off sex. We went for counselling and she realized that she enjoyed the risk-taking, the chance that a pregnancy might happen after all." If modern contraception has freed sexual pleasure from the shackles of procreation, it may have lost something in the process. Lovemaking when you might just conceive a child, in other words, can be the sexiest kind of sex.

sex drive. That said, some women get such relief from very heavy periods or period-type pains that they find themselves more free to enjoy sex.

Abortion

While it's not, technically speaking, a contraceptive choice – given that it takes place after conception – millions of women have abortions every year so as not to have a child. Abortion is therefore covered in this chapter. The vast majority of abortions take place in the first trimester, within twelve weeks of conception, before the foetus officially becomes an embryo. Later-term abortions are relatively rare.

How abortion works

The earliest abortions are usually "medical". This generally means going to a clinic to be given two drugs. The first, mifepristone or RU486, blocks the action of progesterone in the body and breaks down the bond of the embryo to the wall of the uterus. The second drug, prostaglandin, is taken a day or two later. It essentially brings on a miscarriage, during which the pregnancy is lost. Many women go straight home after taking the second drug so that they can miscarry in private, at home. This usually takes place within four to six hours, accompanied by severe cramps, like a heavy period, and perhaps with shivering and nausea. At some point, many women feel the need to go to the toilet and sense something is being expelled.

Symptoms subside quickly afterwards, though some bleeding and cramps, or passing of further clots, can continue for a few days.

Surgical abortions

For some women, a medical abortion allows them to take control of the process and to stay out of the hands of the medical profession and its invasive procedures. It also allows them to go through a kind of miscarriage, with all its attendant emotions. For other women, surgical abortion is a better choice. (And mifepristone can only be used for up to 49 days in the US, or 63 days in the UK.) They find the professional presence reassuring, and the surgical process less upsetting.

In a surgical vacuum abortion, the foetus is removed from the uterus using suction, either in an equipped treatment room or an operating theatre. A thin plastic tube is pushed up into the uterus via the vagina. A vacuum is created using a kind of syringe (Manual Vacuum Aspiration) or an electric pump (Electric Vacuum Aspiration), and the contents of the uterus are drawn into the tube. It takes about ten to fifteen minutes in all. Vacuum abortions are usually restricted to the first fifteen weeks and are generally done using as little anaesthesia as possible, though some women opt for a general anaesthetic. Most women feel moderate period-pain-type cramps, and experience some bleeding for up to two weeks afterwards.

Vacuum abortion is fairly safe – much safer than childbirth, certainly. The main risks are having to come back for further suction treatment, or the procedure causing some damage to the cervix. (The chances are about 1 in 100 either

way.) There's also the possibility of pelvic inflammatory disease. The emotional risks are harder to define. Some women feel upset, some relieved. A few find themselves distressed or even traumatized, but the much-touted 2006 study which showed that young women who had abortions were more likely to experience depression or anxiety later in life shouldn't be taken at face value: it didn't take into account the circumstances which led to those abortions, and what effect they may have had on women's lives.

Later abortions

After 15 weeks, abortion becomes riskier and more problematic. Dilation and evacuation (D&E) is the usual procedure: the foetus is taken apart inside the uterus using surgical instruments and removed using suction. A technique known as dilation and curettage can also be used in which the cervix is widened (or dilated) and the walls of the uterus scraped out with a curette (rather like a spoon). The "D&C" is used by gynaecologists for lots of uterine conditions, but it's increasingly uncommon in terminations.

Two alternatives are used for the very rare later-term abortions that take place after week 20. First, an injection stops the foetus's heart. Hysterotomy abortion is like a caesarean section, and is done under general anaesthetic. Intact dilation and extraction (IDX or D&X) is similar to D&E, except that the foetus's body is removed first, whole, followed by its head, in two stages. In 2007 it was banned in the US by the Supreme Court on the grounds that it represented "partial birth" – a controversial ruling.

Abortion law

In 1995, the United Nations' World Conference on Women, in Beijing, declared that women's human rights included "their right to have control over and decide freely and responsibly on matters related to their sexuality, including sexual and reproductive health, free of coercion, discrimination and violence." A total of 189 countries around the world signed up to the declaration, which appeared to support the right to choose abortion.

Yet at the time of writing, three countries around the world banned abortion outright, even after rape and incest, or where the woman's life was in danger. Stand up Nicaragua, Chile and El Salvador. A further 66 countries, covering more than a quarter of the world's population (and including many predominantly Catholic countries such as Brazil, Ireland and Mexico), ban abortion but make some allowance for situations where the woman's life is at risk. Thirty-four countries officially allow abortion to preserve a woman's physical health; another 23 countries, including Spain, New Zealand and Israel, extend this provision to preserve a woman's mental health as well. Fourteen countries, making up 21 percent of the global population, and including Australia, India and Britain, allow abortion on socio-economic grounds too, and in practice the law is interpreted liberally. Free choice on abortion is permitted by 56 countries – including Canada, much of the EU, South Africa and the United States – making up forty percent of the world's population.

Even countries that allow abortion "without restriction as to reason" – or "on demand", as it's sometimes known – impose limits. In the UK, for instance (with the exceptions of Northern Ireland, where it's still illegal), abortion is only allowed up to 24 weeks of pregnancy, or 28 weeks in cases of serious risk to the woman's life or health, or where there is foetal abnormality. In the US, in

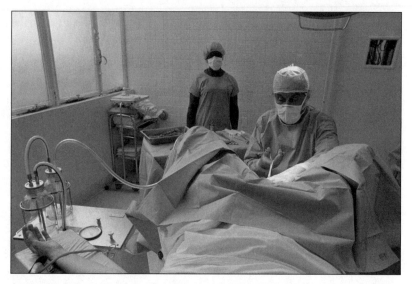

An abortion being performed at St Luke's Hospital, New York, in 1971 – one year after it became legal to do so.

1973 the Supreme Court ruling on the famous case of Roe v. Wade established that abortion was a legal constitutional right – up to the age where the foetus might be able to live outside the womb, that is. That landmark is under constant attack, however. Where exactly "viability" begins is a highly charged issue, and in practice, many states make access problematic after 12 weeks or, to cite just one add-on restriction, require minors to tell their parents.

Some contraceptive myths

• "Having sex during a period is safe." It isn't. A woman's fertility cycle is so much more complicated than that (see p.249).

• "If you don't have an orgasm you can't get pregnant." If this were true, there'd be a whole lot fewer babies born.

• "Washing sperm out of the vagina after sex protects you." Douching, as it's called, may even force sperm deeper in, and it washes away the barrier of the cervical mucus. And no, a shaken-up bottle of coke (or bicarb with lemon) cannot "steam-clean" sperm out of the vagina either.

• "Woman-on-top or standing positions are fine." No position will hold back the millions of very determined sperm in every ejaculation.

• "Using two condoms gives extra protection." Condoms are actually more likely to tear if you "double-bag". Re-using them is even more risky.

• "Sperm and HIV can pass through tiny holes in condoms." Notoriously, some Christian groups have peddled this line, or rather lie.

• "Condoms give you cancer". Condoms protect against the HPV virus, which can cause cancer and genital warts. They also form an effective barrier to sexually transmitted infections.

• "You can't buy condoms till you're 16. Or 18, maybe." In the US, stores have the right to refuse to sell them to minors but it's legal to buy them at any age.

• "Hot baths and hot tubs kill the man's sperm". They might take out a few, but millions more survive just fine.

• "The Pill builds up over time, so it doesn't matter if I miss a few." Women can conceive after missing just one Pill. Women trying to conceive may have to wait a few months longer on average – but it's just an average.

• "Sneezing, running, jumping or dancing stops the egg implanting." Very, very extreme exercise might just bring on a miscarriage, but you'd have to half-kill yourself trying.

• "Oral sex can get you pregnant." Only if sperm also gets into the vagina. Oral sex can pass on infections, however (see p.110).

7

Sexual health

Sexual health

When two people get naked and hot, press their mouths together, lick and poke around in each other's bodies, and generously share a little of their sexual fluids, it's a golden opportunity for sexually transmitted infections (STIs). With the right treatment, most sexually transmitted infections, including chlamydia, syphilis and gonorrhoea, won't kill you. All sexually active people need to know about them, however, as they can make you or your partner very ill or even infertile; HIV–AIDS, of course, still kills.

A significant part of this chapter focuses on HIV and AIDS. This is because there is still no cure and because, around the world, some 40 million people – including men, women and children; gay, straight and in-between; drug-users, social smokers and puritans – are living with the virus. HIV is also hugely important because it has changed sexual culture in a way that nothing since the Pill has done. Everyone is now aware of safer sex – or if they're not, they should be.

This chapter includes a section on dysfunctions and disorders. It might seem strange to yoke this together with pubic lice and advice on how to put on a condom, but physical and mental problems are an intrinsic part of sexual health. Unless you are incredibly fortunate, it's unlikely that you or your partner won't experience some kind of problem at one time or another. Getting sex right also means knowing how to handle it when it goes wrong.

Venus's revenge – infections and parasites

Sexually transmitted infections, or STIs, seem to have been around almost as long as sex. The ancient Egyptian Ebers papyrus, a medical treatise from around 1550 BC, discusses a vulval inflammation, while the biblical book of Deuteronomy (28:27) threatens the chosen people with "the botch of Egypt, and with the emerods, and with the scab, and with the itch, whereof thou canst not be healed". Thankfully, most STIs are now curable. Some, however, present no symptoms – and without diagnosis there can't be a cure.

After the safer-sex campaigns following the HIV scare of the 1980s, new infection rates dipped for a while. Since the mid-1990s, however, they have been growing at extraordinary rates, especially among people under 25 and men who have sex with men. The truth is that if you have sex without a condom, especially if you have many partners, you risk acquiring an infection – or more than one.

The old term "venereal disease", or VD, incidentally, referred to the diseases associated with Venus, the goddess of love. It has given way to the more useful term "sexually transmitted infection", or STI, as infected people may not necessarily have the symptoms that qualify an infection as a disease.

Safer sex – the basics

If you don't have sex you can't, of course, acquire a sexually transmitted infection. But that's a bit like saying if you don't jump out of a plane without a parachute you won't die. There are ways of managing the risk without killing the fun. People with regular partners should get to know their sexual history and encourage them to take a test for STIs. Anyone having sex with anyone else should have safer sex – which means using a condom. And just as it's ill-advised to jump with a shady outfit using a worn-out 'chute, it's unwise to have unprotected sex with sexual risk-takers.

The silent epidemic – chlamydia

Chlamydia is the most common STI of all. In the UK, more than 100,000 people are now newly diagnosed with the infection each year, and the figure is close on a million in the US. The frightening part is that three or more times as many people probably have chlamydia without knowing it, as it exists without symptoms in approximately three-quarters of infected women and half of infected men. It's also quite hard to diagnose accurately. All this is why chlamydia is sometimes known as the "silent disease", or the "silent epidemic".

With those kinds of statistics, everybody who's sexually active should probably get themselves tested. Chlamydia can be spread by oral or anal sex as well as vaginal intercourse, so men who have

The smooth guide to putting on a condom

Condoms are incredibly effective when used properly. They protect against almost all STIs, including HIV (but not against herpes), and are 94–97 percent effective at preventing pregnancy. When they fail, it's almost always because they're put on incorrectly or after a short bout of unprotected lovemaking. When used by experienced people, condoms very rarely break or fall off, though men with unusually large or small penises should seek out special sizes (see p.231). Novice condom-users – both men and women – need practice, and not just because fumbling ineffectively with your genitals doesn't look all that sexy. Try a banana, or any penis that's willing to be experimented on (including, for men, your own).

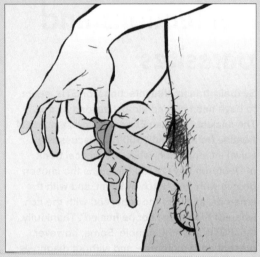

Step 1: pinch the teat.

The dos
Roll a condom onto the penis after it's erect but before it touches the partner's genitals. Open the wrapper by tearing with the fingers (not the teeth, and be careful with long or jagged fingernails) from the side, just below one corner. (The foil is designed to tear open smoothly in one direction, so if it doesn't work, turn the wrapper round 90 degrees and try again.) Pinch the end of the condom to squeeze out any air inside – some have a "teat" (optimistically known as a "reservoir") which makes this easy.

Place the condom snugly on the tip of the penis, like a little beanie hat. Check it isn't inside-out – the roll should be on the outside. Then unroll it smoothly down the penis as far as it will go. If it's inside-out at this point, it won't roll down easily. Uncircumcised men are often advised to pull their foreskins back first before putting on a condom, but some, particularly young men, find this uncomfortable; if so, push the foreskin back

over the head of the penis once the condom is securely on while holding it firmly at the base to keep it secure.

Condoms are much longer than most men's penises, so there'll be some material left rolled up at the base – this can pinch if pubic hair gets caught underneath it, but won't do any harm. For the same reasons of excess length, the condom can hang loose from the end of the penis during sex; this shouldn't be a problem as long as the condom is firmly anchored at the base. If it's slipping off from the base, it could be that the man's erection isn't actually firm enough to have sex, or that a narrow-fit condom would work better.

A water-based lubricant (see p.139) applied to the outside can solve any rubbery lack of glide. After ejaculation, the man should hold the base of the condom as he withdraws from his partner to make sure

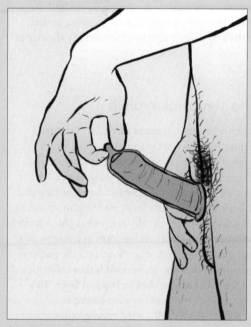

Step 2: unroll.

it stays safely on. Roll up the condom carefully from the base. Tying a knot in its end makes it less messy to dispose of.

The don'ts

Don't reuse condoms. Don't use vaseline or oil as lubricants. Don't wear two condoms – they might rub together and break. If you're anxious, or having anal sex, use thicker condoms with names like "extra safe". Don't flush used condoms down the toilet unless you want to bump into one next time you go to the beach.

sex with men, and women who don't have vaginal intercourse aren't immune. People under 25 or who have had sex with more than one partner should consider having annual check-ups.

Antibiotics are an effective treatment, but it's quite common for people to be reinfected by an untreated partner. If they have symptoms, men will likely suffer from non-specific urethritis (NSU) – burning sensations when urinating and discharge from the penis. In women, chlamydia is potentially a very serious condition. It can spread into the Fallopian tubes, causing pelvic inflammatory disease – which can lead, in turn, to sterility or problems with pregnancy. Some women experience pain during sex, pain in the lower-back or belly, bleeding outside periods, fever and nausea. Tragically, others know nothing about it until they try, unsuccessfully, to get pregnant.

The great pox – syphilis

So deadly and virulent was syphilis when it first appeared, and so large were the chancres (skin ulcers) that it caused, that it was called The Great Pox. Considering the devastation wrought by smallpox, that was really saying something. Though still called "the pox" today, syphilis has become a less serious disease – and penicillin can now cure it. It is usually contracted through sexual activity, though mothers can pass it on to their babies, too. Tiny, coil-shaped, wriggling bacteria called spirochetes pass from an infected person's sores into their partner – either through tiny cuts on the vagina, penis or rectum, or directly through the mucous membranes of the genitals.

Pelvic inflammatory disease

More women become infertile because of pelvic inflammatory disease than for any other reason. The chief causes of PID are the sexually transmitted infections gonorrhoea and chlamydia, which can cause infections of the uterus, ovaries or Fallopian tubes. This can lead to internal inflammation and scarring – which can, in turn, cause appendicitis, ectopic or failed pregnancies, ovarian cysts and, potentially, infertility. The classic symptoms of PID – pain in the belly or during intercourse, bleeding outside the times of menstrual periods, discharge and fever – don't always occur. Prevention, then, is the best defence. Use condoms, have regular tests for STIs and, if you're worried, get yourself examined internally by a gynaecologist.

Condoms protect against infection from penetrative sex. Unprotected oral sex, however, is not safe – in the UK, almost half of all syphilis cases in men who have sex with men were acquired this way. In general, gay men are particularly at risk from syphilis, but the picture is pretty complex. In the UK, diagnoses went up by almost 2000 percent between 1996 and 2005, thanks to a series of outbreaks – the first of which, in Bristol, was among heterosexuals. In the US, rates of infection dropped so much during the 1990s that people began to talk about eliminating the disease altogether. In the early 2000s, however, numbers started to rise again, particularly in the South, in urban areas and among men who have sex with men. In China, similarly, syphilis has exploded recently, with infections surging thirty-fold in under ten years, largely due to changing sexual habits and living patterns – particularly the rise of sex workers in cities.

The stages of syphilis

Syphilis has four stages of infection. The first, Primary syphilis, is the initial chancre, which appears at the point where the spirochetes wriggled across. It can be anything from a scarcely noticeable red spot to a large, oozing and ulcerating sore. It lasts for some three to six weeks. Secondary syphilis usually arrives roughly a month to three months later, in the form of a measle-like rash that doesn't itch, often found on the palms or the soles of the foot, along with futher infectious chancres and aching, headaches and fever. This stage can last for weeks or even months.

Eventually, syphilis goes underground, invading the body ever more deeply even as symptoms vanish. In this latent stage, the sufferer remains infectious. After anything from one to ten years, or even longer, Tertiary syphilis emerges. In some people, tumour-like gummas appear internally, causing chronic inflammation and joint problems. Others have heart problems. Others still have neurological complications, causing emotional disturbances, nerve and spine problems, meningitis-like symptoms, dementia and psychosis. Most notoriously, some late-stage syphilis sufferers experience a dramatic episode of hallucinogenic, violent or paranoid dementia. Unless it's accompanied with HIV, it's now relatively rare for syphilis to progress this far, but in the nineteenth century, syphilitic "madness" was all too well known (see box on p.268).

The origins of the pox

Christopher Columbus may not really have been the first European to sail to the Americas, but he may have been among the first to catch syphilis. Certainly, by his second voyage, of 1493, he was repeatedly feverish, and he remained ill for the rest of his life. The European epidemic kicked off when the French king Charles VIII invaded the kingdom of Naples, just two years after Columbus returned from Hispaniola, in 1495. When Ferdinand II of Spain (who had sent Columbus on his original mission), reinforced his Neapolitan ally, the Spanish soldiers brought syphilis with them – perhaps acquired from the sailors that brought them to Italy, perhaps thanks to the prostitutes that followed them there. The hungry, weary, vastly randy soldiers of three nations, together with their attendant prostitutes, provided the perfect breeding ground. Naples soon succumbed to an appalling plague, and people died in their tens of thousands.

Syphilis spread with incredible speed. People were clearly having a lot of sex outside marriage. By 1496, Paris was trying to impose a curfew on syphilitics. By 1497 James IV of Scotland was quarantining syphilitics on the island of Inchkeith, and threatening branding on the cheek for any

A poster, produced by the American Social Hygiene Association in World War II, warns of the twin evils of prostitution and venereal disease.

that disobeyed. By 1498 the disease had got as far as India. By 1500, one in twenty people in Europe may have contracted the disease. The Neapolitans called it the Spanish disease, the French called it the Neapolitan sickness, while half of Europe called it the French disease, or *morbus Gallicus*. No one then knew that it probably came from America, via Columbus's sailors.

Syphilitics celebrated and notorious

Syphilis in nineteenth-century Europe looked remarkably like AIDS in modern Africa: it was feared, it was apparently incurable, it was everywhere – and yet people largely refused to talk about it, or only in terms of other, secondary diseases. It was associated with terrible guilt. Many men contracted it in brothels, and believed thereafter that their physical sickness was emblematic of moral corruption. If married, they were faced with a terrible choice: between committing to a life of married chastity or taking the risk of infecting their wives.

The dementia of tertiary-stage syphilis was often linked with artistic genius. It killed the Austrian composer Franz Schubert at the age of 32, and may well have caused the insanity and aural delusions of his near contemporary Robert Schumann. In the visual arts, the mental breakdown of Vincent van Gogh and the early death of Henri de Toulouse-Lautrec could have been syphilis-related. French literary figures seemed particularly prone: the poet Charles Baudelaire and the novelists Gustave Flaubert and Guy de Maupassant were all syphilitic. Within fiction, the lead character in Thomas Mann's *Doctor Faustus* derives his genius from syphilitic disturbance, while some critics interpret the madness of Mr Rochester's first wife in *Jane Eyre* in syphilitic terms. The playwright Henrik Ibsen confronted the issue of congenital syphilis head-on in his groundbreaking play *Ghosts*.

Syphilis may even have shaped world affairs. Abraham Lincoln probably had it, as did Benito Mussolini. During World War I, the future Italian dictator's career was supposedly cut short by a shrapnel injury but syphilis might better explain Mussolini's puzzling treatment regimen, his unaccountable silence on the subject of his supposedly heroic hospitalization, and his erratic behaviour – both sexual and political. As for Adolf Hitler, contemporary rumour had it that he caught syphilis from a Jewish prostitute in Vienna. True or not, Hitler certainly liked to fulminate that syphilis was a "Jewish disease" and he is known to have had eye problems, a roseate rash and to be subject to demented rages – all possible symptoms of Tertiary syphilis. Most tellingly, in his terrible last years, he employed a private physician best known for doctoring syphilitics.

Henri Toulouse-Lautrec sleeps it off.

The clap – gonorrhoea

Gonorrhoea has always looked like a common-or-garden sort of STI next to its more lethal neighbours. Unlike syphilis, it was never associated with artistic genius. Unlike HIV, it very rarely kills – though it can cause pelvic inflammatory disease in women, and thus infertility (see p.266). It's also widespread: until the epic modern rise of chlamydia, gonorrhoea was the most common bacterial STI.

No one knows the origins of the slang name "clap". Some say it refers to the stinging of the urethra, others that people used to treat gonorrhoea by clapping the penis on both sides to expel a blockage. (Later treatments including scraping out the inside of the urethra with an unfolding umbrella-like device – like erecting a ship-in-a-bottle inside the penis. Single doses of antibiotics are used today, mostly very effectively – though drug-resistant strains are, inevitably, on the rise.)

In fact, the word probably came from an old French word for a brothel, *un clapier*, though medieval French people usually talked about *la chaudepisse*, or "hot piss" – referring to the common symptoms of urethral infection and stinging during urination. It's a much better word than gonorrhoea, which doctors concocted from the ancient Greek for "seed flow", on the mistaken basis that the discharge had its origins in semen.

Symptoms like stinging or burning during urination, and discharge from the penis or vagina – charmingly known as gleet – usually appear between two and ten days after infection. Many people have no symptoms at all, however, so getting tested is important. Left untreated, the complications can be serious. As well as pelvic inflammatory disease, it can cause infections of the testicals, prostate and epididymis. Women can pass it on to their babies, too, potentially giving them a nasty form of conjunctivitis.

The creeping virus – genital herpes

The herpes simplex virus isn't going to kill you. It isn't even going to make you feel particularly ill – though the first outbreak can feel like a dose of the flu. An outbreak of herpes does increase the chance of acquiring another STI, however, including HIV. So while herpes is incredibly common, and in itself not all that serious, it's also not to be taken too lightly.

Most of the time herpes just dozes quietly in the body. Just when you thought it had gone away, however, it slowly crawls back into action – hence its name, from the Greek word *herpein*, "to creep". When it wakes up, it's not exactly pretty. Most people have seen the ugly, itchy blisters of type-1 herpes – better known as cold sores. The blisters produced by the sexually transmitted kind of herpes, type-2, are much the same, but occur on or around the genital and anal areas. They can be painful the first time they occur, especially if urine touches them.

The blisters are also very infectious, and using condoms doesn't necessarily protect against passing them on. Luckily, they almost always vanish within a month, so most sufferers just take

Visiting a sexual health clinic

" When I got together with my partner, I felt I wanted to make a clean start. I also thought we wouldn't always want to use condoms, so I booked myself in at a sexual health clinic. It wasn't so different from a normal doctors' surgery, though the average age in the waiting room was way younger. First, I had to fill in a questionnaire about my sex life, to help them work out what risks I'd been exposed to. They offered me an HIV test at this point. I was really tempted to say no, just because it sounded frightening, but in the end I decided I'd be mad to pass up the opportunity to know for sure.

The urine and blood tests were fine, obviously, but the one bit I didn't like was when the nurse took a swab from inside my urethra. Literally, he stuck a cotton bud up the hole in the end of my cock. It didn't feel all that sore, just hot and uncomfortable, but it was a very weird sensation. When the nurse got out a second swab and said "this one may hurt a bit" I did think about doing a runner. In fact, it wasn't all that much worse, and over pretty quickly.

The strangest thing was when they asked me how I wanted the result of my HIV test. "Negative, obviously", I thought. Of course they meant how did I want to be contacted: by phone, letter, text or in person. By text? What, beep-beep: "hi you've got HIV"? It turned out that actually they always give a positive result in person, with counselling available. My results were all negative, which changed my feelings about having sex more than I'd thought it would, I felt lucky and maybe more determined to stay out of trouble. "

a temporary vow of celibacy. To be really effective, this vow should include oral sex, as the blisters can change from type-1 to type-2 and cross-infect. Cuddles and stroking are much lower risk than mouth or genital contact.

No cure currently exists for herpes, though vaccines seem to be in the offing, and antiviral drugs can help control outbreaks. If taken soon after initial infection, antivirals may also reduce the severity of future attacks. Women who experience their first attack while pregnant should seek advice, as herpes can pass to unborn babies and cause complications.

An orchard of figs – genital warts and HPV

In about AD100, the scurrilous Roman poet Martial wrote a cutting epigram about a certain fellow citizen who made a poor exchange. "In order to buy some slave boys Labenius sold his garden", Martial wrote. "But now he has only an orchard of figs". The figs in question were actually genital warts – miniature eruptions of the skin that look like tiny heads of flesh-coloured broccoli.

Like herpes blisters, genital warts are caused by a virus – in this case, the human papillomavirus, or HPV. It's highly contagious, extremely common (perhaps 80 percent of UK adults carry one of the 100-odd types) and not currently curable. There is now a vaccine, however, which – if parents can be persuaded to let their young daughters have it – will save many, many lives, as HPV types 16 and 18 are the major cause of the most common kinds of cervical cancer. (HPV types 6 and 11, which cause warts, are less likely to promote any cancerous changes to the cervix.)

Genital warts can actually crop up anywhere around the genital and anal region, though they're most common in men around the tip of the penis, and in women around the edge of the vagina. If you're dedicated enough to apply a cream or lotion daily over a month or so, the warts can be removed that way. More dramatically, they can be blasted with lasers or supercooled nitrogen by a doctor. Even if your own warts aren't numerous enough to look really gross, they're not much of a gift to a sexual partner.

From A to G – hepatitis

The list of different kinds of hepatitis – a kind of jaundice that inflames the liver – seems to get longer all the time. It currently runs from A to G. You might conceivably catch hepatitis A if you manage to ingest a partner's faeces – by rimming, maybe, or slipping a finger up their anus and then touching your mouth. Sexual transmission of hepatitis C – a very serious condition that, if untreated, can kill – used to be regarded as very rare, but is on the rise among men who have sex with men.

The hepatitis to be really aware of, in terms of sex, is hepatitis B, otherwise known as HBV

Oral sex and health

Herpes is the sexually transmitted infection most easily acquired through oral sex, as both types will happily switch from genitals to face, and vice versa. Gonorrhoea is also very eager to transmit itself in this way. For chlamydia and syphilis, transmission by mouth is less common but the potential consequences are that much more serious. The same is true, to an even greater extent, of HIV. HIV isn't frequently passed on by being given a blow job, and the chances are still smaller for someone who is giving a blow job – and one UK study in 2000 found just two cases of HIV infection resulting from cunnilingus. But the risks can rise significantly in the presence of a mouth ulcer or a herpes blister, or even if oral sex occurs within a couple of hours of brushing the teeth, which can open up tiny cuts or cause bleeding gums.

Basically, oral sex should not be considered safe, and if an STI is suspected, or you don't know your partner's status, it's wise to put a barrier between the mouth and the genitals. For fellatio, this means a condom (avoid lubricated models, which mostly taste awful, and consider flavoured ones). For cunnilingus, use what dentists call a dental dam – these small sheets of latex can easily be improvised by cutting up a condom or a piece of cling film; pressure and touch can still be transmitted through a thin enough barrier, though obviously the feel isn't quite the same. It's also a good idea to wash your parts beforehand – this can, of course, be sexy. Avoid giving oral sex if you have cuts or ulcers on your mouth, and receiving it if you have cuts or abrasions on your genitals or, for that matter, if it's your period.

An awkward conversation – contact tracing

> My own test result was negative, but the clinic pointed out that since no test is 100 percent accurate, I ought to consider contacting recent sexual partners anyway, to suggest they get themselves checked out. It was a real dilemma: should I sweep the whole thing under the carpet, speak to everyone I'd had the slightest fling with, or just talk to the few people where there'd been a significant risk? I wasn't necessarily on the best of terms with those concerned, either ... In the end, my conscience had its say. The conversation itself was not so easy. "How is your love life / marvellous new relationship / broken heart these days? Oh and by the way, you should probably get yourself tested for chlamydia." Awkward. Still, at least if you put it that way you're neither apologising nor accusing.

(hepatitis B virus). Like HIV, "hep B" is transmitted through blood or bodily fluids. It's at epidemic levels across much of Southeast Asia. In Western Europe and the US it's generally less common, but men who have sex with men and people who have energetic sex lives are at higher risk. It potentially causes fever, nausea, vomiting and other jaundice-like symptoms, and kills perhaps a million people worldwide every year.

Antiviral drugs are fairly effective as treatment, and the vast majority of adults (some 95%) will cure themselves naturally if they're able to take lots of rest and to follow a nutritious, low-fat diet. Recovering from a serious illness is no fun, however, and babies, younger children, and people who are malnourished or have stressed immune systems may not make it. Even people who are apparently cured, without further symptoms, can become chronic carriers, and may develop liver problems later in life. If in any doubt, a blood test is in order.

Parasites

Not everything you can pick up from sex is an infection. Parasites like pubic lice, scabies mites and the protozoas that cause "trich" just love to take that unrivalled opportunity to jump from one host to another. Luckily, they're quite easy to get rid of. Funguses like thrush aren't usually called parasites but they do live inside people in much the same way, and they too can be passed on (or at least activated) by sexual contact.

Pubic lice

Pubic lice are tiny little grey-white critters about the size of a smallish nail-head. Their ultra-tiny pincers – and their habit of pinching with them, causing unbelievable itching – gives them their popular name of crabs. They're not actually much different from head lice, so-named because they affect the head only. If you're itching anywhere else on the body – eyebrows, underarms, chest hair – it's the pubic louse.

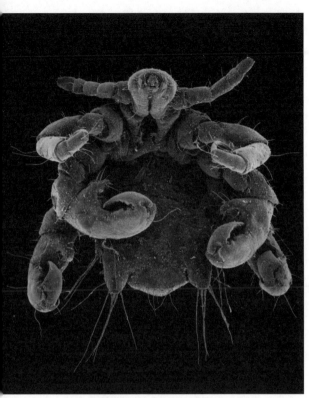

Crabs, aka the pubic louse.

You catch crabs in exactly the same way as schoolchildren catch head lice: through direct contact. (Catching them via bed linen or towels is possible but really unlikely.) Treatment is just the same as for head lice. You can comb your hair through for the nits, but it's easier to just shave. A medicated shampoo or lotion will complete the job, but it's also important to give clothes and bedclothes a hot wash, and dry them thoroughly.

Scabies

The scabies mite doesn't need sexual contact to jump from one person to another, but it really loves it. People rarely get closer to one another's skin, or stay close for longer, than when they're having sex, and scabies mites prefer softer, looser or more moist skin. An infestation, often manifested as a pimply rash, can be so itchy that people scratch themselves sore. Applying medicated lotions, and boil-washing clothes and linen usually gets rid of the mites. Unfortunately, the itching can continue for two or three weeks.

Trichomoniasis

Trichomoniasis, aka "trich", is caused by a minuscule, single-celled creature that's neither plant nor animal but a protozoa called trichomonas vaginalis. Despite its name, it doesn't live only in the vagina but in the male urethra as well. In fact, it takes up lodgings in some 7 million Americans every year. It often gives no sign of its presence, but can cause pain while urinating or having sex, and can result in a discharge described by the Center for Disease Control as "frothy, yellow-green" and having "a strong odour". Most people call the smell fishy, but you wouldn't cook a herring which smelled like that. Like most STIs, trich undermines the body's defences against HIV, so don't have sex during an episode, or at least wear a condom. And get yourself tested. Trich is quite hard to detect, especially in men, but a single dose of the antibiotic metronidazole clears it out.

Thrush

Thrush is usually called a "yeast" infection but it's actually caused by a kind of fungus called candida. Like most funguses, candida likes warm moist environments like the vagina, mouth, or under the male foreskin. It lives inside pretty much everyone quite harmlessly but if irritated or disturbed it can grow out of control. The process is rather like beer where fermentation just keeps on going, except that the yeasty-smelling, often yoghurt-like discharge of thrush is rather less appealing.

Once thrush sets in, it's not the discharge that's the real problem so much as the burning and itching feelings of the accompanying inflammation. This is reason enough to get hold of antifungal drugs, which are usually taken in the form of creams or pessaries inserted into the vagina. Some people swear by natural antifungal remedies like diluted vinegar, live yoghurt, tea tree oil tampons, and garlic (taken in food). To avoid recurrence many people wear cotton underwear and looser clothing, they take a break from inserting tampons, diaphragms, penises and the like.

What seems to set candida off is any kind of interference. It doesn't like internal washing or cleansing with detergents or deodorants, or the use of perfumes or lubricants, especially ones containing glycerin. It's not too keen on people taking the Pill, antibiotics or steroids. Or people having lots of sex. Diabetics are particularly prone. In women, thrush can easily be confused with other genital inflammations – collectively known as vulvovaginitis. Trich and bacterial vaginosis can also produce discharge, itching and soreness. They tend to yield a fishy – rather than a yeasty – smelling discharge but if in any doubt, ask a doctor.

HIV and AIDS

The UN's children's agency, UNICEF, has called the Human Immunodeficiency Virus "the worst catastrophe ever to hit the world". Of course, HIV doesn't just affect children – though some 2 to 3 million children are currently living with the virus worldwide. Neither, contrary to widespread popular belief, does it affect only gay men. In fact, in the vast majority of countries, heterosexual contact is the main way the virus is transmitted.

HIV doesn't actually cause disease, it weakens the body's immune system so that it can't fight off other diseases. When the immune system has become so debilitated that those diseases start to win the battle, someone living with HIV is said to have AIDS, or Acquired Immune Deficiency Syndrome. AIDS is not, then, an infection in itself. It is, however, a killer. While drug therapies now mean that the immune system can be supported and sustained against HIV for many years, the drugs are expensive and they can only buy time. Practising safer sex – which means using a condom properly – is as important now as it ever was.

From chimps to pandemic – the story of HIV

In the spring of 1981, an unusually aggressive type of cancer began appearing in a surprising number of gay men living in New York. Over in Los Angeles, meanwhile, men with a rare kind of pneumonia were starting to seek treatment. Within

Some HIV statistics

People estimated to be living with HIV worldwide (2007)	33 million
People newly infected with HIV worldwide (2007)	2.7 million
People estimated to be living with HIV in the US (2007)	1.1 million
People living with HIV in the UK (2007)	77,400
People newly diagnosed with HIV in the US (2007)	44,000
People newly diagnosed with HIV in the UK (2007)	7370
People aged 25–34 among all new HIV diagnoses (UK, 2007)	43%
Women among all HIV diagnoses (UK, 2008)	37%
Heterosexual contact as cause, among all HIV diagnoses (UK, 2008)	43%
People unaware of their infection, among all living with HIV (UK, 2007)	28%
Men who have sex with men unaware of their infection, among all living with HIV (US, 2005)	48%

a few years, Kaposi's Sarcoma and Pneumocystis Carinii Pneumonia would become notorious as the diseases associated with the onset of a killer disease, and a host of acronyms that hadn't even been invented – from KS and PCP to HIV and AIDS – would become commonplace.

In 1981, no one knew that the Human Immunodeficiency Virus existed. In fact, it had been spreading silently across the world for as long as fifty years. One day, perhaps towards the beginning of the twentieth century, perhaps in the 1940s, a hunter in the forests of West Central Africa – in southern Cameroon, maybe – was out looking for bushmeat. He trapped or shot a chimpanzee. It bit him, or perhaps he had cuts on his hand while butchering it; either way, the ape's virus passed into his bloodstream. This wasn't unique, but on this occasion, the man's immune system was unusually depressed, maybe by malnutrition. The virus was able to adapt itself to its host's body and SIV, the original Simian

Immunodeficiency Virus, became HIV, the human version.

How the virus then spread is a controversial question. Some blame shared needles in the vaccination programmes of the 1950s. Others blame a generalized health crisis in demoralized and malnourished African populations during a time of harsh colonial adminstration. Some think HIV's virulence was enough to do the job on its own. A few conspiracy theorists have claimed that the virus was deliberately spread – or even manufactured – by racist governments; genetic and epidemiological evidence, however, has proved that the virus existed long before the supposedly sinister vaccination or research programs took place.

By the late 1950s, HIV was spreading fast in West Africa. The trade route that followed the Sangha and Congo rivers from southern Cameroon towards the Belgian Congo, later Zaire, provided an artery for the virus to spread. Infected health workers and truckers carried the virus further into

Some trace the origins of HIV to monkeys and the trade in bushmeat.

Africa; sailors, migrants and foreign visitors took it beyond the continent. By 1966, it was in Haiti; from there it spread to the US, by 1969. By the mid-1970s, it was in the gay community. By 1980, HIV was in every continent.

The AIDS pandemic

At first, there was of course nothing to suggest that an outbreak of various diseases among gay men was linked to an African virus. Doctors began referring vaguely to a "gay-related immune deficiency", or GRID, suspecting that it might be sexually transmitted. Then, in 1982, came the first reports that the disease was appearing in haemophiliacs (thanks to tainted blood transfusions), heroin-users (thanks to needle-

sharing) and Haitians (where the disease had spread early). The idea of the "four Hs", four high-risk groups, counting homosexual men, was born. But then came reports that heterosexual women were also becoming infected.

Health officials invented a new name for the symptoms of the mysterious malaise: Acquired Immune Deficiency Syndrome, or AIDS. In May 1983, Paris's Pasteur Institute announced that they'd isolated the virus that caused it, though it took some years before the Human Immunodeficiency Virus (HIV) could be definitively proven to cause AIDS. It was also some years before much was done to halt its spread (see box on p.279).

Things began to change in 1987. UK cabinet minister Norman Fowler shook hands with an AIDS patient in San Francisco – as did Princess Diana, more famously. The British were told "Don't

Dodging the silver bullet – HIV variants

Thanks to the speed with which it replicates, and its power to mutate, HIV is an unusually varied virus, in genetic terms. Finding a vaccine or cure is like shooting in a fairground: you can aim at one target, but other ones keep popping up.

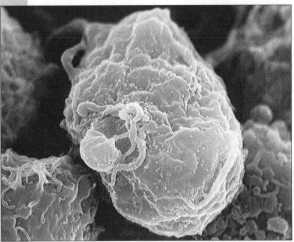

There are two main species of HIV, numbered 1 (pictured right) and 2. HIV-2 is more closely related to the "monkey AIDS" virus, SIV, and seems to have jumped into humans from the Sooty Mangabey monkey rather than from chimpanzees. It's less virulent than HIV 1 and rarely found outside West Africa. HIV-1 is by far the more common species, and it comes in three main groups: M, N and O. The most prevalent of these is group M, which is in turn divided into three subtypes found mainly in different areas of the world. Around half of all HIV infections are HIV-1 M, subtype C, found mostly in Africa and Asia; a further quarter are subtype A, found mostly in Africa; and another 12 percent are subtype B, which is most common in Europe, the Americas, Australia and Japan.

There are no prizes for guessing which subtype of HIV has received far and away the most research and funding from government agencies and pharmaceutical companies. Even if a vaccine is found, it's likely that it would be many more years before it could be adapted for use in Africa, if it could be used at all.

Die of Ignorance"; Americans were warned that "Silence=Death" and given the ratio "1 in 61" (being the proportion of New York babies born with HIV); Australians were shown the Grim Reaper carving his way into men, women and children, lined up like bowling pins.

The first antiretroviral drug treatment (see p.284), AZT, was trialled in 1989, but it only retarded the onset of AIDS, it didn't cure it. In any case, the initial cost of around $7000 per person per year was beyond the reach of most people or governments. In 1991, basketball player Magic Johnson and rock star Freddie Mercury announced they had AIDS, and the World Health Organization estimated that 9–11 million people worldwide were infected with HIV. People in the developed world started wearing red ribbons as a sign of support and compassion.

It was discovered that HIV could be passed on in a mother's milk – but for African women

Patient Zero

For some people, the AIDS epidemic required a scapegoat, and the man unlucky enough to have played that role, for a time at least, was Gaëtan Dugas, aka Patient Zero, the man who supposedly brought AIDS to America. Dugas was a handsome, blond, Quebecois flight attendant who made the most of his sexual opportunities in the late 1970s and early 80s. He claimed to have had more than 2500 sexual partners, in states across the US, before he died in March 1984, his kidneys having finally failed after years of AIDS-related infections.

The accusation that Dugas was the ultimate source of the AIDS epidemic was based on a hostile misinterpretation of an early epidemiological study which traced the sexual contacts of the earliest reported American AIDS sufferers. It came up with a "cluster" of forty men, with Dugas at its centre, all of whom died from AIDS-related infections in the early 1980s. This was enough to start a witch hunt.

It's now known, however, that Dugas could never have been Patient Zero. The original study assumed a year-long latency period for AIDS, when in fact it typically lasts around ten years – meaning that HIV must have arrived in America before Dugas even took his first job with Air Canada. Sufferers from AIDS have now been traced right back to the 1960s, and HIV probably arrived in north America via multiple routes: health workers returning from Africa, sailors who had visited prostitutes, soccer teams on tour, migrant drug-users – these are just some of the candidates.

The early days of the AIDS scare inspired compassion in some and "righteous" homophobia in others.

faced with giving their babies formula made with contaminated water, there was little choice. In the 1990s, infection rates in sub-Saharan Africa soared alarmingly. One in four Botswanans were thought to be living with HIV, while in neighbouring South Africa, official denial helped the disease spread. Across the continent, AIDS orphans were forced into roles once taken only by adults, including childcare and daily labour. Only in Uganda was the disease rolled back. An unusually open prevention campaign made headway into unsafe sexual

Scandal or crisis – AIDS in the 80s

In the early years of the AIDS epidemic, the US and UK governments were unconscionably slow to react. President Reagan did not mention AIDS until October 1987. It wasn't as if he hadn't heard what was going on: in 1985, his former showbiz friend Rock Hudson died from an AIDS-related illness. The following year, during the centennial rededication of the Statue of Liberty, television cameras caught him laughing at a Bob Hope gag: "I just heard that the Statue of Liberty has AIDS", Hope drawled; "but she doesn't know if she got it from the mouth of the Hudson or the Staten Island Fairy."

By the time Reagan finally spoke up, 27,909 Americans had died of AIDS-related illnesses, and some 10 million people worldwide were infected with HIV. Even then, Republican conservatives fought tooth and nail to quash funding for health campaigns. Perhaps they agreed with the outspoken pastor Jerry Falwell, who reckoned that "AIDS is not just God's punishment for homosexuals, it is God's punishment for the society that tolerates homosexuals." Senator Jesse Helms pushed through a bill that banned any education programmes that "encouraged or promoted homosexual activity". In practice, this meant that it was impossible for officials to explain how HIV was passed on during unprotected anal sex – which condemned thousands, perhaps tens of thousands, to infections born of ignorance.

In the UK, Norman Fowler, the minister responsible for health, described Margaret Thatcher's attitude: "her initial instinct was that this was not a big problem," he recalled, "and at any rate the people who get AIDS, it's entirely their own fault." Fowler – a man unable to pronounce the word "vagina" correctly – fought manfully for action on AIDS, often against open hostility from colleagues. Sir Alfred Sherman, Thatcher's intellectual-in-chief, wrote to the *Times* to say that AIDS was a disease of "undesirable minorities … mainly sodomites and drug-abusers, together with numbers of women who voluntarily associate with this sexual underworld". Manchester's Chief Constable, James Anderton – a man who described himself as "very close to God" – described AIDS sufferers as "swirling about in a human cesspit of their own making".

Religious groups were divided. Many advocated a compassionate attitude. Britain's Chief Rabbi, Immanuel Jakobovits, however, complained that the UK's 1987 information campaign "tells people not what is right, but how to do wrong and get away with it – it is like sending people into a contaminated atmosphere, but providing them with gas masks and protective clothing". The Catholic Church refused to modify its opposition to barrier contraception and continued to promote abstinence – a policy proven to be relatively ineffective. Most culpably, many high-ranking Catholics, including the president of the Vatican's Pontifical Council for the Family, Cardinal Alfonso Lopez Trujillo, argued, against all the evidence, that condoms could not prevent transmission of HIV.

behaviour, and a joint Ugandan–US study found that an affordable single dose of the antiretroviral drug nevirapine could significantly reduce HIV transmission from mothers to their babies.

By 2000, any lingering notion that AIDS in the West was a "gay plague" was blown away. In the US and UK, more heterosexuals than homosexuals were being infected – and total numbers were still rising. They still are today. Worldwide, the statistics cry out for urgent action (see box on p.275). In the 25 years since the epidemic was said to have begun, more than 25 million adults and children are though to have died of AIDS-related illnesses.

The progression of HIV and AIDS

HIV doesn't so much cause illness as reduce the body's ability to fight it off. It does this by attacking one of the many kinds of lymphocytes, or white blood cells, which roam around the bloodstream fighting infection. The cells targeted by HIV are the "helper" T cells, otherwise known as CD4+ or T4 cells, which coordinate the immune system's response to all kinds of attack.

If helper T cells are the officers marshalling the troops, HIV is the enemy assassin slipping through the lines – and making for headquarters. Essentially, HIV targets the cells that produce helper T cells, causing their numbers to decline over time. Opportunistic infections can then seize their moment, break through the defences and take up occupation in the body.

Technically, HIV is classed as a retrovirus, which means it is able to reverse the usual flow of genetic information. It is made up of RNA, a relatively simple (single-stranded) molecule which usually acts as a messenger for (double-stranded) DNA, helping it translate genes into proteins. Retroviruses, however, are able to convert their RNA into DNA inside the host. They do this by binding themselves to a host cell (often a helper T cell) and injecting a kind of cocktail into its nucleus. The key ingredients of this cocktail are the RNA of the HIV virus itself and an enzyme called reverse transcriptase, which causes the host cell to create its own copies of the virus's RNA in the form of DNA. This allows HIV to spread rapidly.

Despite its speed, within the family of retroviruses HIV is classed as a lentivirus, from the Latin for "slow", because it tends to have a long incubation period. HIV can lie dormant, or latent, for many years – in contrast to flu, for example, which can be activated within a single day. This is one of HIV's more sinister characteristics: it's possible to carry it for years – and pass it on – without ever knowing you've got it.

The stages of HIV infection

Soon after infection, the HIV virus starts to rapidly create copies of itself, causing the "viral load" to rise sharply. The number of helper T or T4 cells (the cell count) steadily drops as the number of copies of the HIV virus (the viral load) rises. At first, another kind of T cells, CD8+ or "suppressor" T cells, rises hugely in number as they attempt to deal with the infection. During this early stage of "seroconversion", or the development of HIV antibodies, many people develop a flu-like illness variously called acute HIV-infection, primary HIV

Being positive: getting an HIV antibody test

The HIV antibody test is a simple procedure, often a routine part of general screening for sexually transmitted infections – though all tests should be confidential and done only with consent. A clinic or doctor will usually take a small blood sample (though sometimes saliva is used) and test it to see if antibodies to HIV are present. Many clinics offer same-day testing; others send blood to laboratories, which can mean a two- or three-week wait.

If you're seeking testing after a particular encounter, it's worth knowing that treatment within 24 to 48 hours of exposure can be particularly effective. You'll usually only be offered this, however, if you were exposed to a significant risk; if you shared needles or if you had unsafe sex with someone likely to be HIV-positive, for instance, or if you were sexually assaulted. Testing in an early stage

can be misleading, as the body's HIV antibodies usually only appear between one and two months after infection, so many clinics recommend waiting three months and having a repeat test. During this "window period" – after initial infection but before the body's defences are activated – HIV is actually at its most infectious.

If HIV antibodies show up in the test, the diagnosis is that you are HIV antibody positive, or HIV-positive for short. Most clinics, and a wealth of other organizations, offer help and counselling. In the event of a positive test, it's worth bearing in mind that AIDS is no longer the inevitable outcome. In developed countries, roughly a third of people infected with HIV won't develop AIDS within ten years, and with the appropriate treatment (see p.284), the outlook is significantly better.

infection, or seroconversion illness. It can last for anything from a week to a month. Fever, rash, sore throat, mouth sores, aching muscles and swollen glands (or, more properly, enlarged lymph nodes) are common symptoms.

This defensive reaction can cause the viral load of HIV to plummet and stay relatively low for some time. If the body's immune system is strong, this latency period or clinically asymptomatic stage, can last for up to twenty years, though ten years is typical – and in developing countries, where malnutrition and disease are more widespread, the latency period is often much shorter. During the latency period, someone with HIV is still infectious to others.

When AIDS is diagnosed

As the viral load of HIV gradually creeps up over time, the CD4+ cell count drops once more. Different countries measure cell counts differently, but someone with HIV is sometimes diagnosed as having AIDS when they have fewer than 200 T cells per microlitre of blood, which is around a fifth of a typical adult total. Another way to diagnose the onset of AIDS is when the T4 cells drop as a proportion of all the lymphocytes in the body below around 13 percent; 21 percent is regarded as healthy.

AIDS is not a disease, then, but a measurement of the inability of the body's own immune system to cope with infections. The first opportunistic

Being positive

" I didn't in all honesty believe that I could have been HIV-positive at the time. Up to that point I'd always had safe sex – or safer sex, I should say. But there was the odd occasion – condoms weren't the order of the day, then. Most gay men thought about getting a "dose". End of story; you got it sorted out. I had been reasonably careful. But it's like getting pregnant: you don't have to sleep with six men. It's a question of bad luck.

I came down with a very bad bout of flu and went to see my local GP. When I told him about the symptoms, he said, "look, I don't want to alarm you but I suspect you may be HIV positive." Actually, it was the way he approached the whole thing that made me think I'd better go and get it sorted out. I went to hospital and had my test. The nurse specialist sat me in a room, and delivered the news in ... not a pleasant manner, but she was obviously concerned. "Would you like someone to come home with you?", she offered. I came straight back to work and informed my line manager. They asked if I'd like some time off but I just carried on – and that's been the same ever since. Whether it's the positive attitude that has got me through, I don't know.

When I went to a support group, a lot of issues around sex came up, especially on the gay scene. Someone asked, "when I pick someone up, what do I do?" The facilitator said, "There are two roads you can go down: you can meet someone, you like each other,

you don't say anything, you go back with them, things work out very well between you and down the line he finds out you are positive and the whole thing goes up in smoke. On the other hand there's the risk of rejection: you say, 'before we go anywhere, I'm HIV positive' and he says, 'no thank you'. But that's a gamble you're going to have to take."

It's very difficult. You are telling a stranger about something very personal, so you're not just coping with rejection, but thinking "I've told a stranger – how many other people is he going to tell?"

Telling people who are close to you is like coming out in some ways. The reactions are so variable. My mother said, "just make sure that you take care of yourself. But if you need anything, I'm here for you. You're still my son." There was a certain amount of disappointment – like all parents! – but it was definitely a sincere thing, that she would be there for me. I thought, "this is amazing." That was a burden off my shoulders, immediately.

My personal belief is that we need to educate our young. Kids are growing up faster these days but people still think, "my children aren't having sex". So the kids learn about sex on the street – and that's where all the misinformation comes from. It's about making sure your children have the tools they need to be safe, about them being able to communicate at a level where they don't feel they have to be embarrassed about having to ask these questions. "

infections are typically mouth ulcers and infections (herpes, gingivitis, periodontitis, oral hairy leukoplakia and oral thrush), fungal infections of the nails, and respiratory tract conditions such as tonsillitis and sinusitis. As symptoms deepen, they may include severe weight loss, persistent fever and chronic diarrhoea, alongside serious infections and cancers affecting the lungs (tuberculosis, Pneumocystis Carinii Pneumonia, Kaposi's sarcoma, and thrush in the oesophagus) and the nervous system (toxoplasmosis, non-Hodgkin's lymphoma).

Safer sex and HIV

The mantra of conservatives is that if you don't have sex, you can't catch HIV. Not counting blood-to-blood transmission (infection through shared needles, needlestick accidents or tainted blood transfusions, for example), or mother-to-child transmission, this is true. It's not, however, particularly helpful, especially for partners of people infected with HIV, victims of sexual violence, or indeed anyone who believes their sexuality deserves expression.

The highest risk sexual activity is unprotected anal intercourse with someone HIV-positive. In this scenario, it's estimated that the receptive partner (the person being penetrated) will acquire HIV within an estimated 200 encounters. Of course, this doesn't mean it's OK to have unprotected sex 199 times – it's as easy to become infected on the first occasion as on the last. A woman having unprotected vaginal intercourse with a HIV-positive man has something like a 1 in 1000 chance of contracting the infection. The risks for the insertive partner are slightly lower.

How HIV can and can't be transmitted

HIV is passed on from person to person by direct contact with blood, breast milk or sexual fluids (vaginal and rectal mucus, semen and pre-ejaculate). The concentration of the virus in saliva is too low to be an effective route of transmission. It is not, contrary to a bizarre popular myth, "created" through anal sex, nor is it restricted to gay men. HIV can't survive for long outside the human body, so urban legends of people wielding dirty needles as weapons, or mosquitoes passing on HIV, or swimming pools being sumps of infection can be totally discounted.

Safe
Swimming in public pools
Exposure to insect bites
Using sterile needles
Sharing toilet seats, toothbrushes, cutlery, cups, flutes, pipes etc
Coughing, sneezing and spitting
Hugging and kissing – including with tongues
Having a blood transfusion in a developed country, nowadays
Having sex with a (properly used) condom

Unsafe
Unprotected vaginal or anal sex
Oral sex – especially with bleeding gums, mouth sores, ulcers, herpes blisters etc
Sharing needles
Blood transfusions with unscreened blood
Tattoos and piercings with unsterilized equipment

Condoms are the simple solution – though of course they can fail if not used properly (see p.265). Stronger condoms are recommended for anal sex, and they mustn't be lubricated with nonoxynol 9, which can cause tiny abrasions.

Probabilities are rarely what they appear to be to the non-expert eye, however, and the actual risk in any given situation varies hugely depending on lots of factors: the viral load of the infected person; whether either partner has ulcers, cuts or other infections; the age or health of sexual partners (younger people are often more infectious, for instance); and whether or not other STIs are present. Some gay men practice "sero-sorting", whereby they have unprotected sex with people of the same HIV status. Given the high incidence of people who don't know their HIV status – let alone people who might lie about it – sero-sorting is not a safe practice in a casual-sex situation.

ART and science – the treatment of HIV

Treatments for HIV are increasingly effective. They can significantly lengthen the time before someone living with HIV develops AIDS, and dramatically improve the outlook afterwards. Treatment usually begins when the T4 cell count is low (around 350), but before AIDS is diagnosed – so regular immune-system check-ups are needed.

The main approach is Combination Therapy, or Highly Active Antiretroviral Therapy, usually known as HAART or just ART. Combination Therapy is often described as a cocktail of drugs, which makes it sound a whole lot more fun than it

actually is. It's more about throwing enough bullets at the infection to put it out of action for a while. There are four main types of medical ammunition. Nucleoside Reverse Transcriptase Inhibitors (known as NRTIS or, more excitingly, as "nukes") interfere with HIV's ability to copy itself. So too do the non-Nucleoside Reverse Transcriptase Inhibitors (NNRTIS). Protease inhibitors (PIs – not yet known as "magnums") focus on the role of another protein, protease, in the same process. Fusion or Entry Inhibitors are the bouncers of the HIV world, preventing the virus from entering cells in the body.

There are many different drugs within each antiretroviral group, each with its own generic and brand name. Things change fast, but a common treatment programme at the time of writing consisted of the NRTIs lamivudine and zidovudine (or AZT) together with the NNRTI efavirenz. In brand-name terms, this means taking Epivir and Retrovir with Sustiva. Side effects of this particular "cocktail" can include nausea, tiredness, and problems with the heart and the body's insulin, as well as with adipose or fatty tissue which sometimes causes distinctive hollow cheeks or "buffalo humps" of fat on the back of the neck.

Side effects are a major cause of people not persisting with Combination Therapy, and the treatment failing. So too are the demands of the routine of daily, timed pill-popping, and the necessity for regular tests on the viral load to see if a drug-resistant strain of HIV is developing. The cocktail may need to be continually remixed. Drugs taken for the opportunistic infections that characterize AIDS, meanwhile, may interfere with the antiretroviral drugs taken for HIV – as can recreational drugs.

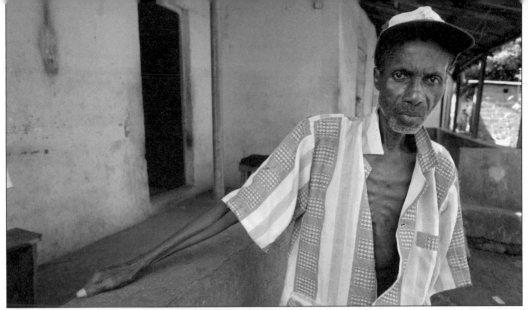

Thirty-three million people worldwide are believed to be living with HIV-AIDS. Twenty-two million of them live in Sub-Saharan Africa.

Combination Therapy requires determination and persistence. But, untreated, many people will die within a year of being diagnosed with AIDS (late-stage AIDS, that is, not HIV). With Combination Therapy, however, people will usually live for some four to twelve years. And more effective and less expensive drugs are being developed all the time.

Post-exposure and mother-to-child treatments

In unusually high-risk situations – if a health worker is injured with a needle after injecting an HIV-positive patient, for instance, or if someone is violently sexually assaulted in an area where HIV is highly prevalent – it's possible to give the body a short, sharp shock of antiretroviral drugs. The sooner this is done, the better: within one hour is ideal, while up to 72 hours can be effective. The side effects of this "post-exposure prophylaxis" can be fairly extreme, but it significantly reduces the risk of infection.

Treatment for prevention of mother-to-child transmission is also relatively effective. Without drugs, anything from 15 to 30 percent of babies born to HIV-positive women will acquire the virus – and breastfeeding will transmit HIV to a further 5 to 20 percent of babies. A single dose of nevirapine at the beginning of labour halves the rate of transmission, and combination therapies further improve the outlook.

Dysfunctions and disorders – and aphrodisiacs

Sexual dysfunction is defined as when the genitals go wrong in such a way that it affects sexual performance – which traditionally, for medics, has meant "gets in the way of vaginal penetration". That said, erectile dysfunction and pain or dryness in the vagina can be obstacles to oral sex and masturbation too. Sexual disorders are dysfunctions of the mind rather than the body. They're about desire rather than its physical cousin, arousal. Of course, they're usually mixed up with sexual dysfunctions: someone with an aversion to sex may well not be having erections or satisfying vaginal lubrication. Two of the most common problems, anorgasmia (see p.174) and premature ejaculation (see p.168), aren't exactly dysfunctions or disorders but lie somewhere in between, as both physical and socio-psychological problems; they are covered separately in the chapter entitled "Orgasm".

Female sexual dysfunction

If you believe the Yale School of Medicine, anything up to half of women have one kind of sexual dysfunction or another. That is, sex doesn't really work for them in the way it should. "Should" should mean "in the way they want it to". Often,

it's a comparison with an imagined norm, which would make it a nice little earner for the doctors and the druggists – something like Viagra, maybe.

Unfortunately, the variability of women's sexual experiences – or Female Sexual Dysfunction (FSD), as the white-coat brigade like to call it – is far more complicated than most cases of erectile dysfunction. For many, many women, sex just isn't about getting it on, getting it up and getting it in. It's not a smooth progression from desire and arousal to penetration and orgasm – what you might call the wham, bam, thank you ma'am approach. So to diagnose women who don't follow this pattern as dysfunctional is blinkered at best, and abusive at worst. All that said, things can and do go wrong down there. And some of these problems can be fixed.

Dryness and tightness – dyspareunia

Feelings of dryness, tightness or pain when a finger, say, or a penis enters or tries to enter the vagina are usually the simple result of not being turned on. Or rather, the not-so-simple result – arousal is, of course, a complex process created by mental and physical cross-feedback. If the vagina isn't cooperative, it could be the whole woman who isn't aroused. Or it could just be her vagina. Or it could be both – sometimes the conversation between mind and groin just doesn't flow, and neither do the juices.

Love, passion and more sensitive, responsive or prolonged stimulation – and perhaps the right lubricant – generally work pretty effectively. If they don't, it's possible that the problem isn't about desire or arousal, but about some other physical or medical factor. Leaving aside psychological, moral or spiritual issues (often lumped together as sexual desire disorders, see p.293), vaginal dryness and pain – or dyspareunia, as doctors call it – can have any number of physical causes, including thrush (see p.274), a urinary infection like cystitis, an STI, ovarian cysts, pelvic inflammatory disease (see p.266) or endometriosis. Hormonal changes in the lifecycle from breastfeeding and going through the menopause can also cause dryness or tightness – as can getting older, or having diabetes. Surgery after childbirth often causes complications, too.

A pain in the nook – vaginitis, vestibulitis and vulvodynia

Vaginitis, or inflammation of the tissue around the vagina, can make vaginal intercourse painful. Lots of different things may lie behind it: thrush, allergic reactions (to condoms, soaps or semen, for example), and STIs such as trichonomiasis, chlamydia and gonorrhoea. More severe pain when the outer part of the vagina (or "vestibule") is touched seems to affect some one in twenty women at one time or another, particularly women in their 20s or 30s. Doctors call this syndrome "vulval vestibulitis", but this doesn't mean they actually know much about it – the term just means "pain in the vestibule of the vulva". Cold cream or local antiseptics may soothe, but left to itself the pain usually vanishes in weeks or, at worst, months.

More generalized burning or aching, especially at night, gets called vulvodynia. Some swear by cold cream, aloe vera and vitamin E oil as a cure for this, others bathe in oatmeal. Others search for allergic causes. If the pain is really bad, doctors

> ## "Women's Viagra"
>
> The pharmaceutical mega-corporation, Pfizer, spent years trying to prove that Viagra worked on women too. If their drug could increase blood flow into the penis, they reasoned, surely it could do the same for the vulva and clitoris. Pfizer failed, miserably: trials showed that Viagra was no more effective than a placebo.
>
> Campaigners against the medicalization of sexual dysfunction in women were delighted by the failure. As Australian sex therapist Rosie King pointed out, "no amount of medication can make up for an unhappy relationship, poor sexual technique, or a tired, exhausted, stressed-out woman". Some would say the same was true of men. Pfizer's experiment wasn't actually a waste of time, however. Both the placebos and Viagra were shown to have a significant effect in that many women who *thought* they'd taken a drug that would make them horny did indeed feel aroused.

may prescribe tricyclic antidepressants. It's not exactly a case of cheering up your vulva – although fighting a generalized depression can have this effect – rather that these drugs act on certain kinds of nerve pain.

Staying tight-lipped – vaginismus

One of the trickiest vulval conditions to treat – though it's not particularly uncommon – is vaginismus. This is where the vagina involuntarily spasms and closes up tight. For some women, this can be connected to sexual distress, perhaps sexual violence in the past, perhaps previous experiences of pain during intercourse. The vagina may be effectively saying, "keep out!" Vaginismus can also relate to more general fears or anxieties about sex. "What if I'm too small?", is a common worry among sexually inexperienced women. Of course, given that most women are able to get a whole baby through there, a mere penis will hardly be a problem. Penetrative success is rarely a question of size, and frequently a matter of lubrication.

Psychological issues are not always at stake. The vagina may just not be listening to the libido, or it may be responding to dryness or inflammation, or it may have picked up a reflex action and needs to unlearn it. If a woman does want to have sex, and can't, vaginismus can be screamingly frustrating. Luckily, with patience and gentleness the vagina can usually be encouraged to relax. Some therapists recommend progressively getting it used to feelings of penetration, starting with a relaxing bath and a well-lubricated little finger, perhaps, and working up to a vibrator or, if so desired, a penis. Some therapists use cone-shaped dildoes in graduated sizes.

Vaginismus should be taken seriously. It can be a sign of underlying issues. If so, these may be best explored in conversation, counselling or psychotherapy. Even if it's purely physical, it's no small matter. In the longer term, feelings of inadequacy can creep in, just as they can for men with persistent erectile dysfunction.

Refusing the fence – erectile dysfunction

Some doctors only diagnose erectile dysfunction, or ED (as impotence is known nowadays), when a man's erection isn't hard enough or long-lasting enough to allow him to penetrate. ED can undermine even the most private of erections, however. Psychologically speaking, this is painful stuff, potentially equivalent to the breaking of a life-long love affair (between man and penis) or to the trauma of losing the ability to walk. Stiffies are the badge and banner of male pride and potency, after all. Just think of those macho metaphors: being "rock-hard" or having a "woody". And think of the opposite: being "impotent" sounds like it's about so much more than not being able to sustain an erection.

Being soft doesn't necessarily mean you can't have an orgasm, but it can be hard work without one. It's not just that erections increase sensation (although they do) but that, for many men, sex and hard-ons go hand in hand. Just like vaginal pain and dryness, erectile dysfunction can be a one-off or occasional thing. An erection can come and then mysteriously vanish. It can merely half arrive, in the form of a "semi".

The penile barometer

Being unable to get it up doesn't have to be a crisis. The man who says he has never failed to rise to the occasion is probably a liar. Occasional ED can be caused by very specific anxiety about sexual performance – perhaps in a new sexual relationship or in a one-night stand where the man is over-eager to impress. Alcohol is a pretty effective erection-killer, too. As Shakespeare famously put it in *Macbeth*, it "provokes the desire but it takes away the performance … it makes him, and it mars him; it sets him on, and it takes him off".

When erections fail on a more regular basis it can be because of deeper background issues: stress, work or financial worries, bereavement, tiredness, anxiety, guilt, confusion about sexual orientation, conflict with a partner, depression. It's as if the penis is a barometer of mental health. If there's a depression hovering, the male mercury can just stays down. Smoking and diabetes are often behind erectile problems, too, as are artherosclerosis, fibrosis and simply ageing. Men's erections just do get softer with time, and after the age of 65, up to a quarter of men are thought to have difficulty getting or maintaining an erection. Among older men with diabetes, the figure may be as high as half. Gone are the boners of yesteryear, those rocket-like erections of adolescence which felt as if they'd lift your whole body away with them.

If erections stay away over a significant length of time, it's usually because the machine itself is faulty rather than because of any psychological issues. An erection is caused by blood filling the spongy tissue of the penis at higher pressure (see p.60). If erections aren't happening, or they aren't lasting, either blood isn't getting into the penis properly or the valve-like device that stops it flowing away again isn't doing its job, or the erectile tissue has got stiff with age and doesn't

The impotence shanty

When sailors asked each other "What shall we do with the drunken sailor … earlie in the morning?", and speculated that their list of treatments would result in "way hay and up she rises" it may not have been the mizzen topsail they were singing about. Is this a list of naval aphrodisiacs? Or ways to get a man with a hangover out of his hammock?

"Put him in a long boat till he's sober
Give him a dose of salt and water
Stick on his back a mustard plaster
Shave his belly with a rusty razor
Put him in the scuppers with a hosepipe on him
Put him in bed with the captain's daughter"

press hard enough against the penile membrane. Or, in long-distance cyclists, if the pudendal nerve is injured.

The way to test for a mechanical malfunction used to be to watch out for involuntary erections at night. Once upon a time, nurses were paid to keep a watchful eye open. Then a ring of perforated postage stamps placed around the penis was found to do the trick. Nowadays, since the concoction of drugs like Viagra and Cialis, doctors just tend to reach for the prescription pad right away, though some sensibly advise trying pelvic floor exercises too – which is particularly effective in younger men. But in the war between urology and psychology for the control of the penis, the urologists have won.

Pumps, potions and pills – the story of Viagra

Imagine the surprise of the pharmaceutical researchers. There they were, in their neat white coats, in the early 1990s, testing sildenafil citrate as a drug for lowering blood pressure in angina sufferers … and up they came, penis after penis springing into erectile life. One can only imagine how quickly the commercial potential dawned on Pfizer, and how many brand names they went through before settling on "Viagra", with its suggestive hints of liveliness and virility, growling tigerishness and raw aggression.

Viagra, the brand name for the chemical, doesn't cause erections, but it helps them happen if a man feels desire. The chemistry is complex, but basically sildenafil citrate inhibits an enzyme called phosphodiesterase type 5 (PDE5). By blocking it, it stops the PDE5 breaking down another chemical, cyclic guanosine monophosphate (cGMP). It's cGMP that relaxes the smooth muscle in the penis, allowing blood to easily flow in. If PDE5 is stopping cGMP doing its job, not enough blood can get in. Viagra, then, doesn't cause erections, it stops the thing that stops them from stopping them.

Viagra's main commercial rivals, Cialis and Levitra (aka Vivanza) have much the same mechanism, albeit using different chemicals. Choosing between them is mostly a matter of what works best for you with fewest side effects – though everyone should see a doctor before taking erectile drugs, and people with any kind of history of blood pressure, heart or penis problems should be especially careful. Viagra's side effects can include headaches, flushing and – more rarely – altered perception of colour, making things look blue. Cialis can cause muscle aches – but then, it can last as long as 36 hours, which means that unlike Viagra and Levitra (which wear off after about four hours), you don't have to be quite as calculating about when you take it. The downside of Cialis, or "the weekend pill", is that it takes around two hours to get to work. It's a long time to improvise on foreplay.

Earlier treatments like inflatable implants – pumped, in some cases, by little balloons in the testicular sack – or bendable rods, are now mostly used only where drugs don't work – and they

Pharmerotics: production of Vardenafil aka "Levitra", a drug designed to treat erectile dysfunction.

Viagra, impotence and satisfying sex

In its first year on sale, Viagra made over $1 billion. For some, this incredible success proves that the old myths about impotence just weren't true. It wasn't the result of witches' spells, as they said in the Middle Ages. It wasn't caused by laziness, luxury and easy living, as they thought in the Renaissance. It wasn't a consequence of masturbation or the "jarring of railway trains", as some Victorians believed. Nor was it created by the ghosts of adolescent incestuous fantasies rising in the minds of men, as Sigmund Freud claimed. It wasn't, in short, mental but physical. To say that 95 percent of cases of impotence were the product of psychological or emotional conflict, as did the sex researchers Masters and Johnson, couldn't have been more wrong.

Or could it? Viagra and its sister pharmaceuticals don't, in fact, have anything to do with increasing desire or arousal. They're not aphrodisiacs – although most people seem to think they are, and of course erections may make some men *feel* more manly. (And it's possible that Viagra enhances orgasm by its side effect of boosting oxytocin levels.) Opponents of the Viagrification of sex point out that it's all very well giving men their erections back, but you can't give them their underlying desires. Getting blood into the penis doesn't get passion into the heart, and turning the penis into a more efficient machine won't make for satisfying sex. An erection means you can achieve penetration, but the rest is up to you.

don't work on everybody. Certainly, few people now inject their penises directly with smooth muscle relaxants, as some were doing in the 1980s – with instant effect. Still less do people use the concoctions and amulets of the more distant past, such as a dish of roasted wolf's penis, an injection of monkey glands, or the tooth of a crocodile worn on a chain – this last being the personal tip of the Latin poet Ovid.

Vitamin V – drugs and recreational use of Viagra

Viagra is designed for people with erectile dysfunction but of course it also makes otherwise perfectly adequate erections that little bit harder. It won't have any effect at all on premature ejaculation, however (see p.168) – it doesn't make erections any "longer lasting" in that way. Viagra can improve the recovery time, of course, in that men may get another, post-orgasmic erection sooner than they might do otherwise. Whether or not this is welcome is another matter.

People who take recreational drugs (including alcohol and cannabis, but especially amphetamines such as speed, MDMA/ecstasy and meth) sometimes take Viagra ("vitamin V") as well, to counteract the fact that many drugs make it difficult to get or keep an erection. Assuming you're getting hold of real Viagra pills anyway – fakes are probably more common than the real thing – then taking this "trail mix", aka "sextasy", pretty much makes you a one-person medical trial. The real danger comes if you mix Viagra with poppers (amyl nitrite), which can cause alarming plummeting of blood pressure, or potentially a heart attack or stroke. The risk people don't talk about so much, meanwhile, is the one of contracting an STI. Smooching around with a boner and your head in the clouds is just asking for trouble (see box on p.296).

The market today – and the average inbox, too – is now saturated with offers of "herbal Viagra", "natural Viagra", "alternative Viagra" and the like. Many are touted as "traditional" remedies from Chile, China, South Africa, India or indeed anywhere that sounds exotic. Many companies promise more than just erections. One Welsh rugby team signed up to taking a Chinese "herbal Viagra" product called "Duro", made from silkworm larvae, the idea being to give their masculine sporting powers a lift. Whether it did the same for fifteen Welsh penises is a matter for speculation.

Priapism

If there's anything worse than not being able to get it up, it's not being able to get it down. This agonizing and potentially damaging condition is known as persistent sexual arousal syndrome or, in men, priapism, after the Roman fertility god Priapus, who was cursed (or blessed, depending on your point of view) with an outsized penis which, in most surviving statues, is shown raised extravagantly aloft. Priapus stood guard on fields and gardens for year after year, but these days, any erection that lasts longer than around four hours should be taken straight to hospital. In fact, most men will probably be on their way to the emergency ward well before then, as an erection that lasts hours at a time can be extremely painful.

The causes of priapism can include blood problems like sickle-cell disease, tumours and

A Roman wall painting of the rustic fertility god Priapus in the guise of Mercury.

injuries of the penis, and multiple sclerosis. Cocaine use can also have a priapic effect, but the most common drugs to cause priapism nowadays are, of course, Viagra and its cousins. Strangely, orgasm rarely has any detumescent effect. Instead, decongestant drugs are the usual treatment, followed by direct drainage of blood from the shaft.

Sexual desire disorders

Sexual desire disorders – which means not wanting to have sex, rather than the "dysfunction" of not being able to – are some of the hardest to diagnose. The boundaries between illness (thryoid disease, perhaps), psychological issues (anxiety, maybe) and just life itself (manifested in an unhappy relationship or libido changing over time) are rarely entirely clear. Even when a diagnosis can be made, the treatment may be less than obvious. Should someone with a lack of desire address their hormonal imbalance, their anxiety issues or their relationship? Should they see a doctor, a psychotherapist or a relationship counsellor? And, given that desire seems so variable between different people and different cultures, and even in a single person at various stages of their life, at what point does low desire become a disorder anyway?

Hypoactive sexual desire disorder

The medical trade was surprisingly slow to come up with Hypoactive Sexual Desire Disorder (HSDD) – which means libido, or desire, that's low enough to cause the sufferer distress. It's characterized not by inability to perform ("impotence" or "frigidity") but by the absence or low-level manifestation of the urge to have sexual activity, and the disappearance or diminution of sexual fantasies.

"Generalized" HSDD is different from a lack of desire for a specific partner – for which psychotherapy, counselling or a change of relationship may be indicated. Generalized HSDD may be lifelong, in which case it's sometimes described as asexuality (see p.294), or it may appear suddenly. Whether or not it causes the "distress" necessary for medical diagnosis, of course, is in no small degree a cultural issue. Levels of desire perceived as normal or acceptable in an urban university campus may be quite different from those found in a rural retirement home.

The potential causes of generalized HSDD are so variable as to make this "disorder" seem more like a symptom. Depression can be implicated, as can anxiety, stress, insomnia and pain. Many drugs affect libido – especially SSRIs (see p.13). Merely ageing is linked with decreasing levels of desire, often because of illnesses such as diabetes, lack of fitness, a thyroid condition or simply a changing hormonal balance.

Testosterone levels are closely linked with libido (see p.10). Whether or not you treat a fall in testosterone with a supplement or accept it as a natural consequence of ageing (or menopause; see p.220) is a matter of preference. The pharmaceutical industry positions itself as fighting for sex itself, and for post-menopausal women in particular. One physician specializing in sexual health opined, rather patronizingly, that "most women have been led to think the problem is simply mind over matter and do not realize that this is a real health issue, a misperception that is not allowing them to reap the benefits of a healthy sex life".

Asexuality

Asexuals don't necessarily lack any sexual feelings whatsoever. Some find the idea of sex repulsive, others are merely indifferent. Some sense a particular orientation – to men or women – but feel it as more emotional than sexual. Some are capable of arousal and may even masturbate for the pleasurable sensations it gives – but don't feel the classic sexual urge to do so. The point is that asexuals don't experience sexual attraction to the extent that they want to do anything about it. There are shades of grey, of course: demi-sexuals or "grey-As", as they call themselves, say they live in the grey area between sexual and non-sexual.

Asexuals are often accused of being in denial, or of having a physiological or psychological problem. If their "condition" causes them distress, they may even be told they have Hypoactive Sexual Desire Disorder (see p.293). Groups like AVEN, the Asexuality Visibility and Education Network exist to support those who want their sexual lifestyle to be respected. They cite studies among animals that show that lack of sexual behaviour is almost as common as homosexuality, or surveys which show that one or two percent of people have never had a sexual experience – and a healthy proportion of them are entirely happy about it.

She may be right. But less sexualized societies are puzzled as to why the modern West regards lowered sexuality as a problem. Many cultures regard sex as a problem to be solved – by abstinence or marriage, for instance – and see a sexless old age as an opportunity for focusing on other human desires: spirituality, for instance. Even the ancient Indian sex manual, the *Kamasutra*, considered that life had three stages with three separate goals: childhood for learning; the prime of life for pleasure; old age for religion. (Amusingly, and pragmatically, it adds an aside to the effect that, really, people should pursue these aims as the opportunities arise.)

The afterword on HSDD may be left to a former soldier who suffered a traumatic injury which had taken away his genitals and, he said, his desire. Asked tactfully by an interviewer about whether he felt terrible loss and distress, he laughed. The wounding was, he said, one of the best things that ever happened to him. Before, he was stressed about finding a partner, about ensuring he had sex, about being attracted to other people. He was conniving, manipulative, selfish and distracted. Without sex in his life, all that had changed. Without sex, he was happy.

Pharmasexuality

GDP-sized fortunes are being spent by drug companies trying to come up with a usable aphrodisiac – not a cure for erectile dysfunction, like Viagra and its brethren, but something which goes straight to the heart and mind: a drug for the libido. Thankfully, no corporation has yet succeeded. In 2006 and 2007 there was much press attention for bremelanotide, aka PT-141, a drug derived from a suntan pill (now there's a company pursuing some admirable health goals) which apparently provoked "genital warmth, tingling and throbbing" as well as "a strong desire to have sex". Unfortunately, bremelanotide also dangerously raised the blood pressure, and not in a metaphorical sense.

Testosterone patches and gels have had more success – as of 2007, the testosterone patch Intrinsa was approved by the European Medicines Agency, and can even be prescribed on the UK National Health Service, although only for post-menopausal women with medically sanctioned sexual desire disorders. In 2009, however, studies began to suggest that the evidence for its effectiveness was "based on highly selected women" and showed only small improvements – with a large placebo factor. The long term safety of taking testosterone was also called into question – and distinctly unsexy side effects such as acne, hair loss, weight gain and insomnia were reported as common.

Sexaholism

The idea of sexual addiction was born in conservative 1980s America, when infidelity – or merely enthusiastic masturbation – could get labelled "problem sex". Sexual expression that's getting out of control, however, or causing distress or hurt to others, is calling out for treatment. Various twelve-step programmes now exist, on the model of alcohol or narcotics anonymous, to help people who have been engaging in endless fruitless affairs, enjoying excessively risky sex, making repeated visits to sex workers or even subjecting others to frotteurism, exhibitionism or assault.

Twelve-steps may help, but sexaholics aren't quite like alcoholics. Leaving aside the gropers and flashers, they're usually told to moderate their behaviour, not to abstain altogether, or only to abstain for up to 90 days. And sexaholics aren't hooked on taking a drug – or not an external one. In this, they may be more like problem gamblers, who start to need the adrenaline and dopamine rush provided by a punt. Sex provides a similar hormonal cocktail, with the added euphoria of orgasmic oxytocin. And many sexaholics suffer from other addictions as well.

The behaviour may be a response to childhood sexual abuse, or express a psychological disorder. Obsessive Compulsive Disorder is a type of anxiety in which sufferers have repetitive thoughts and may feel compelled to perform personal "rituals" – and these can include sexual ones. Histrionic and Narcissistic Personality Disorder are both characterized by personal grandiosity and the seeking of admiration – which can be expressed sexually. Cognitive Behaviour Therapy may, then, be as useful a treatment as a twelve step programme – and in fact they share some of the same goals and language. Others find treatment for depression or anxiety helpful. Finding support, as with all addictions and disorders, is crucial.

Aphrodisiacs and recreational drugs

Love pills may be a pharmaceutical fantasy of the future, but aphrodisiacs – foods and potions that cause desire – have been the dream of centuries past. (The word "aphrodisiac" derives ultimately from the name of Aphrodite, Greek goddess of love.) Many ancient and folk remedies rely on sympathetic magic, or the belief that things can transmit their key qualities. The classic example, the oyster, is probably thought to be an aphrodisiac not because of its high protein, vitamin and mineral content, nor because it changes sex many times over the course of its life, but because an oyster looks or feels or maybe tastes a little bit like a woman's vulva: pearlescent smooth, fresh and ferrous, ozone-salty.

Oysters and rhino horns

The Japanese have linked the oyster with the vulva of the dancing goddess Ama-no-Uzume-no-Mikoto, Chinese theoreticians have considered oysters to be pure, feminine *yin* (though they're used more to encourage labour than conception) while the Akamba women of Eastern Kenya wear girdles of oyster shells until after the birth of their first child. The Danes simply call oysters *kudefisk*, or "vulva fish". Oyster pearls, meanwhile, have been valued as aphrodisiacs by authorities as remote as Cleopatra (see below) and ancient Hindu physicians.

It's often said that the Romans used oysters as an aphrodisiac, but in truth they were seen as one of a number of luxuriously sensual – rather than explicitly sexual – foods. The satirist Juvenal described a gluttonous aristocratic woman who ate giant oysters and drank unmixed wine foaming with unguents out of perfume bowls. That said, Cleopatra drank a cocktail of an oyster pearl dissolved in vinegar (yes, it works) to impress her lover, Mark Anthony. For specific aphrodisiac effects, the Roman historian Pliny served his guests grape-hyacinth bulbs, snails and eggs.

But the most famed Roman aphrodisiac was salep, or the root named *satyrion*, after its satyr-like qualities. It was the tuber of a kind of orchid which resembled the male testicle (the Greek *orchis*

actually means "testicle"); as the sixteenth-century alchemist Paracelsus asked, "is it not formed like the male privy parts?" Unfortunately, the plant was driven to extinction by over-enthusiastic harvesting.

Similar threats now beset rhinos and tigers, whose horns and bones, respectively, are used in some Asian folk remedies. They're not actually classed as aphrodisiacs in Traditional Chinese Medicine, as is often claimed (they're supposed to reduce fevers and suppress arthritic and rheumatic pain instead), but rhino horn is prescribed for virility in parts of north India, while all kinds of tiger parts, including alleged penises, crop up in costly soups across Southeast Asia.

Sex & drugs & STIs

People who have taken drugs, including alcohol, take bigger sexual risks. They may have sex when they otherwise might not have done, or they may not use a condom – or only put one on after penetration (and infection) has already taken place. Statistically, drugs or alcohol roughly doubles the chance that someone will risk unprotected sex.

Young people are especially likely to take sexual chances – because they take more risks generally, because they're less used to handling the effects of drugs or booze (or desire) and because they may be less comfortable with talking about sex and condoms openly. The result is an explosion in the number of sexually transmitted infections in the young. One unlucky, unprotected experience with an infected partner gives an adolescent girl a 50 percent chance of getting gonorrhoea, a 30 percent chance of contracting herpes, and a 1 percent chance of acquiring HIV.

Strangely enough, there's nothing much in rhino horn other than keratine, plus a few amino acids – making this another example of sympathetic magic.

Fragrant plants and stimulant roots

The majority of ancient aphrodisiacs have powerful odours which seem to mark them out as stimulants: the Chinese had ginseng and cloves while the ancient Indians used licorice root, asparagus, honey and sugar – as well as "dog's fang" prickly root, cock's-head root and the juice of a sparrow's egg. The Egyptians enjoyed the fragrant tuber cyperus rotundes, a relative of papyrus. The Greeks called on artichoke, asparagus, candied ginger, shellfish and spring onions. Iowa's Meskwaki people mixed a ginseng-like root with snake meat, gelatine, wild columbine and soil speckled with mica.

The Romans used ginger spread on the genitals in the form of a pounded paste, along with highly aromatic plants such as frankincense and myrrh (which puts an unusual spin on the Christian nativity story), and what the poet Martial called "lubricious rocket" – the same peppery salad familiar from cosmopolitan pizza parlours. Truffles are universally admired – and in fact their giddy aroma is disconcertingly similar to musk, as found in pig and other animals' pheromones (see p.16).

Some roots and plant extracts may actually have had real effects. Ginseng seems to help generate nitric oxide and relax smooth muscle – both important in the mechanism of erection. It may also help fight the libido-suppressing effects of some antidepressants. The West African aphrodisiac yohimbine, made from an oak-like bark, is used in some modern medicines; modern science reckons the natural extract would have only a mild stimulant effect, and then only after a good fortnight's delay – which may seem like excessive forward planning. The side effects of panicky agitation and sleeplessness are off-putting, too.

The weirdly popular European aphrodisiac cantharides, or "Spanish fly" (extracted from a kind of blister beetle) certainly had an effect: it was a powerful poison. The famed seventeenth-century witch "La Voisin" mixed it with mole's teeth and blood to lure Louis XIV into the arms of Madame de Montespan. When the Marquis de Sade gave it in the form of aniseed pastilles to courtesans at one of his orgies, a number died.

Luxury and lechery

Often, sheer decadent rarity seems to be behind aphrodisiac reputations. Roman delicacies such as peacock brains and pregnant lampreys were associated with the kind of parties which could quickly become orgies. Some European medieval aphrodisiacs included anointing the penis with jackal bile or the fat from a camel's hump. Alternatively, you might consume the "sperm" whale's ambergris, or a bezoar stone removed from the gut of a particular kind of ibex. None of these remedies were exactly lying around in medieval times; even leeches rotted in a dungheap – another reputed aphrodisiac – may have been easier to come by.

Exclusive luxury had much to do with the lecherous reputation of theobroma cacao, the drink of the Aztec gods, better known as chocolate. Originally mixed with chilli in the form of a liquid, "chocolate" was reputed to turn even the best-behaved seventeenth-century ladies into lascivious orgiasts. Curiously, chocolate's reputation as an aphrodisiac survived into modern times, when it was suggested that its dose of phenylethylamine (PEA) produced a minor amphetamine-type high similar to the rush of being in love. The urban myth has gathered pace since, even though the scientist who originally proposed the idea has admitted that the PEA in chocolate doesn't seem to get anywhere near the brain.

Recreational drugs and sex

Far the most popular aphrodisiac of modern times is alcohol. It boosts testosterone and, more importantly, peels away inhibitions thanks to its depressant effect on the nervous system. Unfortunately, alcohol also inhibits erection in men and arousal in women, and makes it much harder to reach orgasm. It also encourages sexual risk taking, with the attendant dangers (see box on p.296).

Many recreational drugs have similar effects. Ecstasy can cause a libido surge in many people, and sometimes intensifies orgasm; but it may also replace the sexual urge with a more asexual kind of loving feeling – and it impairs erection in roughly half of men who use it. Similar effects are common with marijuana, which can heighten sensory perception but equally leave the user too lethargic to want to bother.

Amyl nitrite, aka poppers, can increase orgasmic intensity if taken at exactly the right moment, as orgasm begins. It also increases blood flow and therefore erection. But it's potentially dangerous, and highly so if taken with Viagra. Cocaine and amphetamines both cause dopamine surges which can be mildly orgasmic in quality, and many users experience a surge in confidence that can make them feel temporarily horny. Cocaine can also prolong or intensify orgasm. But even discounting legal issues, addictiveness, cost and the appalling ethics of the drugs trade, the sexual downsides of cocaine are pretty major: it's an anaesthetic, so can potentially encourage rough and emotionally chilly sex in the search that elusive prolonged orgasm; it can also cause impotence and loss of libido in the frequent user – not to mention paranoia and relationship breakdown.

The least sexual drug of all is surely heroin. In William Burroughs' drug-addled novel of 1959, *The Naked Lunch*, the character Dr Benway states that "Some of my learned colleagues (nameless assholes) have suggested that junk derives its euphoric effect from direct stimulation of the orgasmic center. It seems more probably that junk dampens the whole cycle of tension, discharge and rest. Orgasm has no function in the junky."

8

Sex and

religion

Sex and religion

Sex threatens religion. It offers an alternative escape from the everyday round of worldly life: it is powerful and potentially chaotic. Sexual desire can undermine the social order on which religion relies, and cut across the lines of patriarchal inheritance that religion has usually defended. According to the German theorist Max Weber, sex is the "greatest irrational force of life". Like food, which religions have also long tried to control, sex is something we crave, and this craving might just get the better of us. This means, for the religious-minded, that it must be kept within the bounds of natural order, as established by God.

Religions are almost universally split between an authoritarian wing, concerned with and often controlling the writing down of laws, and a more permissive wing. It's not hard to find a Christian preacher, a Muslim imam or a Jewish rabbi who'll describe any kind of sex except straight, marital, him-on-top, contraception-free sex as an abomination. But it's no harder to find liberals and mystics who see sex as an expression of god's creativity and a gift of grace.

And in any case, religion isn't just what people say they believe, or what their ancient books or indeed contemporary authorities, want them to believe: religion is also what people do. Seventy percent of churchgoing Catholics in the US, for instance, believe that the Pope should permit birth control devices. So is it true to say that "Catholicism" is against contraception? At best, it's possible to say that religious traditions offer some of the most deeply positive ideas about sexuality. And some of the most deeply negative as well.

Holy sex

When religions have something positive to say about sex, they usually put it something like this: sex is good because it is part of God's creation; why would God have given us something pleasant if he didn't want it to be enjoyed? Protestantism long made a point of promoting itself as sex-positive in this way – in opposition to those celibate, Papist priests and monks and nuns. Islam teaches that not only is all creation beautiful and pure but that the human body is one of its most beautiful and purest parts. An act which pays homage to this creation, therefore, can be a holy act – especially (or only) when it takes place within the holy state of matrimony. Judaism, for instance, has often treated sex as a divine imperative – something which a husband and wife owe to each other and to their community.

Seminal sacrifices

According to writings uncovered in the Ancient Egyptian city of Heliopolis, the first act of creation was a kind of masturbatory sacrifice by the hermaphroditic god Atum, who used his semen to form the twin gods of air and moisture, Shu and Tefênet. Atum's hand was eventually personified as the fertility goddess Hathor, who was said to be visible in the night sky as the Milky Way and was considered responsible for the annual inundation of the Nile, on which all life in Egypt depended.

In Hinduism, semen is seen as a physical manifestation of *tejas*, the brilliant, fiery seed energy

Kosher sex

A bizarre urban legend is apparently widespread in the US: Orthodox (or, sometimes, Hasidic) Jews are supposed to have sex through a hole cut in a bedsheet. They don't. (Or not unless they like the sound of it.) The source of the rumour is hard to pin down. Some think it comes from outsiders seeing a kind of undershirt known as a talit katan, which usually has a hole for the wearer's head. One other theory holds that it stems from the sheet used by some conservatives to allow a woman to be baptized modestly.

Kosher sex, according to the Orthodox rabbi and TV personality, Shmuley Boteach, is something quite different. Kosher sex, he says, "is carnal love that leads to knowledge and intimacy … a journey whose destination is a couple who feel joined not only by the same roof or children, but especially through the enjoyment and pleasure they constantly give each other." It is designed "to sew two distinct bodies together as one flesh." "Great sex", Boteach quips, "is a delight of the body. Kosher sex is a delight of the soul."

that drives the universe. It is semen that allows creation, and semen that contains the divine spark. The *Brihadaranyaka Upanishad*, a work of Hindu philosophy dating back to the sixth or seventh centuries BC tells the story of a young man who asks his father about the meaning of sex. Sex, his father explains, is a kind of sacrificial offering that a man makes to the gods. A woman's vulva is the sacrificial ground, while "her pubic hair is the sacred grass; her labia majora are the Soma-press; and her labia minora are the fire blazing at the centre." The *Upanishad* goes further, likening the sexual act, where "a man, closely embraced by his loving wife, knows nothing without, nothing within" to a state of divine enlightenment.

According to the oral tradition recorded by the Imam Muslim, the Prophet Muhammad told his followers that sex involved *sadaqa*, or worship through giving. Hearing this, Muhammad's companions asked him eagerly if this meant that having sex would actually be rewarded by God. The Prophet answered: "Do you not think that were he to act upon it unlawfully, he would be sinning?", he said. "Likewise, if he acts upon it lawfully he will be rewarded."

Sex in paradise

In Ancient Egypt, sexual desire was regarded as a key element of the life force, and there's good, hard evidence that Ancient Egyptians expected actual sex in the afterlife. Along with other grave goods, for use after death, false penises were added to male mummies. False breasts or nipples were added to female mummies, too, which may indicate an expectation of suckling and therefore procreation, too.

Islam is pretty confident that living in paradise must include some kind of sex (box on p.304.). The Qur'an describes heaven as being well supplied with "pure companions" or *houri*. These are lovely-eyed people, virgins like "hidden pearls" with whom the dead – all righteous Muslim dead, not just martyrs and not just men – will be paired, as a reward for good deeds in life. You could think of them as lovely angels.

The presence of "phallic" *lingams* (see p.309) and a central garba-griha, or "womb-chamber" in temples puts sex at the heart of Hindu religion. But the most astounding explosion of sex into Hinduism is in the medieval temple complexes of Khajuraho and Konarak, where erotic sculptures run amok on parts of the outer walls. Nymphs can be seen displaying their broad hips and high breasts, dancing, washing their hair – and making love in endless acrobatic and extreme postures. The sculptures may symbolize Tantric principles, where sex is a metaphor for union with the divine (see p.314). They may reflect a religious joy in the fertility of all creation, or have acted as magical talismans, deflecting evil spirits from entering the temple. They may have depicted a vision of paradise.

Modern religions seem less sure of what pleasures lie in store. When Jesus was asked which husband a seven-times widow would belong to in paradise, he replied that there was no marriage in heaven. Many take this to mean that there will be no sex either. Others point out that the Church teaches that at the last judgement humanity will be resurrected not in spirit, but bodily. The great theologian St Thomas Aquinas very specifically claimed that those bodies, being perfect, would include the genitals – but that those genitals wouldn't have any sexual purpose.

Buddhists definitely make no room for sex in their nirvana, or heaven. It's not that sex is bad in itself. It's rather that the craving for it is partly what makes this world so sorrowful: sexual desire is one of the strongest, deepest roots of the attachment to this world, which imprisons the mind. Nirvana, by contrast, is characterized exactly by the absence of craving. It is described as cool, still and peaceful. Far, then, from sexual desire.

The southern façade of the Lakshmana Temple at Khajuraho is decorated with highly explicit statuary. The entwined groups may conceal spiritual, Tantric meanings, or have magical-propitiatory significance.

The Song of Songs

When Christians (or agnostics tying the knot in church) pick Bible readings for their weddings, there's a dearth of appropriate material to choose from. Luckily, there's always the Song of Songs. These highly charged verses were legendarily written by the Hebrew King Solomon in praise of his wife, the unnamed "Pharaoh's daughter". "O that you would kiss me with the kisses of your mouth!", he begins, "For your love is better than wine". Later, the poet tells his love "you are stately as a palm tree, and your breasts are like its clusters" – shortly before threatening to "climb the palm tree and lay hold of its branches".

The Song of Songs was clearly known as a deeply sensuous piece of writing from early on. A rabbi complained in the first century AD that it was being sung at feasts. Other rabbis felt the need to explain the poem's surprising inclusion in the Hebrew Bible. It wasn't erotic poetry at all, they claimed, but an allegory of God's burning love for his people. To make sure this interpretation was established as the correct one, Jewish scholars classified the Song of Songs as one of the types of scripture that should only be studied by elderly men. Lines like "Your two breasts are like two fawns, twins of a gazelle that feed among the lilies", it seems, might confuse the young.

Seventy-two virgins

The erotic aspirations of ultra-extremist Muslims have, thanks to the video farewells of suicide bombers, become surprisingly well-known in the West. A number of Islamicist "martyrs" have apparently believed that the paradise waiting for them won't be anything like the sobrely authoritarian state they hope to leave behind. There will be virgins. Seventy-two per man, to be precise. What's more, these virgins will be red hot for it. And having sex with them will be no sin.

The idea isn't exactly mainstream. The notion comes not from the Qur'an, which only talks about lovely-eyed companions (see p.302) but from one of the *hadith* collections, the books accepted by Sunni Muslims as reporting the sayings of the Prophet Muhammad. According to the Imam at-Tirmidhi, "the smallest reward for the people of Heaven is an abode where there are 80,000 servants and 72 *houri*, over which stands a dome decorated with pearls, aquamarine and ruby."

A respected fifteenth-century scholar, Imam Suyuti (who also wrote a number of sex manuals), disagreed on the number of *houri*. Each Muslim would marry seventy, he said, in addition to any women he married on earth – "and all will have appetising vaginas." Suyuti also elaborated on how exactly sex in heaven would work. "Each time we sleep with a *houri*", he explained, "we find her virgin." He doesn't explain why virgins are supposed to be better sexual partners than women with sexual experience. Suyuti does explain away the other problem of sex in paradise, however. "The penis of the Elected", he proclaims, "never softens. The erection is eternal."

In reality, most Muslims treat the promise of 72 virgins much as most Christians treat the idea of lounging around on a heavenly cloud strumming on a harp and eating grapes. It's a nice idea to conjure with, but it'd be rather embarrassingly medieval to actually believe in it. One controversial scholar, Christoph Luxenberg, thinks it's the wrong idea altogether anyway. If certain key words in the Qur'an are read as being in the Syriac rather than Arabic language (and quite why they might be is a very technical matter) then the promised "lovely-eyed companions" become, well, "white raisins of crystal clarity". Which brings us back to the clouds and the grapes.

Christians went further in defusing the Song's erotic charge. Under the influence of the Neoplatonist philosophers, the third-century father of the church Origen wrote ten volumes of commentary on the Song of Songs. He saw it as an extended metaphor of the union of the human soul with God after death, and as a debate on the natures of carnal and spiritual love. There's little doubt which kind of love Origen valued more highly: he castrated himself, after all. Catholic theologians of a later period preferred to recast the poet's desire for his lover as a mystical union between God and the Church, or between God-in-heaven and God-on-earth or even, somewhat strangely, as a passionate outpouring of Jesus's devotion to his mother. They weren't just making this stuff up: poetry of the time really was subject to highly allegorical interpretations. Still, there's little excuse for certain Latin translations, where *ubera*, the word for "breasts", somehow becomes *verba* – as in "your words are sweeter than wine".

Today, the Song of Songs is largely accepted as an erotic poem, its place in the Bible thought to reflect the importance of sexual passion – as long as it's safely within marriage. In fact, the strength of the poet's desire supposedly emphasizes the value placed on monogamy. Anyone who fancied their wife quite that much, surely, wouldn't stray. Just don't think too much about the biblical fact that Solomon, the poem's legendary author, had 700 wives and princesses, and 300 concubines, to boot.

Sex gods and goddesses

Digs across Europe, and beyond, have turned up scores of primitive statuettes with exaggeratedly buxom female anatomy: heavy breasts, broad hips, ripe vulvas. All date from the Paleolithic and Neolithic periods – from around 25,000 BC to 2500 BC – and they outnumber images of male divinities by four to one, leading some archaeologists to speculate that Europe was once in the grip of a goddess cult which venerated sex and fertility.

Of course, the primitive figurines could have been pornography, or sex-education aids, or dolls, or even self-portraits. But there are plentiful myths about men overthrowing female power in some distant age – most commonly among so-called "primitive" peoples in Australia, Melanesia, Africa and the Amazon basin. Does some ancestral memory survive in these parts of the world which, in Europe, patriarchal religion managed to stamp out?

Statue of Artemis Polymastros (many-breasted) at the Ephesus Museum. The Ephesians worshipped her as a fertility goddess and built a large temple in her honour.

The primal androgyne

The oldest myths of creation reflect the oldest kind of reproduction – asexual. Just as single-celled amoeba divide to reproduce, god was supposed to have done much the same in the beginning. One Indian sacred text, the *Brihadaranyaka Upanishad*, says that creation began when the original "Self-existent" being was "itched" by sexual desire. This primordial being was apparently "as big as a man and a woman in close embace", but it divided itself into two parts, created the primal waters with a thought and planted the first seed in them. Which is why, says the *Upanishad*, men and women long to be joined together once more in sex.

In Japan, the twin male–female gods Izanagi and Izanami created the first land (or Japan, or the material world) by thructing a jewelled spear down into the ocean from heaven; the brine dripping from their spear became the first island. Immediately after, Izanagi and Izanami felt the urge to come together in copulation.

The Greek philosopher Plato similarly speculated that humans may desire to return to their "original nature, seeking to make one of two, and to heal the state of man". This was the opinion he ascribed to the playwright Aristophanes, at any rate. The primordial being apparently had "four hands and the same number of feet, one head with two faces, looking opposite ways, and could "walk upright as men now do, backwards or forwards as he pleased" but, when needing to move quickly, could also "roll over and over at a great pace, turning on his four hands and four feet, eight in all, like tumblers going over and over with their legs in the air".

Plato may have been poking fun, but the "primal androgyne" crops up in Norse, Germanic, Persian and Roman creation myths, as well as Indian and Greek. The Hebrew notion that God made Eve from Adam's rib could be yet another version of the story. Christian mystics wondered whether, if God created the original Adam in his own image, before Eve was ever created from Adam's rib, was this original Adam a hermaphrodite? Would this mean that God, too, was both male and female?

The book of Genesis also links this initial creation with the origin of sexual desire. Because of it, "a man shall leave his father and mother and be joined to his wife, and they shall become one flesh." Sex is seen as a way of returning to the original unified state of humanity, just as Plato saw it. The "Gnostic Gospel" of St Thomas even quotes Jesus as saying that entry to the Kingdom of Heaven depends on this mystical unity: "When you make the two one," he says, "and when you make the inner as the outer, and the outer as the inner, and the above as the below, and when you make the male and female into a single one, so that the male will not be male and the female be female … then you shall enter." Admittedly, most church authorities dispute that this gospel reports the authentic words of Jesus.

Or almost stamp out: in ancient Greece, it was said that male priests had once taken control of the female Oracle at Apollo's shrine. Traces of goddess or nature worship crop up in the earliest Indo-European cultures, such as the civilizations of the Minoans, Etruscans and early Greeks. The Mediterranean region, in particular, seems to have venerated mother goddesses, and some think that named deities such as Isis, Artemis and Astarte all refer back to one Great Goddess or god-mother. The Babylonians worshipped the fertility goddess Ishtar (see p.307), while the early Israelites are sometimes said to have worshipped a similar goddess called Asherah who stood in the Temple for hundreds of years (before being driven out by the god who was once her consort, and later became the jealous god of the Hebrews). In Arabia, the triumph of Islam is sometimes described as a victory over a triad of goddesses: as Muhammad said, in one of the *hadith* sayings, before the revelation of the Qu'ran the Arabs worshipped only women. Further east, in India, meanwhile, the many Hindu goddesses are sometimes said to stem from the original Devi, sometimes called Ekakini, "the Only".

Ishtar, queen of heaven

One of the most enduringly popular deities for the Babylonians, who dominated Mesopotamia until the sixth century BC, was Ishtar (or Inanna or Nin), the Queen of Heaven. She was visible as the morning and evening star, which symbolized how she lived a life of sexual licence when night fell, but was reborn pure and virginal at dawn. (Later civilizations would associate this star with Venus,

goddess of love). Ishtar was known for her ruthless love affairs, but was also the wife of Tammuz, the shepherd god (see p.310). She famously travelled into the underworld in search of him, leaving the world in permanent winter, without new growth and without sexual desire. At each of the seven gates of hell she had to remove an article of clothing until she journeyed on entirely naked – a myth which later spawned the idea of a "dance of the seven veils".

Under her Sumerian name Inanna, Ishtar was celebrated in the "bridal songs", love poems which cast her as a joyful bride preparing herself for marriage. In one, she bathes her body and then, as she dresses, she starts to sing a song in praise of herself and in praise of her *gala*, or vulva – in fact, the song may actually be sung *by* her *gala*. Ishtar was plainly not a bashful kind of goddess. She was served by celibate high-priestesses, or *ishtaritu*, as well as upper-class women called *naditu*, who may have performed the famed *hieros gamos* rite, the "sacred wedding" at which the earth's fertility was ensured by acts of symbolic sex between the *naditu* and the earthly king. The exact nature of the rites is not recorded, however, as only the priestesses and the king would ever enter the holy of holies, where the rite was performed.

Erotic Greeks

The chief of the Greek gods, Zeus, was celebrated for his philanderings among goddesses, but his dalliances with mortals were most notorious of all, sparking countless sculptures and paintings in both ancient and modern times. As an eagle, Zeus sired Dionysus (see p.310) with Semele, and abducted and became the lover of the boy-prince, Ganymede of Troy. As a swan, he seduced Leda. As a white bull, he raped Europa. As a cloud, he made love to the maiden Io.

But Zeus was predominantly a god of thunder, a king and a ruler. The pre-eminent erotic Greek deity was Aphrodite. Known to the Romans as Venus (and analogous to the Egyptians' Hathor), she was the goddess of love, beauty, desire – and high-class prostitution. Even Aphrodite's birth was erotically charged: when the horned harvest deity Kronos overthrew his father, the sky god Ouranos, he castrated him and threw his genitals into the sea; as the surf bubbled up, Aphrodite arose from the foam. Artists from Praxiteles, in the fourth century BC, through to Botticelli, Bouguereau and Odilon Redon have dwelled on this moment with lascivious care, making Aphrodite the archetypal female nude (see p.52).

Aphrodite spawned a number of subsidiary erotic divinities, chiefly Eros (the Romans' Cupid or Amor) – he of the wings, bow and love-sparking arrows. The boy-god of desire (or, according to some, specifically male desire) was sometimes said to be Aphrodite's own son but, mythologically speaking, his deep origins probably lie alongside the Aryan god celebrated by the Hindus as Kama, who carries a bow of sugar cane, strung with stinging bees and firing erotically fatal, flower-tipped arrows.

The best-known story about Cupid was told by the second-century spinner of Latin yarns, Apuleius. Cupid was apparently sent by a jealous Aphrodite to instill in the beautiful, mortal girl Psyche "a passion for some low, mean, unworthy being, so that she may reap a mortification as great as her present exultation and triumph".

Unfortunately, Cupid himself was captivated by Psyche's loveliness and, while trying to kiss her, stabbed himself with his own arrow. The pair's succeeding affair is one of the all-time classics of mythology – and their notorious kiss became a favourite theme of Neoclassical erotic art (the depictions by Canova and Bouguereau are perhaps sexiest of all). The ultimate outcome was a daughter, the goddess Voluptas, or "bliss" – also known in Greek as Hedone, from which English gets its word hedonism, meaning the pursuit of pleasure.

Phallic worship

While some archaeologists see mother goddesses everywhere, others see phalluses. Phallic symbols and standing stones have been identified in Mesopotamia, Egypt and the Mediterranean, in the pre-Celtic west, and away across India into east Asia, Polynesia and the Americas. They can be grouped together in stone circles, or stand solo as obelisks and menhirs. Some think the phallus represents the creative god of Nature, a god typically associated with shepherds, or as the "lord of the animals". This god has been worshipped as the ancient Egyptian gods Min (who was usually depicted with an erect penis), Amun, Re and Osiris (see p.310), as the Greek god Pan, and, by the Romans, as Silvanus, Faunus or, most obviously, Priapus – who lends his name to the priapic, or erect, state.

Unfortunately for this phallic cult, if it ever existed, it was met head on by the rising Semitic religions in Europe and the Middle East and there are few signs now of its former power. One is the

Ritual bathing around the Shiva lingam at Gai Ghat, beside the sacred River Ganges at Varanasi.

lingering Mediterranean belief in the "evil eye", a powerful symbol some link to the meatus or "eye" of the penis, whose baleful influence only a quick touch of a man's penis can avert. (The practice of wearing a phallic symbol as jewellery for protection, as classical Romans did, has died out.) Another is the curious Germanic and English custom of getting people (especially young girls) to dance round and round a maypole in springtime (tradionally on May Day). This wasn't always just symbolic sex. One sixteenth-century Puritan

observer disapprovingly recorded how, after the pole was danced, "What clipping, what culling, what kissing and bussing, what smooching and slobbering one of another" went on.

The ithyphallic, or permanently erect god, is worshipped in India today as Shiva, whose stone *lingams*, or penises, are found all over the subcontinent, daubed in holy oils and powders, and garlanded with flowers. Some have argued that Christianity, with its phallic cross and god who dies then rises again – both, arguably, inherited or at least borrowing their symbolic resonance from Osiris – is another phallic survival, but it is a minority point of view.

Osiris and Dionysus

Osiris was known as the Lord of the Pillar, representing stability. His symbol was the *djed*, a kind of pillar topped with a number of spikes. Some interpret the *djed* as an unequivocal phallic symbol, others see it as a representation of the bones of the base of the spine. Either way, it's directly related to semen, which was thought by the Ancient Egyptians to begin life as spinal fluid. Ancient Egyptian myths about the underworld god Osiris took many forms, but the key element was always his murder and resurrection. It symbolized the germination of seeds and the annual flooding of the Nile which allowed the crops to grow. As such, he was the god not only of death but of life – of fertility.

In one version of his myth, Osiris is tricked by his enemies, led by Set, into entering a coffin which is promptly cast into the river Nile. It flows downstream, the dying god trapped inside, before embedding itself in a cedar tree. The tree is afterwards cut down and erected as the central strut of a palace roof. Osiris's wife, Isis, eventually tracks down the pillar and, casting a spell her father taught her, brings her husband back to life for long enough for him to father her child. Unfortunately, Set then comes across the newly dead body, and tears it into fourteen parts. Isis manages to gather thirteen of the dismembered parts together. The missing part, which was eaten by a fish, was, of course, the divine penis.

Undeterred, Isis created a golden phallus and the god was magically brought back to life again.

This weird story had such psychological power that it survived the collapse of Egyptian religion, and took new expression in what became known as the Osiris-Dionysus cult, a group of myths and beliefs that, some say, influenced the growth of stories about the life and untimely death of a Jewish prophet called Jesus. Dionysus himself was a Greek god of wine and fertility, later worshipped as Bacchus. He was celebrated in festivals known as the Dionysian Mysteries in which his followers – notably the sexually unrestrained, skin-clad Maenads – succumbed to what seems to have been a religious-alcoholic, erotic-ecstatic frenzy. In statues, Dionysus was typically depicted in a cooler, more laid-back mood, but he was still louche and lovely – and, fascinatingly, distinctly androgynous.

Counterpart goddesses

Gods of the phallus are typically married – and often also related – to goddesses of fertility or love. The Egyptians honoured both Osiris and his sister-wife, Isis, the Babylonians Ishtar and Tammuz, the Canaanites Ba'al and his furiously warlike sister-lover Anat. The female deities were often particularly fierce – a reflection, perhaps, of the widespread belief that the female represents the active principle.

Kali, the consort of the Hindu god Shiva, is both Mother of the Universe and the goddess of destruction – she even wears a necklace of human heads. She isn't a sex goddess, as New Agers would like her to be, but she is often depicted naked or locked in yab-yum, or sexual union with her husband. Kali requires particularly bloody sacrifices. Cybele, the Phrygian Earth Mother, was even more demanding. Her priests would castrate themselves and offer the amputated part in devotion. (Some think this rite was echoed by the ancient Hebrews in the form of their relatively minor snip, or circumcision.)

Even Christianity, the religion devoted to the Father and Son, has historically made plenty of room in heaven for a quasi-goddess. Veneration of the Blessed Virgin Mary, as *Theotokos* ("Mother of God"), as a "new Eve" and as Queen of Heaven was arguably as important to the medieval Church as worship of God himself, and she retains a hugely important role in the Catholic and Orthodox Churches – above all saints. The Church itself was described as a "Mother". And according to Julian of Norwich, a fourteenth-century mystic and Benedictine nun, God Almighty was a father but God "all-Wisdom" was a mother. And Jesus, according to Julian, was a "precious mother" who nourished humanity with his blood just as a mother suckles her child with milk.

Sex cults and the far-out fringe

If many mainstream religions frown on sex, there is no shortage of alternatives. If there's one factor which most of these fringe movements have in common, however, it's that their sexual ideas or practices aren't really about sex at all. Sex is usually a tool, or a metaphor, to allow devotees to reach towards something beyond – a divine Something that rarely has much to do with sex.

Ancient Egypt

Ancient Egyptian religion was obsessed with fertility – understandable, perhaps, in a land which depended on the Nile bursting its banks every year to make the fields fruitful. This annual inundation was typically described as the joining of man and woman in sexual union, but it was also associated with ejaculation. In the New Kingdom, the coronation of the Pharaoh involved a ritual planting of seed – a rite which some scholars think involved an act of public masturbation by the Pharaoh himself (echoing, perhaps, the original primordial wank – see p.301). The ceremony was presided over by the permanently erect fertility god, Min, whose symbols included an arrow with barbs and the wild prickly lettuce, which exudes a milky sap when torn or broken. A cult image of Min was carried into the fields before harvest, and boys and young men would compete to climb a giant totem pole.

Thirty years after a Pharaoh's coronation, he would celebrate another festival, the Heb Sed, or Feast of the Tail. A *djed*, or pillar of stability (see p.310), would be erected, and the Pharaoh would perform a sacramental run and dance while wearing an animal's tail – probably a bull's, recalling the ancient idea that bull semen was the perfect fertilizer. The Heb Sed ritual symbolized, tested and guaranteed the Pharaoh's continuing potency and fitness for office, and it was intimately bound up with sexual potency: a relief carving reveals that when Queen Hatshepsut had to perform the festival, she had a bull with a very visible penis running alongside her.

In the Ptolemaic period, a festival performed at Edfu featured the goddess Hathor, who was ritually given a phallus to symbolize creation.

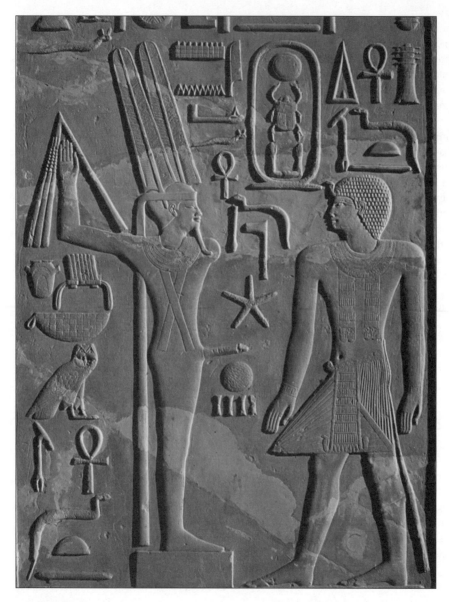

A relief at the chapel of Senusret I at Karnak showing Amun-Re in the form of the permanently erect fertility god Min. He wears a twin-feathered headdress and carries a flail, a symbol of his kingship.

No romance, please, we're Mangaian

The Pacific island of Mangaia, in the Cook Islands, is often cited with awe as a kind of sexually liberated paradise. Sex education, it's said, begins early. Mothers massage and mould their daughters' clitorises, and pull their sons' penises to make them longer and stronger. Masturbation is learned from the age of between seven and ten, and older men teach boys how to do cunnilingus and how to time orgasm, among other vital skills.

Upon reaching adulthood – and after the boys undergo a ritual splitting of the foreskin called superincision – older, experienced women introduce boys to sex itself. Mangaian youths would then indulge in *motoro*, or "sleep crawling", meaning they visit each other's beds and have sex with each other, with parental approval. They don't resort to romantic preliminaries such as kissing, cuddling or petting. In fact, kissing and romantic love itself are supposedly unknown to Mangaian society: the only way of saying "I love you" in the local language is supposedly "I want to copulate with you". Not that this reduces pleasure in sex any: Mangaian men are supposed to be confident of giving their partners orgasms, and capable of averaging three a night themselves.

That's the Mangaian myth, anyway, and it's repeated everywhere – partly because it's such an outstanding example of a sex-positive culture. The truth, however, is almost certainly different. Indeed, this is not a portrait of contemporary Mangaian society – which, post-AIDS and post-Christianity has very different values. (Nowadays, the dress code is "conservative" and on Sundays, there's not only no shopping, but no driving or even swimming.) It may not even be a portrait of pre-colonial Mangaia. The stories all originated with one anthropologist, David Marshall, who visited the island and reported on it in 1971. Some have suggested that he was fooled into taking the beery stories passed around a group of men at face value.

Anthropologist Helen Harris, who visited the island twenty years later, was told that, sure, some men slept around, but "a woman looks for a man who isn't going around with other women and who wants to marry her". Love was very much part of this Pacific Island's culture, she found. In fact, parents even tried to put a stop to it so young people would make more sensible marriages. Could love really have been learned in a single generation?

But perhaps the most sexually adventurous of the Egyptian festivals were the hierogamies or "holy weddings" of the Radiant Festival of the Wadi at Thebes, performed in the era of the New Kingdom. The sacred statue of Amun-Re from Karnak was placed in a boat and ferried across the Nile to visit the shrines of other gods and goddesses on the west bank of the river. This quasi-sexual "rite of incorporation" symbolized the nearness of the living and the dead. During the ecstatic and possibly orgiastic celebrations which accompanied the festival, it's thought that couples would spend the night in and around the shrines, sharing in the electrifying sexuality emanating from the gods.

The real Tantric sex

"Tantric sex" is notorious in the West as a kind of super-athletic, hyper-spiritualized way to make love. It's sold as an authentic, Eastern tradition, but it's essentially a New Age concoction of slow-burn sexual practices mixed with a smattering of Buddhist or Taoist precepts.

The original Tantric philosophers were writing towards the end of the first millennium AD, in India. They were less interested in desire than in overcoming it, and their ultimate goal was not a gratifyingly extended sex session but to tap into the power of the divine. Some Tantric notions are close to the ideas behind Indian Yoga. The universe's supreme power, for instance, is thought to lie in hidden channels in the body. The chief vein, found in the spine, takes the form of the sleeping Kundalini serpent. The Tantrin, or adept, is supposed to awaken the Kundalini through ritual, magical – and, in some rare cases, sexual – practices. This causes the serpent to rise through the various *chakras*, or energy points along the spine, allowing the Tantrin to unite his or her inward male and female spirits – found in the perineal area and the skull, respectively – in a kind of enlightened spiritual sensation known as *ekarasa*.

Ekarasa could be likened to a kind of mystical orgasm, but Tantra's main link with sex is very different. For a few Tantric extremists following the 'left-hand' or 'sinister' path, sex itself could be used to purify the consciousness. It was one of five acts of transgression, known as the five "m"s, along with drinking alcohol (*madya*), eating meat (*mamsa*) and fish (*matsya*), making forbidden gestures (*mudra*) and contemplating sex (*maithuna*).

A few scholars think the left-handers went further than just contemplation of *maithuna*. One of the most powerful Tantric rituals of all, reserved for high-level Tantric initiates only, was *kula prakriya*. Sexual fluids would be expressed, exchanged, offered and consumed – and ritual sex may even have taken place between devotees. The point wasn't to have a mind-blowing orgasm, though. Tantrins were not supposed to find pleasure in the act. They weren't even meant to feel desire, and certainly not any emotional attachment to their partners. The object of sacramental sex was to echo the godlike union of Shiva and female counterpart, Shakti. And, as in Taoism (see p.314), to absorb the life energies of sexual fluids and inwardly transform them into nuggets of spiritual progress.

Shakers and Perfectionists

Protestants may have considered themselves pro-sex but they are not exactly known for warmly embracing pleasure. And when Puritanism met the nineteenth century, the result could be distinctly frigid. The Shakers of nineteenth-century New England, for instance, were so implacably opposed to sex that they remained entirely celibate. Attempts to keep-up the population of their communities by converting sinners and adopting orphans were only partially successful, and by the end of the twentieth century the Church was virtually extinct.

But not all nineteenth-century Puritans were puritanical. The Perfectionists of Oneida, New York, believed that the Second Coming had already come and that, because Jesus said that

older and more godly were supposed to have sex with their spiritual inferiors, to give them a lift up the spiritual–sexual ladder towards perfection. To prevent Oneida being swamped by baby Perfectionists, and to stop some less-than-perfect members breeding out of hand, Noyes taught "male continence", a method of birth control otherwise known as coitus reservatus (see p.253). Teenage boys, who lacked the necessary ejaculatory control, were given sexual mentors in the shape of post-menopausal women.

The drawbacks of celibacy: Bertha Lindsay, one of the last of the Puritan Shakers, looks out across an empty classroom at her community in Canterbury, New Hampshire.

"in the resurrection they neither marry nor are given in marriage, but are like angels in heaven", there should no longer be any marriage on earth either. Which meant, following from the group's communitarian principles, that men and women should share their sexual partners.

The Perfectionists' leader, the charismatic preacher John Humphrey Noyes, called his system "complex marriage". It was designed to do away with sexual jealousy, adultery and "special love", to replace the "I-spirit" with the "we-spirit". The

Sacred prostitution

If the *naditu* women (see p.307) topped the bill in Babylon, the donkey work at temples dedicated to Ishtar seems to have been done by assistants called *kulmashitu*. It's not quite clear whether they were actual temple prostitutes, dedicated to the ritual practice of sex, or secular prostitutes whose earnings simply helped support the temple. But there was definitely a ritual element to their work: they would learn to dance and sing in honour of the goddess, as well as providing nursing services. The Greek historian Herodotus even assured his wide-eyed readers that every single Babylonian woman would have had ritual sex with a foreigner in the temple of Ishtar – just as every Syrian

Papal peccadilloes

Despite some stiff competition, the most infamous of all Popes was Alexander VI, born Rodrigo Borgia. He ascended the papal throne in 1492, as the High Renaissance was in full swing. His conduct wasn't exactly saintly. As well as keeping an "unlawful herd" of female "dancers", Alexander maintained numerous more formal mistresses. One, Vannozza dei Cattani, bore him three sons and a daughter – or rather, three "nephews" and a "niece". Another, Giulia "la Bella" Farnese, also known as the "Bride of Christ", he installed in a palace conveniently located next to the Vatican. Scandalously, Alexander commissioned a fresco depicting himself adoring his lover in the costume of the Virgin Mary. It adorned the papal bedroom for a time before being painted over, and was only rediscovered in 2007.

Among Alexander's more scandalous public actions was the sumptuous party he laid on at the Vatican for the wedding of his thirteen-year-old daughter, Lucrezia Borgia – with whom he was accused of having incestuous relations. Alexander's son, Cesare Borgia, orchestrated an even more scandalous banquet, known as the Dance of the Chestnuts. It featured fifty prostitutes crawling around naked picking up chestnuts, and culminated with a free-for-all orgy at which prizes were given for sexual prowess.

In 1534, Giulia Farnese's brother ascended the papal throne, as Paul III. He was relatively serious-minded, but his image is somewhat tarnished by the fact that he made his grandchildren cardinals at the ages of fourteen and sixteen; and that, like Alexander, he was rumoured to have taken his daughter as a lover. Julius III, who became Pope in 1550, upped the stakes, adopting a beggar boy as his son, and making him his lover from the age of about fourteen. Julius liked to boast of the sexual prowess of the boy who became his official "cardinal-nephew".

The Renaissance Popes didn't have a monopoly on papal misbehaviour. The tenth and eleventh centuries were scarcely more pious. Benedict IX (1032–48) was notorious as a murderer, rapist and adulterer, while John XII (955–64) and John XIII (965–72) were both murdered by jealous husbands. Dying in adultery was the least of John XII's problems. According to the *Patrologia Latina*, a collection of early church writings, he was accused of having "fornicated with the widow of Rainier, with Stephana his father's concubine, with the widow Anna, and with his own niece, and he made the sacred palace into a whorehouse." His sins weren't only sexual: he also went hunting in public, toasted the devil, blinded his confessor, Benedict, and killed his cardinal subdeacon – after castrating him for reasons that history does not record.

An elderly *devadasi* sits by the side of an image of Yellama, also known as Renuka, a goddess whose cult *devadasi* serve by providing sexual services to pilgrims.

woman offered their bodies to their parallel goddess, Astarte.

The Old Testament found it necessary to forbid a man from letting his daughter become a temple prostitute and described, with horror, the *qadeshah*, or "sacred evil", a woman who may have been even more dangerous than the *zonah*, or everyday harlot, because she combined sexual wickedness with religious deviancy. The prophet Josiah found it necessary to clear *quadesh* prostitutes out of the Jewish Temple itself, and to destroy the shrines they had set up for their goddess Asherah – a goddess whom they had

sacrilegiously attempted to marry to the Jewish god Yahweh. Josiah didn't quite manage to stamp out devotion to Asherah, or the associated prostitution. Goddess figurines have been turned up (and then, controversially, suppressed) from digs in Israel at much later sites, and there is evidence of temple prostitution thriving in the last century BC.

In India, the practice of temple prostitution didn't really get going until the sixth century AD. *Devadasis* (or "servants of god") maintained the highest cultural traditions of singing, dancing, worship and sexual prowess. Curiously, some claim that *devadasis* were once celibate priestesses who married a temple deity – in much the same way as Christian nuns are "brides of Christ", or Rome's vestal virgins tended the sacred flame of Vesta, the goddess of the hearth. (The Roman virgins had good reason to stay celibate: they risked being buried alive in special oubliettes otherwise.) During the Muslim era, the *devadasi* tradition was weakened by association with the professional prostitute-dancers or "nautch girls" who performed for aristocrats. The tradition took a further beating from the prudish British and the equally prudish Hindu-reformers who followed them. Today, there are maybe a few thousand *devadasis* left in all of India, mostly in rural areas of Karnataka and Andhra Pradesh, and, for the most part, having only a nominal connection to a religious life.

Regulating desire

The great religions don't embrace sexuality with much enthusiasm. The same negative attitudes emerge again and again, right around the world. First, there's asceticism: religions often see the pursuit of sexual pleasure as a distraction from the serious business of spirituality – or, as Buddhists would put it, the mind clouded by lust struggles to live with right awareness. In the West and East alike, ascetism has led to chastity and virginity being considered exalted states.

The second source of sexual negativity is misogyny: religions tend to mistrust women and attempt to repress or at least control their sexuality.

A third source, currently emerging into the spotlight, is homophobia.

Cynics believe that, as a powerful, emotional force in which one can lose the self, sex offers religion just too much competition. Today, religions insist, almost universally, that sex can only be between a man and a woman, and within marriage, but beyond that, they tend not to pry – although the Catholic and Orthodox Churches retain a deep interest in the use of contraception (see p.253).

Asceticism

The author (and notorious atheist) Mark Twain once complained that "The human being … naturally places sexual intercourse far and away above all other joys – yet he has left it out of his heaven!" Muslims might just have a better time of it (see box on p.304) but otherwise it's a pretty major omission.

Even trying to get to heaven can spoil your sex life. Most religions have celibate religious orders, and respectable studies have shown that lay people with intense religious beliefs have less sex and enjoy it less when they have it. Traditional Christians would say they've exchanged sex for something better. This was the reason given by the early church father Origen, who castrated himself as "a eunuch for the kingdom of heaven". In fact, the feelings and rewards of sex and religion may be closely linked. Religious enlightenment through self-denial and orgasm are both supposed to result in a unique kind of "loss of self". Freud even thought that orgasmic feelings lay at the root of all religious ecstasy.

Sexless gods

The themes of asceticism, patriarchy and misogyny come together in the person of the Christian God, often imagined as a kind of male head-of-the-family. If he isn't quite the stereotypical old man with a beard, he certainly isn't seen as a sexual being – despite being a fatherly figure. He doesn't have a wife or divine consort, for instance. Jesus is even less sexualized, being both celibate and born to a virgin mother (the heretical suggestion in one Gnostic gospel that he may have been on kissing terms with Mary Magdalen is far from orthodox). The Christian "Holy Ghost", however, is perhaps the ultimate expression of asexual divinity, as it lacks a body – or gender – altogether. The same sexless, bodiless dualities are traditionally ascribed to Yahweh, the God of the Jews.

Things are little sexier in the East. The Buddha Siddharta Gautama, for all that he was "handsome, pleasant to look upon, inspiring trust, gifted with great beauty of complexion, fair in colour, fine in presence, stately to behold", left his wife and set off to live a life of unworldly contemplation with a group of largely male hangers-on until, finally, there was "no passion of lust left in him".

Hinduism is a little more divided in its opinions, with a powerfully ascetic strain competing with a more rampant, fertility-obsessed wing. Or as the poet Bhartrihari put it, there are two paths in the world: the religious devotions of the sages which is, apparently, "lovely because it overflows with the nectarous waters of the knowledge of truth" and "the lusty undertaking of touching with one's palm that hidden part in the firm laps of lovely-limbed women". You choose.

The prophet Muhammad, as described by the oral tradition of the *hadith*, is the grand exception to all this religious sexual severity. He was married many times, and was said to have been able to satisfy all his wives equally, even in one night, because he had the vigour of thirty normal men. Some traditions hold that he had two concubines as well, and passed on specific instructions on "treating your woman right", by advocating foreplay and general sexual considerateness. He wasn't above authorizing his followers to use the withdrawal method of contraception, either. Muhammad, of course, was human.

Body versus spirit

If religious hostility towards sex can be blamed on anything, it's probably dualism – the age-old philosophical notion that the body and soul are separate entities. Religion being in the business of souls, it pretty much follows that bodies are viewed with some suspicion.

A Hindu holy text, the *Maitri Upanishad*, tells how the legendary monarch Brihadratha left his kingdom to his son and ran away to the wilderness to stand with his arms held aloft, gazing up at the sun. He did this for 1000 days. Why? Well, he said, "in this ill-smelling, unsubstantial body, which is a conglomerate of bone, skin, muscle, marrow, flesh, semen, blood, mucus, tears, rheum, faeces, urine, wind, bile and phlegm, what is the good or enjoyment of desires?" Or, as St Paul puts it in his letter to the Galatians: "Live by the Spirit, I say, and do not gratify the desires of the flesh. For what the flesh desires is opposed to the Spirit, and what the Spirit desires is opposed to the flesh."

Eros and agape, kama and prema

In the first of his letters to an early church group in Corinth, as collected in the New Testament, St Paul emphasizes a particular kind of love. He calls it *agape* (pronounced "a-ga-pay" and sometimes translated as "charity"), implicitly contrasting it with the more common Greek word for love, *eros* (hence "erotic"). He argues that *agape* is a higher and distinctively selfless form of love – very different from the possessive, earthly, sexual kind. "Love suffereth long, and is kind", he says; "love envieth not; love vaunteth not itself"; true love, for St Paul, "is not puffed up".

Hinduism also distinguishes spiritual and profane love. There is carnal desire, on the one hand, and heavenly longing on the other. In the holiest of Hindu sermons, the *Bhagavadgita*, the god Krishna savages *kama*, or sexual desire, calling it "a fire insatiable" which "smothers wisdom". He urges his followers to "strike down this evil thing!". The ideal, instead, is *prema*, a kind of sacred love stripped of sensuality, characterized by passionlessness renunciation of the sensual world.

St Paul got his big idea from the Ancient Greeks, who shared many notions with the ancient Hindus. In Plato's *Symposium*, the character Pausanias – who is notable for being the lover of Agathon (a man) – suggests that there are two goddesses called Aphrodite, one "Common", the other "Heavenly". Ignoble love, as represented by the Common Aphrodite, is about "completing the sexual act", and nothing more.

The other kind of love, presided over by the Heavenly Aphrodite, is "free of the lewdness of youth", and leads the mind on to higher things. For Pausanias, then, love is not in itself praiseworthy, it simply "depends on whether the sentiments it produces in us are themselves noble". (Buddhists, incidentally, agree that sex in itself isn't the problem, it's the things which sexual desire makes us do.) This is the origin of the phrase "Platonic love" – not, originally, a sexless love, but rather a love of beauty which ultimately inspires more spiritual thoughts.

It wouldn't be fair to say that the church has always equated *eros* with "bad love", and *agape* with good. Most Christian theologians think there's a continuity between the two extremes. This view was even supported by the very first encyclical, or official pronouncement, released by the new Pope Benedict XVI, in 2005. *Eros* and *agape*, the Pope said, "can never be completely separated. The more the two, in their different aspects, find a proper unity in the one reality of love, the more the true nature of love in general is realized."

Again, Hinduism agrees. For all that *kama* or desire is an obstacle to spiritual success, it's also one of the three basic goals of existence, alongside religious and worldy duties. *Kama* also provides the basic urge which can be transformed by adoration of god into a higher kind of love. Guided right, *eros* can become *agape*.

Paul was drawing on a rich pre-Christian legacy of dualism which stemmed ultimately from the ancient Greeks. In Plato's philosophical work, the *Phaedrus*, the rational mind is likened to a stern charioteer driving two powerful horses. One is long-necked, white and well-bred, the other squat, black and unruly. The black horse represents desire or the unrestrained passions (characterized as female), the white, rational or moral impulses (characterized as male). The mind's goal, Plato says, is to ascend upwards towards divine beauty. If the charioteer gives the black horse its head – by, say, "rushing on like a brutish beast to enjoy and beget" – he'll fall back down. Only the white horse is capable of carrying his chariot out of this world towards a place of true, divine beauty.

This kind of anti-sensual dualism was given its classic Christian spin by St Augustine of Hippo (see box on p.323). Before graduating as the early church father who did more than any other to shape Christian ideas on sex, Augustine spent time as a Manichean. This Persian cult, inspired by the prophet Mani, saw the world in terms of divine, spiritual (and, incidentally, male) light, and earthly, fleshly (and, as for Plato, female) darkness. For Augustine, it was sex, above all, which sucked the spirit down into the mud and prevented it flying up towards God – as if the body was literally weighing down the soul.

The dualist vision has proved incredibly influential. Even the great rethinker of sexual motivations, Sigmund Freud, was still considering the difference between spiritual and sexual love in dualist terms. (Though, typically, Freud spun the notion on its head, describing spiritual desire as a re-channelling of a thwarted libido – for him, sexual not spiritual desire was

at the root of everything.) And today, the dualist idea lives on: every protest of a "higher" kind of love, every dismissal of more overtly sexual feelings as being "just physical" is evidence of its shaping force.

Lust, sin and guilt

Judaism gave the world the idea of Eve the temptress, and linked sex with uncleanness or ritual pollution. The Greek Stoic philosophers established the notion that sexual pleasure, as Seneca put it, "has been given to man not for enjoyment but for the enjoyment of his race" – not for pleasure, then, but for procreation. Christianity, as a hybrid of both cultures, turned sex into a subset of lust. And lust was a sin.

For early Christians, sex was a constant reminder of the fall from grace, when Eve (tempted by the serpent) persuaded Adam that they should both disobey God and eat the fruit of the Tree of Knowledge – this being the original "Original Sin" with which all humans are supposedly tainted. St Augustine wrote that it was lust which originally undermined Adam and Eve's willpower. Sex was the cause of the Fall, then, and also the result. Only after the expulsion from Eden did sex enter the world: it was only then that Adam and Eve became ashamed of their genitals and covered them with leaves.

The medieval theologian St Thomas Aquinas described sex as being a kind of filth. He associated it with words such as stain, foulness, vileness, disgrace or disease. Even marital sex was disturbing. A pious husband and wife might try to have sex like Adam and Eve – as a pure act,

Adam and Eve by Albrecht Durer (1504). Eating the forbidden fruit brought sin into the world – and caused the first couple to cover their nudity in shame.

without any stirrings of lust – but lust would keep creeping into their thoughts. St Jerome considered there was nothing filthier "than to have sex with your wife as you might do with another woman". At best, marital sex meant that those who weren't able to be chaste – like priests and holy men – could avoid the worse sin of adultery. As St Paul put it, "it is better to marry than to be aflame with passion". Or as the Anglican Book of Common Prayer put it in 1662 – a phrase repeated in many marriage ceremonies today (though some make discreet cuts) – "Holy Matrimony … is not by any to be enterprised, nor taken in hand, unadvisedly, lightly, or wantonly, to satisfy men's carnal lusts and appetites, like brute beasts that have no understanding; but reverently, discreetly, advisedly, soberly, and in the fear of God."

For centuries, Catholics were encouraged to defend themselves from Satan by confessing their sins in the confessional. This included, or even focused on, their sexual sins. These weren't just actual acts – masturbation or adultery, for instance – but sinful thoughts: wanting to masturbate; feeling attracted to someone. Only if such thoughts were acknowledged (and confessed, and forgiven), could evil be kept at bay. As a result, stray sexual thoughts were supposed to be mentally noted so that they could be confessed later. The intended result was that sexual urges would provoke guilty internal surges, and these would quickly nip any sexual feelings in the bud. On the other side of the confessional, one can only imagine the impact that intimate sexual confessions might have on a young and celibate priest.

Augustine of Hippo

Saint Augustine is the fall guy for Christianity's negative attitudes towards sex, although in truth he only put in writing what a lot of other early Christians were thinking. Born in around 354, he didn't start out as a model of piety, converting from pagan Manicheanism to the new religion only at the age of 29, after he'd had a child with his partner – and after he'd sown some very wild oats. "As a youth I had been woefully at fault", he later confessed, "particularly in early adolescence". He remembered praying to God, saying, "Give me chastity and continence, but not yet." While he waited, he made good use of his time, remembering that "I kept not the measure of love … but out of the muddy concupiscence of the flesh and the bubblings of youth, mists fumed up which beclouded and overcast my heart … I boiled over in my fornications".

Once Augustine got religion, however, he got it bad. He claimed that the doctrine of "original sin" didn't refer to the eating of the apple of the Tree of Knowledge, and the loss of God's grace, but to Adam and Eve having sex with each other. Weren't they ashamed of their nakedness afterwards, he argued? Weren't their genitals disobedient to their will, just as they were disobedient to God? Didn't the sex act take place between the places where people defecated and urinated? Because all humans were the result of a kind of filthy disobedience, all humans inherited the original sin of Eve and Adam. Sex was the conduit through which sin passed from generation to generation. And because lust, Augustine believed, began in the mind, good Christians had to keep a stern watch not only over their sexual actions, but over their sexual thoughts as well.

Who and how – Christians and control

Despite one of the Ten Commandmants forbidding adultery, Judaism is famously more interested in controlling food than sex; for Christianity, it's the other way around. For the early Christians, even sex within marriage wasn't necessarily safe. The second-century writer Clement of Alexandria advised husbands and wives to pray for the gift of sex without passion. The Council of Nicaea, held in AD 325, banned bishops (but not yet priests) from sex and, in 342, all kinds of non-penetrative sex were ruled out. In the seventh century, Theodore of Tarsus, the Archbishop of Canterbury, was a little more specific. Fornication (or sex outside marriage), adultery (sex with someone married), incest and bestiality were obviously out, but so were masturbation, fellatio, anal sex, or sex during menstruation – even for married couples.

The three big names in Christian thinking on sex before the Reformation are St Paul, who laid down the foundations just after Jesus's death, St Augustine of Hippo, who moved sex centre stage in the fourth century (see box on p.323), and the theologian St Thomas Aquinas, who provided the intellectual framework in the thirteenth century. Aquinas described how the cardinal virtue of Temperance needed to combat the vice of Lust. "Natural" lusts, which were those that could theoretically result in procreation, could be more easily forgiven. "Unnatural lusts", such as masturbation, anal sex or bestiality, acquired the name of sodomy, and were more serious. In the medieval period, church law took care of the practice. Sex was theoretically outlawed on a Sunday, but also on Wednesdays or Fridays, or at any time during the feasts of Lent or Advent, or on holy days, or for three days after communion, or during pregnancy, or for forty days after birth, or during breastfeeding, or menstruation. For anyone dutifully obeying the rules, the window of opportunity was all but tight shut. The one escape route for men was prostitution, which thinkers from Aquinas onwards accepted as a necessary evil.

Taking a position

Where Rome, India, China and the Middle East saw sexual positions as opportunities for sexual creativity, on the whole, medieval Christianity saw them as moral traps. It's not just Christianity's fault. Greek Stoic philosophers were teaching man-on-top as the only moral position as early as the third century, and ancient physicians worried that any other postures risked provoking anything from abscesses in the loins to hernias and penile eruptions. The Jewish tradition wasn't free of hang-ups, either. The pre-tenth-century text the *Alphabet of Ben Sira*, told the cautionary story of Lilith, Adam's first wife, who was forced out of Eden because she refused to "lie below", insisting on her equality to her husband.

The idea that Christian missionaries actually taught the "missionary position" to their converts isn't quite true (see p.127), but Christianity certainly extended its theory of "natural" versus "unnatural" sexuality to positions. In the fourth century AD St Augustine of Hippo defined sexual misconduct as either outright unnatural, as in oral or anal sex,

Abstinence education

Sexual abstinence, as the key to moral, physical and religious health, is taught in government schools across the US, and actively promoted in developing countries abroad. Teenagers are encouraged to take public pledges of virginity, and even to wear "purity pledge" rings to signify their vows. Unfortunately, information about contraception is typically restricted or misrepresented and study after study has shown that abstinence education is not an effective way to reduce either rates of teenage pregnancy or sexually transmitted infections – which is what it's supposed to do. Of course, abstinence is not really about public health. To listen to the preachers' rhetoric, it's more concerned with lengthening the supposedly sexless "innocence" of childhood in the face of the apparently terrifying nature of adult sexuality. It's also designed to bolster the institution of marriage against the sinful vortex of disease, pregnancy, out-of-wedlock birth, single-parenthood, homosexuality and general godlessness which apparently threatens to destroy it.

or natural but "defective in mode", which probably referred to unorthodox postures. By the thirteenth century, theologians were ranking positions in order of deviance. Albert the Great of Cologne thought side-on was unacceptable, while sitting and standing positions were grossly deviant, and sex from behind "in the manner of mules or dogs" was an outrage. Aquinas devised a formula for working out how sinful a position was: the further removed a position was from the "natural manner", he said,

the worse the sin. In general, sexual variations were not thought to be mortal sins, although they could be a sign of "deadly concupiscence", or a tendency to do evil.

Rights and obligations

As long as it's safely corralled within marriage, most religions stress the importance of sex. Even the famously squeamish Victorians thought sex between a husband and wife was a key part of the spiritual bond between them. Christians today stress the loving bond of marriage as a version of God's contract with his people in microcosm. Sex, and the desire to raise children, makes marriage different from other relationships. As Mark's gospel puts it, man and wife will become "one flesh". Sex doesn't just symbolize the sanctity of marriage, it creates it.

According to the Jewish lore collected in the Talmud, a man isn't just supposed to have sex with his wife, he is supposed to satisfy her. The Jewish mystical tradition, collected in the Zohar, instructs men to have sex with their wives after the ritual bath that signals the end of menstruation. As soon as the law permits it, in other words, sexual relations should be restored. Similar obligations applied in ancient China, where Confucius said that wives and concubines had the right to sexual satisfaction at least once every five days.

Perhaps more than any other religion, Islam has underlined the importance of sex within marriage. The Qur'an itself encourages sexual relations, saying that it is rewarded in heaven (see p.302) and that men should approach their wives on the night of the fast, because "they are your garments and ye are their garments". The

Religious circumcision

In Jewish law, male circumcision takes place on the eighth day after birth. It's usually performed by a medically trained Mohel.

Ancient Egyptians, Canaanites, Moabites and other ancient Mediterranean cultures are known to have circumcised their boys. Some historians believe Jews actually began doing it at the time of the Second Temple, in the last centuries BC. It was supposedly a way in which Jews could affirm their Jewishness in the face of a dominant Greek culture in which a long foreskin was deemed beautiful. Another theory would have it that circumcision symbolizes a marriage between God the father and mankind, and the spillage of blood represents a token menstruation, signalling mankind's obediently feminine role in that relationship.

Many religions and cultures practice ritual scarring or blood-spilling as a rite of passage and a symbol of inclusion. In Judaism and Islam (and among the Masai), it takes the form of circumcision, or the removal of the penis's foreskin. For Jews, brit milah is a sign of identity, a ritual that binds a boy into his community – usually at eight days old, unless there are medical reasons otherwise. The practice officially stems from the Book of Genesis, where the patriarch Abraham is told he should "walk before God and be perfect". He is also told to cut off his foreskin as a sign of the contract he is making with God.

The Qur'an doesn't actually mention circumcision, but the practice is endorsed by certain *hadith*, or sayings of the Prophet, where it is said to be part of the *fitrah*, the natural order of human creation. Other such "hygienic" acts include cutting the fingernails, the armpit hair and the moustache. Islam also sees itself as descended from the religion of Abraham, so Muslims mark their own covenant with God in the same way. In some Muslim countries and traditions, the rite is obligatory; in others, it is merely recommended. It can be done within a week of birth or at the onset of puberty – though late circumcision is falling out of favour for medical reasons, and converts are rarely expected to have it done. In some countries, particularly in Africa, genital cutting is also performed on young women or baby girls (see FGM, p.67), but this is more of a cultural practice and rarely endorsed by Islamic teachers.

Male circumcision is falling out of favour in some communities (see box on p.70). Muslim converts are not generally expected to get themselves circumcised, for instance. And some Reform Jews do not circumcise their children. Other Jewish campaigners believe that circumcision could just as easily involve a token removal of the very tip of the foreskin, and blame the more aggressive surgical form on the anti-masturbatory hysteria of the nineteenth century (see p.338). Certainly, the idea that the operation can be done without anaesthetic, on the basis that it's a mere snip, is mistaken; babies may not react much because they go into a state of semi-comatose shock.

Christianity dropped circumcision very early on, within a generation of Jesus's death, as the new religion spread into the Gentile world. It didn't stop Christians continuing to celebrate the circumcision of Jesus – who was, after all, a Jewish boy – as a feast day. Numerous medieval churches even claimed to possess the Holy Prepuce itself. One such relic was lost in the sixteenth-century Sack of Rome; others vanished in the Reformation. But claims for ownership of the relic were still clamorous enough that, in 1900, the Vatican banned all discussion of the matter under pain of excommunication.

Qur'an also describes a man's wife as being like a field to be ploughed – not an image that women might appreciate, but implying nonetheless that sexuality in marriage needs to be cultivated. Early Sufi thinkers elaborated on this idea. Mohammed al-Ghazali observed that "sex should begin with gentle words and kissing". According to al-Daylami, no man should treat his wife like an animal – and the woman should always come first.

Misogyny and homophobia

At the root of much religious mistrust of sex is misogyny, the fear or hatred of women. The third-century church father, Tertullian, even called women the conduit through which Satan arrived on earth. Well, he was only going on what it says in the Bible: for both Judaism and Christianity, evil begins at the very beginning, in the garden of Eden, when Eve takes the apple. Disease, sex, death are all her fault, thanks to one little chat with a serpent.

The Greek origin myth about Pandora is just as hard on women. According to Hesiod, Zeus first created a race of men alone. (They presumably don't have sex with each other or have children though Hesiod doesn't say.) Zeus holds back the secret of fire from mankind until it is stolen by the hero, Prometheus. As punishment, Zeus orders his blacksmith to create the first woman, Pandora, a beautiful but deceitful creature whom he calls a "lovely evil" and a "great infestation" wished upon the human race. Zeus gives Pandora a jar (today it's usually refered to as "Pandora's box", with no pun

Model women: A'ishah, Sita and the Marys

For Hindu wives, the ultimate role model is Sita, a goddess sent to earth to show how well women can bear suffering. She endured plenty of it. Kidnapped by the demon king Ravana, Sita was forced to defend her honour against him. Eventually rescued, she then had to prove her chastity to Rama by passing unharmed through fire. Even then, Rama sent her away to protect his reputation. Pregnant, and alone, Sita successfully raised two children before sending them back to their father – and promptly dying.

The principle role models in Islam are Muhammad's wives. His first, Khadijah, was a successful merchant, and his boss for some years. After her death, Muhammad married A'ishah, the only one of the Prophet's wives to have been a virgin on their wedding night (the others were all widows). Like Sita, A'ishah was accused of adultery. After vanishing from camp to look for a lost necklace, she was rescued by a man. Muhammad had to defend his wife against insinuations but fortunately, a divine revelation quickly confirmed her innocence – incidentally providing the Qur'anic ruling that accusations of adultery had to be backed up by four witnesses.

A'ishah is admired by Sunni Muslims not only as Muhammad's favourite wife, but as a learned and strong woman. She played an important political role after her husband's death, and is responsible for a large proportion of the *hadith*, or oral traditions, concerning the Prophet's life and opinions. Hindus revere Sita for her strength and her steadfastness. The stories of both women, however, focus on the question of sexual loyalty.

No such doubts were raised about Christianity's prime example of womanhood – even though she conceived a child without having sex with her husband. The "Blessed Virgin" Mary was meek, obedient and perfectly pure. The Catholic doctrine of the Immaculate Conception even proposed that she herself was miraculously conceived without her own mother, Anna, being "defiled". The fourth-century pope, Siricius, even ruled that she must have had no other children after Jesus's birth, as this would have defiled the "hall of the Everlasting King" that was her womb. As the philosopher Simon Blackburn provocatively puts it, this is rather like "being suspicious of a public lavatory not because of who might have been there, but because of who might follow".

Christianity's other notable Mary is Mary Magdalene. The Gospels describe her as a woman of independent means and, crucially, the first witness to the Resurrection. The Gnostic Gospel of Philip calls her Jesus's *koinonos*, or "companion" and observes that he "loved her more than all the disciples and used to kiss her often on the mouth" – a detail made much of in *Holy Blood, Holy Grail* and *The Da Vinci Code*. Mary Magdalene's reputation didn't sit too well with the patriarchal worldview, so in the sixth century, Pope Gregory pronounced that she was actually the same woman as another Mary mentioned in the Bible – a "sinner" who had washed Jesus's feet with her tears. "Sinner" somehow became "penitent ex-prostitute". As a scarlet woman, she made a neat foil for the Virgin Mary's pure, celestial blue.

apparently intended) which holds all the evils of the world: disease, pain and death.

Religions may have their feet in misogyny, but it's a moot point whether the religions themselves are to blame or just the prevailing culture at the time of their birth. At the millennium, Pope John Paul II apologized for seven kinds of sin committed by the Catholic Church over the years. Among them were sins against love, peace and culture, and sins against the dignity of women. Most religions now offer more positive messages about women, and about female sexuality. The Anglican Church now has female vicars (but not yet bishops), for instance, and the Islamic feminist movement is burgeoning. Among religions invented in more recent times, the Baha'i faith has as one of its core beliefs the fundamental equality of all humans, while many people are attracted to Wicca, the New Age concoction of witchcraft and nature worship, precisely because the goddess – and female power and sexuality generally – plays such an important part in its theology.

Unequal before God; unequal before the law

Women don't do well by religious law. One Hindu Upanishad recommends beating a wife if she refuses sex. The Qur'an advises husbands to beat their wives if they think they might rebel or disobey, and says that if a single male witness can't be found to support a legal claim, two female witnesses are needed instead. According to the Torah, men can divorce women (for unspecified "indecency") but women can't divorce men. Wives are guilty of adultery if they have sex with any other man; husbands if they have sex with a married woman. Men can have multiple wives (though most Jewish communities gave up polygamy in the early Middle Ages) but women can't have more than one husband. One passage in Exodus suggests fathers can even sell their daughters into slavery.

Jesus's teaching largely went against Judaism's misogynistic leanings. He condemned divorce for men as well as women. When an adulterous woman was brought before him, he agreed that the official penalty was indeed stoning to death, but advised that the person without sin should cast the first stone. Unfortunately, Jesus's followers largely rejected this kind of radicalism. In his letters to Christian communities around the Mediterranean, St Paul advised that men were in charge of woman just as God was in charge of man, that women were not to speak in public – not among the Greeks, at least – and that if women wanted to know anything they should ask only their husbands. It wasn't all one way, however. Paul also proclaimed that "because all of you are one in the Messiah Jesus, a person is no longer a Jew or a Greek, a slave or a free person, a male or a female". All were equal in the eyes of God.

It is easy to cherry-pick religious texts for misogynistic or sexist passages, and most religions preach at least tolerance and kindness to women, if not outright equality. But women today are not priests or imams, and only sometimes rabbis (outside the Orthodox community) or vicars (in the Church of England, for instance). Buddhism and Christianity both accept nuns, but then they're in the convent nicely kept away from trouble. One deep reason for this structural inequality is ritual purity. A Jewish or Muslim man who touches menstrual blood or semen is supposed to ritually cleanse himself, for instance,

Christ and the Woman Taken in Adultery (c. 1540) by Lucas Cranach the Elder. The Jesus of the Gospels is typically tolerant of human frailty and intolerant of hypocrisy.

and Hindu women who have their period are supposed to stay away from fire and water – which means stopping cooking, and also rules out most kinds of worship. A woman, it's clear, isn't supposed to mediate between God and man because she might just be bleeding.

Temptresses and semen-stealers

All the major religions have myths of male saints whose meditations were disturbed by the great temptresses: women. In many Hindu myths, sages meditate in the high Himalayas, accumulating ever-greater levels of psycho-spiritual energy, or *tapas*, as they retreat ever further from the world. Unfortunately, this makes the gods jealous of their powers, so they send sexy nymphs as a distraction, hoping to cause the sages to spill some semen and precipitate a kind of spiritual bankruptcy.

Christianity has the hermit St Anthony, whose saintly life in the desert was undermined and interrupted by "filthy and maddening thoughts" – as his fourth-century biographer Athanasius himself put it. Or St Jerome, who despite having only "scorpions and wild beasts as companions", was "often surrounded by dancing girls". Athanasius himself was even visited by the Evil One, in the form of a woman (strapped naked to a cross, according to one artist) – but to no avail. Athanasius remained chaste.

Medieval persecutions of witches often focused on their supposed sexual liaisons with the devil, or the way they tempted or charmed men into sexual misdemeanours. It was believed that beautiful demon creatures known as succubi would visit men in their sleep, draining them of semen. (To be fair, their male counterparts, the incubi, were hardly less wicked: they used this semen to impregnate women, thus spawning demonic children.)

Religious homophobia …

On the face of it, Judaism, Islam and Christianity are united in their condemnation of homosexuality. (Male homosexuality, that is: lesbianism hardly registers a flicker of interest from any religion – which is fascinating in itself.) Surah 26 of the Qur'an promises utter destruction to those who "approach males", leaving the wives Allah created for them. During the bloody aftermath of the Iraq war, the pre-eminent Shia

Cultural blow jobs – the "Sambians" of New Guinea

In the early 1970s, the anthropologist and sex researcher Gilbert Herdt went to study an ethnic group in a remote part of Papua New Guinea. They had one extremely unusual cultural belief. In order for a prepubescent boy to grow into a man, it was thought, they had to ritually ingest semen from older boys. They did this by "eating penis". To protect the identity of his subjects, Herdt gave them a pseudonym: the "Sambians".

From the age of about seven or eight, Sambian boys leave home to live in an all-male house. There they learn to perform the rituals of their society – which include playing the flute and bringing on major nosebleeds to purge the body of the ritual pollution caused by previous contact with women. Boys also learn to milk older, post-pubescent boys for their seminal fluid. It's not seen as a sexual act, and the boys performing fellatio do not say they enjoy it (many have to be coerced to do it at all), but some eventually start to seek out partners seen as attractive and may get erections during the process. Once they've passed puberty, the boys become donors of semen in their turn. In receiving oral sex, the power of their semen is being built up, turning them slowly into young warriors capable of fathering a child. After marriage, all male-to-male sexual contact stops. His penis is now contaminated with womanliness, and his semen has another job to do.

Gene Robinson, the openly gay Bishop of New Hampshire, attending a Gay Pride Parade in Boston. His ordination caused great controversy within the Anglican church, and homosexuality remains a divisive issue among Christians.

cleric, Grand Ayatollah Sistani, recommended that homosexuals "should be killed in the worst, most severe way of killing". Plenty of vigilantes took him up on his suggestion.

The biblical book of Leviticus famously calls homosexuality an "abomination" and preaches death as a punishment, while the Sodomites are famously destroyed with fire and brimstone for trying to gang rape (or possibly just being hostile towards, depending on your interpretation) Lot's visiting angels. St Paul's letter to his followers in Corinth, from the New Testament, warns that the immoral will not enter heaven – and among thieves and drunkards he also lists prostitutes and "homosexual offenders". In his letter to the Romans, Paul condemns men who, among a host of other sins, put aside the "natural" love of women and commit indecent acts with men.

Why can't I own Canadians?

In the 2000s, an anonymous email addressed to "Dr Laura" forwarded its way round tens of thousands of inboxes, after US radio pundit Laura Schlessinger called homosexuality a "biological error", citing biblical law. "When I burn a bull on the altar as a sacrifice," the email begins, "I know it creates a pleasing odour for the Lord (Lev. 1:9). The problem is my neighbors. They claim the odour is not pleasing to them. Should I smite them?" Another question is no less troubling: "I know that I am allowed no contact with a woman while she is in her period of menstrual uncleanliness (Lev. 15:19–24)", the writer asks. "The problem is, how do I tell? I have tried asking, but most women take offense". A third question is even more of a puzzle: "Lev. 25:44 states that I may indeed possess slaves, both male and female, provided they are purchased from neighbouring nations. A friend of mine claims that this applies to Mexicans, but not Canadians. Can you clarify? Why can't I own Canadians?"

But looked at more closely, few scriptural condemnations are quite what they seem. The Prophet specifically attacks men who leave their wives seeking satisfaction of their lust for men; he says nothing about love between men, or male unions. Leviticus specifically rules out anal sex between two Jewish men, and does so in the context of warning of the dangers of aping pagan fertility cults. The story of the Sodomites is actually about sexual assault – of men and women – and the abuse of Jewish laws of hospitality. And Paul's anger appears to be directed against Christian heterosexuals who copy Greco-Roman sexual manners for their own gratification – he says nothing about homosexuals in loving relationships.

Hinduism officially frowns on sex between men, but its chief books of law, the *Laws of Manu* and the *Arthashastra*, recommend only a ritual bath or a fine as punishment. A third ancient text, the *Kamasutra*, embraces sex between men enthusiastically, discussing people of the "third nature" and giving recipes for different ways to "suck the mango" (see p.112). Despite this relatively liberal heritage, the right-wing nationalist strain of modern political Hinduism is just as fiercely anti-gay as, say, its evangelical equivalent in the US. And that's not friendly. The hugely influential preacher Pat Robertson once counselled the city council of Orlando, Florida, against sporting the gay-friendly rainbow flag by warning, "You're right in the way of some serious hurricanes, and I don't think I'd be waving those flags in God's face if I were you."

Buddhism is more nuanced. It stresses the intentions behind any act and the potential harm it might do, and any homosexual act or relationship would be judged by this standard alone. Some gay rights activists openly admire the Buddhist stance, but the truth is that Buddhism is troubled by sexual desire in general – and would certainly question the very idea of people defining themselves according to sexual preference.

... and religious tolerance

The gap between law and religious practice is nowhere wider than in sexual behaviour. In the medieval period, many Arab countries celebrated male love in much the same way as did the ancient Greeks (see p.28) and Sufi Muslims were criticized in the same era for heretically seeking the reflection of God's face in the gaze of their beloved (male) partners. The Buddha himself used to nuzzle his beloved disciple Anand like a deer, and some Buddhistic monastic movements, such as those in Tibet and Japan, have historically tolerated sexual relations between monks. The Catholic Church has been a haven for gay men for centuries – and still is – while the Anglican Church is currently considering supporting the right of bishops to be gay (even if the Church's conservative and African wings threaten to secede from the communion because of it).

There are gay rights movements now in every religion, drawing on long-standing traditions of compassion and respect for the dignity of the individual. Liberal Christians point out that Jesus had a habit of sticking up for the oppressed – and for those whose sexual behaviour was criticized in particular. The former Anglican Archbishop, Desmond Tutu, once stated that persecution of homosexuals was "every bit as unjust a crime against humanity as apartheid". Making gay men and women "doubt that they too are children of God", he said, "must be nearly the ultimate blasphemy."

9
Sex and society

Sex and society

Uniquely among the pleasures, sex generally takes place in private – or at least, the invitations to join in are usually very restricted indeed. This doesn't mean, of course, that sex doesn't take place in a social context. Sex is surrounded by social influences and assumptions, by pressures and restrictions. The ways in which people have sex (and the ways in which they want to have sex) are profoundly conditioned not just by what they experience with others but by what they hear or read about – and, in the case of pornography, by what they see.

The historical secrecy surrounding sex means that, for a long time, laws reflected a narrow version of what society expected sex to be. As scientists and writers and activists revealed the breathtaking diversity of what people actually did behind those closed doors, both laws and social mores shifted. They had to. Leaving aside the whole issue of marriage and civil partnerships, sex is now restricted in just a few key areas. First, there's the age of consent: partner sex is almost universally agreed to be an adults-only affair. Then there's sexuality: some cultures still struggle to conceive of sex as more than just something that takes place between men and women. Then there's sexual violence and the crucial issue of consent.

Less common practices and preferences are called either "perversions" or "paraphilias", depending on how strongly you disapprove. Many are treated with an amused or faintly shocked tolerance, but those that cause harm are rigorously banned. The other area of social anxiety concerns sex-for-sale, whether that's first-hand sex bought from a sex worker or prostitute, or second-hand sex in the form of erotica and pornography. For better or worse, most societies clearly feel uncomfortable about sex that's public in this way. There remains a core belief that part of what makes sex so precious is its privacy, delicacy and intimacy. Sex that's so tangibly rooted in all the world's earthiness is, for some people, too much to accept.

Rights and repression

In Western countries, nowadays, the law generally stays out of the bedroom. Ever since Revolutionary France set the agenda by establishing sexual privacy and calling for an end to "phoney offences", adults, by and large, have been free to do what they want – so long as they both (or all) agree to it and so long as it doesn't harm anyone (and sometimes even if it does).

This relative liberalism is a historical freak. Legal history is stuffed with odd prohibitions against what was often loosely called sodomy – which generally meant any kind of sex that wasn't between husband and wife and didn't have the intention of conceiving a child. Buggery, which usually meant either anal sex or sex with an animal, was a particular target of legal hostility, and laws criminalizing or restricting sex between men have only recently come off the statute books.

Most countries' legal codes still invade bodily autonomy and sexual privacy in a few key areas. Children are forbidden to have sex until they

Yemeni heroine: when her father forced her to marry a 30-year-old man, Nojoud Nasser, aged 8, took both father and husband to court, although not before she had been beaten and raped. A judge later annulled the marriage.

Going blind: masturbation hysteria

The playground urban myth that masturbation makes you go blind is not, of course, true, but neither is it the product of childish imagination. It was invented by the medical profession, arguably as a conscious act of sexual repression. Religious authorities around the world had long warned of the dangers of wasting the "life force" supposedly found in semen (see p.170), but they were more bothered by non-solitary abuses, which they labelled "sodomy". Shakespeare rued the "unthrifty" lover who did "spend upon thyself thy beauty's legacy", but the first ever medical discussion of the perils of masturbation was a pamphlet passed around in London in about 1712, entitled *Onania: or, The Heinous Sin of Self-Pollution, and all its Frightful Consequences*. Its soft-porn-peddling author warned of the potentially fatal effects of compulsive practice – and advertised a "Prolific Powder" and "Strenghtening Tincture" as remedies.

This alarmist tract should have passed into pulp as a piece of simple quackery, but was picked up almost fifty years later by the celebrated Swiss nerve specialist Samuel-Auguste Tissot. In his sensation-causing 1760 treatise, *L'Onanisme* (which, like the earlier text, took its name from the biblical character, Onan, who spilled his seed on the ground), he argued that semen was an "essential oil", the wastage of which could cause nervous disorders, gout, rheumatism, migraine and, of course, blurred vision.

Enlightenment thinkers pounced on Tissot's thesis, turning masturbation into the ultimate threat to the virtues of moderation (masturbation was gluttonous), rationality (it relied on fantasies) and officially sanctioned sexuality (it was private, and could scarcely be controlled). No lesser lover than Casanova wrote that in the West it was believed that "young men who

Chief Scout, Lord Baden-Powell (far right), casts a fatherly eye over some "cheery" boy scouts.

indulge in the practice impair their constitutions and shorten their lives".

The Victorians, of course, went overboard, inventing all kinds of terrifying toothed contraptions to stop boys misusing themselves. Parents could buy pocketless trousers or even a "Mechanical Penis Sheath" which cheerily advertised "great physical pain and possible mutilation". *Excessive Venery*, an 1888 publication by the American physician, Joseph Howe, warned that masturbators could go blind, impotent or insane, or suffer from "suppurating pustules" on the face. Many doctors agreed that "self-abuse" caused physical and moral degradation, marked by rings under the eyes and an ape-like, dragging posture.

In his original, 1908 manual, *Scouting For Boys*, Baden-Powell avuncularly advised his boy-readers that "You all know what it is to have at times a pleasant feeling in your private parts, and there comes an inclination to work it up with your hand or otherwise. … A very large number of lunatics on our asylums have made themselves ill by indulging in this vice although at one time they were sensible cheery boys like you."

One lunatic who didn't heed this kind of advice was the ultimate literary self-examiner, Marcel Proust, who, at around the same time as Baden-Powell was writing, recalled how, as a boy looking out of a leaf-framed window, he had explored "an untrodden path which for all I knew was deadly, until the moment when a natural trail like that left by a snail smeared the leaves of the flowering currant that drooped around me". Proust never looked back and, thankfully, neither did future generations of happy masturbators – all of them with perfect eyesight.

reach a certain age. Women in some countries do not have free access to contraception or abortion. Gay men and lesbians are frequently denied state sanction of their relationships in the form of marriage, or civil partnership with the same rights as heterosexual couples. Adults are not allowed to talk about sex in certain media, notably in particular times or in particular ways on television, or in schools. And there are usually state controls on paid-for sex.

The age of consent

The tide of sexual rights has crept towards liberalism in the last 150 years or so in all areas but one: children and sex. At the same time as the age of puberty (see p.194) has dropped, the "age of consent" – at which people are allowed to have sex – has gone up. In the nineteenth century, children could often get married or have sex at anything between twelve and fourteen years of age. Nowadays, the average is sixteen.

Many countries set the barrier even higher. In California, Florida and a number of backwoods US states, for instance, a boy and a girl are supposed to be eighteen years old before they can have sex – five years or so after puberty usually begins. Across much of the Middle East you have to be both eighteen and married. Some countries have "Romeo and Juliet" exceptions, which specify a lower age of consent when both partners are of similar age. Teenagers may be allowed to have sex with their peers, in other words, but not with adults or people in authority. Other countries have higher age limits for sex between men or between women, or for sex work or appearing in pornography.

Age-of-consent laws have many motivations. Applied to older, post-pubescent children, they're designed to help avoid pregnancy in girls regarded as too young to cope, and to discourage sexual behaviour among boys and girls vulnerable to hurt or exploitation. Applied to younger children, they are a crucial defence against sexual abuse by peers or adults. They work to a limited extent in that they may be able to make it easier for children to say "no". In many people's minds these laws also exist to preserve the "innocence" of childhood. This well-meaning notion is based less on reality than on the foundations of a contemporary Western culture that infantilizes even older children to an unusual degree. Young people are debarred from the chief areas that define adulthood: work, social responsibility, and sex.

Opponents of age-of-consent laws argue that children have as much right to pleasure and to bodily autonomy as adults. They also point out that making teen sex illegal criminalizes teenagers who will almost certainly end up having sex anyway, and makes it harder for young people to access the very services that will protect them from actual harm, namely sex education and contraception.

Women's sexual rights

Alongside medical science, which came up with the era-defining contraceptive pill in the late 1950s (see p.237), feminism is rightly lauded for its battle to win, for women, what are often called "reproductive rights". These are the right for a woman to control her own body and her own reproductive cycle: to decide on the "number, spacing and timing" of her children, as the

World Health Organization puts it. There are still major threats to these rights from states that wish to control information about and access to contraception and, especially, abortion. (For more on abortion law, see p.259.)

Less often praised, but arguably just as great an achievement, is feminism's proclamation of women's sexual rights. Foremost among these, in the public imagination, is the right to say "no". The clarity of the "no means no" message, and its assertion that what counts is explicitly given consent – not how a woman behaves or dresses or whether she flirts or what her sexual history may be – has been a major weapon in the campaign against sexual violence.

A woman's right to say "yes" is no less of an achievement of the women's movement. Once upon a time, a woman could be described as a passive vessel, a sexless being who required the touch of a husband to turn her on; either that or she was a whore who had relinquished the respect due to her as a woman. Either way, women's sexuality was generally respected only in its relation to men – until feminism got to work. Only on the basis of political equality, it was argued, can equal, just and sincere male–female sexual relations flourish. It's dispiriting, then, that feminism is popularly dogged by a perception of it as being somehow hostile to sex or romance – or perhaps it's a misogynistic conspiracy to damn feminists as aggressive man-haters. The perception is largely inaccurate, though some radical "second-wave" feminists from the 1970s liberation movement, most notoriously Andrea Dworkin, employed assertive language which alienated some, confused others and enraged a good few more (see box, opposite).

Sex is rape?

The radical feminist Andrea Dworkin is often reported as having said that "all sex is rape and all men are rapists". She didn't (and neither, incidentally, did her fellow anti-pornography campaigner, Catherine MacKinnon) but she did assert that male culture, especially pornographic culture, often links penetration with violation. Dworkin also wrote that intercourse can be "a means, or the means, of physiologically making a woman inferior: communicating to her, cell by cell, her own inferior status, impressing it on her, burning it into her by shoving it into her, over and over, pushing and thrusting until she gives up and gives in – which is called surrender in the male lexicon". Some of Dworkin's colleagues argued that men had created a presiding "rape culture" in which individual acts of sexual violence served to keep women subjugated as a class. Most, however, merely used the rhetoric of rape to emphasize an obvious truth: that as long as gender relations are unequal, women's sexual choices cannot be entirely free.

The "third-wave feminism" of the 1980s and 1990s was, in parts, a reaction to the perceived hostility to sex, or to male sexuality, of the second wave. (Feminist dissident, Camille Paglia, provocatively quipped that "leaving sex to the feminists is like letting your dog vacation at the taxidermist".) Many feminists chose to embrace and celebrate female sexuality, including heterosexual relations, as a positive force. Even pornography (which Andrea Dworkin really did link to rape, saying it "depends for its continued existence on the rape and prostitution of women") and sex work were reconsidered in terms of women's empowerment. Sex-positive feminists such as Candida Royalle, Susie Bright and Annie Sprinkle emerged within the erotica industry, producing woman-oriented pornography and headlining a new "raunch culture". Traditionalists complained that metaphorically putting on lipstick and high heels wasn't empowerment; it was the internalization of male sexual fantasy. The feminist "sex wars" continue to this day.

Sodomites

The gay rights movement has had to contend with a long and virulent history of religious, legal and social hostility to homosexuality. But the roots of gay history run no less deep. (For lesbian back-history, see p.30.) Despite draconian medieval laws against "sodomy" – which were even used against a king, Edward II of England, and (posthumously) a pope, Boniface VIII – men were evidently having sex with men, and women with women right through the pre-modern era.

Much "queer history" has been lost, or buried, but a few flowerings of homosexual freedom or at least homosexual expression stand out. Most famously, there's ancient Greece (see p.27), while Renaissance Florence may have been a kind of San Francisco of its day: "Florentiner" was contemporary German slang for "gay", and artists including Michelangelo, Leonardo da Vinci, Benvenuto Cellini and, most obviously, Giovanni "Il Sodoma" Bazzi, revelled in their male lovers. (As did William Shakespeare, in England, along with many other courtiers and poets.) As the scholar Helmut Puff (really) has shown, the German Reformation movement even took strength from associating Italian Catholicism with "sodomy".

The arrival of the industrial revolution, and large cities, made homosexuality more possible, and urban areas developed what might be called gay subcultures. Revolutionary France was one of the first states to do away with laws against victimless sexual crimes (much as it briefly supported female emancipation) and a few other liberal regimes copied its radical lead (though it took the UK until 1967 to finally repeal its sodomy laws).

Science turned its attention to homosexuality from roughly the mid-nineteenth century onwards; it came hand in hand with early activism. The British traveller and proto-anthropologist, Richard Burton, charted the existence of what he called an Oriental "Sotadic Zone" in which male–male desire flourished free of the restrictions and hatreds of the West. Scholars began to look again at what the ancient Greeks got up to. In Germany, in the 1860s and 1870s, Karl Heinrich Ulrichs published a twelve-volume scientific–polemical study of *Researches on the Riddle of Man–Manly Love*. His coinage "urning" or "Uranian" didn't catch on, however, and it was left to a Hungarian scholar, Karoly Kertbeny, to concoct the word "homosexual" (homos is Greek for "the same" – and has nothing to do with Latin homo, meaning "man"; sexus is Latin for "sex" as in "gender").

Ulrich's lead was taken up by the gay scientist and "father of sexology", Magnus Hirschfeld, who proposed the idea of a hormonally determined "intermediate sex" and set up Berlin's pioneering Institute for Sexual Science. In Britain, some rather eccentrically original thinkers set to work on the phenomenon, including the radical psychologist

Countries where homosexuality is illegal

If a man has sex with another man in Iran, Mauritania, Saudi Arabia, Sudan, the United Arab Emirates and Yemen, and is arrested, he risks the death penalty – possibly by being stoned, thrown off a cliff, crushed under a wall, sliced bodily in half or having his throat cut. The same is true in those parts of Nigeria, Pakistan and Somalia where Muslim sharia law is applied. In total, male homosexuality is illegal in some 85 to 90 countries (definitions vary), and legal in more than 100. Lesbians, on the whole, are less vigorously oppressed – by the law at least. In scores of countries (especially, but far from exclusively, in Africa, the Caribbean, the Middle East and South Asia), gay men and lesbian women are at risk of physical violence from vigilantes and police. And across the world, almost anyone with non-mainstream gender or sexual identity risks homophobic violence, discrimination or bullying.

and sexologist Havelock Ellis, who preached tolerance of what he called "inversion" (and whose wife was a lesbian), and Edward Carpenter, a gay former Anglican vicar (who also promoted healthy sandal-wearing and vegetarianism). The legal sideshow of the 1895 Oscar Wilde trial – he sued the Marquess of Queensberry, his lover's father, for calling him a "posing somdomite" [sic] – greatly increased awareness for what Wilde called "the love that dare not speak its name"; but Wilde was actually defending pederasty, and his flamboyance may have exacerbated social intolerance.

LGBTIQ

The modern rights movement took shape alongside the campaigns for civil and women's rights. In the postwar period, the pathologizing term "homosexuality" was gradually rejected in favour of the identity-asserting, celebratory "gay". Fighting off medical and social attempts to "normalize them" and state attempts to repress them, gay and lesbian campaigners came together. The acronym LGB (lesbian, gay and bisexual) was born – eventually becoming LGBT with the addition of "transgender" (see p.76) and soon after, LGBTI, with "intersexual" (see p.76).

The 1969 Stonewall riots in New York, where gays and lesbians in the Greenwich Village Stonewall Inn fought back against police harassment, was the most celebrated of a number of acts of assertion. In the 1970s, Gay Pride marches swelled in number and size across the West and, gradually, anti-gay laws were repealed. The HIV-AIDS crisis of the 1980s brought a good deal of anti-gay hatred into the open, but simultaneously engendered a culture of state openness, as many governments were forced to create policies aimed at what was now increasingly recognized as the gay community.

From the late 1980s, many theorists and activists reappropriated the once-derogatory term "queer" to express the feeling that celebrating difference, or being on the margin, was more the point than fighting for a "gay" identity alongside

Pink power: Gay and lesbian activists preparing for a parade in Des Moines, Iowa in 1983.

Homophobes are GAY!

In 1996, researchers at the University of Georgia persuaded 64 straight men (of whom half were deemed "homophobic") to hook themselves up to a machine monitoring penile arousal and watch porn with gay, straight and "lesbian" themes. Just about all the men had erections while watching straight or woman-on-woman porn. When it came to gay porn, however, 24 percent of the non-homophobes had erections compared to 54 percent of the homophobes.

It rather looked as if homophobia was less fear of homosexuality than fear of becoming homosexual: those erections seemed to indicate repressed desire – an idea that would no doubt discomfort those gay-bashing politicians, priests, rappers, rabbis and imams. Unfortunately, the discomfort is often shared by young gay people struggling to deal with their own internalized homophobic feelings. "Accepting yourself" is one of the greatest challenges faced if you're young and gay, and the difficulty of the task surely contributes to the monstrously high suicide rates among gay teens. Not all homophobes are hypocrites; some are simply in distress.

mainstream hetero culture. Being "queer" covered all kinds of sexual or gender variation, and was political as much as sexual or biological. With basic sexual liberties largely won in the West, much activism in the 1990s and 2000s focused on demanding gay rights for non-Western countries (see box on p.342). Many try to argue that homosexuality is some kind of corrupt Western import. Similar arguments were once used about racism – by Apartheid South Africa, for instance – and still are about women's rights as well. Homosexuality certainly takes many social forms, but it is found in every society (not to mention the animal kingdom; see p.34).

Perhaps the highest-profile gay rights campaign of recent years is a return to the issue of civil rights: in this case, the right of gay men and lesbian women to form legal partnerships or marriages on the same terms that heterosexuals enjoy. Despite many countries signing up to international charters avowing an end to discrimination on the grounds of sexuality or gender identity, few have honoured these promises in the matter of marriage. "The institution of marriage" remains one of the last great bastions of conservative dogma.

Sexual violence

Sexual violence is a hostile targeting of someone's sexuality that hurts and degrades. It infringes two core sexual rights: the first is a person's right to decide who, how, when or whether their body is touched by another person – their right to give or withhold consent, in other words. The second is their right to choose when any given situation becomes sexual; most insidiously, sexual violence potentially undermines the ability to enjoy intimacy in the future.

Rape and sexual assault are the most obvious and brutal forms of sexual violence, along with sexual slavery and trafficking (see p.360) and child sexual abuse (see p.348). Some would add Female Genital Mutilation (see p.67) to the list, along with denial of access to contraception and abortion. Sexual harassment and bullying, homophobic and unwanted sexual comments are less explicit kinds of sexual violence, but they certainly infringe sexual rights and are violent in their core nature.

A perpetrator's motivations for sexual violence are not necessarily sexual: they may be as much about sadism, or rage, or power, or hatred, or politics. War rape, for instance, is often used to terrorize and intimidate a population; it goes hand in hand with ethnic cleansing and acts of nationalistic ot tribal revenge. Many rapists are more intent on inflicting suffering or evacuating their own internal hatred or distress than on gratifying their own sexual desires – though in practice these psychological circuits may be hopelessly entangled.

Rape

One of the most disturbing kinds of sexual violence – because of the emotional damage it can cause and just because it's so appallingly common – is rape. The word conjures up one image in many people's minds: that of a strange man having vaginal, penetrative sex with a woman against her will. But the vast majority of rape attacks are committed by someone the victim knows, is dating, is in a relationship with, or is married to. One US study found that stranger rapes made up only 2 percent of cases; acquaintance rape made up the other 98 percent with "steady dating partners" the most likely perpetrators.

Legal definitions of rape vary, but many agree that the crime can be committed with a hand or an object, as well as a penis, and it can be directed against the anus or mouth, as well as the vagina. Some states call these acts sexual assault or similar names but, terminology aside, it's telling that at least one in ten rapes are committed against men: usually but not always by another man. Men can and are raped by women, however: they can get erections even when they don't want to have sex, they can be pressured or blackmailed into sex, or they can be penetrated themselves.

Rape statistics are notoriously variable, largely because it's such an under-reported crime. Studies tend to show that somewhere between 5 and 50 percent of women have been raped or sexually assaulted, depending on country and community; in Europe and North America somewhere between one in four and one in ten is the likely figure.

The number of men who have committed rape is inevitably comparable, though this is a statistic that's much less frequently pondered. What's clear

Andrea Dworkin's experience of rape

❝ I started hating every day. I hated seeing the sun rise. I couldn't put one foot in front of the other and I wanted to put a butcher's knife into my heart behind my ribs ... My body was a curse and had betrayed me. I couldn't figure out why they would want to do this and why they would want to do it to me. ❞

What "no" means

Obtaining sexual consent doesn't just mean eliciting a "yes". It also means not creating conditions where someone feels pressured to say yes, or frightened of, or worried about, saying no. It means finding out what they actually mean by yes – discovering where they're setting the boundaries. And it means creating the opportunity for them to say no – asking them carefully and explicitly, checking in again later (one entry isn't a free all-areas pass) and never making assumptions. Consent requires talking. Where a "no" is spoken or indicated, it means exactly and immediately that: "no".

It's undeniable that many societies conceive of sexual relations between men and women as a kind of game, where men pursue and persuade, and women withhold or delay. Many same-sex partnerships find the same dramatization successfully fulfilling. Many heterosexuals do it with the traditional gender roles in reverse. However it's played out, the game provides the thrill of many relationships and encounters, as the pursuer relishes in their own prowess and the force of their yearning, and the pursued tastes and revels in their desirability and control. It's a kind of grand enjoyment of sexual power by both parties. And sex itself often flirts dangerously with the tiltings and shiftings of power balances. It may be spiced with a kind of violence, too, with feelings of possession or relinquishing, with danger or roughness. Some people actively enjoy tasting humiliation or pain.

But the golden rule always remains the same: "no" means "no". (In fact, straight sex could take advice from the bondage and sadomasochism scene, where passwords are often used to ensure that a real "no" is never misunderstood – see p.136.) However someone may have behaved to date, whatever they've said or done or suggested or promised (or drunk, or taken, or worn), wherever they've gone or whoever they've gone with, they retain an absolute veto, to be exercised whenever they choose. They have the right to set the boundaries of their sexuality wherever they want.

is that there cannot be a "typical rapist", though propensity to rape has been linked to factors such as hostility to women, use of violent pornography, and bullying or aggressive or controlling behaviour. Rapists are also, overwhelmingly, young men, and many rapes take place when alcohol or other drugs are being used.

Dealing with rape and sexual assault

If you are raped or assaulted, find somewhere safe. Try to stay warm. Contact a friend. Most major cities have dedicated organizations or centres for victims of sexual assault, accessible through the emergency services. Medical care facilities can, of course, treat

Who cares if you've been battered?

Victim Services does.
And we'll help.
Call our 24-hour hotline.

VICTIM SERVICES
212-577-7777
TDD 212-233-3456 9am - 5pm

A woman answers the telephone at the New York Victim Services Agency, a coalition of groups supporting the victims of criminal, domestic and sexual assault.

any injuries and provide information on emergency contraception (see p.342) and tests and treatment for sexually transmitted infections. Acquiring HIV from a single sexual contact is by no means inevitable, and preventive medication is most effective if begun within 72 hours.

Medical centres can also take forensic evidence. You can, potentially, add weight to any future police case by not washing or going to the toilet or changing clothes or brushing teeth or eating and drinking in the aftermath. Unfortunately, these are exactly the things many people want to do. Even if you just store clothing somewhere, it can help. If you do report the assault to the police, ask to be put in contact with a trained police officer.

Paralyzing fear, anger, acute embarrassment and anxiety are common emotions, and may last a long time – and future sexual experiences, however positive, can re-trigger these feelings. Many people feel shame or blame themselves for provoking the assault or failing to resist or avoid it. But rape is only ever the fault of the rapist. No behaviour, however sexual or risky, justifies rape. And many victims are gripped by a "frozen fear response" during the attack which makes them unable to resist. Some are rendered helpless by spiked drinks. Others have an entirely rational fear of injury, and remain passive so as not to antagonize their assailant.

Dealing with rape or sexual assault in the longer term will take time and support. The best advice for friends and partners is, first of all, to believe someone who says they've been raped. Let them talk; don't focus on how the rape "might have been avoided"; don't belittle the potential effects or rush the recovery. And don't deny your own feelings of hurt, though expressing anger towards the attacker is unlikely to help.

Friends, family or partners cannot always offer the right kind of help. Counselling is almost always available from government agencies or women's organizations – and most will happily refer male victims of rape to dedicated men's support networks. Many survivors find therapy helpful – either group therapy, alongside other survivors, or cognitive behavioural therapy. The latter, known as CBT, can be especially helpful in dealing with anxiety or post-traumatic stress disorder – which is very commonly experienced by survivors of rape or assault.

Child sexual abuse

Sexual contact with a child is a form of violence. Even leaving aside the fact that prepubescent and pubescent children do not have the sexual responses of adults, and do not want sexual contact, any person under the age of legal majority, whether post-pubescent or not, cannot legally or morally consent to sexual behaviour. Studies vary, but to say that one in five women and one in ten men were sexually abused in some way as children would be a realistic estimate. It's a shocking statistic, but there's at least this comfort in it for survivors: they are not alone. Many people have made the journey towards recovery before them.

Child sexual abuse does not only mean rape. Its most obvious, physical forms may be vaginal or anal penetration, oral sex, and intimate kissing or touching. But taking inappropriate photographs is also a form of abuse as, in certain circumstances, is watching a child undress; so, too, is instigating an inappropriate conversation, or encouraging sexualized contact between children. Different degrees of abuse may have different effects, but in essence, any form of sexual contact between an adult or someone in authority and a child amounts to an attack on the core sexual feelings: trust and intimacy as well as physical or sexual response.

Most abusers are not the child-snatching paedophiles of the tabloid press. Roughly half are well-known to the family; perhaps a third are actually family members – a phenomenon historically called incest. Many abusers are adolescents, engaging in what could be called a vicious form of sexual bullying. The theory that abusers were themselves abused is not well supported; statistics show that only half of convicted molesters suffered abuse themselves, and some believe that paedophiles often claim to have been abused in order to diminish the perceived responsibility they have for their actions. Certainly, most victims of child sexual abuse do not develop paedophiliac tendencies – for a start, a majority of victims are female while some ninety percent of perpetrators are male. That said, the reports of female abusers, as with crimes perpetrated by women generally, are rising.

The consequences of child sexual abuse

Perhaps the worst thing about child sexual abuse is that it occurs before positive sexual feelings have had a chance to be established, and while the very sense of self is in its infancy. This can have a powerful impact on a child's self image, and any damage done to the identity is likely to continue into adulthood.

Leaving aside physical injuries or marks, the initial psychological signs of abuse may be very effectively buried. Some children may become anxious, have nightmares, or become unusually aggressive or withdrawn. They may avoid certain people or situations. Some exhibit surprisingly sexual behaviour or language, others express dislike of their bodies. School performance or behaviour at home may change. Children may try to tell parents or caregivers, but may not have the language.

The full effects of abuse may only emerge in later life. Survivors often experience depression, anger, guilt, loss and pain. Low self-esteem can lead to unhealthy relationship choices, and even to further abusive relationships. Some survivors develop eating disorders; some pursue unhappy promiscuity or take sexual risks; some self-harm; others self-medicate using alcohol or drugs.

Many struggle to find positive sexual feelings and have problems maintaining healthy relationships. Distressingly, arousal may become linked to fantasies about the original abuse, which can cause guilt and confusion. Sex, or specific acts or feelings within sex, may trigger powerful memories of the original trauma. Some experience sex as a duty or obligation, finding no pleasure in it for themselves.

Recovering from child sexual abuse

The journey of recovering from child sexual abuse or sexual violence is a long one, and discovering or rediscovering positive sexual feelings can be one of the toughest stretches. Sexual symptoms, including difficulties in becoming aroused or reaching orgasm are often treated in isolation, and the same is often true of non-sexual responses to sexual trauma, such as depression, anxiety, alcohol and drug abuse, and chronic pain. Treating the original source of trauma may be much harder, but potentially more effective.

Staci Haines, author of the positive and practically minded classic, *Healing Sex* (2007), observes that "turning and facing pain isn't the easy road, but if offers a sense of dignity and power". Speaking of her own experiences, she compared it to "being willing to walk into a deep and dark underground tunnel, knowing the only way out was through it." Haines' own book is an excellent place to start, and further reading can be found in the Resources section which follows this chapter. Community organizations, especially women's groups, offer valuable support to survivors. In the UK, NAPAC (napac.org.uk) and Rape Crisis (rapecrisis.org.uk) offer frontline help; in the US, sites such as jimhopper.com, darknesstolight.org and malesurvivor.org are a good place to start.

The most in-depth way to turn and confront the trauma is counselling and therapy. Psychoanalysis, Freudian or otherwise, is probably not the best way forward: it can be a lengthy and in-depth process which some survivors may find too destabilizing. Psychotherapy, by contrast – and cognitive behavioural therapy and cognitive analytic therapy in particular – can be practical and effective. It offers guidance in leaving behind habits of thinking and behaviour that may be "maladaptive" – unhelpful to your life, in other words. Dialectical behavioural therapy offers many of the same benefits, while also emphasizing that even if you can't make your pain go away, it is possible to learn to accept or tolerate it. It draws on Buddhist ideas of "mindfulness", or calm awareness.

The most positive and uplifting thing ...

" In therapy, the psychotherapist kept bringing up the past and at first I couldn't see why it was so important. But when I started talking about what had happened, I couldn't believe the effect it had on me, bringing it out. Half of me was angry, but half just felt such shame, and guilt. I was angry, because it was hurting me so much. I'd carried a sense of blame throughout my entire life but I learned that these feelings were put into me as a child – I'd been brainwashed.

Bringing it all out helped me start to look at life in a different, more positive way. I went to work with kids who had been abused. I was giving something back, and it was good to feel wanted, to be able to turn a negative experience into a positive one. It did bring up more feelings, but I also found a strength I'd never had before. I decided to confront my abuser and the case went to court. He was found guilty.

It was the most positive and uplifting thing. It changed the way I felt about sex. When I first started getting interested in boys, I wouldn't go with them. I felt dirty, I used to get a very uncomfortable feeling. I thought anybody who wanted anything like that was some kind of pervert. So I lost a lot of people I liked. By going into things, I didn't only open up my past, I didn't only find answers, I changed my feelings as well. It's not just that I've got justice, I've got peace of mind: peace and wellbeing. Everything is moulded together. I did not realize that being able to accept that I was abused would bring me so much comfort. "

Healing can also take place within sexuality itself. Staci Haines recommends a somatic or body-and-mind process: "you gotta feel your way out of this", she says. She recommends not just talking therapies, but bodily exploration and relearning: masturbation, for instance, "will help you learn … through your own experiences, that your sexuality is yours, and that you are not 'damaged' or 'bad'. " Ellen Bass and Laura Davis's *The Courage to Heal* (2002) agree, though they emphasize that learning to "say no to unwanted sex is perhaps the first step." Later on, with a sympathetic partner, survivors will be able to talk, and maybe "try a little teenage sex", slowly beginning to "make room for desire".

Taboos and fetishes

What's normal – and what's weird, kinky, or perverted – depends on who you're asking, and when. It's not so long since homosexuality was legally and medically defined as either a perversion or a sexual deviation. (It was only removed from the US's Diagnostic and Statistical Manual of Mental Disorders (DSM) in 1973, and some psychoanalysts still attempt to "treat" the "condition".) Oral sex and anal sex, for a good many people, are obscene, unnatural or perverted acts. And more than a few people even consider any form of sex that isn't aimed at procreation to be "wrong".

In the past 150 or so years, the West has gone through a number of sexual revolutions. Each transformed-formerly invisible, unheard-of or unthinkable sexual practices into ones which were more visible, more openly discussed, more widely thought about – and perhaps more frequently enjoyed. Psychologists, psychoanalysts and scientists in the later nineteenth and early twentieth century invented the main categories of sexual identity, including "deviant" sexual behaviour and homosexuality – though this was usually described as an "inversion" rather than a "perversion". In the 1960s and 1970s, feminism made it clear that genital, penetrative sex was not necessarily the be-all and end-all. And from the 1980s, "queer" political theorists and radicals investigated and theorized about sexual subcultures, among them transgender people and the bondage and sadomasochism scene.

The liberal West may have pushed back its sexual boundaries, but it keeps the outer edges in good repair. Behaviours that stand outside that moral or clinical or legal fence, it calls "kinky", "paraphiliac", "disordered", "deviant" or "perverted". The words carry different nuances and weights of moral disapproval but amount to the same thing: sexual behaviour which mainstream society considers as unusual or unacceptable. Above all, using sex to cause real harm – to the self or another – is always defined as a sexual perversion. Anything does not, in fact, go.

Perversions and paraphilias

In 1886, the pioneer sexologist Richard von Krafft-Ebing distinguished between involuntary perversion, which he thought was a form of mental disease, and wilful perversity, which he called a vice. The same basic distinction exists today, albeit with less judgemental terminology. Virtually all adults, it's recognized, are capable of being aroused by pretty bizarre images or activities – and most will occasionally or frequently have fantasies so strange as to astonish themselves (see p.39). Everyone, it seems, is occasionally perverse; some are sufficiently disinhibited or sexually explorative to be frequently perverse.

For a minority, sexual exploration can lead to long-term fascination, and choice is replaced by recurrent or obsessive interest – or, in "exclusive" cases, by compulsion or dependency for arousal on a particular "paraphilia". Perversity, as Krafft-Ebing would have said, becomes perversion. Psychologists typically diagnose paraphilias where sexual behaviour gets in the way of a balanced life, or gets in the way of reciprocal affection, or simply causes the paraphiliac more distress than it gives them sexual pleasure.

Naming obscure paraphilias, and presenting utterly bizarre "the man who loved..." case studies is something of a nerdy sexological hobby, and Latinate terms run the alphabet from acrophilia (being aroused by giddy heights) to zelophilia (being turned on by jealousy). The most common paraphilias are fetishism – which Freud called the "master perversion" – and partialism; exhibitionism and voyeurism; toucherism and frotteurism; sadism and masochism. Among the more celebrated rarities are coprophilia (love of faeces), urolagnia (urine), zoophilia (animals) and necrophilia (corpses).

Krafft-Ebing pointed out that a perversion (or a paraphilia) wasn't just any alternative sexual preference. Society had to regard it with horror or disgust. If sex was hunger, he said, a perversion would be the "impulse to eat spiders, toads, worms and human blood". In terms of sex, it could be acts which focus on bodily taboos, such as those surrounding urine or faeces, or which focus on pain or humiliation, rather than the more positive sexual goals of pleasure and affirmation.

According to philosopher Thomas Nagel, a paraphilia is "wilfully abnormal". If sex was gastronomy it would be a preference for eating cookbooks or for fondling a napkin in a favourite restaurant – acts that are disconcertingly specific, or perhaps narcissistic, or unbalanced. A paraphilia is a preference, Nagel says, for "truncated acts" rather than the circular reciprocity of mutual lovemaking. It betrays an unusually reflexive or double way of thinking about the desired object. It focuses more on what it can take from the experience rather than on giving. It constructs identity around a particular sexual act, rather than being willing to surrender the self in the merging of sexual union.

Causes and origins

At least nine out of ten paraphiliacs are men, which suggests that paraphilias are at least partly physical in origin, and possibly related to testosterone or brain development. Certainly, "exclusive" paraphiliacs (who cannot get aroused or have an orgasm without their particular trigger) are much more likely to have brain abnormalities, hormone imbalances or chromosomal disorders than the average man.

Paraphiliacs are also much more likely to be socially inadequate. Physical abnormalities may not so much cause paraphilias as contribute to social problems – which may then encourage a paraphilia to develop. If you're unlikely to find a "normal" sexual relationship, you're more likely to try to develop one with an object, or within the supportive framework of a subculture. Paraphilias may be self-medicating for tension, anger or low self-esteem. Just as people eat when they're feeling bored, some men seek sexual satisfaction when they're stressed, depressed or anxious. (Women in

Richard von Krafft-Ebing, the pioneering author of *Psychopathia Sexualis* (1886).

Is rape a paraphilia?

Sex with non-consenting adult partners, tellingly, isn't usually regarded as a "perversion", but more as a criminal, immoral exaggeration of a "normal" sex drive. It only becomes "perverted" if the focus of the act is not on penetrative, vaginal sex. Traditionally, in English law, rapists were jailed as criminals, rather than being humiliatingly flogged for deviant behaviour, in the manner of those convicted of exhibitionism or transvestite transgression. In this book, rape is discussed as a form of sexual violence (see p.345). So too is child sexual abuse, even though the preference for pre-sexual partners can be seen as a paraphilia.

parallel situations are statistically more likely to shoplift, self-harm or develop anorexia.)

Going through the cycle of arousal and orgasm while focused on the paraphilia may relieve tension or anxiety, or lift self-esteem due to feelings of excitement, danger or control. Thanks to conditioning, such repeated "positive" experiences reinforce the paraphilia, rather as a river cuts into its own channel. Negative reinforcement also plays a role: as when, for instance, "normal" sexual activity fails to come to fruit, or proves unsatisfying, or altogether elusive. Eventually, the paraphiliac may become incapable of being aroused in any other way, or they may become effectively addicted to the behaviour. The channel may be cut too deep, in other words, to escape – or not without the help of cognitive behavioural therapy or treatments.

What actually causes the paraphilia to develop in the first place is less clear. Formative emotional experiences, often traumas, can shape, distort or "imprint" the developing sexual mind in infancy or adolescence. So, too, can sexual or emotional repression: if the sex drive or libido is an energetic natural force, like a plant, it can be trained or cultivated – and cut short, thus forcing it to find new directions. Sex may become a way to express hatred and relieve anxiety rather than to express love and create intimacy.

Psychoanalysts believe that people may bond to sexual objects which were either present at or symbolically represent the moment at which the natural development of the libido was first challenged. For psychoanalyst Robert Stoller, paraphiliacs seek sexual experiences which symbolically "convert the childhood trauma to adult triumph". Other psychoanalysts see paraphiliac sexuality as being stuck at an immature or transitory stage, short of the final goal of mutual, reciprocal lovemaking. Psychoanalysis is often criticized for seeing vaginal, penetrative sex as normal, but Freud himself noted that children were "polymorphously perverse" and that it was society which shaped and channelled that early, instinctive, all-embracing sexual instinct into socially acceptable directions. He felt that the "sexual instinct" (or basic drive) and the "sexual object" (the thing which triggers arousal), were "merely soldered together".

Freud also considered that sexual disorders could arise from the idealization of women. If a man thinks that by giving in to his sexual advances a woman proves herself unworthy of his attentions (by being "dirty" or a "slut"), he might well attempt to compensate for those feelings, possibly by revelling in things which are dirty or forbidden. Fear and hatred of one's own sexuality (as in the case of victims of child abuse), including internalized homophobia, may have similar consequences. It's also possible that the gender stereotype where men pursue and women say "no" (or, occasionally, "yes"), puts less socially competent men in an impossible position – and gives them an obvious motivation to retreat into sexual practices which can, unlike unpredictable, reciprocal relationships, be controlled.

Fetishes and partialism

When Portuguese mariners landed in West Africa, in the fifteenth century, they were struck by the reverence paid to certain objects and idols, which they called *fetico*. The same awestruck focus on things characterizes sexual fetishes. Technically, fetishism is the need for non-living objects in order to achieve arousal. (This isn't at all the same as using objects for pleasure – a vibrator is not a fetish object unless it is the focus of the user's desire.) The object should also be slightly unusual. Many men have modest fetishes for women's underwear, but this is so mainstream that few would count it as a proper, paraphiliac fetish – unless it becomes so intense as to displace other forms of eroticism.

Many fetish objects are ornamental and highly coded to gender, social class or subculture: jewellery, wigs, piercings, gloves, shoes and underwear are common fetishes of this type. Transvestite fetishists – being men who need to wear women's clothing to become aroused, as opposed to transvestites or cross-dressers, who wear women's clothing without seeking arousal (see p.77) – may incorporate many different fetish objects to achieve the total effect.

Fetish objects are commonly made of highly textured, deep-coloured, or scented and scent-retaining materials – rubber, leather, lace and fur, for instance – and are often worn next to the skin. Some think this makes them "super-stimuli", exaggerated versions of or symbolic substitutions for more workaday triggers like hair or skin. They may also represent "transitional objects", which, according to psychoanalytic theory, are used to replace the mother–child bond along the journey to adult sexual relationships. The psychologist Alfred Binet, who coined the term fetishism in 1887, thought that fetishes were a sign of an inability to "fully possess" the desired person; they were the sign of someone who didn't really want to get past the wrapping, in other words.

Some fetishists are obsessive collectors, building up private little harems of shoes or garters or masks or whatever. Others develop elaborate rituals around their fetish object. These are similar in many ways to the rituals of childish games or religious ceremonies; where they differ is in their hub-like position within the cycle of arousal and orgasmic discharge.

A fetish for a particular body part, rather than an object, is a partialism. Genitals and secondary erogenous zones are too commonly desired to count as partialism, though different countries differ in their emphasis. American straight male culture, for instance, could easily be described as partialist in its obsession with women's breasts. So, too, could some gay cultures in their focus on the penis – just check out the pictures on cruising websites.

Underwear and high heels are such common fetish objects that they're often not even seen as fetishes.

Exhibitionism, voyeurism, toucherism, frotteurism

Posting a picture of your own penis on the Internet could be seen as a mere advertisement. It can also be exhibitionism, though technically, the person "flashed" has to be surprised or unwilling. The flasher is generally a man, too; female self-exposure may still be frowned on by the kind of conservative who says "cover yourself, young lady", but women with exaggerated décolletage or ultra-short skirts are rarely thought to be sexually deviant.

Like telephone "scatalogs", who make "dirty" or "heavy breather" phone calls, exhibitionists may get their thrills from the shock or distress they

cause – which is one reason why the vulnerable or innocent are generally selected as victims. Many exhibitionists persuade themselves that their victims are aroused by their actions, however, and imagine that their display could lead to sexual contact. Such delusions are typical of the poor empathy skills of many sex offenders. Pornography may support the delusion: the woman surprised and miraculously aroused by the mere sight of a penis is a staple of low-grade erotica.

Having sex in a public place is a rather different form of exhibitionism, though it also uses danger to create arousal. There may be an element of sado-masochistic humiliation or egocentric triumphalism, too, in exposing the self or the partner to intimate public view. There could also be a flirtation with group sex or stranger-sex: the door is left open, as it were, to a passing stranger.

Voyeurism is the desire to watch people having sex. Again, to qualify as a paraphilia, the coupling couple should be unsuspecting and, again, the adrenaline rush of risk or danger is likely to be at work. Similar mechanisms are at play in toucherism (bottom-pinching, breast-brushing and the like) and frotteurism (rubbing the genitals up against a stranger's body, stereotypically in a crowded train carriage), though these paraphilias could also be described as a halfway house between "hands-off" exhibitionism and rape.

Sadomasochism and BDSM

Sadism and masochism look like an opposing pair. The sadist enjoys inflicting pain or humiliation, the masochist receiving it. So ideally, sadists

Sacher-Masoch and the Marquis de Sade

The original Sadist and the original Masochist were both distinctly high-minded novelists who spent the last years of their lives in an asylum. Their names were first attached to sadism and masochism, respectively, not by themselves but by Richard von Krafft-Ebing, the German psychiatrist who first examined "perversions" scientifically in the 1880s.

Leopold Ritter von Sacher-Masoch (1836–1905) was an idealistic writer from the Austro-Hungarian kingdom of Galicia, in modern-day Ukraine. His love of pain and humiliation began, he confessed, when as a boy he witnessed his aunt, "the Countess Zenobia", having illicit sex with a young man while he hid in a cupboard, watching. The "countess" wore a "magnificent green velvet jacket trimmed with squirrel". Upon discovering her young

nephew in hiding, she whipped him vigorously, her "cruel blows" only giving him intense pleasure. "This event", he wrote, "became engraved on my soul as with a red-hot iron" – an outcome which today would be called imprinting. It inspired a lifetime's pursuit of women who would dominate, hurt or humiliate him.

Von Sacher-Masoch's first wife beat

him with fists, whips and birches. His mistress, Fanny Pistor, made her "slave" sign a contract to "comply unreservedly, for six months, with every one of her desires and commands". He encouraged his second wife, Aurora Rumelin, to take lovers and to whip him with a nail-studded cat-o'-nine-tails. He novelized his life in the brilliant and radical *Venus In Furs* (1870).

Donatien-Alphonse-François de Sade, a French count, was no less radical, a philosopher and revolutionary who spent much of his life in prison: not for revolutionary fervour, however, but for two rather sordid escapades in a lifetime of dedicated libertinism. He was first imprisoned in 1768 for whipping a young beggar woman until she bled and keeping her wounds open with a knife. Four years later, he gave sweets laced with "Spanish fly" – a potentially lethal irritant which then had a reputation as an aphrodisiac – to prostitutes in a Marseillaise brothel. He had sex with men, boys, women and girls, all with equal malevolent intent.

In July 1789, de Sade was one of the very few prisoners in the notorious Bastille prison two weeks before it fell to the revolutionary mob. While incarcerated he wrote his masterpiece, *The 120 Days of Sodom*. Focusing on the retreat by four monstrous libertines into a fantastical debauch in a sealed-off château, it is an unsettling mixture of libertine philosophy, virulent pornography and riotous, Rabelaisian glee in extreme sexual violence. One of his characters seems to speak for de Sade when he says, "It's always the filthy thing that attracts our fuck; and the filthier it is, the more voluptuously it flows."

and masochists should be paired up. Certainly, sadists who enjoy causing pain to non-consenting partners should seek therapy; their concerns are not discussed here.

In truth, S/M is less black/white and more midway grey. Some psychologists think masochism can be a defence against buried or feared sadistic instincts, while many people who begin their S/M life as masochists change, or enjoy "switching". In practice, sadism is characterized as much by issues of domination and control as by pain, and masochism may be as much about deferring or delaying gratification, and finding "permission" to enjoy sex as being actually humiliated or hurt. For this reason, some see it as a dramatized or exaggerated version of everyday sex, which plays with domination rather more often than it plays with pain (unless you think arousal and orgasm are parallel to pain responses).

Krafft-Ebing thought sadism and masochism were versions of traditional masculine and feminine active/passive roles. He thought coy women got pleasure from the male's "final victory", for instance, while the man enjoyed demonstrating his superior strength – hammering home his conquest, as it were. Researchers since have pointed out that S/M only exists in aggressive and unequal societies; if so, then S/M practitioners may be playing out social frustrations and complexes as much as gender ones.

The majority of people occasionally play with sadomasochistic tensions in their lovemaking at least to some degree. A few develop a more intense interest, usually in late adolescence. They may find that hurt or humiliation are ways to express or manage feelings such as guilt, low self-esteem, or fear of rejection. They may just enjoy the sensation, and the sexual liberation. Perhaps half of sadomasochists feel mainly masochistic, a quarter mainly sadistic, and another quarter "switch" either way.

A small minority of people get involved in what's usually called the bondage-domination-sadism-masochism (BDSM) "scene". It's not just tying up and spanking, though bondage and flagellation may be the focus of sex itself. Far from it – BDSM typically incorporates any number of paraphiliac-type or fantasy-based activities within a safe and consensual environment.

"Subs" and "doms" may agree to be master/slave, guardian/child, employer/employee, or whatever. They may wear fetish or bondage gear of leather or rubber, with masks or uniforms or hyped-up versions of lingerie. They may use ties, ropes and handcuffs; gags, hoods and blindfolds; paddles, whips and chains; clamps, swings and cages. They may play with ritualized humiliations or "hypermasculine" displays such as fisting and cockbinding. They may play sexually with urine and faeces in "golden showers" and "scat" (short for scatology, also known as coprophilia or being turned on by shit – usually shitting on someone or being shat upon). Many, but not all, people on the BDSM scene practise group sex or partner-swapping.

One of the curiosities of BDSM is how strongly scripted (not to mention clichéd) many encounters are. Participants agree roles, boundaries and, ideally, "safewords" which stop proceedings. They know what to expect and only push the limits enough to make the scenario feel realistic. People entering a BDSM scene are expected to play by the rules and speak the lingo.

In some ways, BDSM is rather like golf, amateur dramatics or any hobbyists' club: inward-looking, slightly nerdy and, if you don't enjoy the game, deathly dull. For those inside the club, it can become a passionate, life-enhancing interest. This clubbish, scripted element leads some psychologists to believe that many S/M practitioners are seeking sexual safety or, to put it in a more hostile way, they are avoiding the risk of unscripted, openly emotional encounters. Many enthusiasts would disagree. As one happy sadomasochist commented, a "good scene" is a "healing process … it doesn't end with orgasm, it ends with catharsis". And there's nothing more emotional than that.

Unusual partners – zoophilia and necrophilia

Lonely shepherds have long been reputed to have turned to their flocks for solace, and many adolescents have tentative or exploratory sexual interactions with pets – perhaps getting the animal to tongue their genitals. Some dogs are all too willing. The 1948 Kinsey Report calculated that almost half of Americans living near farms had "sexually interacted" with animals.

There's a difference between using an animal's orifices for sexual gratification, however, and the practices of avowed zoophiles, who engage in what they persuade themselves are full, consensual sexual relationships with their pets. Zoophiles may even look down on those practising self-pleasuring "bestiality". Even leaving aside the mainstream taboo on cross-species sex, the element of control or dominance in any master-pet relationship makes sexual interaction problematic, much as teacher-pupil relationships are often seen to be.

Despite its prominence in popular myth, true necrophilia is extremely rare. "Romantic" or "inhibited" necrophiles who literally will not let go of departed loved ones are clearly focused on the memory of the living. A few violent sex offenders and serial killers may rape or sexually mutilate their victims but this "sadistic necrophilia" does

In Greek mythology, satyrs were followers of the gods Dionysus and Pan, and were associated with wild, animalistic sexual energy.

not amount to actually desiring dead bodies. The Marquis de Sade conceived of some baroque sexual tortures, for instance, but their goal was pain and humiliation, not death. Most of the blindings and burnings and savage assaults which conclude *The 120 Days of Sodom* are continued only for as long as the victim survives – or, in one case, until the lightning rod in her anus attracts a bolt.

One 1989 study found only a handful of authentic case studies of necrophilia, and of those only 15 percent were characterized by attraction to corpses. Funeral parlour scandals very occasionally emerge, including that of Karen Greenlee, who called herself a "morgue rat" and claimed to have encountered others. She praised the death smell of a freshly embalmed corpse and the way it would purge blood from its mouth when she was on top of it. Other scandals may well be hushed up. According to Herodotus, ancient Egyptian families reportedly kept attractive female corpses back for a few days before delivering them to the embalmers, to prevent "any indecency being offered to their persons".

Sex as work

Prostitution – or "sex work" to call it by a less loaded name – is often wryly called the world's oldest profession. The 4000-year-old *Epic of Gilgamesh* certainly features a splendidly powerful whore, Harimtu, who trains the hero Enkidu in the ways of civilization – including sexual learning. And "harlots" appear frequently in the Old Testament, albeit accompanied by patriarchal flapping about sons being seduced from righteousness.

In Greece, the sixth-century-BC Athenian legislator, Solon, established brothels to defend the city against social chaos, and a hierarchy soon grew up, from the pornai at the bottom – who wore sandals with soles imprinted with the words "follow me" – to the socially influential and exquisitely cultivated hetaerae, at the top. (The hetaerae became fantasy figures for generations of classically educated European men; Simone de Beauvoir sniffily described them as "women who treat not only their bodies but their entire personalities as capital to be exploited".) India's third-century *Kamasutra* described a similar range of prostitutes, from servant women (especially those who carry water, for some reason), dancers and artists to the highly accomplished ganika or "courtesan de luxe".

The Romans were famously keen on buying sex (see p.372), and the ancient Roman statesman Cato the Elder even praised a young man for visiting a brothel on the grounds that this was better than "grinding away at the wives of others". It didn't mean that the Romans entirely approved, however. Harlots were far from respectable, pimps came in for a lot of abuse, and clients were said to stink of the soot of cheap brothel lamps.

Christianity was even more disapproving, though even St Augustine agreed with Cato that "remove prostitution from society and you will throw everything into confusion". Until the twentieth century, this pragmatic opinion prevailed. Prostitution wasn't approved of, but it was tolerated because it acted as a release valve for male sexuality. Married men could more easily defend their ownership of their wives' bodies. Poor women had a means of survival. Bachelors could

Turning tricks in a toga – Roman prostitution

You could buy sex just about anywhere in ancient Rome. The rich got it in-house; slaves and servants performed sexual services as much as other duties. The lower classes had to find theirs on the street – and at the circus, among the columns beneath the theatre, by city gates and in stables, hot baths, courthouses, taverns and any number of other public places. In the emperor Caligula's time, city inspectors noted the existence of 64 established brothels, along with 35,000 female and 2000 male prostitutes. Female prostitutes, uniquely among women, were supposed to wear the male *toga*. Whether this was to distinguish them from respectable, *stola*-wearing matrons, whether it symbolized their masculine-type independence, or whether it just looked sexy isn't known.

The city of Pompeii is sometimes said to have had 35 brothels servicing a population of only 10,000 or so. Walls all over town are covered with graffiti such as "Narcissus, cock-sucker extraordinaire", "Successa the slave girl's a good

lay" and "Maritimus licks cunt for four *asses*" (he was quite expensive). But as the classicist Mary Beard points out, if you see "Donna sucks you off for a fiver" daubed on a bus shelter you don't assume that Donna really does. And many of the Pompeiian brothels counted by awestruck archaeologists may be no such thing. The notorious *cellae meretriciae* (little off-street cells with a built-in stone bed and a phallus over the entrance) weren't necessarily cheap knocking-shops – they could just have been shelters; and phalluses were a good-luck symbol used everywhere in Pompeii.

Beneath its volcanic ash, Pompeii has preserved one undoubted brothel. It has five small cells, each with a built-in bed, and the walls are covered with erotic paintings and boastful graffiti. Some scrawls praise the talents of particular women. Curiously, most had Greek or eastern names – which is probably a sign that migration for sex work was as common in ancient Rome as it is today.

practise – although they mightn't have learned much about female satisfaction.

The global marketplace

As sex outside marriage became more common in the twentieth century, paid-for sex began to cater for the losers in the non-commercial sex market: the unattractive, the unconfident, the inexperienced and the un-partnered. It also

increasingly served "special interest" clients, including men who wanted to have sex with men but didn't want to embrace a gay lifestyle or identity, and devotees of unusual fetishes.

Estimating the number of sex workers in the world today isn't like counting up lawyers or plumbers. Most trade sex for cash informally, occasionally or periodically. (Five years, off and on, is a fairly typical career length; after that, a sex worker's price starts to go down, unless he or she starts specializing.) Outside the rare

The most public side of sex work: a "punter" negotiates with a "streetwalker" in Marseilles.

registration schemes in liberal countries, few sex workers declare themselves to the government (and certainly not for tax purposes). Still, it's fairly safe to say that between one in a thousand and one in fifty women are involved in "transactional sex" of some description, around the world; that's somewhere between 3 million and 60 million women. In some urban parts of the Americas, Southeast Asia and sub-Saharan Africa, it may be more like one in twenty.

Male sex workers are significantly fewer in number, while those serving female clients are rare indeed. As regards clients, roughly 10 percent of the world's men paid for sex in the last year. Countries where non-commercial sex is relatively available have lower rates. In the US, some 16 percent of men have paid for sex at some point in

their lives – it's a dramatic reduction from the 69 percent reckoned up by Alfred Kinsey in the 1940s, but still a whole lot more than the UK's modest 7 percent.

Whores, hustlers and CSWs

Most people talk about "prostitutes", a word which comes from the Latin for "standing in front" but now carries a strong pejorative charge. To "prostitute yourself" means to do something for money alone, without pride or self-respect. Most people actually "on the game" prefer the terms "pro", "girl" or "sex worker", while experts refer to commercial sex workers (CSWs). Male sex workers tend to go by "hustler" and "rent boy" – or

Buying sex

Every sex worker has their own rules and codes and boundaries, but certain guidelines are regularly set out on sex workers' websites. They typically ask clients to wash thoroughly, brush their teeth, avoid being drunk or otherwise incapacitated and to wear a condom – of course, a sex worker who's willing to work without one is much more likely to pass on an infection. They ask clients to be clear about what they want and what they're paying for, but respect the worker's limits – including the agreed time limit. They ask for payment up front, and no negotiation on prices. Above all, as Chezstella.org puts it, "remember that sex workers are people, like everyone else. Give us the same respect that you give to yourself and to others". That respect should certainly extend to making quite sure that the sex worker is over-age and not trafficked.

supposed to protect or market them. They're also prone to drug and alcohol dependency. "Turning a trick" for a "street girl" is often about finding a fix, hence the US slang term "crack whore".

Street work is a relatively small part of prostitution. More common are "call girls" who arrange appointments – either an "in-call" or an "out-call" to a trusted client's home – by phone or, increasingly, via the web. Many use an agency for screening customers, perhaps with an online presence, or have an arrangement with a hotel, a club, a massage parlour or an established brothel. Some share costs with other professionals, others give a cut to a brothel's "madam". An agency cut might be something like 30 percent, a reputable brothel is more likely to take at least half. Disreputable brothels, of course, may well keep migrant sex workers in virtual or actual slavery, holding back their passports, charging extortionate fees for illegal entry or threatening and performing sexual or other violence to their victims – or to their families back home.

just "rent". Some campaigners proudly proclaim themselves "whores", a word which derives, curiously enough, from the same root as Latin *carus*, French *chère*, Italian *cara*, Welsh *cariad* and Sanskrit *kama* – all meaning something along the lines of "dear" or "desired". It's all a long way from "ho", the misogynistic American slang term.

Leaving aside sexual slavery, "hookers" or "streetwalkers" who advertise themselves in person and in public are at the bottom rung of the ladder. They earn the least (though it's still some way above entry-level shop work), and they're much more vulnerable to violence and abuse – from police, punters (or "johns") and the pimps who are

Why do it?

The fantasy of the prostitute who does it for pleasure is just that. Sex workers do it for money, and because the alternatives for them and their families may be grimmer than comfortable anti-prostitution campaigners can easily imagine. Prostitution *can* be an unusually flexible and independent kind of employment – pimps, police, traffickers and dealers aside – and it's telling that many female sex workers are single mothers or carers.

A minority of clients see sex as something that can be bought, so that's what they do. A good many just can't get sex elsewhere: they might be shy or unconfident, or have a mental or physical disability. Many punters can't get the *kind* of partner or sex they want elsewhere: they might be ashamed of their particular fetish or their desire for bondage, and don't want to involve their partner in it, or they might prefer acts to which few partners would willingly consent.

Men ask for oral sex more often than anything else – an act which, statistically, women don't like doing half as much as men like getting. They also frequently ask to be dominated or degraded, though this might just mean she's on top. The client may need to feel in control of the sexual transaction, but statistics show that they like playing passive. Wanting the prostitute to "take charge" may be motivated by male performance anxiety or by the common fantasy of the "dirty" or "rampant" whore. Mingled feelings of fascination, awe and disgust can combine with a sense of transgression – that the punter himself is doing something "filthy" – to create a potent sexual cocktail.

A surprisingly large number of punters say that they're searching for an emotional connection, for the "big-hearted whore". They complain that prostitutes are too often "cold". This sounds like self-justification (or self-delusion) but many sex workers do provide longer-term clients with companionship or a kind of therapy.

The law

Most countries have become more moralistic about prostitution in the last half-century or so. Even in the countries where sex work is not actually illegal, it's usually hemmed in by laws preventing,

A strip club in London's Soho. Many sex workers congregate in so-called "red light districts".

say, kerb-crawling, living off immoral earnings, brothel-keeping and "soliciting" – which means advertising. Police harassment is commonplace and can range from interference with work to the withdrawal of basic protections (notoriously, prostitutes may be told they "cannot be raped") and actual violence. Shockingly, the public prosecutor in the case of the "Yorkshire Ripper", who murdered thirteen British women in the 1970s, commented that "what is saddest of all is indeed that some of the murder victims were not in fact prostitutes".

iSex

It began with phone sex. For a fee levied through the phone company any lonely guy could ring up and listen to a woman saying she was taking off her top now, and would he like to touch himself? It was rarely convincing, but at least if offered the interactivity pornography lacked. And it was a whole lot safer and less guilt-inducing than paying for real, live face-to-face sex with a prostitute. The conditions for the call workers were better too.

Then, with the web, came cybersex. Now a man could enter a chatroom and talk dirty while practising a bit of one-handed typing – and, this time, the sex was free. On the downside, the chat was more likely to be with a geeky adolescent playing it for laughs than with an actual, horny woman. But it didn't matter as long as disbelief was kept nicely suspended. Webcams improved matters: now men could see what they were getting. Unfortunately, the lack of women interested in this kind of sex took them back to paying for it, unless they were lucky enough to be gay.

Web 2.0 brought online social networks and games, and a further step into virtual sexual reality. Within virtual worlds such as Second Life, punters could buy and build themselves gorgeous second selves. (Curiously, it's reckoned that around half the female avatars in online gaming are actually men offline – and if exaggerated breast size is any kind of clue, the figure is probably higher.) They could either try out animated sex within the game world – rarely very satisfying – or use the game to arrange something more old-fashioned, such as phone sex, sexting or video cybering with that old webcam. Gender-bending aside, there were two big problems with sex 2.0. Rapid response and easy availability tended to make most encounters, well, nasty, brutish and short. And of course people using social networking sites for sexual interaction were still reliant on themselves for actual physical stimulation.

That was where teledildonics stepped in. Devices such as the Sinulator, the MagMag-Hole ("with 9 separate motors!") and the Wiibrator allowed people to plug a vibrator or an artificial vagina into a USB socket. Some allowed a "partner" with a matching device to control its speed or action remotely, others allowed scripted virtual encounters with porn stars. More imaginative devices included the Mutsugoto, which allowed couples to draw on each other's bodies remotely, using light. The ibuzz, meanwhile, created its particular frisson by means of an MP3 player, a cock ring, a bullet vibrator and a bunch of cables.

The drawback of teledildonics is that the interaction is as limited as the sex toys themselves. According to sex entrepreneurs, the future may lie with virtual reality "love suits", similar to those worn by actors for motion-capture movie animations. These would be hooked up either to "hardcore software" or an online partner or sex worker. The technology will have to come a long way, however, before a suit can provide anything like the complexity of stimulation offered by old-school masturbation or intercourse. And society will have to come some way before strapping yourself into an electric gimp suit doesn't seem just a little weird. It's more likely that research into the physiology of orgasm will come up with better ways to artificially induce sexual pleasure. But for now, the possibility of buying yourself an "orgasmatron" seems almost as distant as when Woody Allen came up with the idea in his 1973 sci-fi comedy, *Sleeper*.

Relatively few countries regulate rather than ban. Their systems are widely regarded as far more effective, but most governments are too afraid of being seen to "condone prostitution" to follow suit. Central Europe – at least, Germany, Austria, Switzerland and Hungary – mostly allows prostitution, as does Nevada (since 1971) and New Zealand (since 2003). Sweden, Norway and Iceland, along with Scotland, have reversed the usual policy and made selling sex legal but purchasing it criminal. At the positive extreme, Switzerland, Denmark and the Netherlands may fund "sex therapists" to visit disabled people – an important clientele for sex workers.

The sensitive legal issue of the moment is how to deal with the explosion in "human trafficking" or "sexual slavery" that has accompanied globalization. Unfortunately, many governments and campaigners confuse the issue by accounting willing migrant sex workers as trafficked people. The Coalition Against Trafficking in Women, for instance, argues that "all children and the majority of women in the sex trade" are "victims of trafficking", just as "all prostitution exploits women, regardless of women's consent". Not everyone would agree.

Ethics and attitudes

The conservative position on sex work is that it's immoral because it's a form of adultery or promiscuity. And where prostitution was once seen as a defence against social instability, it's now often seen as an attack on ordered society. Prostitutes have also long been feared as carriers of disease, for instance, and this anxiety is reinforced by the fact that many sex workers today are migrants from countries known to have high rates of HIV-AIDS. Some communities fear that prostitutes will infect the healthy "native stock", in other words, or seduce their clients, or other young women, into an underworld seething with crime and drug abuse. Leaving aside a few token glamorous, globetrotting, confession-publishing call girls, the media is saturated with images of murdered addicts and trafficked children, not independent women (still less men) making rational choices.

Mixing sex with money is also controversial. It's often not clear which of "filthy lucre" or "dirty sex" is regarded as tarnishing the other more. In European history, virgins were typically described as "clean"; going on this standard, a modern-day sex worker, who may entertain anything from 500 to 1500 clients a year, would be very "dirty" indeed. And for a great many people, sex in itself is seen as a dirty (or brutish) act that is only cleaned up (or civilized) when it takes place in the context of an emotional, spiritual or perhaps marital relationship. Sex for the sake of sex (and for money, too) obviously doesn't provide this context.

Feminists have long been hostile to prostitution as a form of exploitation, and many anti-prostitution groups still define sex work as something like "the abuse of a person's sexuality by abrogating that person's human right to dignity, equality, autonomy, and physical and mental well-being". An alternative feminist line, however, takes its lead from abortion campaigns and from sex workers themselves; it proclaims a woman's right to do what she chooses with her own body. On this understanding, a woman doesn't sell her body, still less "sell herself", she simply contracts out her sexual services for an agreed price.

For Camille Paglia, the prostitute is "not the victim of men, but rather their conqueror". Karl Marx more drily observed: "prostitution is only a specific expression of the general prostitution of the labourer". If so, then the conditions of work really need improvement. Selling sex is rarely a transaction between economic equals, and sex workers have a severely heightened exposure to sexually transmitted infections (including HIV-AIDS), drug dependency, legal discrimination, police harassment, assault, rape and murder.

Conditions are unlikely to improve without state intervention, police protection – for which legalization is crucial – and unionization. One of the early campaigning groups, the US's COYOTE ("Call Off Your Tired Old Ethics") has now given way to a host of International Prostitutes Collectives and the like, many affiliated to trade unions. In the UK, the GMB union campaigns for chapel recognition by lap-dancing clubs; the Netherlands' Red Thread group is part of the massive FNV labour movement, while two Australian sex workers' activist groups joined that country's Liquor, Hospitality and Miscellaneous Workers Union as long ago as 1995. In some arenas, the fact that sex work involves sex is no longer overshadowing the fact that it also involves work.

Erotica and pornography

Ever since humans could paint on a cave wall or mould a figurine, they've created images to arouse and titillate. And if ancient myths are anything to go by, they've told sexy stories for just as long. Today, films or photographs or books that are specifically designed to cause arousal are described as either erotica or pornography – and the difference between the two is much disputed. The ancient Greek roots of the word pornography mean "writing about prostitutes", and the word still has a more commercial edge than erotica, which considers itself to be a little more soft-focus. You could say that erotica dresses itself up in the silks and cottons of romance or art, where pornography is only interested in bare, naked fucking.

Cynics say that erotica is pornography of which you approve; or, following the porn actress Gloria Leonard, they reckon that the difference between the two is nothing more than a question of lighting. But broadly speaking, women read erotica while men watch pornography. The difference may reflect a basic gender gap in sexuality, or just the fact that porn tends to aim itself at male pleasure. It's also very evident that emotions – and love most of all – are forbidden in pornography, whereas erotica positively roils with strong feeling.

Dirty books

Medieval poetry could be unabashedly bawdy and Renaissance love poetry highly sensual, but, arguably, the first true works of modern erotica were the early sixteenth-century "luxurious sonnets" of Pietro Aretino, a man known as the "scourge of princes". The poems included outrageous lines such as "Open up your thighs,

The early, pioneer photographers quickly learned to explore the camera's erotic potential. This "naughty" French postcard dates from around 1900.

then, so I can clearly see / Your pretty arse and cunt, full visible to me", and their illustrations – known as the sixteen "postures" and drawn by none other than Raphael's pupil, Giulio Romano – became a kind of pornographic fable after the originals were destroyed.

Such heights of debauchery were only reached again when the free-thinking libertine tradition got going. The poet laureate of libertine obscenity was undoubtedly John Wilmot, Earl of Rochester (1647–80), but less highbrow works were more popular. In Blessebois' notorious *L'Ecole des filles* (1655), an experienced woman instructs a virgin about sex, sparing no details: "she feels his yard entering her cunny as gently as you could dream of", she explains;

"I think I should rather like to try this thing", her pupil replies. Translations found their way all over Europe; the diarist Samuel Pepys thought it the "most bawdy, lewd book that ever I saw" and burned his copy – after reading it, of course.

L'Ecole des filles and many works which followed it – *The Cabinet of Love*, Chorier's *Satyra Sotadica*, *Venus in the Cloister* – were all dialogues, and erotica proper was only born alongside the novel. The first great erotic fictions both appeared in 1748: John Cleland's *Memoirs of a Woman of Pleasure*, better known as *Fanny Hill*, is a first-person romp through the exuberant sexual career of a free-living adventuress; Denis Diderot's *Les Bijoux Indiscrets* focuses on a magic ring which

Lesbian landmarks and gay greats

Great love between men has inspired great fiction ever since the Greek myth of Damon, who was willing to die for his friend Pythias, and Patroclus, who did die for Achilles, beneath the walls of Troy. Only rarely was the erotic nature of that love made clear – even Homer was not entirely explicit about Achilles' relationship with his "concubine", though later Greeks certainly assumed the two men were lovers. Only in the late nineteenth and early twentieth centuries did writers begin openly to explore same-sex love.

The two first, great gay landmarks couldn't be more contrasting. *Teleny, or the Reverse of the Medal*, was probably composed as a sort of round-robin by Oscar Wilde and his friends, and was privately printed in 1893 – its no-holds-barred eroticism made publication entirely impossible. It centres on the passionate affair between Camille des Grieux and the magnetically attractive pianist, René Teleny. "A kiss", the novel declares, "is the breathing forth of two enamoured souls. But a criminal kiss long withstood and fought against … is a fiery brand that burns deep, and changes the blood into molten lead or scalding quicksilver". The second great, early gay novel is E.M. Forster's infinitely more reticent *Maurice*, which was completed by 1914 but remained unpublished until 1971, after Forster's death. The novel is the story of two great loves: the eroticized friendship between Maurice and his Cambridge friend, Clive Durham, and Maurice's consummated love for the gamekeeper, Scudder. The novel ends on an affirming note but is troubled in mood: "only a struggle", Forster wrote, "twists sentimentality and lust together into love."

The twin landmarks of early lesbian literature, Virginia Woolf's strange epic, *Orlando*, and Radclyffe Hall's *The Well of Loneliness*, were both published in 1928 but, couldn't be more different. Woolf played down her novel's lesbian content (and masked the identities of her models, Vita Sackville-West and Violet Trefusis) by allowing her hero to shift gender over the course of his/her centuries-long life; the novel was subtle and radical and became Woolf's breakthrough bestseller. *The Well of Loneliness*, by contrast, was oddly old-fashioned. It was also banned as obscene – not so much because its heroine discovers Parisian lesbian subculture, but because Hall was explicitly campaigning on behalf of "inversion", culminating with a plea for "the right to our existence".

Today, gay and lesbian fiction has a place in bookshops in all but the most conservative cities, and novels by gay and lesbian authors such as Rita May Brown, Julia Darling, Patrick Gale, Alan Hollinghurst, Armistead Maupin, Sarah Waters, Edmund White and Jeanette Winterson are read by millions, of whatever sexuality.

enables a sultan to hear the reminiscences of his court ladies' vaginas. Both are witty, zestful and highly literate, but by the end of the century, the erotic novel had exhausted itself as a genre. The late landmarks of libertinism, de Sade's *Justine* and Restif de la Bretonne's *L'Anti-Justine* strive to outdo each other in outrageousness, but erotic effect is secondary.

Pornography, as we know it, was born in the mid-nineteenth century – an era as remarkable for how much it talked and wrote about sex as for how much it claimed to disapprove of doing it. Despite ever more restrictive laws (see p.372), backstreet porn, including illustrated books and the first pornographic magazine, *The Pearl*, boomed around an apparent upsurge in fetishism. Lesbianism, flagellation, the defloration of virgins and sexual tourism among the lower classes were particularly popular. Gay erotica got started with *Teleny* (see p.368) and, for the first time, fictional "confessions" by young ladies were matched by semi-fictional memoirs by gentlemen. The most astonishing Victorian memoir is undoubtedly *My Secret Life*, which exactingly details the seemingly endless erotic adventures of its author, "Walter".

From the late nineteenth century onwards, literary fiction – notably Bram Stoker's *Dracula* and the novels of Emile Zola – tested sexual boundaries even as erotica pushed at literary ones. For much of the twentieth century, Paris took the lead: Guillaume Apollinaire and Georges Bataille wrote some of the first highbrow erotica there in the 1910s and 1920s; Henry Miller and Anaïs Nin tried their hand at art-porn in the 1940s; and, in the 1950s and 1960s, the Paris-based Olympia Press funded its publication of mould-breaking novels such as *Lolita* and *The Naked Lunch* by virtually bombarding the UK and US with pulp erotica, including the notorious sub/dom novel, *Story of O* (1954).

As photographic pornography became more widespread – peep-show postcards smoothly morphed into the high-gloss magazines familiar today – and the erotic was allowed to enter mainstream fiction (due largely to the 1960 Chatterley trial – see p.376), erotica found itself pushed into a niche. It survives today largely under the guise of "romantic fiction" from companies such as Mills & Boon, and as a sub-genre of sci-fi and fantasy. The latter isn't just a question of lesbian vampires and the like. "Slash/het" (gay/straight) fan-fiction, in which characters from much-loved fantasy novels find themselves in situations their creators could hardly have imagined, is hugely popular online. The possibilities for *The Lord of the Rings*, in particular, seem boundless.

Money shots – the porn industry

The emergence of pornography is one of the great cultural changes of the last hundred years. Where once erotica was underground and illicit – and so actively prosecuted that it was effectively restricted to a few enthusiasts with the time and money to seek it out – it is now available to anyone with access to the Internet or cable television. And millions take advantage – to the extent that one Swedish survey reckoned that two-thirds of the time men spent on the Internet was accounted for by use of pornography. Pornographic styling and behaviour, aka "raunch culture", is embedded in mainstream media. Pop videos borrow "porno chic" styling while magazines advise readers "how to have sex like a porn star" – a surprising ambition, really, given that porn actors are faking.

Porn flicks have existed almost as long as film itself; the earliest known "stag film", *Free Ride*, dates to 1915 and features a man picking up and having sex with two female hitchhikers.

Pornography hasn't changed much since, but the laws hemming it in have. The great cultural and technological shift began in the 1960s. Denmark legalized pornography in 1969, West Germany in 1970, Sweden in 1971 – and other countries eventually followed. The so-called "golden age" of porn ensued, with full-length features such as *Deep Throat* (awful, and probably exploitative) and *Behind the Green Door* (much more ambitious) appearing in mainstream movie theatres in 1972. Home video soon ushered porn into the privacy of the home, sending quantity soaring and quality plummeting. The domestication of porn was furthered by the arrival of the Internet, which let people watch and buy porn without even having to leave their bedrooms.

If size was everything, the porn industry would easily outgun mainstream cinema. Some 10,000 adult films are shot each year in the US alone, mostly in California's San Fernando Valley; Hollywood knocks out a mere 400 or so. "Adult entertainment" grosses some $12 billion in US sales, which is some $3 billion more than Hollywood – and that's not counting some of the huge profits made out of porn by hotel and telecoms companies (profits they generally keep quiet about). Globally, the porn industry is thought to be worth some $50–60 billion. These figures don't even account for the booming amateur (or semi-amateur) porn sector, which now enthusiastically splurges itself all over x-rated versions of YouTube – sites with imaginative names like "youporn" and "xtube".

The future for porn may have much to do with women. Studies suggest that anything from 40 to 80 percent of younger women have watched online porn, and "woman-centred" porn from directors like Anna Span and Candida Royalle is a growing genre. Recent research suggests that older lab tests, which found that women weren't nearly as turned on by visual stimuli as men, unwittingly skewed their own results by showing women pornography designed for men. Given the right stimulus, women are just as physiologically aroused by porn as men – though there still seems to be a relative shortfall in their psychological arousal. Most fascinatingly, women seem to respond to all kinds of sexual footage, while men need porn that's oriented to their sexuality and specific erotic interests.

Problems in pornland

Porn is cheap, commercial, unambitious and formulaic – so it's pretty much the opposite of art, by most definitions. It aims at the lowest common denominators of male arousal, playing up again and again to the same tired old erotic formulas, enlivened only by a bit of half-intended humour. (Porn film titles can be pretty lively, though: *Freddy vs Jason* becomes *Freddy Does Jason*; *Edward Scissorhands* becomes the even more tragic *Edward Penishands*.)

Germaine Greer compared the rise of pornography to the simultaneous rise of the potato crisp: a "food that fattens and does not feed", which is "designed to leave the consumer unsatisfied." (Given the addictiveness of pornography, others have thought cocaine a better comparison.) But the bigger problem with porn isn't quality but politics. Even leaving aside the sex workers who produce the stuff, and the health risk they face, antiporn feminists have long complained that porn exploits, degrades and objectifies women in general. Which is all true – but then gay porn routinely degrades its male objects, too.

An anti-pornography demonstration in New York City in 1979.

Degradation is partly what porn is all about. At least, as the erotic theorist Georges Bataille observed, "nothing heats the passions more than irregularity", so porn basically shows people transgressing what are generally regarded as sexual norms. It shows people having sex in public (porn is effectively a technological kind of voyeurism, even if – usually – the actors are only pretending). It shows them having sex in a way that's totally unrestricted by manners, politeness, sensitivity, mutual respect, shame or any of the other rules and emotions that hold society together (and unrestricted by normal physical constraints, too.) And it shows sex acts that have long been regarded as transgressive – from oral, anal and group sex to acts of violence or degradation.

Few people can explore far into porn without coming across scenes they find disturbing, and if they feel simultaneously aroused, as is often the case, the result can be confusing or distressing: "am I really so vile as to find this sexy?" It's estimated that less than 10 percent of even hard-core pornography (that is, porn that shows the genitals) shows outright aggression, and a tiny proportion of that shows physical violence or rape, but even the "ordinary" penetrative sex shown in pornography is far more pumpingly aggressive than real sex. And the use of women's bodies in heterosexual porn – notably in the universal "money shot", which shows ejaculate landing on a woman's body, typically her face – could be seen as, well, a little hostile. Maverick porn actor Bill Margold claims that the industry exists "to satisfy the desire of the

Fig leaves and indices

Censorship and liberalization have gotten along for years like a sea and a shore, with waves and tides alternating advance and retreat. Occasionally, however, a freak wave appears – and two of the biggest hit in the late 1550s. First, Pope Paul IV ordered that Michelangelo's frescoes in the Sistine Chapel be destroyed. The problem wasn't just nudity. Michelangelo's classically naked statue of David was fine – it depicted heroism. The problem was nude saints and naked virgins. Even the scurrilous poet Pietro Aretino (see p.366) said the frescoes' "licentiousness" made him blush, while a papal official called them "shameless" and "better suited to a brothel" than a papal chapel. Protests from artists made Paul relent, and in the end draperies and fig leaves were strategically added.

In 1559, the Vatican published the first *Index librorum prohibitorum*: an infamous list that banned books not just for heresy, but for scurrilousness and sexual decadence. It survived for over four hundred years – roughly the time it took for Europe to start seriously swinging towards liberalism. Mussolini was still adding fig leaves to nude statues in 1932 (well, they were over seven metres tall). The *Index* was only abolished in June 1966, and the Sistine Chapel's modesty drapes were still in place until the grand restoration project of the 1980s and 1990s.

get … So we come on a woman's face or somewhat brutalize her sexually: we're getting even for their lost dreams."

The antiporn feminist Robin Morgan famously declared that "pornography is the theory; rape is the practice" and while there's no evidence that violent porn triggers sexual attacks on women, it may well reinforce myths about women's sexuality – including, in the most dangerous cases, the myth that women enjoy forced sex. Porn also seems to condition the sexual triggers of frequent users, over time, and may have a significant impact on young people's developing sexuality. One 1981 study showed that men exposed to sexually violent films had more accepting attitudes about violence to women – though aggression, rather than sex itself, does seem to be the main trigger.

Most insidiously, the camera-oriented, repetitious and often brutal sexual techniques used in porn can't do much to increase the overall sexual sophistication of society. And porn-star bodies – hairless vaginas, huge penises, inflated breasts and so on – can't exactly be a positive influence on porn-viewers' self-image, nor on their expectations of others.

Two hundred years of obscenity – a quick guide to censorship

The roots of modern censorship – like the roots of most sexual attitudes – are grounded in the nineteenth century. From 1802, the Society for the Suppression of Vice campaigned for

men in the world who basically don't much care for women". Even the most satisfied Casanova, he claims, "has always wanted somebody he couldn't

Hot off the press, 3 November 1960: *Lady Chatterley's Lover* finally becomes legal.

legislation to defend the British public against what Lord Campbell called "a poison more deadly that prussic acid and strychnine or arsenic". He meant pornography or, specifically, anything "offensive to modesty or decency, or expressing or suggesting unchaste or lustful ideas, or being impure, indecent or lewd". (As so often, the fulminations of the censors sound almost as sexually charged as the material they condemn.) Lord Campbell's Obscene Publications Bill was passed in 1857, and the Act stood for over a hundred years – it still stands in England and Wales, in a modified form.

In the US, freedom of speech has been regarded as sacred since the writing of that First Amendment – but it didn't stop the country's first obscenity trial taking place in 1821, when a Boston printer was prosecuted for daring to publish John Cleland's pornographic novel, *Fanny Hill*, and thus "corrupting, debauching and subverting" the morals of youth. Twenty years later, the US Tariff Act prohibited imports of "obscene" books and, twenty years after that, in 1865, it became criminal to send obscene publications through the mail. Most repressive of all, however, were the Comstock Laws of 1873, which pretty much banned the mailing of

Too hot to handle – seven banned films

I Am Curious Yellow (Vilgot Sjöman, 1967). A Swedish art house movie, influenced by the French New Wave, *I Am Curious Yellow* unflichingly depicted sexual acts and body parts – the kissing of a (flaccid) penis causing particular consternation (and not because it was flaccid). The film follows the activities of a politically and sexually curious young woman, Lena Nyman (playing a version of herself), who, in between interviewing various real figures (Martin Luther King, Olof Palme), enjoys lively sexual relations with a car salesman and the film's director. Its intial banning in the

US was lifted by the Supreme Court in 1971, paving the way for greater explicitness in mainstream cinema throughout the 1970s.

Last Tango in Paris (Bernardo Bertolucci, 1972). This bleak portrait of an affair between a grieving widower and an aimless young woman – brilliantly played by Marlon Brando and Maria Schneider – attracted most attention for its butter-assisted but brutal anal sex scene. In the UK, censors cut the key scene but the distributors were nonetheless sued (unsuccessfully)

Lena Nyman and Börje Ahlstedt get it on in *I Am Curious Yellow* (1967), blazing a trail for the erotic cinema of the 1970s.

under the Obscene Publications Act. In Italy, police seized prints of the film, the Supreme Court ordered negatives burned and Bertolucci was briefly jailed. Schneider later claimed that she "felt a little raped" during the screening and that Brando himself "felt manipulated, raped by Bertolucci".

Salò or the 120 Days of Sodom (Pier Paolo Pasolini, 1975). Pasolini's earlier literary adaptations – versions of Bocaccio's notorious *Decameron*, Chaucer's saucy *Canterbury Tales* and the louche *Arabian Nights* – have a jaunty eroticism, but this film, based on de Sade's monstrous novel (see p.356), is utterly, remorselessly, bleakly different. Despite being updated to 1940s Italy in order to serve as a satire on fascism, and despite being so upsetting that audiences around the world (where it was allowed to be shown, at least) walked out, it was almost universally banned or savagely cut. Pasolini was murdered in the same year as the film was released – supposedly by a rent boy, though many believe it was that most extreme form of censorship, a contract killing.

Ai No Corrida / In the Realm of the Senses (Nagisa Oshima, 1976). This arty film, set in 1930s Japan, shows a man and a prostitute journeying into experimental eroticism. It draws on Japan's tradition of shunga woodblock pornography, but aims to provoke as much as celebrate – especially in its upfront depiction of genitals and pubic hair – depictions unacceptable in Japan – not to mention its asphyxiation and castration scenes. It was seized by US Customs and suppressed by the British Board of Film Censors until 199. In Japan, Oshima was unsuccessfully prosecuted for obscenity.

Caligula (Tinto Bass, 1979). Purporting to be about the final years of the depraved Roman Emperor, with a script by renowned US novelist Gore Vidal, the final 170-minute cut was a pornographic extravaganza of equal degrees of explicitness and incoherence. Producer Bob Guccione (of *Penthouse* magazine fame) had duped both Vidal and the film's stars – Malcolm McDowell as Caligula, Helen Mirren as his wife Caesonia – by shooting reels and reels of orgiastic footage unbeknownst to them and then editing it into the more "serious" scenes. Universally panned by critics, it existed in various censored versions only receiving BBFC approval in 2008.

Crash (David Cronenberg, 1996). Based on the 1973 novel by J.G. Ballard, this focuses on a group of fetishists whose thing is … car crashes. The British Board of Film Censorship thought it so good that they passed it with an 18 rating; the next day, the right-wing newspaper *The Daily Mail* proclaimed "Censors's Yes to Depraved Film". London's Westminster Council quickly banned it anyway.

Baise-Moi (Virginie Despentes and Coralie, 2000). In this wilfully low budget art-shocker, two women are raped and then go on a sex-and-killing revenge spree. Despite using porn actors, its directors claimed to be setting out to challenge and disturb, not arouse. Pressure from right-wingers caused the Conseil d'État, a kind of supreme court, to make it the first film to be banned in France for nearly thirty years. In the UK, the BBFC at first refused it even the highest R18 rating, but after cuts to a rape scene that the Board ruled "eroticised sexual assault", it got its certificate.

anything whatsoever to do with sex. From that year, not just pornography but educative materials on sex and contraception were pushed underground.

Liberalization began in the late 1950s, on both sides of the Atlantic. Following the prosecution of "Broadway Sam" Roth (for distributing, among other things, Allen Ginsberg's poem *Howl*), the US Supreme Court ruled in 1957 that obscenity rested on whether "the average person, applying contemporary standards" would think the "dominant theme … appeals to the prurient interest." Law would try to reflect society, in other words, not shape it. In 1960, obscenity prosecutions against the publishers of D.H. Lawrence's *Lady Chatterley's Lover* in the UK and US failed. Two million copies of the novel were sold in a single year, and publishers fell over themselves to sell other erotic books, from Philip Roth's novel of masturbation, *Portnoy's Complaint*, to the *Kamasutra*.

The floodgates had opened, but conservatives carried on trying to hold back the waters. Supreme Court Justice Potter Stewart famously observed in 1964 that he didn't need to define obscenity, "I know it when I see it". In 1989, a passionate Jesse Helms waved photos by Robert Mapplethorpe at fellow Senators, imploring them to "look at the pictures", such as one showing a black man urinating into a white man's mouth. (Just to be clear, Helms wanted Mapplethorpe's photos banned.) Most recently, the British Labour party introduced the Criminal Justice and Immigration Act (2008) which, on the one hand, abolished blasphemy and, on the other, made it a criminal offence to possess extremely violent pornographic images – even if the participants had consented and weren't harmed.

Rated X – film censorship

In the 1930s, the Motion Picture Producers and Distributors of America drew up a set of guidelines, known as the Hays Code, in order to stave off the threat of federal censorship. The idea was to ensure that all the Hollywood studios toed the same moralizing line. Like most acts of self-censorship, the rules were particularly rigorous. Most concerned sex. According to the code, movies were to avoid showing "excessive and lustful kissing", "nakedness and suggestive dances", "sex perversion" (which meant homosexuality) and any implication "that low forms of sex relationship are the accepted or common thing".

The import of high-class (but Hays Code-breaking) foreign films in the 1950s caused the system to begin to break down, but its principles broadly persisted in the new ratings system administered by the Motion Picture Association of America, from 1968. Again, the MPAA ratings were voluntary, but any film that got itself stamped with anything stronger than an "R" (for "restricted") could kiss goodbye to distribution or advertising (at least until the NC-17 rating snuck in under the non-rated "X" category in 1996). Films ever since have been shot or cut to fit the ratings standards, in an institutionalized version of self-censorship.

In the UK, censorship is imposed by law, with the British Board of Film Censorship having wielded both the razor and the rubber stamp from 1912 to the present. The BBFC is somewhat secretive about its criterion for awarding certificates or making cuts, but was long rumoured to employ the "Mull of Kintyre test", which measures the "angle of the dangle" against the phallic-looking peninsula of that name on the west coast of Scotland. Even if this story isn't true (and the BBFC did "pass" an erection in Lars von Trier's 1998 *The Idiots*), the Board has a curious focus on nakedness and genitalia. One examiner admitted that "simulated" sex generally gets an "18" rating, while the "R18" category, restricting sale to licensed sex shops, is applied when there are "clear images of real sex". To the BBFC, "real sex" apparently means penetration with genital exposure, rather than sex that's actually being done for pleasure. Still, the BBFC has at least abandoned the old rule where the man had to be on top.

Guides and gurus, sexperts and sexologists

If you wanted to find out more about sex at any time during most of the last two thousand years, you had a bit of a problem. Apart from religious texts, which were only really interested in prohibition or disapproval, there was very little written down on the subject. This meant that folk wisdom handed down by word of mouth held sway – with all the problems that can cause. Even as science and medicine slowly edged towards the scary subject in the early modern era, social and legal restrictions tightened – which meant that what few researchers there were dared publish very little.

This atmosphere of throttled secrecy was perfect for the nurturing of hysteria and pseudoscience – most obviously as in the great masturbation scare (see p.338). Science developed on one track, popular wisdom on another (the latter expressed in misguided manuals). Only the mainstream was big enough to be visible; anyone on the margins might well feel that they were entirely alone. What saved the situation was the late nineteenth-century mania for classification. Suddenly, sex was subjected to the same rigorous inspection and analysis as, say, flower taxonomy or Bible authorship. Slowly, the awareness of sexual diversity spread and the understanding of sexual complexity grew. Even more slowly, writers of sex advice began to reflect that awareness and understanding in their books. The two tracks, sex science and sex practice, were coming together. Astonishingly, this convergence took the best part of a hundred years to complete.

Perverts or pioneers?

If European medical knowledge remained largely a mixture of ancient Greek and Arab ideas and home-grown herbalism until the nineteenth century, sexual knowledge was even more mixed up. It was commonly (and inexplicably) believed that women could only get pregnant if they had an orgasm, for instance, and that they produced or ejaculated a female seed to match that of men. In the late ninteenth century, a few mavericks began to take a more objective view.

At the vanguard were several German men who, from the 1890s onward, used science to reconcile what was then thought of as "aberrant" sexuality –

often enough their own – with growing medical and biological understanding. A doctor specializing in mental health, Richard von Krafft-Ebing, came to believe that sex was "the most important factor in social existence" and wrote up hundreds of clinical case studies of what were called "perversions" (see p.351) in his *Psychopathia Sexualis*. Karl Heinrich Ulrichs, the "grandfather of gay liberation" declared himself to be a born *urning*, or homosexual man, and determined to justify himself scientifically and philosophically "against all the humiliations that have been laid onto me up to now". The physician Magnus Hirschfeld began the first scientific study of sexuality, focusing first on (his own) homosexuality; the Nazis eventually destroyed his work.

Albert Moll, a Berlin neurologist, theorized about the sexual impulse and how it grows in childhood. His work profoundly influenced Sigmund Freud (1856–1939), the soon-to-be famous Viennese doctor who originally specialized in nervous disorders. In his famous 1905 *Three Essays on the Theory of Sexuality*, Freud suggested that children pass through different psychosexual stages, beginning with "oral" and "anal", and passing through "phallic" and "latent" towards – as long as no psychic shocks or conflicts get in the way – the adult goal of the genital. Freud later came up with the notions of the "Oedipus complex" (boys want to kill their fathers and marry their mothers), "penis envy" (girls want one) and "castration anxiety" (boys fear girls will take theirs away). Despite the bizarre, fairy-tale qualities of Freud's theories, and their very evident masculine bias, they proved incredibly influential: the entire trade of psychoanalysis was founded upon them.

It took a while for the Anglophone world first to catch up with the Germans, and then to get over their obsession with Freud. The great early pioneer was Havelock Ellis (1859–1939), who argued that homosexuality was inborn, and that masturbation was a pleasurable and harmless act. He followed Freud in believing that sex was a kind of accumulation and discharge of energy (what Freud called libido), but he was primarily a scientist, not a spinner of yarns. He reckoned that Freud's insistence on the primacy of vaginal orgasm, for instance, proved that he didn't know much about women. (Ellis's own personal sexual preference, curiously, was what he called "undinism", now better known as urolagnia, or being turned on by female urination.)

The science of sex

While Europeans were developing theories of sexuality, a few American scientists were getting on with surveys, observations and experiments. An early pioneer was Robert Latou Dickinson (1861–1950), a gynaecologist who interviewed female patients on their sexual histories and, in a few cases, observed them masturbating to orgasm. He made sketches and notes with unprecedented detail, such as "2 fingers making about inch stroke about 1 to 2 a second – not hard pressure but sway of pelvis and contraction of levator and thigh adduction – rhythmically once in 2 sec or lost" – which is about as good a description of how to masturbate as a woman might hope to find.

Dickson's thoroughness impressed the sexologist Alfred Kinsey (see box, opposite), but his research focused mostly on interviews – the mores of the 1950s ensured that his plan to film thousands of ejaculations and "couplings" couldn't come to fruit. Kinsey did secretly film colleagues masturbating

Alfred Kinsey, reporting for duty?

Zoologist Alfred Kinsey (1894–1956) was much praised by fellow scientists for his maniacally thorough study of gall wasp populations and their taxonomy. He only came to wider attention, however, after he was asked to coordinate Indiana University's course on "marriage". He was appalled to find there was almost nothing of worth in the campus library – and he wasn't about to re-peddle the moralizing misinformation his colleagues had for so many years – so he launched the biggest and most thorough sex survey ever undertaken. With three meticulously trained colleagues, he interviewed 18,000 American men and women, asking each literally hundreds of questions about their sexual experiences. He published his results in two volumes: *Sexual Behavior in the Human Male* (1940) and *Sexual Behavior in the Human Female* (1953).

The "Kinsey Reports", as they became known, caused an uproar which has yet to die down. The biggest shockers were that 37 percent of American men had reached orgasm through homosexual contact at least once and that 26 percent of American women had "engaged in extramarital coitus". America just wasn't the steady, conservative nation it pretended to itself it was, and its laws were massively out of step with what people were actually doing. Human sexuality was revealed to be rich and diverse. At last, Americans could stop worrying about straying from the straight and narrow.

Conservatives couldn't accept Kinsey in the 1950s – they relentlessly attacked both him and his funding – and they still can't today. He is criticized for taking a skewed sample including too many volunteers (the kind of daring people who were willing to talk about sex) and too many prisoners (whose criminality implied all sorts of moral turpitude). In fact, statistical methods such as "group sampling" compensated for these faults fairly well, but it is true that later surveys have found marginally less sexual diversity than Kinsey found in late-1940s America.

The most vehement attacks on Kinsey centre around the idea that he was a kind of pervert who embarked on a "covert crusade" to undermine American values. The perversion charge is based on his somewhat surprising experiments on himself (which included stimulating himself to orgasm with a toothbrush up his urethra), the films he made of colleagues having sex with their wives (and other women), the sexual relationships he and his wife had with other people (including, for Kinsey, some men) and the interviews he recorded with a multiple-offending paedophile and a number of children (whose parents were always present). Kinsey's defenders point out that all his activities were typical of the all-devouring curiosity which motivated his scientific greatness. But it is also true that most sexology pioneers have in some way stood at the margins of the sexual mainstream. And in putting science before prejudice, and curiosity before fear, Kinsey was certainly a long way wide of many of his critics.

Kinsey and his colleagues discuss the final changes to *Sexual Behavior in the Human Male*.

and having sex in his own attic – all for the sake of science – but a true, laboratory-based study had to wait until gynaecologist William Masters took up the sex baton, alongside his psychologist assistant (and, later, wife), Virginia Johnson.

Where Kinsey habitually sported a slightly fun bowtie, Masters and Johnson were very much wearers of clinical white coats. But, from 1954, their respectable-sounding Reproductive Biology Research Foundation began not just filming but measuring what they called the "orgasmic phase expression" of "reacting units" with the help of "stimulative literature" – in other words, they gave couples porn and monitored them as they got on with it. They used a battery of scientific tools, including a "penile plethysmograph" (rubber ring) to measure erectile blood flow and an "artificial coition machine" (see-through plastic dildo) to film what was going on inside the vagina as a woman stimulated herself to orgasm. Their results, published in the more permissive climate of the mid-1960s, cast astonishingly clear light on what was actually going on during sex. They devised a four-phase model of arousal (see p.6), and worked out exactly what role each body part played in stimulation and orgasm.

Since Masters and Johnson, researchers have penetrated sex on an ever more microscopic level. Endocrinologists have started tapping into the role that hormones play in attraction and arousal, and, of course, in the menstrual cycle; neurologists, with the help of fMRI scanners, have started to produce the first blurry pictures of what's going on inside the brain; geneticists are beginning to unravel DNA's contribution to sexuality; and medical researchers have, well, created a drug that makes men's penises harder. Psychologists and social scientists, meanwhile, have refined their understanding of attitudes, and created more effective therapies for sexual dysfunction.

In the social sciences, the greatest step forward was taken by the psychologist John Money when, in 1955, he borrowed the term "gender" from linguistics, using it to differentiate the qualities of "femininity" and "masculinity" from the physical facts of female or male biological sex. This conceptual leap opened up an entire field of study. In the 2000s, the study of "heterosexuality" – now seen as a phenomenon in itself, rather than a neutral norm – is at last starting to catch up with all the work done to date on same-sex attraction.

Only fifty years after Kinsey was forced into the attic, sexology is a respectable discipline, with the whole apparatus of International conferences, journals and papers. Sex surveys and laboratory studies are still controversial enough to be much rarer than they should be, but at least the breakthroughs of sex science are unusually well-publicized, courtesy of a media eager to provide its readers with titillation. Some research even filters through into the parallel world of sex manuals.

Great sex guides of the past …

After the Romans had departed, Europe seems to have been plunged into a sexual dark age. The best books on offer were medical treatises cobbled together from the theories of Greek physicians like Galen and Hippocrates (such as the madly misogynistic *De Secretis Mulierum*, or

The ancient wisdom of the orient

The oldest sex guides still in existence today are Chinese and Indian. The Greeks and Romans seem to have had manuals – notoriously the "little books of Elephantis" which illustrated a range of positions – but they either got lost in the medieval period or, more likely, were destroyed. The most ancient Chinese texts date back over two thousand years (copies on strips of silk or bamboo were discovered in Hunan's third-century Mawangdui tombs). They were primarily medical textbooks aimed at the conservation of sexual or seminal energy (see p 170), but they also include painstaking detail on the ins and outs of the sex act, alongside helpful dialogues between a mythical "Yellow Emperor" and various female sexperts he turns to, notably the "Plain Girl". Chinese sex education flourished in succeeding centuries as a respected branch of medical science.

Just as venerable is India's erotic tradition, which probably dates back well before the second-century *Kamasutra*. Known as "the Sixty-Four", the *Kamasutra* was actually more than a mere manual: it detailed far fewer positions than advertised, and instead portrayed the ideal bachelor lifestyle in gorgeous detail, and discussed the rights, wrongs, obligations and duties surrounding pleasure. It remains one of the most readable and intelligent of all sex books (and inspired a whole Oriental tradition of medieval manuals, from the Indian *Ananga Ranga* to the Islamic *Perfumed Garden of Sheik Nefzaoui*). Unfortunately, and unaccountably, the *Kamasutra* did not mention the clitoris.

"Secrets of Women") or bizarre fantasies about women's Satanic and sexual activities – which included, according to the frothy-mouthed, fifteenth-century witch-hunters' bible, the *Malleus Maleficarum*, stealing men's penises and squirrelling them away in birds' nests.

Two proper sex manuals finally arrived in the seventeenth century. Both mentioned the clitoris (at last) and proved so wildly popular that they remained in print, astonishingly, well into the twentieth century. *Aristotle's Masterpiece* was an eccentric family medical encyclopedia that concentrated on "venery", or conception and childbirth; it didn't see fit to mention contraception but did at least discuss "the use and action of the several parts in Women appropriated to generation". Its chief rival, Nicolas Venette's *Conjugal Love*, discussed how not to get pregnant, argued that women were "hot in constitution and vehemently desirous of commerce with man", and described the clitoris as "the fury and rage of love".

Censorship and hysteria about the dangers of masturbation (see p.338) ensured that things didn't improve much until well into the nineteenth century. Only a few left-wing radicals dared write sensibly on the subject of sex. One of the first was Richard Carlile. A bookseller, he saw a ladies' maid "scampering away delighted" with a copy of *Aristotle's Masterpiece*; on looking through the book himself, he was so shocked that he resolved to write his own (a story familiar to most sex writers). Carlile's *Every Woman's Book* was published pseudonymously in 1826. Its chief aim was to advertise contraception but it also proclaimed that sex was a healthy and "natural passion". It quickly inspired two classics: Charles Knowlton's much-banned *Fruits of Philosophy* (which recommended douching) and Robert Dale Owen's *Moral Physiology* (which preferred coitus interruptus), but the nineteenth-century smash-hit bestseller was George Drysdale's *Elements of Social Science* (1854) which enthused about the use of condoms, warned of the "evils arising from abstinence" and advocated free love (rather than dangerous self-abuse) as the cure.

Unfortunately, most nineteenth-century radicals were more interested in stopping the working classes breeding than helping anyone towards orgasm. At the decadent-flavoured end of the century, however, a number of books were published in order to excite and instruct – the book-collecting upper classes, at least. The first English *Kamasutra* was privately (and expensively) published in 1883, and promoted by the outrageous explorer Sir Richard Burton. In 1889, *The Horn Book: A Girl's Guide to Good and Evil* revealed 62 extravagant positions including the "wheelbarrow reversed" and "the elastic cunt". Joseph Weckerle's collectors' edition of the *Golden Book of Love* (1907) went more than one better, with its list of no fewer than 531 positions.

Such books were more pornographic than practical. Truly useful advice only emerged when a few pioneering women, many of them proto-feminist American doctors, established the genre of the marriage manual. In her 1884 book, *The Human Element in Sex*, Dr Elizabeth Blackwell argued that sexual passion was not "the exclusive attribute of men". In 1896, the esoterically minded Dr Alice Stockham advocated retrograde ejaculation or "karezza" (see p.123). In the 1890s and 1900s, Ida Craddock was persecuted under the Comstock laws (see p.373) for mailing out handy pamphlets such as *The Wedding Night* and *Right Marital Living*.

... and modern sex manuals

As obscenity laws were slowly relaxed in the twentieth century, writers could stop railing against what couldn't be said and start saying it. The most influential books by far were Marie Stopes' *Married Love* (1918) and Theodoor van de Velde's *Ideal Marriage* (1926). Between them, they sold literally millions of copies, and jointly ushered in the modern era of sex writing – which is quite surprising for two books written, on the one hand, by a virtual virgin who "had never been fully penetrated by a normal male organ" (as she put it) and by an elderly Swiss physician. Both books were designed to prevent others from paying what Stopes called the "terrible price for sex-ignorance": Stopes' marriage to her sexually inadequate first husband was annulled; van de Velde ran away from a loveless marriage aged 36.

Married Love was the first book with the panache and the punchiness to sell sex to its readers, and to praise the power and complexity of a woman's sexual response. It warned that "instinct is not enough. In every other human activity it has been realized that training, the handing on of tradition, are essential". If Stopes was also an eccentrically committed eugenicist, it didn't stop her sex and contraception advice being sound. *Ideal Marriage* vowed to "keep the Hell-gate of the realm of sexual perversions firmly closed" but still taught readers about "gentle and soothing caresses with lips and tongue", and masturbation for wives unsatisfied by intercourse. "What is physiologically sound", van de Velde advised, "may also be considered ethically sound".

Over the next half-century, numerous doctors and activists published any number of marriage manuals. Some were good, but most had what Alex Comfort called "a Stopesian squareness which is enough to make one abandon the project before the banns are up". They tended to trip over themselves to emphasize that sex was only for married couples, and strongly disapproved of aberrations like oral sex; and few took any account of the many advances in sex science. Then, in 1969, Dr David Reuben's *Everything You Always Wanted to Know About Sex (But Were Afraid to Ask)* hit US bookstands. Reaching tens of millions of readers, it proved that Americans no longer *were* afraid to ask. A second big impact was created by Alex Comfort's 1972 *The Joy of Sex*; again, it was written by a physician, but it had an earthy, colourful, hippyish style, and intended to treat sexuality "as Indian and Arabic works have treated it – at the level of ballroom dancing". As an art and a pleasure, in other words, not as a marital duty.

Since Comfort's classic, sex manuals have ditched the beards and the hippy tone, and taken on board the message of safe sex (usually to a lawyer-friendly fault). They've increasingly oriented themselves not at married couples (except for the Christian market) but at either straight women or lesbian women or gay men – as if having a different sexuality necessarily means you have different tastes. They've also crept closer to the sex industry, focusing increasingly on vibrators, lubes, fetish gear and DVDs, while borrowing a lot of their styling from pornography.

Many books are authored by semi-celebrity "sexperts" who write agony columns, appear on the sofa in daytime chat shows and endlessly regurgitate "hot new positions" for men's magazines. A few experts moonlight in the sex-confessional genre, which blends reportage with memoir and soft-core pornography. Some writers are a cut above: Paul Joannides, for instance, or Suzi Godson, or most of the people writing for Cleis Press, whose niche publications cover anything from disability and recovery from sexual trauma to anal sex. But in general, the modern manual market is stuck in a pattern where each book tries to exceed the erotic experimentalism of the last. More tongues, more toys. More fetishes, more fantasy. More (of the same old) positions. All of these books try to cover everything and anything concerning the body (where anything, needless to say, goes). Few dare, however, to imagine sex as something that also takes place beyond the bedroom: in the deeper spaces of human culture, the soul, and the mind.

Resources

Resources

This is not a complete list of all the books and websites used to research this book – far from it. It is, instead, a shortlist of the more interesting, useful, important, provocative or just readable of resources for those who want to explore a little deeper. The selection emphasizes more recent publications, but if you think a real classic is missing, let us know: sex@roughguides.com.

Advice and expertise

Books

The Courage to Heal Ellen Bass and Laura Davis (2002). This acknowledged classic draws on the personal experiences of survivors of child sexual abuse.

The Clitoral Truth Rebecca Chalker (2000). Well written feminist handbook, arguing that the clitoris is only the tip of a much larger structure.

Contraception: Your Questions Answered John Guillebaud (2008). Aimed at doctors, so incredibly detailed. **Contraception: A User's Guide** (2000) is more user-friendly but needed updating at the time of writing.

The Sex Book Suzi Godson with Mel Agace (2006). One of the clearest, most sensible books on the market, with excellent illustrations,

though it doesn't go much beyond the practicalities.

Guide to Getting It On Paul Joannides (2004). A down-to-earth approach with lots of personal testimony from enthusiastic readers.

The Ultimate Guide to Sex and Disability Miriam Kaufman, Cory Silverberg and Fran Odette (2007). The most useful self-help book on the subject, it also covers how to combine a sex life with chronic pain and illness.

She Comes First: The Thinking Man's Guide to Pleasuring a Woman Ian Kerner (2004). Sober, thoughtful book about how men can understand and approach female sexuality.

Sex in Loving Relationships Sarah Litvinoff (1999). A wise little book from the UK's respected relationship counselling organization, Relate.

Is It A Choice? Eric Marcus (2005). Frank and useful "answers to 300 of the Most Frequently Asked Questions about Gay and Lesbian People".

The Whole Lesbian Sex Book: A Passionate Guide for All of Us Felice Newman (2004). Practical and affirming, with detail on communication, finding partners, and relationships, as well as hands-on detail.

How to Make Love to the Same Person for the Rest of Your Life – And Still Love It Dagmar O'Connor (2003). Deals with practical issues like creating the mood and handling family commitments, as well as giving physical advice.

Gay Sex, Gay Health Alex Vass (2006). This doctor-authored book is definitely gay-oriented but contains lots of stuff equally relevant to straight men.

Good Vibrations Guide to Sex Cathy Winks and Anne Semans (2002). A comprehensive guide from the pioneering feminist sex store. Good on the how-to side of things as well as what to buy.

The Erotic Bondage Handbook (1998). and **SM 101: A Realistic Handbook Jay Wiseman** (2000). The classic texts for people who want to explore BDSM.

Websites

asexuality.org Open-minded, supportive and fascinating discussion boards from AVEN, the Asexual Visibility and Education Network.

bettydodson.com The frank and fascinating site of the original sex-positive US feminist: educator, orgasmic expert and author of *Sex For One*.

fpa.org.uk The UK's leading sexual health charity. Offers reliable, clear, up-to-date fact sheets for download, and can point Brits towards clinics and free contraception.

goaskalice.columbia.edu Columbia University's health Q&A has one of the best archives of sex worries and sex advice.

informedconsent.co.uk The UK's leading BDSM society offers online chatrooms, event listings, personal ads, and a handy BDSM dictionary for those new to the scene.

ourbodiesourselves.org Superb resource from the feminist Boston Women's Health Book Collective covering all aspects of women's bodies, health and sexuality.

plannedparenthood.org The major advocacy group and provider of sexual health services in the US. Provides emergency contraception.

rapecrisis.org.uk UK support organization offering information, advice and emotional support not just to people who have been raped, but to survivors of all kinds of sexual violence.

relate.org.uk The UK's respected Marriage Guidance Council is one of the best providers of relationship support. Offers an excellent range of straightforward, well-targeted publications, too.

sda.uk.net The Sexual Dysfunction Association offers support and some good online fact sheets written by medics on all aspects of male and female sexual dysfunction.

teenagehealthfreak.org Website and series of books offering "cringe-free health information specific to teenagers". Covers everything from sunburn to smoking, and cystitis to small penises.

the-clitoris.com A plain-speaking educational website for all ages. Learn about anatomy, sexual function, orientation, masturbation and more.

Science and psychology

Books

Women: An Intimate Geography Natalie Angier (1999). A personal and up-tempo account of everything from the clitoris and testosterone to breast milk, puberty and the evolution of desire.

Secrets of Love and Lust: The Science and Psychology of Sex, Love and Marriage Simon Andreae (1998). Wide-ranging survey of the debate over male and female differences in desire, and how the institutions of marriage and Christianity have shaped it.

The Evolution Of Desire: Strategies of Human Mating David M. Buss (2003). Classic socio-biological tale by one of the key researchers in the field. Asserts that inter-gender relations are evolutionarily hardwired.

Why We Love: The Nature and Chemistry of Romantic Love Helen Fisher (2004). Fisher is an anthropologist who works with MRIs, combining behavioural psychology with evolutionary theory. Best of all, she knows how to write. Her earlier book, **Anatomy of Love** (1993), is a fascinating cultural study of marriage and fidelity.

Love, Sex and Intimacy: Their Psychology, Biology and History Elaine Hatfield and Richard L. Rapson (1995). This textbookish but wide-ranging and extremely informative study, from a wife–husband team, focuses on sex in the context of passionate love and relationships.

The Psychophysiology of Sex edited by E. Janssen (2007). Five hundred pages of serious research papers – but it's such a major resource, especially on sexual response, arousal and dysfunction, that it has to be included.

Sex and the Psyche Brett Kahr (2007). Written by a Freudian but much heavier on surveys, statistics and thoughtful commentary on sexual fantasies than on psychoanalysis.

The Scent of Eros: Mysteries of Odor in Human Sexuality James Vaughn Kohl and Robert T. Francouer (2002). One of the best books on smell and sexuality, covering history, culture and science.

Sex and Sexuality Richard D. McAnulty and Michele M. Burnette (2007). This three-volume set of scholarly essays covers most conceivable subjects – from adolescence and identity to race, gender and prostitution.

The Science of Orgasm Barry R. Koimisaruk, Carlos Beyer-Flores and Beverly Whipple (2006). Splendid digest of all the research to date on the physiology and neuroscience of orgasm by three of the leading authorities.

The Case of the Female Orgasm Elizabeth Lloyd (2005). A scientist's demolition job on the bad reasoning and assumptions behind the various evolutionary theories for the existence of female orgasm. Her view is that it's "for fun".

The Naked Woman: A Study of the Female Body Desmond Morris (2005). Unsophisticated and somewhat sexist, but offering an engaging mix of speculative evolutionary notions, cultural anecdote and human zoology. **The Naked Man** (2008) does the same thing for the male, albeit with a cooler tone.

Bonk Mary Roach (2008). Sceptical, wisecracking science journalist takes a wry look at science's attempts to understand – and improve – sex, focusing mainly on the modern era.

The New Psychology of Love **Robert J. Sternberg and Karin Weis** (2006). Serious collection of high-powered essays on evolutionary, cultural and psychological theories of romantic love, presenting all the latest ideas.

Websites

faceresearch.org/demos Test out the attractiveness-equals-averageness theory by merging online photos. You can even use your own uploaded faces.

kinseyinstitute.org Homepage of Alfred Kinsey's original institute: still doing pioneering sex research in Indiana. Lots of online resources.

sexscience.org The Society for the Scientific Study of Sexuality is a professional body "dedicated to the advancement of knowledge". You can download and read journal articles from the *Journal of Sex Science* and the quarterly newsletter, *Sex Science*.

History and culture

Books

Gay Life and Culture: A World History Robert Aldrich (2006). Fantastic coffee-table book distilling academic research into a highly readable history of gay culture – and, inevitably, of the oppression that pursued it.

The Story of V: Opening Pandora's Box Catherine Blackledge (2003). Fascinating study of the vagina in human culture, covering vaginal veneration, anatomical understanding, the science of conception and orgasm.

Virgin: The Untouched History Hanne Blank (2007). Enthralling history of virginity – everything from vampires and vestals to Female Genital Mutilation and the modern abstinence movement.

Cross Dressing, Sex and Gender Vern L. Bullough and Bonnie Bullough (1993). A survey of cross-dressing from two of the leading authorities on the history of sexual science.

The Greeks and Greek Love James Davidson (2008). Dismisses the old idea that what mattered to the Greeks was chiefly who penetrated whom, and exposes a vibrant and nuanced culture of homosexuality.

Intimate Matters: A History of Sexuality in America John D'Emilio and Estelle B. Freedman (1997). Superbly researched study of sex in America, with an emphasis on the ongoing argument between repression and liberalism.

Epidemic: A Global History of AIDS Jonathan Engel (2006). Humane and urgent general history of HIV–AIDS, from the origins of the virus, its spread, and the political and social issues surrounding it, to modern-day medical research.

A Mind of Its Own: A Cultural History of the Penis David M. Friedman (2001). Intelligent, wide-ranging, absorbing and sometimes funny too – if not exactly ideal reading for the beach.

Pox: Genius, Madness and the Mysteries of Syphilis Deborah Hayden (2003). A controversial but enthralling history of syphilis, with a whole section of celebrated (probable) syphilitics of the past – including Hitler.

Alfred C. Kinsey: A Life James H. Jones (1997). The classic, scandalous but authoritative biography of Kinsey, which delves deep into his personal life and discovers a troubled man.

Casanova: Actor, Lover, Priest, Spy Ian Kelly (2008). This highly readable and very sympathetic biography focuses on the many guises of the great eighteenth-century Venetian lover.

Solitary Sex: A Cultural History of Masturbation Thomas Laqueur (2003). Laqueur's study of masturbation and the anxiety that long attached itself to it is an eye-opening, if heavy-going, read.

The Technology of Orgasm: "Hysteria", the Vibrator, and Women's Sexual Satisfaction Rachel P. Maines (1998). This entertaining and impeccably researched book unmasks the medicalization of women's sexuality over the centuries, focusing on hysteria and its "cures".

A History of Contraception Angus McClaren (1990). Almost certainly the most authoritative single book on the subject. Detailed without ever being dry.

The Book of Love: In Search of the Kamasutra James McConnachie (2007). Puts the *Kamasutra* back in its Hindu context, and explores why this ancient manual created such a furore in the West and in modern India.

Put What Where John Naish (2005). Alternating hilarious quotations from sex guides with a brief but well-researched overview of their development.

The Facts of Life: The Creation of Sexual Knowledge in Britain, 1650–1950 Roy Porter (1995). Porter was *the* authority on the history of medicine and this, and his **Sexual Knowledge, Sexual Science: The History of Attitudes to Sexuality** (1994) are defining surveys of the territory, covering medical understanding as well as popular sexual knowledge.

Websites

bestsexbloggers.com Why restrict yourself to the erotic escapades and musings of one blogger? This site links to scores of them and also features reviews of sex toys.

http://digital.library.upenn.edu/women/ stopes/married/married.html The online text of Marie Stopes' classic 1918 manual, **Married Love**.

glbtq.com The excellent Encyclopedia of Gay, Lesbian, Bisexual and Queer Culture. Offers potted biographies, features and articles, plus an active discussion board.

www2.hu-berlin.de/sexology/IES/ Robert T. Francoeur's International Encyclopedia of Sexuality, published online through the respected Magnus Hirschfeld Institute of Sexology, in Berlin. Features summaries of sexual politics, health and cultural factors in scores of countries around the world. Elsewhere on the sexology part of the site you can find key books by leading sexologists, plus the thorough (if uninspiring) Encyclopedia of Human Sexuality.

lesleyahall.net Fascinating exploration of gender and sex history. There's recommended reading and resources for researchers, including how to make a sheep-gut condom.

sacred-texts.com/sex Includes full online texts of the "Burton" editions of the **Kamasutra**, the **Ananga Ranga** and **The Perfumed Garden**, along with other nineteenth-century oddities, and translations of Sappho, Ovid and the like.

world-sex-news.com Trawls the web for sex-oriented news stories, featuring half a dozen or so a day – anything from Paris Hilton's latest press release to research into sperm quality.

Issues, ethics and religion

Books

Global Sex Dennis Altman (2002). Sociological overview of the effect of globalization on sex, covering such topics as HIV–AIDS, sex workers and migration, and the economics of porn.

No-Nonsense Guide to Sexual Diversity Vanessa Bair (2007). Pithy summary of gay and transgender issues. The emphasis is on politics but it also covers history, science and religion.

Lust Simon Blackburn (2004). Enjoyable musings on the sin of lust from a philosopher who wears his learning lightly.

The Shere Hite Reader: New and Selected Writings on Sex, Globalization and Private Life Shere Hite (2006). The 1976 *Hite Report* revealed what American women were thinking, not just what they were doing. This reader focuses on feminism and the politics of sexuality.

The Horseman: Obsessions of a Zoophile Mark Matthews (1994). A man realizes he loves his horse more than his wife – and not in a cowboy way. Intelligent defence of "zoophilia".

Sex and Social Justice Martha C. Nussbaum (1999). Political and ethical essays from a feminist social philosopher. Topics include genital mutilation, gay rights and ancient Greek sexuality.

The Philosophy of Sex edited by Alan Soble (2007). Collection of excellent essays, followed by coursebook-style follow-up questions.

Porn Studies edited by Linda Williams (2004). Academic essays on contemporary issues from Japanese porn comics for women to online issues, edited by the original "professor of porn".

Websites

www.avert.org/aofconsent.htm Lists ages of consent around the world, for male–female, male–male and female–female.

www.ewtn.com/library/CURIA/CDFCERTN. htm Declaration on Certain Questions Concerning Sexual Ethics, from the Sacred Congregation for the Doctrine of the Faith – better known as the Inquisition.

www.islamawareness.net/Sex/ Overview of Islamic ideas on sex, without the dubious scholarship of the fatwa-issuing sites, or the hostility of US many "Islamic awareness" sites.

isna.org The Intersex Society of North America: for "a world free of shame, secrecy and unwanted genital surgery".

mariestopes.org.uk Marie Stopes International runs over 400 birth-control clinics worldwide. It also provides safe abortions.

nerve.com/specialissues/christiansex/ Lively and upfront set of articles on anything from St Augustine to the sex appeal of Catholic boys from Nerve magazine.

religioustolerance.org/homosexu.htm Discussion of religious attitudes to homosexuality from a site promoting tolerance in North America.

www.reproductiverights.org Campaigning group for freedom of choice. Good resources on abortion laws around the world, with a printable full-colour poster-map.

www.who.int/reproductive-health/family_ planning/ Focuses on government policies, but with links to cutting-edge research and surveys of attitudes and practices around the world.

A dozen erotic classics

The Life of an Amorous Man Ihara Saikaku
(1682). A hedonistic aristocrat sets himself adrift
in Japan's floating world, passing from one sensual
adventure to another. A little-known classic.

Memoirs of a Woman of Pleasure aka **Fanny
Hill John Cleland** (1748). This splendidly bawdy
and explicit romp is often called the first erotic novel.
The heroine, Fanny, may lose her virtue but never her
insouciant charm.

Justine, or the Misfortunes of Virtue De Sade
(1787). The eponymous heroine of this mannered
and sophisticated satire is repeatedly, relentlessly,
rudely punished for her efforts to resist a world of
sexual cruelty and human injustice.

**Teleny, or the Reverse of the Medal Oscar Wilde
and others** (1893). Probably written by a group of
friends, including Wilde, the "first gay novel" is a
throbbingly passionate story of a man falling for a
charismatic pianist, and his induction into a decadent
world of homoerotic pleasure.

Story of the Eye Georges Bataille (1928). The
great French theorist of the erotic tells a wilfully
disturbing tale of the descent of two lovers into ever
greater deviancy. The eyeball scene at the end is
notorious.

Lady Chatterley's Lover D.H. Lawrence (1928).
Frustrated aristocratic wife falls in love with her
earthy gamekeeper, and discovers the passion
behind sex. The failure of the book's obscenity trial
in 1960 was a landmark in publishing history.

Tropic of Cancer Henry Miller (1934).
Fierce, passionate delving into the stream of
consciousness of a highly sexed man exploring
the possibilities of Paris – a man not unlike Miller
himself. As the narrator says, it's "a gob of spit in
the face of Art".

The Story of O Anne Desclos (1954). A woman,
called only "O" – as a hole or orgasmic mouth –
becomes the willing but much-abused sex slave
of various debauched men. Written under the
pseudonym Paulie Réage, the book was notorious
for decades.

Lolita Vladimir Nabokov (1955). Subtle and
sympathetic, wayward and witty, this is a novelistic
occupation of the mind of a man who becomes
erotically obsessed (and involved) with a twelve-year-
old girl.

Beautiful Losers Leonard Cohen (1966).
Experimental and distinctly wry novel exploring an
erotic quadrangle in which two of the participants
may not actually exist.

Couples John Updike (1968). As one adulterous
New England housewife tells her lover, "welcome to
the post-Pill paradise". But, in this tightly written story of
early 60s sexual boredom, it's more of a purgatory.

Delta of Venus Anaïs Nin (1978). Kooky but
intelligent – and beautifully written – these interlinked
erotic short stories are set in a dreamy Parisian demi-
monde. Originally written for private consumption in
the 1940s.

Index

flashing 355
foreplay 115–118
foreskin 57
Foucault, Michel 7
fourchette 50
frenulum 50, 59
frequency of sex 209
Freud, Sigmund 5, 13, 164, 185, 193,
    321, 378
Friday, Nancy 42, 119
frotteurism 355
fucking – see penetrative sex

G

G-spot 47–48
Galen 152, 172, 183, 197, 380
gay history 341
gay literature 368
Gay Pride 343
"gay uncle" theory 33
gender, sex and 74–80
genes, male and female 191
genital herpes 269
genital warts 270
genitalia 45–64
    female 45–55
    male 56–64
    slang for 76
gods and goddesses 305–311
Godson, Suzi 90, 383, 386
gonadotropins 194
gonorrhoea 269, 271
Gräfenberg, Ernst 48, 171, 246
Greece, Ancient 307
Greer, Germaine 165, 370
group sex 132
guilt, religious 321–323

H

hair, removal of body 65–67
Hardy, Thomas 156
Hartman, William 158, 161, 162, 176
Hathor 301, 308, 311
Hays Code 376
headaches from sex 180
Helms, Jesse 376
hepatitis 271
Hepburn, Katherine 77
hermaphrodites 79
Hermaphroditus 79
Herodotus 315
heroin 298
her-on-top 121
herpes, genital 269
heterosexual script, the 117
hickeys 90
Hinduism 301, 307, 319, 320, 330, 380
Hippocrates 197, 380
Hirschfeld, Magnus 342, 378
Hite, Shere 161, 165, 174, 223
Hitler, Adolf 268
HIV 271, 274–285
    antibody test 281
    history of 274–280
    progression of 280
    transmission of 283
    treatments 284, 285
    variants of 277
Homer 368
homophobia
    and AIDS 279
    as symptom of repressed desire 344
    in religion 331–334
homosexuality
    in animals 34
    countries where illegal 342
    and identity 25
    research into origins of 29–34

Hormone Replacement Therapy 222
hormones, role in attraction 10
HPV 270
HSDD 293–295
hymen 50
Hypoactive Sexual Desire Disorder
    293–295
hypothalamus 5
"hysteria" 182–185

I

I Am Curious Yellow 374
Ideal Marriage 382
implants, contraceptive 241
    effectiveness 241
    pros and cons 229
    side effects 241
impotence – see erectile dysfunction
In the Realm of the Senses 375
Inanna – see Ishtar 307
incest – see child sexual abuse
injection, contraceptive 253
    effectiveness 253
    pros and cons 228
    side effects 241
intercourse – see penetrative sex
intersexuality 76
Intrauterine Device – see IUD
irrumation 113
Ishtar 307
Isis 310
Islam 157, 302, 304, 307, 325, 328
IUD 247
    effectiveness 247
    history of 246
    pros and cons 228
    side effects 247
IUS 248
    pros and cons 228
    side effects 249

Picture Credits